Pit bikes
Service and Repair Manual

by Penny Cox

Models covered

(6035-240)

Pit Bikes with 4-stroke air-cooled horizontal (lay-down) engines, specifically the
Lifan semi-automatic 1P52FMH, and 4-speed Lifan 1P52FMI, Lifan 1P56FMJ (YX140),
Zongshen 1P60YMJ (ZS155).

Applicable brands: Stomp, WPB, Demon-X, LMX, M2R, Slam, Thumpstar, SSR,
Orion, YCF, PitsterPro, Piranha, G2 Moto, Coolster, Motovert.

© Haynes Publishing 2016

ABCDE
FGHIJ
KLMNO
PQRST

A book in the **Haynes Service and Repair Manual Series**

ISBN 978 1 78521 035 8

Library of Congress Control Number 2016934501

British Library Cataloguing in Publication Data
A catalogue record for this book is available from the British Library

Printed in the USA

Haynes Publishing
Sparkford, Yeovil, Somerset BA22 7JJ, England

Haynes North America, Inc
861 Lawrence Drive, Newbury Park, California 91320, USA

Haynes Publishing Nordiska AB
Box 1504, 751 45 Uppsala, Sweden

*Printed using 33-lb Resolute Book 65 4.0 from Resolute Forest Products Calhoun, TN mill. Resolute is a member of World Wildlife Fund's Climate
Savers programme committed to significantly reducing GHG emissions. This paper uses 50% less wood fibre than traditional offset. The
Calhoun Mill is certified to the following sustainable forest management and chain of custody standards: SFI, PEFC and FSC Controlled Wood.*

Contents

LIVING WITH YOUR PIT BIKE

Introduction

Specifications

Bike stands

MAINTENANCE

Routine maintenance and servicing

Contents

REPAIRS AND OVERHAUL

REFERENCE

Pit bike roots

The pit bike takes its name from the small bikes (or even bicycles) used by riders and pit crew to get around the pit area of motocross and road race events. Going back years, it was Honda's Z50 mini-bike or monkey bike which almost exclusively did this job. It was small, cheap and easy to ride and over time the Z50's later incarnation, the XR50, had developed into the benchmark style of today's pit bikes.

Popularity of the Honda Z50 and XR50 grew outside of the race pits and paddocks, especially in the US, once it became evident that you could have a lot of fun on these little bikes. They were ideal for young riders cutting their teeth on their first bike, and also for full-size riders once the aftermarket parts world developed and offered larger diameter wheels, uprated taller suspension and higher bars. At the same time performance products were been developed to increase bore size and power output. Within a short time there was sufficient interest for a series of dedicated pit bike races operating in much same way as dirt bike or motocross events.

The power house of the pit bike has always been the single cylinder air-cooled four-stroke engine, distinct from all others by its horizontal top-end, or 'lay-down cylinder' as

it's sometimes known. The roots of this engine go way back in Honda's history to the Cub, ATC, CT/ST ranges. Engine displacements range from 50 to 200 cc and transmissions are either manual or semi-automatic like the Cub. Apart from electronic ignition control little has changed in terms of engine development, a result no doubt of keeping production costs low and not being swept along with the legislation applied to road bikes. This style of pit bike remains in Honda's range as the CRF50 and 70. Kawasaki and Yamaha have theirs too, the KLX110 and TTR110 respectively.

By far the biggest development in pit bike production has been from factories in China, now a manufacturing base for many of the world's motorcycle and scooter manufacturers. Continuity is maintained in

the use of the lay-down engine, but USD forks, hydraulic brakes and wavy discs, plus striking bodywork and graphics, set these bikes apart from traditional brands. With low purchase costs and comprehensive model ranges, backed up by good spares supply and a wide range of aftermarket products, these bikes offer good value to the pit bike rider.

Nowadays riders have the option of race events (MX and supermoto), stunt riding and freestyle motocross. With pit bikes being very affordable they're an ideal way to start on the road to a full MX bike and even if you just want to have some fun on one, they're easy to put in the back of pick-up and take to a pit park or track. The pit bike community is also supported by clubs and forums providing a good source of information.

Riders leaving the start line at the Pit Bike Trophy

Frame number location

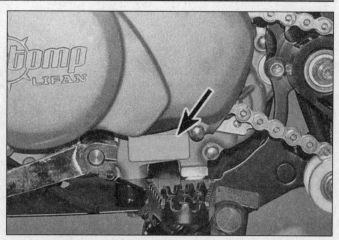

Engine number location

Frame and engine numbers

The frame serial number is stamped into the steering head and the engine number is stamped into the left-hand side of the crankcase. Both of these numbers should be recorded and kept in a safe place so they can be given to law enforcement officials in the event of a theft.

Note that the first part of the engine number denotes the engine type, e.g. 1P52FMI.

Buying spare parts

There are two places to purchase parts – a pit bike dealer or an on-line parts supplier. They will be able to offer OE (original equipment) parts plus aftermarket performance parts. Spark plugs, chains, sprockets, tyres and lubes can be purchased from a wider range of bike dealers. Note that you may need to supply dimensions, such as distance between mounting holes, number of sprocket teeth or length of cable, to ensure you get an exact match; always keep the old part until the new one arrives just in case you need to do a comparison.

Parts for pit bikes are on the whole very cheap so it's rarely worth fitting second-hand parts.

Acknowledgements

Our thanks are due to Stomp Racing Ltd, who supplied the machines featured in the illustrations throughout this manual. We would also like to thank NGK Spark Plugs (UK) Ltd for supplying the colour spark plug condition photographs and Draper Tools Ltd for some of the workshop tools shown.

About this Manual

The aim of this manual is to help you get the best value from your motorcycle. It can do so in several ways. It can help you decide what work must be done, even if you choose to have it done by a dealer; it provides information and procedures for routine maintenance and servicing; and it offers diagnostic and repair procedures to follow when trouble occurs.

We hope you use the manual to tackle the work yourself. For many simpler jobs, doing it yourself may be quicker than arranging an appointment to get the motorcycle into a dealer and making the trips to leave it and pick it up. More importantly, a lot of money can be saved by avoiding the expense the shop must pass on to you to cover its labour and overhead costs. An added benefit is the sense of satisfaction and accomplishment that you feel after doing the job yourself.

References to the left or right side of the motorcycle assume you are sitting on the seat, facing forward.

We take great pride in the accuracy of information given in this manual, but motorcycle manufacturers make alterations and design changes during the production run of a particular motorcycle of which they do not inform us. No liability can be accepted by the authors or publishers for loss, damage or injury caused by any errors in, or omissions from, the information given.

Professional mechanics are trained in safe working procedures. However enthusiastic you may be about getting on with the job at hand, take the time to ensure that your safety is not put at risk. A moment's lack of attention can result in an accident, as can failure to observe simple precautions.

There will always be new ways of having accidents, and the following is not a comprehensive list of all dangers; it is intended rather to make you aware of the risks and to encourage a safe approach to all work you carry out on your bike.

Asbestos

● Certain friction, insulating, sealing and other products - such as brake pads, clutch linings, gaskets, etc. - contain asbestos. Extreme care must be taken to avoid inhalation of dust from such products since it is hazardous to health. If in doubt, assume that they do contain asbestos.

Fire

● Remember at all times that petrol is highly flammable. Never smoke or have any kind of naked flame around, when working on the vehicle. But the risk does not end there - a spark caused by an electrical short-circuit, by two metal surfaces contacting each other, by careless use of tools, or even by static electricity built up in your body under certain conditions, can ignite petrol vapour, which in a confined space is highly explosive. Never use petrol as a cleaning solvent. Use an approved safety solvent.

● Always disconnect the battery earth terminal before working on any part of the fuel or electrical system, and never risk spilling fuel on to a hot engine or exhaust.

● It is recommended that a fire extinguisher of a type suitable for fuel and electrical fires is kept handy in the garage or workplace at all times. Never try to extinguish a fuel or electrical fire with water.

Fumes

● Certain fumes are highly toxic and can quickly cause unconsciousness and even death if inhaled to any extent. Petrol vapour comes into this category, as do the vapours from certain solvents such as trichloro-ethylene. Any draining or pouring of such volatile fluids should be done in a well ventilated area.

● When using cleaning fluids and solvents, read the instructions carefully. Never use materials from unmarked containers - they may give off poisonous vapours.

● Never run the engine of a motor vehicle in an enclosed space such as a garage. Exhaust fumes contain carbon monoxide which is extremely poisonous; if you need to run the engine, always do so in the open air or at least have the rear of the vehicle outside the workplace.

The battery

● Never cause a spark, or allow a naked light near the vehicle's battery. It will normally be giving off a certain amount of hydrogen gas, which is highly explosive.

● Always disconnect the battery ground (earth) terminal before working on the fuel or electrical systems (except where noted).

Electricity

● When using an electric power tool, inspection light etc., always ensure that the appliance is correctly connected to its plug and that, where necessary, it is properly grounded (earthed). Do not use such appliances in damp conditions and, again, beware of creating a spark or applying excessive heat in the vicinity of fuel or fuel vapour. Also ensure that the appliances meet national safety standards.

● A severe electric shock can result from touching certain parts of the electrical system, such as the spark plug wires (HT leads), when the engine is running or being cranked, particularly if components are damp or the insulation is defective. Where an electronic ignition system is used, the secondary (HT) voltage is much higher and could prove fatal.

Remember...

✗ **Don't** start the engine without first ascer-taining that the transmission is in neutral.

✗ **Don't** suddenly remove the pressure cap from a hot cooling system - cover it with a cloth and release the pressure gradually first, or you may get scalded by escaping coolant.

✗ **Don't** attempt to drain oil until you are sure it has cooled sufficiently to avoid scalding you.

✗ **Don't** grasp any part of the engine or exhaust system without first ascertaining that it is cool enough not to burn you.

✗ **Don't** allow brake fluid or antifreeze to contact the machine's paintwork or plastic components.

✗ **Don't** siphon toxic liquids such as fuel, hydraulic fluid or antifreeze by mouth, or allow them to remain on your skin.

✗ **Don't** inhale dust - it may be injurious to health (see Asbestos heading).

✗ **Don't** allow any spilled oil or grease to remain on the floor - wipe it up right away, before someone slips on it.

✗ **Don't** use ill-fitting spanners or other tools which may slip and cause injury.

✗ **Don't** lift a heavy component which may be beyond your capability - get assistance.

✗ **Don't** rush to finish a job or take unverified short cuts.

✗ **Don't** allow children or animals in or around an unattended vehicle.

✗ **Don't** inflate a tyre above the recommended pressure. Apart from overstressing the carcass, in extreme cases the tyre may blow off forcibly.

✔ **Do** ensure that the machine is supported securely at all times. This is especially important when the machine is blocked up to aid wheel or fork removal.

✔ **Do** take care when attempting to loosen a stubborn nut or bolt. It is generally better to pull on a spanner, rather than push, so that if you slip, you fall away from the machine rather than onto it.

✔ **Do** wear eye protection when using power tools such as drill, sander, bench grinder etc.

✔ **Do** use a barrier cream on your hands prior to undertaking dirty jobs - it will protect your skin from infection as well as making the dirt easier to remove afterwards; but make sure your hands aren't left slippery. Note that long-term contact with used engine oil can be a health hazard.

✔ **Do** keep loose clothing (cuffs, ties etc. and long hair) well out of the way of moving mechanical parts.

✔ **Do** remove rings, wristwatch etc., before working on the vehicle - especially the electrical system.

✔ **Do** keep your work area tidy - it is only too easy to fall over articles left lying around.

✔ **Do** exercise caution when compressing springs for removal or installation. Ensure that the tension is applied and released in a controlled manner, using suitable tools which preclude the possibility of the spring escaping violently.

✔ **Do** ensure that any lifting tackle used has a safe working load rating adequate for the job.

✔ **Do** get someone to check periodically that all is well, when working alone on the vehicle.

✔ **Do** carry out work in a logical sequence and check that everything is correctly assembled and tightened afterwards.

✔ **Do** remember that your vehicle's safety affects that of yourself and others. If in doubt on any point, get professional advice.

● If in spite of following these precautions, you are unfortunate enough to injure yourself, seek medical attention as soon as possible.

Engine

Spark plug type	
Original fitment	A7TC
Aftermarket replacement	NGK C7HSA or Denso U22FS-U
Spark plug gap	0.6 to 0.7 mm (0.024 to 0.028 in)
Compression pressure	125 to 190 psi range (150 psi measured)
Valve clearances	
Intake valve	0.10 mm (0.004 in)
Exhaust valve	0.15 mm (0.006 in)
Idle speed	1400 ± 100 rpm
Piston-to-bore clearance	0.01 to 0.04 mm (0.0004 to 0.0016 in)
Service limit	0.15 mm (0.006 in)
Cylinder bore taper or out-of-round limit	0.10 mm (0.004 in)
Clutch cable freeplay	4 to 5 mm (0.16 to 0.20 in) at lever bracket
Throttle grip freeplay	2 to 4 mm (0.08 to 0.16 in) at twistgrip flange
Brake lever freeplay (drum front brake)	4 to 5 mm (0.16 to 0.20 in) at lever bracket
Brake pedal freeplay (drum rear brake)	10 to 20 mm (0.4 to 0.8 in) at pedal tip
Crankshaft big-end side clearance	0.01 to 0.35 mm (0.0004 to 0.0137 in)
Service limit	0.60 mm (0.0236 in)

Chassis

Drive chain size	420 (6 mm thick sprockets) or 428 (7 mm thick sprockets). Check chain length when ordering.
Drive chain freeplay	30 mm (1.2 in) with gearbox in neutral, bike on its wheels and without the weight of the rider
Sprocket size	
Front	14T, 15T, 16T, 17T, 18T
Rear	37T or 41T
Match sprocket thickness with correct chain width – 420 or 428	
Tyre sizes	
10 inch wheels	2.50-10, 2.75-10, 3.00-10
12 inch rear wheel	80/100-12
14 inch front wheel	60/100-14
Tyre pressure	
Front	20 to 25 psi (1.4 to 1.7 Bar)
Rear	25 to 30 psi (1.7 to 2.1 Bar)
Brake fluid	DOT 4
Brake pad thickness (disc brake)	1 mm (0.04 in) service limit
Brake shoe thickness (drum brake)	3 to 3.5 mm (0.12 to 0.14 in) when new, 1.5 mm (0.06 in) service limit
Wheel rim run-out (axial and radial)	2 mm (0.08 in) service limit
Wheel axle run-out	0.2 mm (0.008 in) service limit

Lubricants and fluids

Engine oil type	Semi-synthetic 10W/40 motorcycle engine oil to API SG
Engine oil capacity	approx. 800 ml
Drive chain	Aerosol chain lube
Cables	Aerosol cable lube
Steering head bearings	Multi-purpose grease
Front forks	5W or 10W fork oil
Front fork oil capacity	see Chapter 5
Brake caliper slider pins	Silicone grease
Brake operating cam and post pivots	High melting point grease
Pivot points	Aerosol lubricant or multi-purpose grease
Fuel	Unleaded gasoline (petrol), minimum 91 octane

Torque wrench settings

Spark plug	10 to 12 Nm (88 to 106 lb-in)
Engine oil drain bolt	25 Nm (18 lb-ft)
Cylinder head nuts	11 Nm (97 lb-in)
Cylinder head bolts	10 Nm (88 lb-in)
Camshaft sprocket bolts	9 Nm (80 lb-in)
Generator rotor nut	41 Nm (30 lb-ft)
Clutch nut	42 Nm (31 lb-ft)
Crankcase bolts	12 Nm (106 lb-in)
Exhaust mounting bolt (to frame)	26 Nm (19 lb-ft)
Wheel axle nuts	47 Nm (35 lb-ft)

Standard torque values (dimensions are thread diameter, not hex size)

5 mm bolt and nut	5.2 Nm (46 lb-in)
6 mm bolt and nut	10 Nm (88 lb-in)
6 mm flange bolt and nut	12 Nm (106 lb-in)
8 mm bolt and nut	22 Nm (16 lb-ft)
8 mm flange bolt and nut	27 Nm (20 lb-ft)
10 mm bolt and nut	34 Nm (25 lb-ft)
10 mm flange bolt and nut	39 Nm (29 lb-ft)
12 mm bolt and nut	54 Nm (40 lb-ft)

Bike stands

Maintenance and repair jobs will be a lot easier with the bike held securely upright with its wheels off the ground. The flat base of the engine bashplate is an ideal platform for a stand. The method of supporting the bike will depend on the job you're doing and what access you need. Here are some suggestions **(see illustrations)**.

Dedicated pit bike, dirt bike or MX bike stands are available, many with a lift handle, or you can substitute this with a crate, wood blocks or axle stands. If you are going to combine the stand with lifting the bike up high on a motorcycle ramp, use tie-downs to hold the bike steady in case it falls.

If raising the bike up on a ramp use tie-down straps to prevent it toppling towards you

Rear paddock stands with adjustable width fittings work well. Choose one with cushioned pads on the lift pieces

A motocross bike stand or even a stout crate provides good support for getting both wheels off the ground

Wood blocks allow adjustment of height, but make sure they're completely flat and securely stacked

Axle stands provide secure support under the frame during engine removal

Chapter 1
Routine maintenance and servicing

Contents

Degrees of difficulty

Easy, suitable for novice with little experience 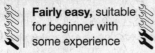	**Fairly easy,** suitable for beginner with some experience	**Fairly difficult,** suitable for competent DIY mechanic	**Difficult,** suitable for experienced DIY mechanic	**Very difficult,** suitable for expert DIY or professional 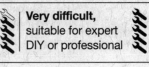

1 Maintenance schedule

Note 1: *It is recommended that you apply time intervals (based on hours use) to the Main and Extended service items. Typically perform the main service every 5hrs and the extended service every 15hrs. Experience is the best guide, so if the bike is ridden hard, raced and/or the suspension gets a hard workout, reduce the intervals accordingly.*
Note 2: *If your bike comes with an owner's manual, use the maintenance schedule it contains.*

Pre-ride checks
- [ ] Check the tyre pressures
- [ ] Check the engine oil level
- [ ] Check the throttle operates smoothly and returns when the grip is released
- [ ] Check each brake holds the wheel firmly when applied and frees off fully when released. Make a visual check of the brake fluid level through the master cylinder window on disc brake models.
- [ ] Compress and release the front and rear suspension, checking that it operates correctly
- [ ] If the bike has a sidestand, check that it stays up when retracted
- [ ] Check the suspension settings are correct for what you're doing
- [ ] Check there's enough fuel in the tank

Post-ride checks
Note: *If the bike is really dirty, clean it. You'll discover any defects much easier on a clean bike.*
- [ ] Check tighten all nuts and bolts. Many will have slackened after a couple of hours riding.
- [ ] Check the rear wheel spoke tension
- [ ] Check that there's no sign of oil leakage from the front forks and rear shock
- [ ] Clean and lube the chain. Check chain freeplay
- [ ] Turn the fuel tap OFF. If you're going to lay the bike up for a while consider draining the fuel from the carburettor
- [ ] If the air filter is visibly dirty, give it a clean before the next ride
- [ ] Apply a squirt of cable lube to the throttle and clutch cables
- [ ] Apply a squirt of cable lube to the front brake cable on a drum brake set-up

Main service
- [ ] Clean and lube the chain, then check the chain and sprockets for wear. Check chain freeplay
- [ ] Check all chain guards, guides and sliders are in good condition and securely mounted
- [ ] Clean and regap the spark plug
- [ ] Change the engine oil (and on models with a paper oil filter change it)
- [ ] Clean the air filter
- [ ] Check the fuel hose
- [ ] Check the crankcase breather hose
- [ ] Check the engine idle speed
- [ ] Check throttle cable freeplay
- [ ] Check clutch cable freeplay
- [ ] Lubricate the throttle and clutch cables
- [ ] Lubricate the front brake cable (drum brake)
- [ ] Check the steering head bearings for play
- [ ] Check the condition of the front fork tubes and seals
- [ ] Check the rear shock and swingarm bearings
- [ ] Check the brake pads and discs for wear (disc brake)
- [ ] Check the brake cable/operating rod freeplay (drum brake)
- [ ] Check the brake fluid levels and hose condition (disc brake)
- [ ] Check the wheel bearings for play
- [ ] Check the wheel spoke tension
- [ ] Check tyre pressure and tyre condition
- [ ] Lubricate stand, footrest, brake pedal and handlebar lever pivots
- [ ] Check the tightness of all nuts and bolts

Extended service
Note: *Carry out all items under the 'Main service' heading plus the following:*
- [ ] Clean the engine oil filter screen, and where fitted the centrifugal filter
- [ ] Fit a new spark plug
- [ ] Check the valve clearances
- [ ] Clean the fuel tap filter (inside the tank) and where fitted renew the in-line filter
- [ ] Fit a new air filter
- [ ] Grease the throttle twistgrip
- [ ] Change the front fork oil
- [ ] Regrease the steering head bearings
- [ ] Change the brake fluid and bleed the brakes (disc brake)
- [ ] Examine the brake shoes for wear (drum brake)

2 Drive chain and sprockets

Chain freeplay check

1 A neglected drive chain won't last long and will quickly damage the sprockets. The chain will stretch in use and need regular adjustment to maintain the correct amount of freeplay. It will also need regular lubrication.

Caution: If chain adjustment is neglected the chain is likely to become so slack that it will come off the sprockets and damage the chainguard, guides, engine casing and possibly the rider.

2 Chain freeplay should be checked with the bike on its wheels and upright (without the rider seated). Hold a ruler vertically against the lower run of the chain at a point midway between the sprockets. Measure the total up and down movement of the chain at this point, using just finger pressure to apply tension **(see illustrations)**. Chain freeplay should ideally be 30 mm (1.2 inches). Note that the chain will not stretch evenly over its entire length so move the bike forwards to enable the freeplay to be measured on other sections of the chain. If adjustment is required, make it at the tightest point of the chain.

3 If the chain looks dry and rusty, corrosion and dirt may have caused the links to bind and kink, effectively shortening the chain's length and making it tight **(see illustration).**

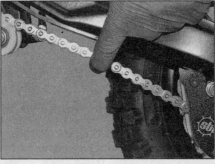

2.2a Pull up…

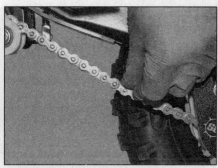

2.2b …and push down on the chain…

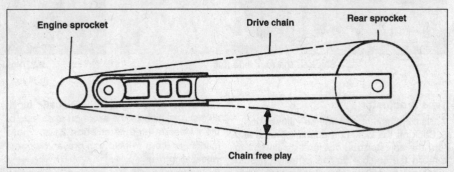

2.2c …measuring the total up and down freeplay

In this case use aerosol chain cleaner to scrub the chain and work free any seized links. Wipe the cleaner off the chain then apply chain lube. Take the bike for a ride to warm the chain and allow the lubricant to penetrate the links. Repeat the chain freeplay check after the ride and adjust it to the correct amount.

4 Check the entire length of the chain for damaged rollers, loose links and pins. Also check that the spring clip of the split link is fitted correctly **(see illustration)**. Fit a new chain if necessary, noting that it is good practice to fit new sprockets at the same time.

Chain freeplay adjustment

5 Move the bike so that the chain is positioned with the tightest point at the centre of its bottom run.

6 Several different adjuster types may be encountered, referred to as Types A, B and C for the purpose of this manual **(see illustrations)**. Regardless of the type, the adjuster enables the rear wheel axle to be moved rearwards within the swingarm slots.

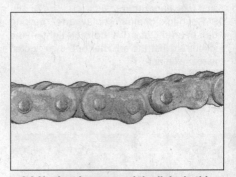

2.3 Neglect has caused the links in this chain to kink

2.4 Spring clip correctly fitted, with closed end facing the direction of chain travel

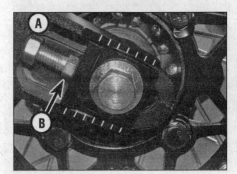

2.6a Type A – Locknut (A) and adjuster bolt (B). Alignment marks provided

2.6b Type B – Locknut (A) and adjuster nut (B)

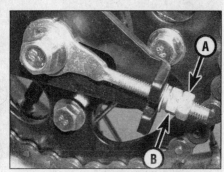

2.6c Type C – Locknut (A) and adjuster nut (B)

2.7 Slacken the rear axle nut

2.8 Tensioning the chain – Type A adjuster

Type A adjuster

7 Slacken the rear axle nut **(see illustration)**.
8 Back off the locknut a couple of turns and turn the adjuster bolt out (anti-clockwise) to tension the chain – do this equally on both sides of the wheel **(see illustration)**. Note

where the front edge of the adjuster block aligns in relation to the scale on each side of the swingarm **(see illustration 2.6a)**. These marks are there to help you preserve correct wheel alignment.
9 Recheck chain freeplay after making

adjustment. Once it's correct tighten the adjuster locknuts, then tighten the rear axle nut.

Type B adjuster

10 Slacken the rear axle nut **(see illustration)**.
11 Back off the chain adjuster locknut a couple of full turns and turn the adjuster nut (front nut) clockwise to tension the chain – do this equally on both sides of the wheel **(see illustration)**. If there isn't a scale on the swingarm, measure the length of threaded adjuster on each side and check that it is the same **(see illustration)**.
12 Recheck chain freeplay after making adjustment. Once it's correct tighten the locknut against the adjuster nut, then tighten the rear axle nut.

Type C adjuster

13 Slacken the rear axle nut **(see illustration)**. Back off the locknut a couple of turns and turn

2.10 Slacken the rear axle nut

2.11a Adjusting chain tension

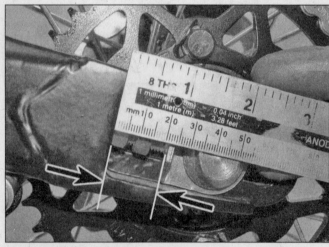

2.11b Ensuring each side measures the same should ensure perfect wheel alignment

2.13a Type C – counterhold the head of the axle and slacken the axle nut...

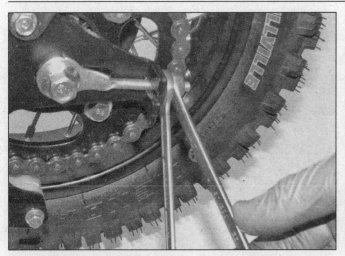

2.13b ...slacken the locknut and make adjustment

2.14 Measure from the index mark in the chain adjuster to the face of the adjuster bracket

the adjuster nut (front nut) inwards (clockwise) to tension the chain – do this equally on both sides of the wheel to preserve good wheel alignment **(see illustration)**.

14 If there's a scale of scribed lines on the swingarm you can check that the index mark on each chain adjuster aligns with the same mark on each side. The type shown has no scale, but in such cases it is possible to measure the distance from the index mark to a reference point at the end of swingarm and check that this is the same on the other side of the wheel **(see illustration)**.

15 Recheck chain freeplay after making adjustment. Once it's correct tighten the adjuster locknuts, then tighten the rear axle nut.

Chain cleaning and lubrication

16 Spray the chain with an aerosol chain cleaner, using a soft brush to work any dirt out if necessary **(see illustration)**. Wipe the cleaner off the chain and allow it to dry. If the chain is excessively dirty remove it from the bike for a thorough clean (see Chapter 6).

17 Use a dedicated motorcycle chain lube, these have properties which will allow the lubricant to stick to the chain and not be flung off like motor oil. Apply the lubricant to all areas of the chain **(see illustration)**.

 Warning: Take care not to get any lubricant on the tyre or brake components. If any of the lubricant inadvertently contacts them, clean it off thoroughly using a suitable solvent or dedicated brake cleaner before riding the bike.

Sprocket check

18 Remove the front sprocket cover **(see illustration 12.4a)**. Check the teeth on the front sprocket and the rear sprocket for wear **(see illustration)**. If the sprocket teeth are worn excessively, renew the chain and both sprockets as a set.

19 With the sprocket cover removed check for wear and damage on the chain slider

2.16 Specially shaped chain cleaning brushes make the job of cleaning easier

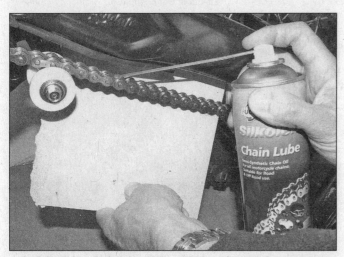

2.17 Applying chain lube. Note use of card to catch overspray

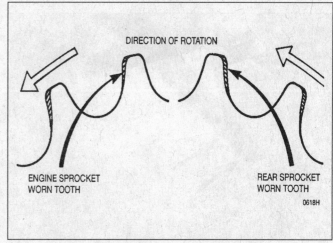

DIRECTION OF ROTATION

ENGINE SPROCKET WORN TOOTH

REAR SPROCKET WORN TOOTH

0618H

2.18 Check the sprockets in the areas indicated to see if they are worn excessively

2.19a The chain slider is secured to the swingarm by screws top and bottom...

2.19b ...and can easily be removed from around the swingarm pivot

around the front of the swingarm – if the chain has worn through the rubbing surfaces of the slider fit a new one (see illustrations).

20 Also check the security of any guards or guides which the chain passes through or over.

3.2a Cap threads must be resting on the cover when checking oil level

3.2b Oil level should be between the upper and lower marks (arrowed)

3 Engine oil level

1 Check the engine oil level when the engine is cold.

2 Unscrew the dipstick from the right-hand engine cover. Wipe the oil off the end of the dipstick. Holding the bike upright, reinsert the dipstick so that its cap threads are resting on the cover aperture, not screwed in (see illustration). Withdraw the dipstick and note where the oil is against the hatched markings on the dipstick end (see illustration).

3 To top up, add oil via the filler hole, then recheck the level (see illustration). A semi-synthetic 10W/40 motorcycle oil is recommended.

Note: Use a motorcycle oil, not an oil designed for car engines otherwise clutch slip could occur

4 Fit the dipstick and screw its cap into the cover.

4 Engine oil change

1 Consistent routine oil changes are the single most important maintenance procedure you can perform. The oil not only lubricates the internal parts of the engine, transmission and clutch, but it also acts as a coolant, a cleaner, a sealant, and a protector. Because of these demands, oil changes should not be neglected.

⚠ **Warning: Be careful when draining the oil, as the exhaust pipe, the engine, and the oil itself can cause severe burns.**

2 Run the engine for a few minutes so the oil will drain easily. Stop the engine and support the bike upright on a crate or stand on level ground. Position a clean drain tray below the drain plug; the plug is accessed through a cut-out in the bashplate.

3.3 Use of a funnel saves spills when topping up the engine oil

4.3 Remove the dipstick

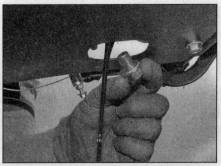

4.4a Unscrew the 17mm drain plug and allow the oil to drain into the tray

4.4b Fit a new sealing washer to the drain plug

3 Unscrew the oil filler cap/dipstick from the clutch cover to vent the crankcase and to act as a reminder that there is no oil in the engine **(see illustration)**.

4 Unscrew the oil drain plug and allow the oil to flow into the drain tray **(see illustration)**. Hold the bike upright to ensure all the oil drains out – this may take some time. Check the condition of the sealing washer on the drain plug – it's good practice to fit a new washer **(see illustration)**.

5 Fit the plug and tighten it securely **(see illustration)**. Do not overtighten it as the threads in the engine are easily damaged.

6 There are no oil capacity volumes given by the engine manufacturers. You can get an idea of the amount of oil required by pouring the old oil into a measuring vessel (we measured around 800 ml), or you can start with half a litre and then continue adding small amounts of oil whilst repeatedly checking where it comes on the dipstick, this being the definitive measurement.

Note: *Make sure you measure the oil level with the bike held upright.*

7 Check the oil level and add more until it is correct according to the dipstick markings (see Section 3).

8 Start the engine and let it run for two or three minutes. Shut it off, wait a few minutes, then recheck the oil level. If necessary, add

4.5 Tightening the oil drain plug

more oil to bring the level close to the upper line on the dipstick, but do not go above it.

9 Check that there are no oil leaks from the drain plug.

10 The old oil drained from the engine cannot be re-used and should be disposed of

Note: It is illegal and anti-social to dump oil down the drain. To find the location of your local oil recycling bank in the UK, call 03708 506 506 or visit www.oilbankline.org.uk

OIL CARE FOLLOW THE CODE

4.6 Add the correct type and amount of oil via the filler hole

properly. Check with your local refuse disposal company, disposal facility or environmental agency to see whether they will accept the used oil for recycling. Don't pour used oil into drains or onto the ground.

Oil filter – paper element

Note: *Certain engines have a renewable paper cartridge oil filter. That shown here is fitted to the Zongshen 1P60YMJ engine.*

11 Fit a new filter as part of the engine oil change.

12 Remove the cover from the oil filter chamber noting the position of the O-rings as the cover is removed **(see illustrations)**.

4.12a Remove the filter cover bolts...

4.12b ...noting the location of the O-rings (arrowed)

4.14a Fit the spring...

4.14b ...and the new filter

4.14c On this engine the cover was secured by two short bolts and one long bolt

Remove the old filter noting which way round it is fitted and retrieve the spring from the housing.

13 Wipe the inside of the housing and cover clean, taking care to return any O-rings to their original locations if disturbed.

14 Fit the spring over the boss inside the housing then install the new filter with its closed end inwards **(see illustrations)**. Install the cover and secure it with the bolts **(see illustration)**.

15 Dispose of the old oil filter responsibly.

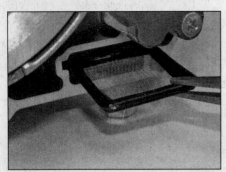

5.1 Oil filter screen will catch oil debris

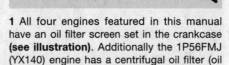

5 Engine oil filter screen

1 All four engines featured in this manual have an oil filter screen set in the crankcase **(see illustration)**. Additionally the 1P56FMJ (YX140) engine has a centrifugal oil filter (oil spinner).

2 Access to these filters requires the removal of the engine right-hand cover (clutch cover). Refer to the appropriate engine chapter.

3 The filter screen can be removed, its deposits washed off in solvent, and refitted. Similarly oil deposits can be wiped from the surfaces of the centrifugal filter. There is no need to renew either filter, although check the relevant procedure for any gaskets you'll need.

6 Clutch cable (manual transmission)

1 Check that the clutch lever operates smoothly and easily.

2 If the clutch lever operation is heavy or stiff, lubricate both the cable and the lever (see Section 20). If the cable is still stiff, replace it with a new one.

3 With the cable operating smoothly, check that it is correctly adjusted. Periodic adjustment is necessary to compensate for wear in the clutch plates and stretch of the cable. Measure the amount of freeplay between the lever and its bracket before you feel the cable operating the clutch; this should be 4 to 5 mm **(see illustration)**.

4 If adjustment is required, this can be done first at the lever end of the cable. Slacken the lockring and turn the adjuster in or out until the required amount of freeplay is obtained **(see illustration)**. To reduce freeplay, thread the adjuster out of the bracket. To increase freeplay, thread the adjuster into the lever bracket.

5 Make sure that the slot in the adjuster is not aligned with the slot in the lever bracket – these slots are to allow removal of the cable, and if they are all aligned while the bike is in use the cable could jump out. Also make sure the adjuster is not threaded so far out of the bracket that it is only held by a few threads

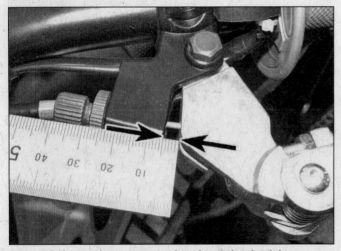

6.3 Use a ruler to measure freeplay at the clutch lever

6.4 Slacken the lockring (A) and turn the adjuster (B) as required

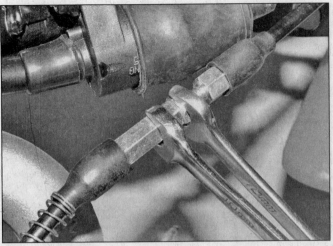

6.6 Slacken the locknut and turn the adjuster nut

7.1 Check the breather hose and its routing

– this will leave it unstable and the threads could be damaged.

6 On all models, if no more adjustment is available at the lever, thread the adjuster all the way into the bracket to give the maximum amount of freeplay, then back it out one turn, making sure the slots are offset – this resets the adjuster to its start point. Now use the in-line adjuster set midway in the cable length **(see illustration)**.

7 Crankcase breather

1 Check the crankcase breather hose for cracks, splits and damage **(see illustration)**. Where its end is open to the atmosphere check that it is not becoming clogged

with road dirt or trapped between frame components. Renew the hose if necessary.

2 The breather hose on competition bikes may be routed into a catch tank **(see illustration 8.4)**.

8 Fuel system

⚠️ *Warning: Petrol (gasoline) is extremely flammable, so take extra precautions when you work on any part of the fuel system. Don't smoke or allow open flames or bare light bulbs near the work area, and don't work in a garage where a natural gas-type appliance is present. If you spill any fuel on your skin, rinse it off immediately with* soap and water. When you perform any kind of work on the fuel system, wear safety glasses and have a fire extinguisher suitable for a Class B type fire (flammable liquids) on hand.

1 Check the tank, the fuel hose, and the in-line fuel filter (where fitted) for signs of leaks, deterioration or damage **(see illustration)**. Make sure the fuel hose is secure on its stub at the tap and carburettor with a clip in place. Fuel hoses deteriorate over time – renew it every three years making sure the new hose is the correct internal diameter, suitable for carrying petrol (gasoline) and the same length as the original.

2 If an in-line filter is fitted, note that it cannot be cleaned **(see illustration)**. If there are signs of contamination visible through the filter body, fit a new one. Note that most filters have an arrow on the body indicating the direction of fuel flow.

8.1 Check that there's no leakage from the tap-to-tank join and from the fuel hose

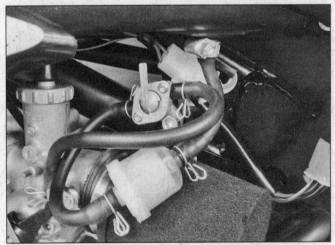

8.2 Some models have an in-line fuel filter

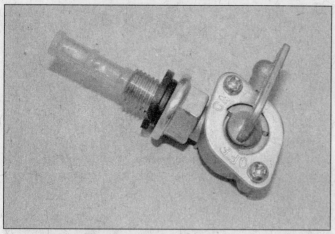

8.3 Fuel tap incorporates a gauze filter

8.4 Catch tank must meet competition regulations

3 All models have a gauze type filter incorporated in the fuel tap **(see illustration)**. The filter can't be inspected without removing the tap, but if fuel starvation has been experienced the filter probably needs cleaning. Remove the tank and then the filter (see Chapter 3).

4 Where the bike is fitted with a catch tank for collecting fuel and oil spills in the event of dropping the bike, check the hoses are in good condition and the tank is securely mounted and empty **(see illustration)**.

5 Check that the fuel cap breather is clear. Pull the cap off the end of the tube and blow through the cap. Also blow through the tube to check the hole in the filler cap is clear. A blocked breather will create a vacuum in the fuel tank, and lead to the engine cutting out.

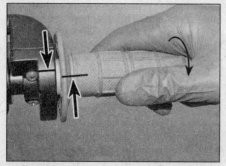

9.2 Throttle cable freeplay is measured in terms of twistgrip rotation

9 Throttle cable

1 With the engine stopped, make sure the throttle grip rotates smoothly and freely from fully closed to fully open with the front wheel turned at various angles. The grip should return automatically from fully open to fully closed when released. If the throttle sticks, lubricate the cable.

2 Check for 2 to 4 mm of freeplay in the cable, measured in terms of the amount of twistgrip rotation before the throttle opens **(see illustration)**. If it's incorrect, adjust the cable as follows.

3 The adjuster is at the handlebar end of the throttle cable, although on some models you may also have an in-line adjuster part way down the cable. Back off the locknut and rotate the long hex piece to alter the freeplay **(see illustration)**. Tighten the locknut back up against the adjuster hex when the freeplay is correct.

4 If the adjuster has reached the end of its adjustment range, fit a new cable.

Cable and twistgrip lubrication

5 If the throttle sticks, this is probably due to a cable fault. Remove the cable (see Chapter 3) and lubricate it (see Section 20). Check that the inner cable slides freely and easily in the outer cable. If not, fit a new cable.

6 With the cable disconnected, make sure the throttle twistgrip rotates freely on the handlebar – dirt combined with a lack of lubrication can cause the action to be stiff. If necessary pull the twistgrip off the end of the bar and clean old grease from the bar and the inside of the tube **(see illustration)**. Smear some multi-purpose grease onto the bar, then refit the twistgrip.

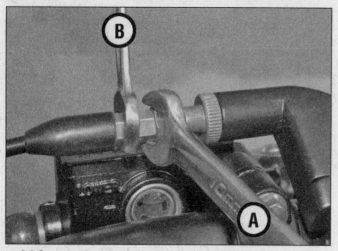

9.3 Spanner A on the locknut, and spanner B on the adjuster

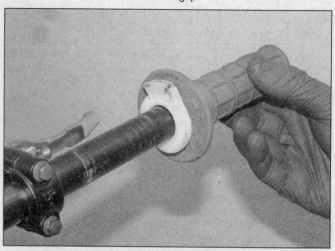

9.6 Lack of lubricant between the twistgrip and bar can cause throttle drag

10.1 Pull the cap off...

10.2 ...then unscrew the plug

7 Install the cable, making sure the routing is correct (see Chapter 3). If this fails to improve the operation of the throttle, fit a new cable. Note that in very rare cases the fault could lie in the carburettor slide.

⚠️ *Warning: Turn the handlebars all the way through their travel with the engine idling. Idle speed should not change. If it does, the cable may be routed incorrectly. Correct this condition before riding the bike.*

10 Spark plug

1 Pull the cap off the plug **(see illustration)**.
2 Using either the plug spanner supplied in the bike's toolkit or a 16 mm plug socket, unscrew and remove the plug **(see illustration)**.
3 Before cleaning the plug refer to the colour spark plug chart at the end of this manual and compare your plug's firing end to those shown, identifying any abnormal condition and assessing its cause if necessary.
4 Clean the electrodes using a wire brush – if you can't remove the deposits fit a new plug. Cleaning the spark plug by sandblasting is fine as long as you blow out any residue and clean the plug with a high flash-point solvent afterwards. Also clean any deposits off the white ceramic body of the plug.
5 Check the condition of the cleaned electrodes. Both the centre and side electrodes should have square edges and the side electrode should be of uniform thickness. Check for evidence of a cracked or chipped insulator around the centre electrode. Check the plug threads, the washer and the ceramic insulator body for cracks and other damage.
6 If in doubt concerning the condition of the plug, replace it with a new one, as the expense is minimal.
7 If the plug can be re-used check the gap between the electrodes with a wire type

gauge or feeler gauge **(see illustrations)**. The gap should be 0.6 to 0.7 mm. If the electrodes have worn and the gap is wider than it should be, or for some reason the gap is narrower than it should be (if the plug has been dropped for instance) carefully bend the outer electrode as required to restore the correct gap **(see illustration)**.
8 Thread the plug into the head by hand until finger-tight, making sure it does not cross-thread **(see illustration)**. Once the plug is finger-tight, tighten it using a spanner on the tool supplied or a socket drive. Tighten the spark plug to the recommended torque – 10

to 12 Nm. Otherwise, if a new plug is being used tighten it 1/2 a turn after the washer has seated, and if the old plug is being reused tighten it by 1/8 to 1/4 turn after it has seated, according to feel. Do not over-tighten it.
9 Fit the cap onto the plug and push it down so it is fully seated.

HAYNES HiNT *Stripped plug threads in the cylinder head can be repaired with a thread insert – see 'Tools and Workshop Tips' in the Reference section.*

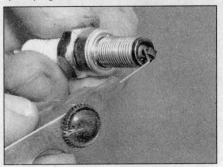

10.7a Using a wire type gauge to measure the spark plug electrode gap

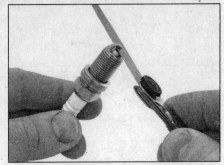

10.7b Using a feeler gauge to measure the spark plug electrode gap

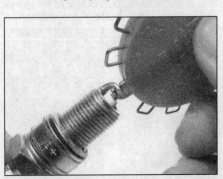

10.7c Adjust the gap by bending the side electrode – a wire gauge is fitted with the correct tool for this

10.8 Thread the plug in by hand

11.1 Slacken the clamp to free the air filter

11.2 Most foam filters have inner and outer sections

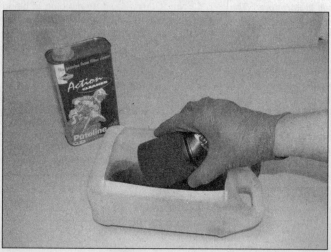

11.3a Wash the filter in the cleaner…

11.3b …then re-oil it

11 Air filter

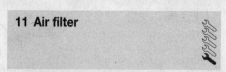

1 Slacken the filter clamp and pull the filter off the carburettor intake **(see illustration)**.

2 Separate the inner and outer foam sections **(see illustration)**.

3 Use foam filter cleaning and lubricating products to clean all old dirt from the filter and to re-oil it ready for re-use **(see illustrations)**. Having oiled the filter, squeeze out excess oil (don't wring it or the foam may tear) so that the filter is oily to touch, but not wet. If the filter is torn or badly contaminated, fit a new filter.

4 Assemble the two filter pieces and fit the filter back on the carburettor at the correct angle, tightening the clamp screw to secure it.

12 Valve clearances

1 The engine must be completely cold when checking the valve clearances. Note that it helps when checking the exhaust valve clearance to raise the bike up on a ramp so that you can see what you're doing. Also position a support under the bashplate so that the front wheel is off the ground; this tips the engine back enough so that oil won't be lost when the exhaust valve inspection cover is removed.

2 Remove the spark plug – doing so makes it much easier to turn the engine over (see Section 10).

3 Remove the two valve inspection covers **(see illustrations)**.

12.3a Valve covers either have a hex shaped head…

12.3b …or will be retained by two bolts

12.4a Remove the engine cover…

12.4b …turn the engine anti-clockwise (as shown by the arrow) with a spanner on the generator bolt…

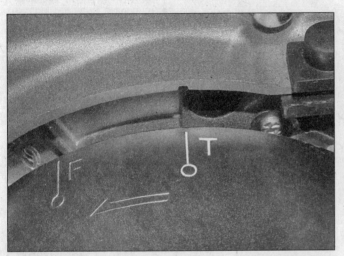
12.4c …to align the line next to the T mark with the notch in the casing

12.5 Insert the feeler gauge between the base of the adjuster on the arm and the top of the valve stem as shown

4 Remove the engine left-hand cover for access the generator rotor; the cover will be retained by two or three bolts (see illustration). Rotate the generator clockwise until the line next to the T mark on the rotor aligns with the notch in the casing (see illustrations). Watch the valves whilst doing this – if on the compression stroke both valves

will be closed and you should be able to feel slight freeplay at the adjuster. If one valve is open, rotate the rotor 360° and realign the T mark – both valves should now be closed.
5 With the engine in this position, check the clearance of each valve by inserting a feeler gauge of the same thickness as the correct valve clearance (select the mid-point in the

range) in the gap between the rocker arm and the valve stem (see illustration). The intake valve is on the top of the cylinder head and the exhaust valve is on the bottom. The gauge should be a firm sliding fit – you should feel a slight drag when you pull it out.

| Intake clearance | 0.10 mm (0.004 inch) |
| Exhaust cleance | 0.15 mm (0.006 inch) |

6 If the gap (clearance) is either too wide or too narrow, slacken the locknut on the adjuster in the rocker arm and turn the adjuster as required using long-nose pliers until the feeler gauge is a sliding fit (see illustration). Tighten the locknut and check the clearance hasn't changed (see illustration).
7 When the clearances are correct install the inspection covers; the cover O-rings should be fine to re-use, but if there's sign of oil leakage fit new ones. Install the spark plug and engine cover.
8 Start the engine and check the idle speed (see Section 13).

12.6a Slacken the locknut then turn the adjuster until the gap is correct

12.6b Check that the setting doesn't change when you tighten the locknut

13.2 Idle speed adjustment

15.4 Checking for play in the steering head bearings

15.5a Slacken the stem nut (or bolt)...

13 Idle speed

Note: *If other engine-related service items are to be carried out (i.e. spark plug, air filter, valve clearances), do these before checking the idle speed.*

1 The engine must be at normal operating temperature, in neutral, and with the choke OFF when the idle speed is checked. As there's no rev counter fitted the idle speed can only be assessed by rider preference, the main consideration being that the engine doesn't falter or stall, and that it's not obviously too high.

2 If you need to adjust idle speed, turn the throttle stop screw on the side of the carburettor body. The screw is central in terms of the throttle slide (which its inner end connects with) and should not be confused with the mixture screw **(see illustration)**.

3 Snap the throttle open and shut a few times after adjustment, then recheck the idle speed.

4 Note that the idle speed shouldn't change as the handlebars are turned from lock-to-lock. If it does, the throttle cable may not be adjusted or routed correctly, or may be

worn out. This is a dangerous condition that can cause loss of control of the bike. Be sure to correct this problem before proceeding.

14 Sidestand

1 Check the stand spring for damage and distortion. The spring must be capable of holding the stand retracted when the bike is in use. If the spring is sagged or broken it must be renewed.

2 Lubricate the stand pivot regularly (see Section 20).

3 Check the stand and its mount for bends and cracks. Stands can often be repaired by welding.

15 Steering head bearings

1 Steering head bearings can become dented, rough, loose or corroded. In extreme cases worn or loose bearings can cause potentially dangerous handling problems.

Freeplay check

2 Raise the front wheel off the ground using a crate or stand placed under the engine.

3 Point the front wheel straight-ahead and slowly move the handlebars from lock to lock. Any dents or roughness in the bearing races will be felt and if the bearings are too tight the bars will not move smoothly and freely. Again point the wheel straight-ahead, and tap the front of the wheel to one side. The wheel should 'fall' under its own weight to the limit of its lock, indicating that the bearings are not too tight (take into account the restriction that cables and wiring may have). Check for similar movement to the other side.

4 Next, grasp the bottom of the forks and gently pull and push them forward and backward **(see illustration)**. Any looseness or freeplay in the steering head bearings will be felt as front-to-rear movement of the forks. If play is felt, adjust the bearings as described below.

Adjustment

5 Slacken the steering stem nut (or bolt) and the fork clamp bolts in the bottom yoke **(see illustrations)**. Engage a C-spanner in one of the adjuster nut cut-outs and turn the nut to take up the free play – only a small adjustment will be required **(see illustration)**. Carry out

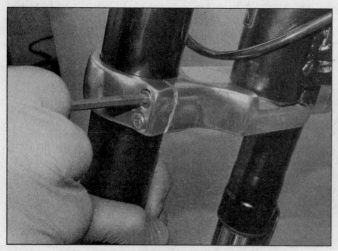

15.5b ...and the fork clamp bolts on each side

15.5c Adjusting the head bearings

16.2 Compress the forks to check their action

16.3 Check each inner tube (arrowed) for pitting on the front facing surface and signs of oil leakage near the seal

the freeplay check again and if good, tighten the stem nut/bolt and the fork clamp bolts.
Caution: Take great care not to apply excessive pressure because this will cause premature failure of the bearings.
6 If the bearings cannot be correctly adjusted, disassemble the steering head and check the bearings and races (see Chapter 5).

Lubrication

7 Over time the grease in the bearings will be dispersed or will harden, or have been washed out by the use of a pressure washer. If the steering action feels rough or gritty, chances are the bearings are dry and worn. Dismantle the steering head and either lubricate the bearings with fresh grease or if they're worn fit new bearings (see Chapter 5 Section 10).

16 Suspension

1 The suspension components must be maintained in top operating condition to ensure rider safety. Loose, worn or damaged suspension parts decrease the bike's stability and control.

Front suspension check

2 While standing alongside the bike, apply the front brake and push on the handlebars to compress the forks several times **(see illustration)**. See if they move up-and-down smoothly without binding. If binding is felt, the forks should be overhauled (see Chapter 5).
3 Inspect each fork inner tube for scratches, corrosion and pitting in the area of travel through the seals **(see illustration)**. Pitted fork tubes will quickly lead to oil seal damage and you'll see tell-tale signs of oil leakage.
4 For front fork adjustment and oil change refer to Chapter 5, Section 13.

Rear suspension check

5 Rear shock life on a pit bike can be measured in terms of hours, especially OE units. If yours is getting a hard life, consider upgrading to a professional shock. Inspect the shock body for fluid leakage and tightness of its mountings. If leakage is found, the shock must be renewed – rebuilding is not cost effective (see Chapter 5).
6 Compress the rear suspension several times **(see illustration)**. It should move up-and-down freely without binding. If any binding is felt, the worn or faulty component must be identified and checked (see Chapter 5). The problem could be due to the shock absorber or the swingarm.
7 Support the bike on a crate or stand under the engine (not a paddock stand under the swingarm) so that the rear wheel is off the ground. Grab the swingarm and attempt to rock it from side-to-side **(see illustration)**. If you can feel movement and it's not due to the pivot bolt being loose (check it's tight), the swingarm bearings are probably worn. To confirm this, recheck with the rear wheel and rear shock removed.
8 Next, grasp the top of the rear wheel and pull it upwards – there should be no discernible freeplay

16.6 Compress the rear suspension to check its action

16.7 Checking for play in the swingarm bearings

before the shock absorber begins to compress. If you can feel freeplay here the bushes in the rear shock mounting points are probably worn. Check first that the shock mounting bolts haven't loosened.

9 For rear shock adjustment refer to Chapter 5 Section 13.

17 Disc brakes

Fluid level check – front brake

1 With the bike upright check the fluid level through the inspection window in the master cylinder. It must be above the LOWER level line cast into the body of the reservoir **(see illustration)**. The level will change as the pads wear, but at a very gradual rate. If you notice a sudden drop in fluid level then there's likely to be a leak in the system.

2 To top up you'll need some DOT 4 brake fluid. Undo the cover screws and carefully

lift off the cover and diaphragm **(see illustrations)**. Top up so that the level is above the lower mark **(see illustration)**, as shown in photo 17.1. Do not overfill.

Caution: Be careful when handling DOT 4 fluid not to spill any on the bike's painted or plastic components – it's an effective paint stripper.

3 Wipe any moisture off the diaphragm and make sure it's folded correctly. Fit the cover and secure it with the two screws.

Fluid level check – rear brake

4 With the bike upright check the fluid level through the window in the master cylinder. The level should be at the top of the window **(see illustration)**. The level shouldn't drop rapidly – if it does there's probably a leak from the seals in the caliper, master cylinder or the hose unions.

5 To top up you'll need some DOT 4 brake fluid. Undo the two screws and remove the cap and rubber diaphragm **(see illustrations)**. Top up the fluid until the level is correct – you shouldn't need much **(see illustration)**. Make

17.1 Keep brake fluid level above the LOWER line (arrowed)

sure the diaphragm is folded correctly and refit the cap **(see illustration)**.

Brake pad wear check

6 The best way to check the front brake pads is to unbolt the caliper and slide it off the disc **(see illustration)**. If the friction material on either pad has worn down to 1mm or less, fit a new set of pads **(see illustrations)**. The

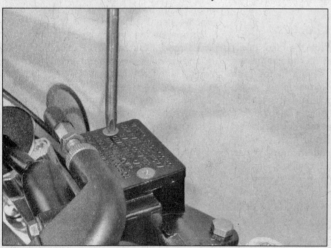

17.2a Undo the reservoir screws…

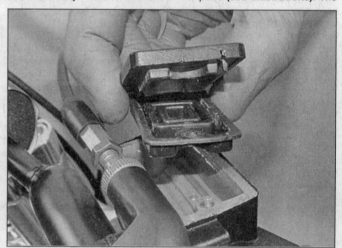

17.2b …remove the cover and diaphragm…

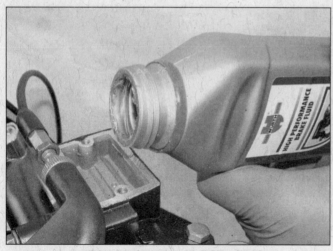

17.2c …and top up with DOT 4 fluid

17.4 A bubble in the top of the inspection window (arrowed) indicates the fluid level is correct

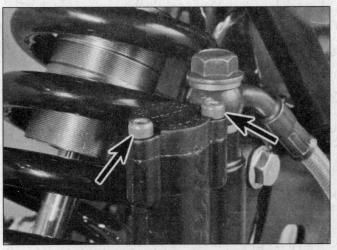

17.5a Master cylinder cap screws (arrowed)

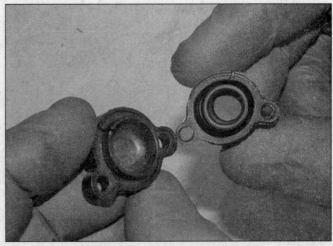

17.5b Master cylinder cap and diaphragm

17.5c Top up with DOT 4 to the level mark...

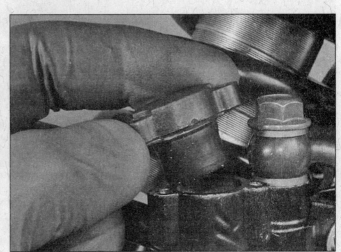

17.5d ...and refit the cap

17.6a Depth of new pads on a single piston front caliper...

17.6b ...and a twin-piston front caliper

17.7 Rear brake pad friction material (new pads) – single piston caliper type shown

17.10 Check there's no leakage from the hose banjos

brake pad change procedure is covered in Chapter 6. Note that some pads have wear grooves which show the allowable limit of pad wear.

7 View the rear brake pad friction material with the caliper in situ **(see illustration)**.

8 If the pads are so dirty that you can't measure the amount of friction material remaining, remove them for inspection (see Chapter 6). If the pads have worn to the backing material check the brake disc for scoring (see Chapter 6). From time to time check the thickness of the disc and renew it if badly worn. The disc is fairly thin and is likely to bend with any sideways pressure from rocks or deep grooves – renewal is the only real solution.

Brake system check

9 Check the brake lever and pedal pivots for sloppy or rough action, excessive play, bends, and other damage. Replace any damaged parts with new ones (see Chapter 5). Clean and lubricate the lever and pedal pivots if their action is stiff or rough (see Section 20). If the lever or pedal is spongy, bleed the brakes (see Chapter 6).

10 Check that there are no leaks from the banjo connections **(see illustration)**. Most models will have braided steel hoses; these are tougher than plain rubber hoses but are still likely to leak if their lining deteriorates.

11 Also inspect the master cylinders and calipers for any sign of fluid leakage due to failed seals. Leakage from the master cylinders is unlikely, but the caliper pistons can become corroded over a period of time leading to seal damage.

18 Drum brakes

1 Put the bike on a crate or stand so that the wheel is off the ground. Hold the brake on and check that the wheel is locked. Release the brake and check that the wheel spins freely.

2 If the brake won't hold this could be due to worn or glazed brake shoes, a build-up of brake dust in the drum or a seized brake operating arm. Brake shoe friction material will wear in use, but you'll need to remove the wheel to check it.

3 If the brake drags when the front brake lever is released this could be due to a dry or sticking cable. Brake drag on the front or rear drum brake can also be caused by weak or broken shoe return springs.

4 Drum brake maintenance usually requires

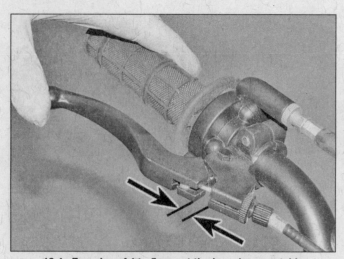

18.4a Freeplay of 4 to 5 mm at the lever is acceptable

18.4b Front brake cable adjuster (arrowed)

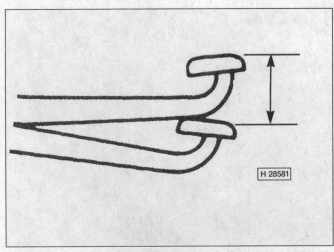
18.4c The amount of pedal freeplay is largely a matter of rider preference

18.4d Rear brake cable adjuster (arrowed)

no more than adjustment to cable freeplay. To reduce excessive lever travel on the front brake turn the adjuster nut at the cable end clockwise **(see illustrations)**. To reduce excessive pedal travel on the rear brake turn the adjuster nut at the end of the brake rod clockwise **(see illustration)**. Note that the face of the adjuster nut must seat fully against the trunnion rather than on its peaks.

5 After making adjustment, check that the wheel is able to rotate freely with the brake released.

19 Wheels, wheel bearings and tyres

1 Clean the wheels thoroughly to remove mud and dirt that may interfere with inspection or mask defects.

Wheels

2 Inspect the wheels for dents and flat spots on the rim and for broken or loose spokes; a loose spoke will produce a dull sound compared to the others when tapped lightly with a screwdriver **(see illustration)**. Rim damage is unlikely to be a problem unless the wheel is buckled or out of round due to accident damage.

3 Visually check the spokes for damage and corrosion. A broken or bent spoke must be renewed because the load taken by it will be transferred to adjacent spokes which will soon in turn fail.

4 Starting at the tyre valve, tighten the first spoke a quarter turn, then miss two spokes and tighten the next, do this all the way around the wheel until you're back at the valve, then move to the next spoke and go round again, and finally the next spoke so that all spokes receive an even amount of tightening. Turn the adjuster at the rim using a spoke adjustment tool or an open-ended spanner, noting that it is turned anticlockwise. **(see illustration)**. Routine spoke tightening is only really necessary on the rear wheel because of the high loads placed on it.

5 Unevenly tensioned spokes will promote rim misalignment – refer to information on wheel runout in Chapter 6 and seek the advice of a wheel building specialist if the wheel needs realigning, which it may well do if many spokes are unevenly tensioned. If the wheel is badly damaged the simplest solution would be to purchase a new wheel complete with tyre.

Wheel bearings

6 Worn wheel bearings will produce handling problems.

7 Support the motorcycle upright on a crate or stand so that the wheel being examined is off the ground.

19.2 Tap each spoke lightly with a screwdriver to show up which ones are loose

19.4 A spoke key or small open-ended spanner will be needed for spoke tension adjustment

19.8 Checking for play in the wheel bearings

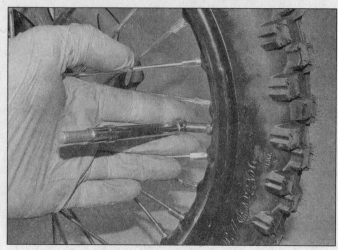

19.10 Press the gauge head squarely onto the valve to check tyre pressure

8 Check for any play in the bearings by pushing and pulling the wheel against the hub **(see illustration)**. When checking the front wheel turn the handlebars to full lock on one side and hold the wheel against the lock. Also rotate the wheel and check that it turns smoothly and without any grating noises (bearing in mind that the brakes and chain make some noise – do not confuse them).

9 If any play is detected in the hub, or if the wheel does not rotate smoothly (and this is not due to brake or transmission drag), the wheel should be removed and the bearings inspected for wear or damage (see Chapter 6).

Tyres

10 Check tyre pressure when the tyres are cold **(see illustration)**. Recommended pressures for off-road are 20 psi (1.4 Bar) front, and 30 psi (2.1 Bar) rear.

11 Always refit the dust cap after checking the pressure because it keeps dirt out of the valve core and also check the valve locknut is against the rim **(see illustration)**.

12 If a rim lock bolt is fitted (usually to a rear wheel) check that its nut is tight against the rim **(see illustration)**.

13 Off-road bikes are not subject to tyre tread depth regulations, but check the tread and sidewall areas for cuts, bulges and anything which might penetrate the tyre and puncture the inner tube. A tread depth of less than 3 mm in the centre can be considered worn.

20 Pivot points and cable lubrication

Pivot points

1 Since the controls are exposed to the elements, they should be checked and lubricated periodically to ensure safe and trouble-free operation.

2 The footrest pivots, clutch and brake lever pivots, brake pedal and stand pivots should be lubricated frequently.

3 An aerosol lubricant applied to the pivot joint gaps and will usually work its way into the areas where friction occurs. If however, the area is dirty or the pivot is stiff to operate it is preferable to dismantle the parts and clean off all corrosion, dirt and old lubricant first.

4 If motor oil or light grease is being used, apply it sparingly as it may attract dirt (which could cause the controls to bind or wear at an accelerated rate). **Note:** *One of the best lubricants for the control lever pivots is a dry-film lubricant (available from many sources by different names).*

Cables

5 The occasional squirt of cable lube into the top of the clutch cable, and on a drum brake

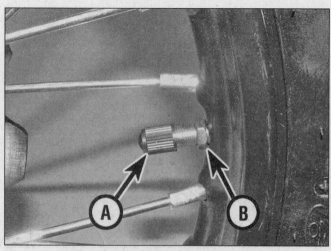

19.11 Tyre valve dust cap (A) and locknut (B)

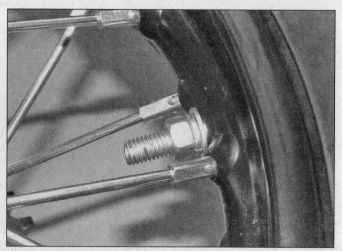

19.12 Nut on the rim bolt must be tight against the rim

20.5 Regular lubrication will keep cable movement free

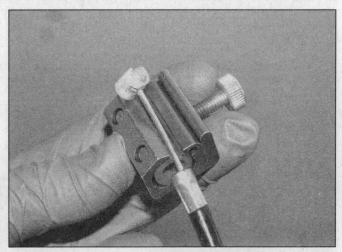

20.6a Fit the cable into the adapter and tighten the screw to seal it in...

20.6b ...then apply the lubricant via the nozzle inserted in the hole in the adapter

model the front brake cable, will usually keep them free **(see illustration)**.

6 If cable action becomes stiff, use a pressure adapter and aerosol lubricant to force lubricant through **(see illustrations)**. You'll need to disconnect the cable at each end.

21 Nuts and bolts

1 Vibration of the bike will loosen nuts, bolts and screws. Go around the bike check tightening all fasteners, particularly the following.
a) Spark plug
b) Engine oil drain plug
c) Generator nut and engine sprocket bolts (you'll need to remove the sprocket cover for access)
d) Lever and pedal bolts
e) Footrest and sidestand bolts
f) Engine mounting bolts
g) Shock absorber bolts
h) Swingarm pivot
i) Handlebar bolts
j) Front fork clamp bolts
k) Steering stem nut (or bolt)
l) Wheel spokes
m) Front wheel axle nut
n) Front wheel axle clamp bolts (where fitted)
o) Rear wheel axle nut
p) Rear sprocket bolts
q) Chain guard and guide bolts
r) Brake caliper and master cylinder mounting bolts
s) Brake hose banjo bolts and caliper bleed valves
t) Brake disc bolts
u) Exhaust system bolts/nuts

Chapter 2 Part A
Engine – Lifan 1P52FMH

Contents

Degrees of difficulty

Easy, suitable for novice with little experience	**Fairly easy,** suitable for beginner with some experience	**Fairly difficult,** suitable for competent DIY mechanic	**Difficult,** suitable for experienced DIY mechanic	**Very difficult,** suitable for expert DIY or professional

1 General Information

1 The 110cc horizontal engine/transmission unit is an air-cooled single cylinder of unit construction **(see illustrations opposite)**. The two valves are operated by rocker arms actuated by a single overhead camshaft that is chain driven off the left-hand end of the crankshaft. The crankcase divides vertically.

2 The crankcase incorporates a wet sump, pressure-fed lubrication system that uses a single rotor trochoidal oil pump that is gear-driven off the cam chain. Oil is filtered by a strainer in the bottom of the crankcase.

3 The generator is on the left-hand end of the crankshaft. The ignition timing trigger is on the outside of the generator rotor, and the pick-up coil is mounted on the stator plate.

4 Power from the crankshaft is routed to the transmission via the primary gears. The clutch is mounted directly to the end of the crankshaft and is operated by the gearchange shaft, effectively it is automatic in operation. The transmission is a four-speed constant-mesh unit. Final drive to the rear wheel is by chain and sprockets.

2 Component access

Operations possible with the engine in the frame

1 The components and assemblies listed below can be worked on without having to remove the engine from the frame. Note however that removal of the engine is fairly straightforward and it is recommended if a number of items require attention, or if the bike cannot be raised up to a convenient working height on a ramp or platform.

a) Cylinder head, camshaft, rockers and valves
b) Cylinder barrel and piston
c) Clutch
d) Oil pump and oil strainer
e) Primary gears
f) Gearchange mechanism
g) Generator rotor and stator plate
h) Cam chain, tensioner and guides
i) Kickstart return spring

Operations requiring engine removal

2 It is necessary to remove the engine from the frame and split the crankcases to gain access to the following components.

a) Crankshaft and connecting rod
b) Gearshafts and bearings
c) Selector drum and forks
d) Kickstart shaft, drive gear and ratchet

3.4a Select the correct adapter (10 x 1.0 mm) to match the spark plug threads

3.4b Thread the gauge hose into the adaptor

3 Compression test

Note: *Special tool: A compression gauge and 10 x 1.0 mm threaded adaptor are required to perform this test.*

1 Poor engine performance may be caused by leaking valves, incorrect valve clearances, a leaking head gasket, a worn piston, worn piston rings or worn cylinder walls. A cylinder compression check will highlight these conditions.

2 Make sure the valve clearances are correctly set (see Chapter 1, Section 12).

3 Run the engine until it is at normal operating temperature. Remove the spark plug (see Chapter 1, Section 10).

4 Screw the threaded adaptor into the spark plug hole making sure that it seats securely and there are no air leaks **(see illustration)**. Connect the compression gauge to the adaptor **(see illustration)**.

5 With the kill switch OFF, kick the engine over for about 4 or 5 kicks until the gauge reading has built up and stabilised **(see illustration)**.

6 A reading of around 150psi is good. If the reading is low, it could be due to a worn cylinder bore, piston or rings, failure of the head gasket, or worn valve seats. To determine which is the cause, pour a small quantity of engine oil into the spark plug hole to seal the rings, then repeat the compression test. If the figures are noticeably higher the cause is a worn cylinder, piston or rings. If there is no change the cause is a leaking head gasket or worn valve seats.

7 Although unlikely, if the reading is high there could be a build-up of carbon deposits in the combustion chamber. Remove the cylinder head and scrape all deposits off the piston and the cylinder head.

4 Engine removal and installation

Caution: The engine is not particularly heavy (around 18 kg), but the aid of an assistant is handy to install the mounting bolts when manoeuvring it back into the frame.

Removal

1 Support the bike on a rear paddock stand, making sure it is on level ground. Work can be made easier by raising the machine to a suitable working height on an hydraulic ramp or a suitable platform. Make sure the motorcycle is secure and will not topple over, and tie the front brake lever to the handlebar to prevent it rolling forwards.

2 Remove the bodywork complete (see Chapter 5, Section 2).

3 If the engine is dirty, particularly around its mountings, wash it thoroughly. This makes work much easier and rules out the possibility of caked on lumps of dirt falling into some vital component.

4 Drain the engine oil (see Chapter 1, Section 4).

5 Remove the exhaust pipe (see Chapter 3, Section 10).

6 Remove the carburettor (see Chapter 3, Section 5). Keep the insulator with the carburettor.

7 Pull the spark plug cap off the plug and secure it clear of the engine **(see illustration)**. Trace the wiring from the generator and disconnect it at the bullet connectors

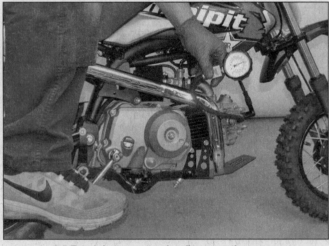

3.5 Read the compression figure on the gauge

4.7a Pull the cap off the spark plug

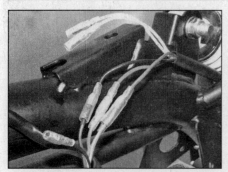

4.7b If necessary remove the fuel tank to access the generator wiring

4.8a Make an alignment mark then unscrew the bolt and slide the gear lever off

4.8b Mark the end of the shaft where it aligns with the slot in the kickstart lever then remove the pinch bolt

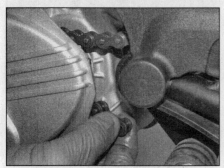

4.9 Threading the drive chain off the sprocket

4.10 A strong hook is useful for stretching the spring to lift it off its anchor

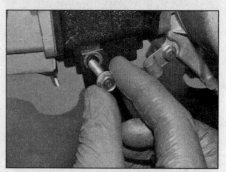

4.11a One bolt on each side secures the bashplate to the barrel…

under the tank on the left side (see illustration).

8 Make a mark where the slot in the gear lever aligns with the shaft (see illustration). Unscrew the pinch bolt and slide the lever off the shaft. Mark its position and remove the kickstart lever in the same way (see illustration).

9 Disconnect the drive chain at the joining link and thread the chain off the engine sprocket (see illustration).

10 Disconnect the rear brake pedal return spring from the rear engine mounting bolt nut (see illustration).

11 Remove the engine bashplate bolts from each side of the cylinder barrel and the two

bolts at the rear of the bashplate; these pass through the footrest bracket (see illustrations). Remove the bashplate. Remove the two bolts which thread through the footrest bracket and directly into the crankcase. Take the weight of the engine and manoeuvre the footrest bracket (complete with sidestand) past the rear brake pedal (see illustration).

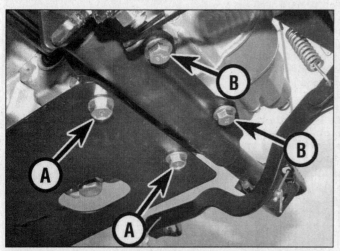

4.11b …and two retain it at the back (A). Footrest bracket bolts (B)

4.11c Removing the footrest bracket and sidestand

4.12a Slackening the top mounting throughbolt and nut

4.12b Slackening the rear mounting throughbolt and nut

4.12c Undo the chain slider clamp bolt...

4.12d ...and manoeuvre the slider off the swingarm pivot

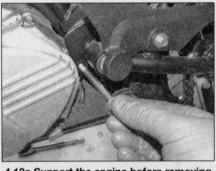

4.13a Support the engine before removing the rear...

4.13b ...and top mounting bolts

12 Remove the nuts from the top and rear engine mounting bolts (see illustrations). On the model shown it was necessary to remove the chain slider to allow the rear mounting bolt to be removed (see illustrations).

13 Withdraw the rear through-bolt (see illustration). Hold the engine and remove the three bolts from the top mounting together with the brackets (see illustration). The engine can now be lifted out.

Installation

Note: *It is advised to smear copper grease onto the engine mounting bolt shafts, not the threads, to prevent the possibility of them seizing in the engine or frame due to corrosion.*

14 Lift the engine into position, aligning its rear mounting lug with the frame's bolt location, and have an assistant install the engine's top and rear mounting bolts; thread their nuts lightly into place.

15 The remainder of the installation procedure is the reverse of removal, noting the following points:

● The rear brake pedal return spring can be difficult to attach because of its tension. It's best to fit the spring over the end of the engine rear mounting bolt before fitting the footrest. Doing this will enable you to position the rear brake pedal higher and there'll be less tension on the spring.

● Note that the bashplate was found to be under considerable tension – take care

to align its mounting holes fully when threading the bolts into the cylinder barrel and crankcase.

● When fitting the gear lever and kickstart levers, align the slit in the arm with the mark you made on the shaft.

● Remake the drive chain noting that the closed end of the clip must face in the normal direction of chain rotation. Check drive chain slack (see Chapter 1, Section 2).

● Refill the engine with oil to the correct level (see Chapter 1, Section 4). You'll need just under 1 litre of oil.

● Start the engine and check that there are no oil or fuel leaks. Check the valve clearances and idle speed (see Chapter 1 Section 12). After the engine has been run and the oil circulated, recheck the oil level and top up if necessary.

HAYNES HiNT *Refer to the section 'Building a bike from the crate' in Reference for details of how to refit the rear brake spring.*

5 Engine overhaul – general information

1 Refer to Chapter 2B, Section 5 for information.

6 Cylinder head removal and installation

Removal

1 If the engine is in the frame, remove the bashplate (Section 4), exhaust (Chapter 3, Section 10) and carburettor (Chapter 3 Section 5). Shift the gearbox into neutral. Drain the engine oil (Chapter 1, Section 4).

2 Unscrew the spark plug (see illustration 4.7a) and unscrew the two valve adjustment caps (see illustration). Remove the long bolt from the right-hand side of the

6.2a Unscrew both valve adjuster caps – they can be tight

6.2b Long bolt with washer retains sprocket cover

6.3a Generator cover bolts (arrowed)

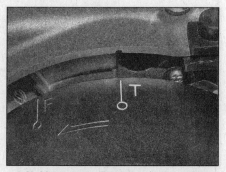

6.3b Line next to T mark on rotor aligns with cut-out in casing

6.3c Punch mark on sprocket and cut-out in head (arrowed)

6.5a Tensioner cap bolt and spring

6.5b Tensioner plunger (note black-tipped end goes in first)

head to free the sprocket cover from the left side (see illustration).

3 Remove the generator cover from the left-hand side of the engine (see illustration). Turn the generator rotor anti-clockwise by hand to align its TDC mark (line next to the T mark) with the cut-out in the top of the casing (see illustration). At this point the punch mark on the cam sprocket should align with the cut-out in the cylinder head at 9 o'clock position (see illustration). You should be able to feel slight play in each valve rocker, indicating that both valves are closed and the engine is on its compression stroke. If one valve is open, rotate the engine forwards 360° and realign the marks.

4 Slacken the three cam sprocket bolts (see

illustration 6.3c). Hold the rotor if required to stop the engine turning.

5 Now slacken off tension on the cam chain to enable it to be detached from the sprocket. Do this by removing the cam chain tensioner; remove the large tensioner plug from the lower left side of the crankcase, followed by the spring and tensioner plunger (see illustrations). Be prepared for some oil loss through the tensioner bore.

6 You should be able to see the tension come off the cam chain as the tensioner arm in the crankcase automatically relaxes pressure on the chain. Now remove the three sprocket bolts and ease the sprocket off the end of the camshaft at the same time as working the chain off the sprocket (see illustration).

7 Remove the single bolt which retains the head to the barrel on the left-hand side (see illustration). Slacken the four domed nuts at the top of the head evenly and in a diagonal sequence. Remove them with their washers followed by the finned cover (see illustration).

8 Lift off the cylinder head (see illustration 6.12). You may need to tap around the head-to-barrel joint with a soft-faced hammer to break the seal between the two components. Remove the old head gasket and retrieve the dowels and seals. Lay the cam chain down across the face of the barrel.

9 Clean all traces of old gasket material from the cylinder head and cylinder barrel. If a scraper is used, take care not to scratch or gouge the soft aluminium. Be careful not to let

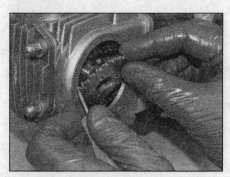

6.6 Disengaging the sprocket and cam chain

6.7a Head-to-barrel bolt (arrowed)

6.7b Four domed head nuts

6.11a Fit the plain dowels (A) and oilway sealing ring (B)

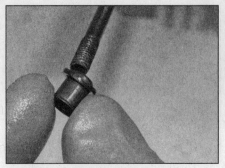

6.11b Fit the short dowel and seal over the bottom right stud...

6.11c ...and fit as shown

6.11d Lay the new head gasket on the barrel

6.12 Fitting the cylinder head over the studs

6.13a Fit a new gasket and the finned cover

any of the gasket material fall into the cylinder bore or the oil passages. If there's a build up of corrosion on the studs or dowels, remove it carefully with wire wool. The dowels should come out easily, but if they are stuck in the underside of the head or top of the barrel, use thin-nose pliers to extract them.

10 Check the cylinder head gasket and the mating surfaces on the cylinder head and cylinder barrel for signs of leakage, which could indicate warpage. Refer to Chapter 2B, Section 7 and check the cylinder head gasket surface for warpage.

Installation

11 Fit the dowels into the cylinder barrel; the two plain dowels go in the top right and bottom left stub locations and there's a seal around the oilway **(see illustration)**. The short dowel (rimmed end outwards) with seal goes over the bottom right stud location **(see illustrations)**. Place a new head gasket onto the face of the barrel **(see illustration)**.

12 Carefully fit the cylinder head over the studs and feed the cam chain up through the tunnel as you do, and making sure the head locates correctly onto the dowels **(see illustration)**. Ensure the head seats fully against the barrel surface.

13 Place a new gasket over the studs, following by the finned cover, noting that its cast arrow points downwards. Fit the washers, noting that the copper washer is on the lower right stud, aluminium washers are

on the three other studs **(see illustration)**. Fit the four domed nuts and tighten them evenly and in a diagonal sequence. Correct tightening is important – the recommended torque is 11 Nm. Refit and tighten the single bolt down the left side of the head **(see illustration 6.7a)**.

14 Make sure the generator rotor TDC mark is correctly aligned (see Step 3). Pull the cam chain up into the camshaft area **(see illustration)**. Line up the sprocket, noting that its holes are offset so it can only be fitted one way, and use a small screwdriver to work the chain over the teeth **(see illustration)**. Make sure the punch mark on the sprocket's outer face aligns with the cut-out in the head and seat the sprocket on the camshaft shoulder.

6.13b Note the copper washer on the lower right stud (arrowed)

6.14a Using a magnetic rod to pull the cam chain into the head

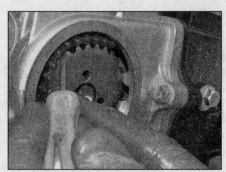

6.14b Use a finger to hold the sprocket in place whilst you install the chain over its teeth

Fit the sprocket bolts and tighten them lightly **(see illustration)**.

15 Now install the chain tensioner plunger (black tipped end first) **(see illustration 6.5b)**. Locate the shaped end of the spring in the end of the plunger **(see illustration)** and push both components into position with the the cap bolt **(see illustration 6.5a)**. You'll see the chain tension be taken up as the plunger is installed. Check that the TDC mark on the rotor and the punch mark on the sprocket correctly align with their cut-outs, then tighten the three sprocket bolts and the tensioner plunger cap bolt.

16 Fit a new gasket to the circular end cover on the left side of the head. Insert the cover so that the lug on its inner face fits between those cast in the head **(see illustration)**. Secure with the long bolt from the other side of the head **(see illustration)**.

17 Clean and refit the spark plug.

18 Check the valve clearances, especially if the head has been worked on and new valves fitted. Fit the valve inspection covers.

19 Refit all other components in a reverse of the removal sequence and fill the engine with fresh oil to the correct level (Chapter 1, Section 4).

7 Camshaft, rockers and valves

1 Refer to the procedure for the Lifan 1P52FMI engine (see Chapter 2B, Section 7). Note that a decompressor is not fitted. The camshaft lobe height measured 26.4 mm intake, and 26.6 mm exhaust on this engine.

8 Cylinder barrel

Removal

1 Remove the cylinder head (see Section 6).

2 Remove the bolt from the left-hand side of the barrel and hook the cam chain guide wheel out of the tunnel **(see illustrations 8.17b and a)**. Remove the bolt which

6.14c Align the holes and install the sprocket bolts

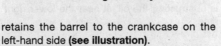

6.16a Fit a new gasket and locate the cover lug correctly

retains the barrel to the crankcase on the left-hand side **(see illustration)**.

3 Pull the cylinder barrel off the crankcase, supporting the piston so the connecting rod does not knock against the engine, and allow the cam chain to pass down through the tunnel **(see illustration)**. If the barrel is stuck, tap around the joint faces with a soft-faced mallet. Do not attempt to free it by inserting a screwdriver between the barrel and crankcase mating surfaces – you'll damage them.

4 Remove the base gasket and discard it – a new one must be used. If they are loose, remove the dowels from the crankcase or the underside of the barrel and retrieve the O-ring seal.

6.15 Locate the tightly coiled end of the spring in the base of the plunger

6.16b Long bolt with washer secure the circular cover

5 Stuff clean rag into the cam chain tunnel and around the connecting rod to protect and support it and the piston and to prevent anything falling into the engine.

6 Clean all traces of old gasket material from the cylinder barrel and crankcase. If a scraper is used, take care not to scratch or gouge the soft aluminium. Be careful not to let any of the gasket material fall into the engine or to block the oil feed jet and return oilway.

Inspection

7 The cylinder barrel is a cast iron one-piece unit. Examine the bore surface for signs of deep scoring and excessive wear **(see illustration)**. If damaged or worn renew the barrel and piston either with original

8.2 Remove the barrel-to-crankcase bolt

8.3 Carefully lift the barrel up off the crankcase

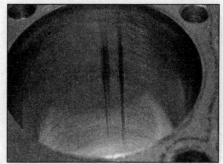

8.7 Wear will occur on the thrust faces of the bore and piston. In this case the marks are not deep.

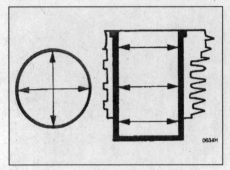

8.8a Measure the cylinder bore in the directions shown

8.8b Use a telescoping gauge to measure the bore…

8.8c …then measure the gauge with a mircrometer

equipment parts or a big-bore kit which increases bore diameter from 52 to 54 mm and gives a resultant 125cc capacity; either way the parts are sold as kit and the expense is minimal.

8 Wear limit figures for the bore are not available, but it is possible to measure the piston diameter and subtract this from the bore diameter to obtain the piston-to-bore clearance. Generally a clearance of 0.01 to 0.04 mm is acceptable. Using a telescoping bore gauge and a micrometer, check the dimensions of the cylinder to assess the amount of wear, taper and ovality. Measure near the top (but below the level of the top piston ring at TDC), centre and bottom (but above the level of the oil ring at BDC) of

the bore, both parallel to and across the crankshaft axis (see illustrations).

9 If the cylinder studs are badly corroded or loose in the crankcase, remove them using one of the stud extraction methods described in Tools and Workshop Tips in Reference. Use a drop of non-permanent thread locking compound on the new or refitted stud and tighten it in the crankcase.

Installation

10 Check that the mating surfaces of the cylinder barrel and crankcase are free from oil or pieces of old gasket and that nothing is obstructing the oil jet near the lower right stud.

11 Remove the rags from around the piston, taking care not to let the piston/con-rod fall against the crankcase. Fit the dowels over the studs and into the crankcase and push them firmly home. Fit a new base gasket over the dowels (see illustration). The sealing ring locates around the oilway (see illustration). Never reuse the old base gasket.

12 Ensure the piston ring end gaps are positioned at 120° intervals before fitting the cylinder barrel.

13 Rotate the crankshaft so that the piston is at its highest point (top dead centre). Lubricate the cylinder bore, piston and piston rings with clean engine oil.

14 Carefully lower the barrel over the studs and onto the piston until the crown fits into the bore, holding the underside of the piston to prevent it dropping. Carefully compress and feed each ring into the bore as the cylinder is lowered (see illustration). Feed the cam chain up the tunnel and slip a piece of wire through it to prevent it falling back into the engine (see illustration).

15 When the piston and rings are correctly located in the bore, press the cylinder barrel down onto the base gasket, making sure the dowels locate.

16 Hold the barrel down and turn the crankshaft to check that everything moves as it should. Fit the bolt which retains the barrel to the crankcase on the left-hand side (see illustration 8.2).

17 Insert the guide wheel into the cam chain

8.11a Fit a new base gasket over the two dowels (arrowed)

8.11b Insert the O-ring seal around the oilway

8.12 Ring end gaps (arrowed) correctly positioned

8.14a Take care with the rings as they're brittle and easy to break

8.14b Slip the chain up through its tunnel before seating the barrel

8.17a Insert the guide wheel in through the chain…

8.17b …and secure it with the pivot bolt

9.1 IN (intake side) marking on piston crown

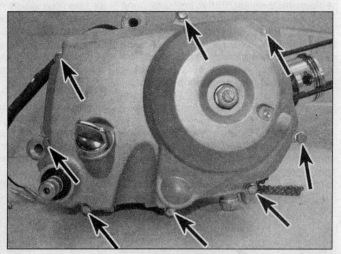

10.3 Clutch cover bolts (arrowed)

and hold it in position whilst the retaining bolt is installed **(see illustrations)**.

18 Install the cylinder head (see Section 6).

9 Piston and rings

1 Refer to the procedure for the Lifan 1P52FMI engine (see Chapter 2B, Section 9), noting the following **(see illustration)**:

● The piston IN marking is located towards the centre of the piston crown, but represents the intake side as with all other engines (see illustration).

● The original equipment pistons rings are marked WLF on their top surface (compression rings).

● Remove the piston ring circlips with a small flat-bladed screwdriver unless a removal tang is provided.

10 Clutch

Removal

1 Drain the engine oil (see Chapter 1, Section 4).

2 Mark the position of the kickstart lever on its shaft, then remove the pinch bolt and pull the lever off the shaft splines **(see illustration 4.8b)**. If there's signs of oil leakage from the seal obtain a new seal for use on installation. Remove the rear brake pedal (see Chapter 5, Section 3).

3 Working evenly in a criss-cross pattern, unscrew the clutch cover bolts **(see illustration)**. Remove the cover, being prepared to catch any residual oil. Note that you may find some resistance from the kickstart shaft. If the

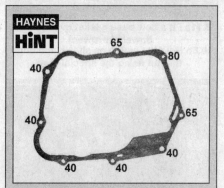

Store the cover bolts in a template of the cover (either draw around the actual cover or produce a sketch) to record the bolt locations. On this engine bolts were of 40, 65 and 80 mm lengths.

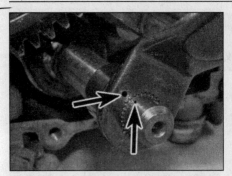

10.4 Punch marks (arrowed) align lifter arm on gearshaft

10.5 Undo the 4 screws and remove the lifter plate

10.6a Work the locking tab out of the slot in the clutch nut

engine is in the frame you'll have to manoeuvre the cover past the footrest as it clears the end of the kickstart shaft. Remove the gasket and discard it. Remove the two dowels from either the cover or the crankcase if they are loose **(see illustration 10.19)**.

4 Remove the clutch lifter arm and ramp plate noting that the position of the arm on the gearchange shaft is referenced by punch marks **(see illustration)**.

5 Remove the four countersunk screws from the clutch lifter plate and withdraw the plate with its gasket **(see illustration)**. The plate holds the thrust bearing. Hold the clutch drum with a strap wrench as shown or as described in the next paragraph.

6 Use a small screwdriver to ease the locking tab out of the clutch nut slot **(see illustration)**. Hold the body of the clutch to stop the crankshaft turning, and unscrew the clutch nut using the special tool shown **(see**

illustration). You can hold the clutch using a strap wrench as shown, or by removing the generator cover and holding the rotor with a strap wrench or with a socket and extension bar on the generator rotor nut. The clutch nut was found to be very tight so you might find the help of an assistant useful at this point.

7 With the nut slackened, thread it off the crankshaft followed by the tab washer and lockwasher **(see illustrations 10.14c, b and a)**. Grasp the complete clutch assembly and draw it off the crankshaft **(see illustration)**.

Inspection

8 The clutch is sold as a complete unit. It is possible to dismantle it to inspect for wear but check first whether you can purchase individual parts. Also you'll need a means of holding the clutch compressed – hand pressure isn't enough.

9 After an extended period of service the clutch

friction plates will wear and promote clutch slip, and the plain plates can distort. The plates can also take on a glazed appearance and smell burnt and the clutch springs will weaken.

10 Assemble the puller across the outer face of the clutch and the inner hub, tightening its centre bolt to compress the two components sufficiently to allow the large circlip around the periphery to be hooked out of its groove **(see illustrations)**. Remove the puller and lift out the plates and centre – keep them in order as a guide to reassembly.

11 Inspect the the inner teeth of the clutch plates and the slots in the clutch centre. Wear of this nature will cause clutch drag and slow disengagement during gear changes as the plates will snag. The friction material will wear over time, causing the clutch to slip; note that new single-sided plates measure 2.6 mm thick (inner and outer plates) and the double-sided plate measures 3.8 mm thick **(see illustration)**.

10.6b Hold the clutch as shown and undo the nut using the special tool

10.7 Draw the complete clutch assembly off the crankshaft

10.10a Assemble the puller across the front...

10.10b ...and back of the clutch, tightening it to take pressure off the large circlip

10.10c Hook the circlip out of its groove

10.11 Friction plate thickness can be measured to check for wear

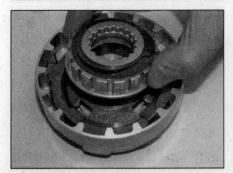

10.12a Insert the clutch centre

10.12b Install the backing plate with its spring posts uppermost...

10.12c ...and fit a coil spring over the four posts

10.12d The first plate is fitted with its friction material towards the backing plate

10.12e The double-sided friction plate tang cut-outs fit around the coil springs

10.12f The second single-sided plate is fitted with its plain side towards the friction plate

12 To rebuild the clutch, seat the clutch centre against the spring plate in the drum, then install the backing plate and place a coil spring over each of its four posts **(see illustrations)**. Install one of the single-sided plates, the double-sided plate and the other single-sided plate **(see illustrations)**. Finally fit the spring seat plate **(see illustration)**. Assembly the puller as for removal to hold the clutch centre compressed and work the large circlip into its groove in the housing **(see illustration)**. Make sure at least one end of the circlip is supported in the cast

groove **(see illustration)**. Remove the puller and check that the circlip remains in its groove.

Installation

13 Remove all traces of old gasket from the crankcase and cover surfaces.
14 Fit the clutch onto the crankshaft end and engage it over the reduced teeth of the primary gear; only the shallow part of the gear sits inside the clutch. Fit the tab washer, the lock washer with its OUTSIDE marking

10.12g Short posts in the spring seat plate locate in the tops of the 4 coil springs

10.12h With the clutch compressed, work the large circlip into the groove...

10.12i ...leaving the open end as shown

10.14a Fit the tab washer...

10.14b ...the lockwasher (OUTSIDE mark faces outwards)

10.14c Thread the slotted nut onto the shaft...

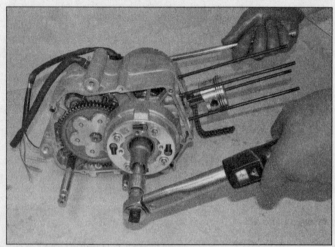

10.14d ...and tighten it whilst holding the generator rotor as shown

10.14e Tab of washer bent into slot of nut (arrowed)

10.15 Fit a new gasket to the lifter plate

10.16a Instal the ramp plate and lifter arm...

facing outwards, then the clutch nut (see illustrations). Using the method employed on removal to lock the crankshaft and the tool to fit the nut (see Step 6), tighten the nut (see illustration). There is no set torque figure for the nut, but we tightened it to 42 Nm. Bend one of the tab washer tabs into one of the slots in the nut (whichever one aligns) (see illustration). If none align, tighten the nut fractionally more until it does – never back the nut off for this purpose.

15 Lubricate the bearing in the lifter plate. Fit the lifter plate (with its gasket) and secure it to the clutch with the four screws (see illustration).

16 Insert the ramp plate centre into the bearing and align the lifter arm on the end of the gearchange shaft (see illustration). Aligning the punch marks will bring the arm and ramp plate directly into line, although one spline out will make such a different that you are sure to notice any error (see illustration).

17 The ramp plate detents locate against the rollers set inside the clutch cover (see illustration). Note that the contact pressure between the two is adjusted via the screw and locknut on the outside of the cover (see the end of this section).

18 Note that engine oil is fed from the pump via a passageway in the clutch cover, through the centre of the adjuster mechanism and into the end of the crankshaft for lubrication of the

10.16b ...so that their centres align as shown

10.17 Rollers and bracket inside the clutch cover

10.19 Locate a new cover gasket over the two dowels (arrowed)

10.20 Thin end of oil filter screen goes in first

big-end bearing. Seals in the roller bracket and behind the lifter plate bearing prevent loss of oil pressure.

19 Fit the two dowels into the crankcase if removed, then fit a new gasket, locating it over the dowels **(see illustration)**.

20 Before fitting the cover, it's a good time to clean the oil filter screen set in the bottom of the crankcase. Use long-nose pliers to pull the screen out. Clean any debris and oil sludge off the screen using a soft brush and solvent. When inserting the screen note that its narrow edge goes in first **(see illustration)**.

21 Check the kickstart oil seal set in the clutch cover. If it has shown signs of leaking or is obviously damaged, prise it out of the cover and tap a new seal into place **(see illustration)**. Fit the new seal with its markings facing outwards.

22 Lubricate the kickstart shaft end with engine oil as this will help protect the seal lips as the splined end of the shaft passes through. Fit the cover and make sure it seats fully onto the gasket and dowels. There may be resistance around the kickstart shaft – grasp the kickstart shaft end and very gently wiggle it to aid seating of the cover.

23 Return the cover bolts to their original positions and tighten them in a diagonal sequence (see Haynes Hint).

24 Freeplay should be checked at this

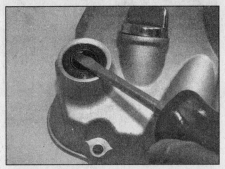
10.21 Prising the kickstart shaft oil seal out of the cover

point, particularly if a new clutch has been fitted. Hold the adjuster screw then slacken its locknut off by a couple of turns **(see illustration)**. Now turn the adjuster screw in until light resistance is felt, then back it off a quarter turn. Hold the adjuster in this position whilst the locknut is tightened.

25 Fit the kickstart lever back onto its shaft, aligning the marks make on removal to get the lever angle right. Tighten the pinch bolt.

26 Fill the engine with the correct amount of 10W/40 semi-synthetic motorcycle oil (see Chapter 1, Section 4). Just under 1 litre will be required, the precise amount being determined by the dipstick level mark.

10.24 Adjusting clutch freeplay

11 Primary drive gears

Removal

1 Remove the clutch (see Section 10). Slide the primary drive gear off the crankshaft followed by its bush and stepped spacer **(see illustrations)**.

2 The large primary driven gear is retained to the gearbox input shaft by a circlip. Use circlip pliers to expand the circlip and remove it from its groove **(see illustration)**. Slide the

11.1a Primary gear...

11.1b ...its bush and spacer can be slipped off the crankshaft

11.2a Use circlip pliers to free the driven gear circlip

11.2b Pull the driven gear off the shaft splines

11.3 Ensure that the circlip locates fully in the shaft groove

11.4 Fit the stepped spacer as shown

12.2a Oil pump screws (longer screw A)

12.2b Note the bush which will either come out with the pump or remain on the driveshaft

the slot in the back of the pump engages the tab on the end of the shaft.
5 Take this opportunity to clean the oil strainer screen at the bottom of the casing. Pull it out with long-nose pliers and clean it in solvent. Note that the strainer is installed narrow edge inwards **(see illustration 10.20)**.
6 Install the clutch cover.

13 Gearchange mechanism

driven gear off the shaft **(see illustration)**. No dismantling of the driven gear is possible. The gear incorporates a shock absorber arrangement which isolates the ring gear from the hub.

Installation

3 Fit the driven gear onto the input shaft making sure it's the correct way round. Install the circlip making sure it locates in its groove **(see illustration)**.
4 Install the spacer on the end of the crankshaft **(see illustration)**. Lubricate the drive gear bush and slide it onto the crankshaft **(see illustration 11.1b)**. Fit the drive gear so that its section with reduced depth teeth is facing outwards and mesh the drive and driven gears together **(see illustration 11.1a)**.
5 Install the clutch (see Section 10).

12 Oil pump

Removal

1 Remove the clutch cover (see Section 10).
2 Unscrew the three screws and remove the pump from the crankcase **(see illustrations)**.
3 The pump can be dismantled to check the rotors but note that spare parts are not available. Drive for the oil pump is via a spindle which is driven off the cam chain on the left side of the crankcase.

Installation

4 Fit the pump onto the crankcase using a new gasket **(see illustration)**. Make sure that

Removal

1 Make sure the transmission is in neutral. Remove the clutch (see Section 10) and primary driven gear (see Section 11).
2 Make a mark where the slot in the gear lever aligns with the shaft **(see illustration 4.8a)**. Unscrew the pinch bolt and slide the lever off the shaft.
3 Wrap a single layer of thin insulating tape around the gearchange shaft splines to protect the oil seal lips as the shaft is removed.
4 Note how the stopper arm spring ends locate and how the roller on the arm locates in the neutral detent on the selector drum cam, then unscrew the stopper arm bolt and remove the arm and the spring, noting how they fit **(see illustration)**.
5 Note how the gearchange shaft centralising spring ends fit on each side of the locating pin in the casing, and how the pawls on the selector arm locate onto the pins on the end of the selector drum. Grasp the end of the shaft, then push the selector arm down until it clears the pins and withdraw the shaft/arm assembly **(see illustration)**.

Inspection

6 Check the selector arm for cracks, distortion and wear of its pawls, and check for any corresponding wear on the pins set in the end of the selector drum **(see illustration)**. Also check the stopper arm roller and the detents in the camplate for any wear or damage, and make sure the roller turns freely **(see illustration)**. Fit a new selector shaft assembly if wear is found.
7 Inspect the shaft centralising spring, the selector arm spring and the stopper arm

12.4 Use a new gasket and engage the slotted drive correctly

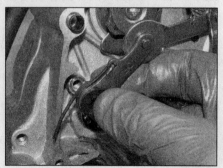

13.4 Remove the stopper arm pivot bolt, arm and spring as a unit

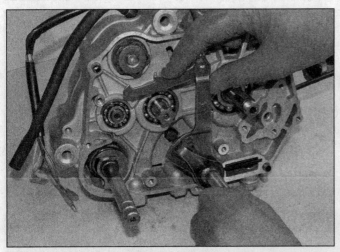

13.5 Lower the arm and withdraw the shaft/arm assembly, noting how it fits

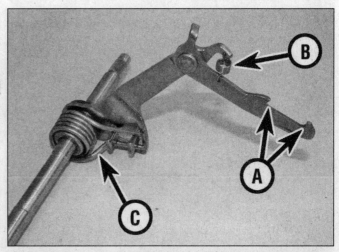

13.6a Check the pawls (A), pawl spring (B) and shaft centralising spring (C)

13.6b Stopper arm roller must be unworn

13.11 Gearchange mechanism correctly installed

return spring for fatigue, wear or damage. Also check that the centralising spring locating pin in the crankcase is securely tightened. If it is loose, remove it and apply a non-permanent thread locking compound to its threads, then tighten it.

8 If the bike has been dropped on its gear lever and there are problems selecting gears, the gearchange shaft may be bent. Fit a new gearchange shaft assembly rather than attempting to straighten it. Also check the condition of the splines on the shaft end, although any damage is more likely to be found on the gear lever splines. Also check the condition of the shaft oil seal in the left-hand side of the crankcase. If it is damaged, deteriorated or shows signs of leakage it must be replaced with a new one – lever out the old seal with a seal hook or screwdriver. Press or drive the new seal squarely into place using your fingers, a seal driver or suitable socket.

Installation

9 Check that the shaft centralising spring is properly positioned. Apply some grease to the lips of the gearchange shaft oil seal in the left-hand side of the crankcase. Slide the shaft into place and push it all the way through the case until the splined end comes out the other side, and push the selector arm down as its pawls engage the change pins **(see illustration 13.5)**. Locate the centralising spring ends onto each side of the locating pin in the crankcase.

10 Fit the stopper arm spring onto its post with the ends facing back and the curved end outermost. Fit the bolt through the stopper arm. Apply a drop of non-permanent thread locking compound to the bolt threads. Install the arm, locating the roller into the neutral detent on the selector cam and making sure the free end of the spring is positioned correctly against the crankcase **(see illustration 13.4)**.

11 Check that all components are correctly positioned **(see illustration)**. Install the primary driven gear (see Section 11) and the clutch (see Section 10).

12 Slide the gear lever onto the shaft, aligning its slit with the punch mark on the shaft. Fit the pinch bolt and tighten it.

14 Kickstart

1 The kickstart return spring and its guide are accessible after removing the clutch and primary driven gear. The crankcases must be separated to access the kickstart shaft. The procedure is the same as for the 1P52FMI engine (see Chapter 2B Section 15).

15 Generator

Removal

1 Remove the engine left-hand cover; it is retained by two bolts **(see illustration 6.3a)**.

15.3 Holding the rotor via its slotted holes

15.4 Operating the centre-bolt puller

15.5 Woodruff key (arrowed) locates the rotor on the crankshaft

2 Trace the generator wiring from the top of the crankcase to the connectors just beneath the fuel tank and disconnect them (see illustration 4.7b). Note that not all wires connect into the loom unless the lighting coil is being utilised.

3 Hold the rotor with a using self locking grips which engage the slotted holes in the rotor (see illustration) or using a strap wrench around its periphery (but take care not to damage the pick-up coil if you do). With the rotor held, undo and remove the rotor nut.

4 You'll need a centre-bolt type puller to pull the rotor off its taper on the crankshaft. The type shown can be obtained through pit bike part suppliers and is not expensive. Back off the puller's centre bolt and thread the body of the puller into the rotor. Note that the thread is left-hand, so it must be turned in an anti-clockwise direction. Turn the puller's centre bolt in so that it contacts the end of the crankshaft then hold the body with an open-end spanner and tighten the centre bolt until the rotor comes free of its taper (see illustration).

5 The rotor has a slot in its boss which locates over a key (Woodruff key) set in the crankshaft taper. If the key is loose, remove it and keep in with the rotor for now (see illustration). The key prevents the rotor attempting to spin on the crankshaft end.

6 Drain the engine oil (see Chapter 1, Section 4).

7 Remove the two countersunk screws which retain the stator plate and gently pull the assembly out of the crankcase (see illustrations).

8 Note the large O-ring around the periphery of the stator plate, the two small O-rings at the screw mounting points and the oil seal set in the centre of the stator plate. All prevent the escape of oil from the cam chain and inner crankcase areas.

9 Refer to Chapter 4 for details of generator coil testing.

Installation

10 Check the condition of the stator plate O-rings and the oil seal set in its centre. If there are signs of oil escaping into the outer cover area, the seals must be

15.7a Stator plate screws

15.7b Gently lever the stator plate free if it is stuck on its O-ring

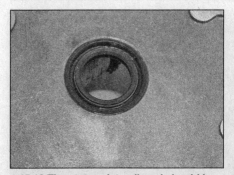

15.10 The stator plate oil seal should be changed if oil has been leaking past the crankshaft

15.11 Stator plate large O-ring (A) and two small O-rings (B – bottom shown)

15.13a Align the rotor slot with the Woodruff key...

15.13b ...fit the nut...

15.13c ...then hold the rotor and tighten the nut

renewed. To remove the oil seal prise it out from the back of the stator plate (see illustration) and press a new seal into position; the seal must be fitted so that its spring side faces inwards towards the crankcase.

11 Make sure the two small O-rings are in their recesses in the crankcase then fit the stator plate (see illustration). Press it into position and secure it with the two screws – you should be able to hear it click into place as the large O-ring seats. Position the wiring grommet into the cut-out in the top edge of the casing.

12 Refill the engine oil (see Chapter 1, Section 4).

13 If removed, install the Woodruff key back into its slot (see illustration 15.5). Instal the rotor so that its cut-out fits over the key, noting that the pull of its magnets will be felt as it passes over the coils (see illustration). Fit the rotor nut and tighten it (see illustration). Hold the rotor to enable the nut to be fully tightened (see illustration). A torque figure of 41 Nm is recommended for the nut.

14 Reconnect the generator wiring and fit the left-hand engine cover.

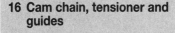

16 Cam chain, tensioner and guides

Cam chain tensioner

1 The tensioner is automatic in operation (see illustration).

2 The tensioner plunger and spring can be accessed easily from the lower left side of the engine although first the engine must be set to TDC compression as described in the cylinder head removal procedure (see Section 6). This procedure covers removal of the engine bashplate, then the tensioner cap bolt, spring and plunger. Note that valve timing must be checked after refitting the plunger particularly if the crankshaft has been rotated with tension off the chain.

Tensioner arm and guide sprocket

3 Remove the generator and its stator plate to access the tensioner arm (see Section 15).

4 Set the engine to TDC and remove the tensioner cap, plunger and spring as described in the cylinder head removal procedure; this will release tension on the cam chain (see Section 6).

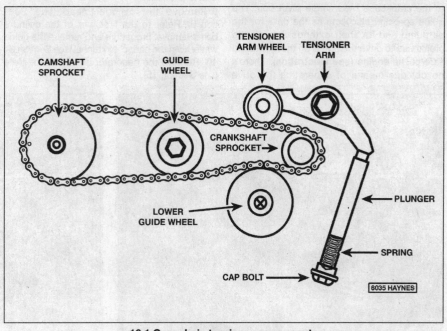

16.1 Cam chain tensioner components

16.5a Tensioner wheel can be slipped off its pivot

16.5b Guide sprocket and oil pump shaft viewed from inside the crankcase

16.11 Lift the cam chain off its sprocket and out of the engine

5 Lift the wheel off the tensioner arm (see illustration). The tensioner arm is retained to the crankcase by a single pivot bolt. The guide sprocket also acts as the drive for the oil pump and its shaft extends through the crankcase to drive the pump on the right-hand side of the engine (see illustration). There's no obvious means of separating the drive sprocket from its shaft; they are likely to be bonded together at the factory.

6 Installation is a reverse of the removal procedure. Note that the valve timing must be checked after refitting the tensioner plunger particularly if the crankshaft has been rotated with tension off the chain.

Cam chain guide wheel in cylinder barrel

7 Remove the cylinder head (see Section 6). Refer to the first part of the cylinder barrel removal procedure and remove the guide wheel from the cam chain tunnel (see Section 8).

8 Installation is a reverse of the removal procedure.

Cam chain

9 Remove the cylinder head (see Section 6). Refer to the first part of the cylinder barrel removal procedure and remove the guide wheel from the cam chain tunnel (see Section 8).

10 Remove the generator and its stator plate (see Section 15).

11 Remove the wheel from the tensioner arm (see illustration 16.5a). Withdraw the cam chain from its sprocket on the crankshaft (see illustration).

12 Check the chain for binding, kinks and any obvious damage and replace it with a new one if necessary.

13 Installation is a reverse of the removal procedure.

17 Crankcase separation and reassembly

1 The procedure is the same as for the 1P52FMI engine apart from the following (see Chapter 2B Section 18).

2 This engine has a plain washer under the bolt at the left end of the selector drum rather than the contact plate (see illustration).

3 Crankcase bolt positions are the same but bolt lengths differ (see illustration).

17.2a Bolt and plain washer retain the selector drum

17.2b Crankcase bolt positions and length (* denotes clip location)

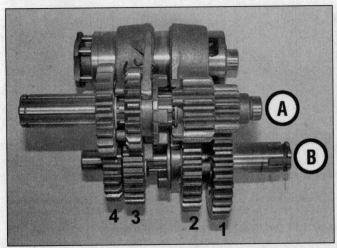

20.2 Input shaft (A) and output shaft (B) – gear positions numbered

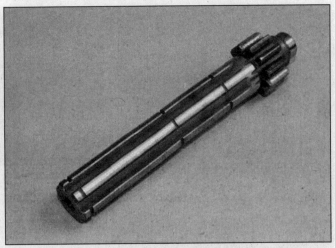

20.5a Input shaft – First gear is integral with the shaft

18 Crankcases and bearings

1 Refer to the information on the 1P52FMI engine (see Chapter 2B, Section 19).

20.5b Second gear dogs face away from first gear...

19 Crankshaft and connecting rod

1 Refer to the information on the 1P52FMI engine (see Chapter 2B, Section 20). Note that the oil pump drive gear is not mounted on the crankshaft on the 110cc engine.

20 Gear shafts and selector drum

Gear shafts

1 Remove the transmission shafts from the crankcase.
2 If the gear pinions show signs of stripped or chipped teeth or excessive wear, e.g. from missing a gear, it's best to renew them (see illustration). A complete pair of shafts can be

purchased very cheaply. If you wish to strip the shafts it's a straightforward operation. Use the appropriate circlips pliers when removing circlips and take care not to strain or distort them.
3 Inspect the dogs and the dog holes in the gears for cracks, chips, and excessive wear especially in the form of rounded edges. Make sure mating gears engage properly.

Input shaft

4 Slide the 4th gear (largest gear) off the shaft followed by the thrust washer. Use circlip pliers to remove the circlip from its groove in the shaft, then slide off the 3rd gear. Remove the circlip and thrust washer and slide off the 2nd gear. First gear is part of the shaft.
5 Build up the gears according to the photo sequence (see illustrations). During reassembly, apply engine oil to the mating surfaces of the shaft, pinions and bushes. When installing the circlips, do not expand their ends any more than is necessary. Install the stamped circlips and washers so that their

20.5c ...washer and circlip retain second gear

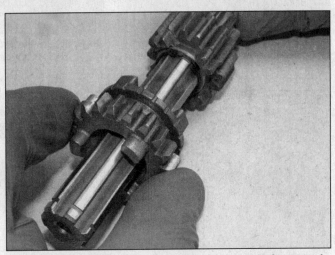

20.5d Fit the third gear with its fork groove towards the second gear...

20.5e ...slide on the circlip and fit it into the shaft groove

20.5f Install the washer...

20.5g ...before fitting the fourth gear (dog holes towards third gear)

20.7a Output shaft – fit all components over the right-hand end of the shaft starting with the bush...

chamfered side faces away from the thrust side.

Output shaft

6 Remove the thrust washer, 4th gear (smallest gear), thrust washer, 3rd gear and thrust washer. Use circlip pliers to remove the circlip from the shaft groove and slide the 2nd gear off. Free the remaining circlip from the shaft and slide off the thrust washer, the 1st gear and its bush.

7 Build up the gears according to the photo sequence (see illustrations). During reassembly, apply engine oil to the mating surfaces of the shaft, pinions and bushes.

When installing the circlips, do not expand their ends any more than is necessary. Install the stamped circlips and washers so that their chamfered side faces away from the thrust side.

Selector drum and forks

8 Inspect the selector forks for any signs of wear or damage, especially around the fork ends where they engage with the groove in the gear pinion (see illustration). The fork ends (tips) will wear rapidly if you do clutchless gearchanges – always use the clutch when changing gear.

20.7b ...and the 1st gear over the bush (dog holes away from the shaft shoulder)

20.7c Secure the 1st gear with the splined washer...

20.7d ...and circlip, locating it in the groove against the gear

20.7e Fit the 2nd gear with its dogs towards the 1st gear...

20.7f ...and the circlip in the shaft groove

20.7g The splined copper thrust washer locates against the circlip

20.7h Fit the third gear with its dogs facing the 2nd gear...

20.7i ...followed by the thrust washer...

20.7j ...4th gear pinion (chamfered teeth facing the 3rd gear)...

9 Check that each fork fits correctly in its pinion groove. Check closely to see if the forks are bent. If the forks are in any way damaged the complete selector drum and fork assembly must be renewed.

21 Running-in procedure

1 Make sure the engine oil level is correct (see Chapter 1, Section 3). Make sure there is fuel in the tank.
2 Turn the engine kill switch to the RUN position and shift the gearbox into neutral. Set the choke to ON.
3 Start the engine and allow it to run until it reaches operating temperature.
4 Check carefully that there are no oil or fuel leaks and make sure the gearbox and controls, especially the brakes, function properly.
5 Treat the bike gently to make sure oil has circulated throughout the engine and any new parts installed have started to seat.
6 Even greater care is necessary if a new piston and rings have been fitted; the bike will have to be run in as when new. This means not over-revving the engine, change up a gear instead, and not running it at more than two thirds throttle. Apply this running-in period for the first two hours of the bike's use. After that, change the engine oil, check the valve clearances and the idle speed and make sure all nuts and bolts are tight.

20.7k ...and final thrust washer

20.8 Inspect the fork ends for wear

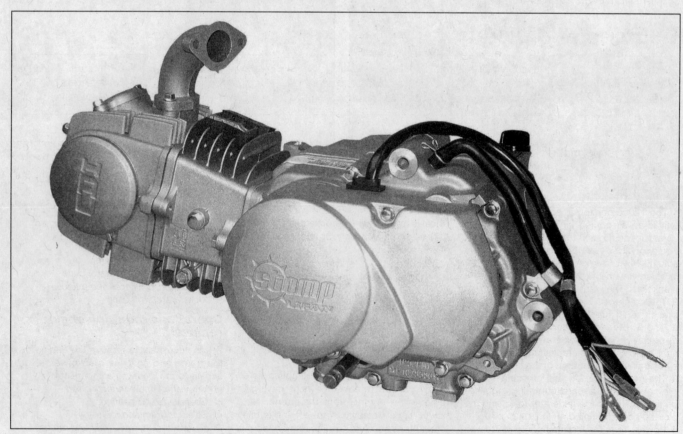

Chapter 2 Part B
Engine – Lifan 1P52FMI

Contents

Degrees of difficulty

Easy, suitable for novice with little experience	**Fairly easy,** suitable for beginner with some experience	**Fairly difficult,** suitable for competent DIY mechanic	**Difficult,** suitable for experienced DIY mechanic	**Very difficult,** suitable for expert DIY or professional

1 General Information

1 The 120cc horizontal engine/transmission unit is an air-cooled single cylinder of unit construction **(see illustrations opposite)**. The two valves are operated by rocker arms actuated by a single overhead camshaft that is chain driven off the left-hand end of the crankshaft. The crankcase divides vertically.

2 The crankcase incorporates a wet sump, pressure-fed lubrication system that uses a single rotor trochoidal oil pump that is gear-driven off a separate gear on the right-hand end of the crankshaft. Oil is filtered by a strainer in the bottom of the crankcase.

3 The generator is on the left-hand end of the crankshaft. The ignition timing trigger is on the outside of the generator rotor, and the pick-up coil is mounted on the stator plate.

4 Power from the crankshaft is routed to the transmission via the primary gears. The clutch is of the wet multi-plate type and is mounted directly to the right-hand end of the crankshaft. The clutch is operated by cable. The transmission is a four-speed constant-mesh unit. Final drive to the rear wheel is by chain and sprockets.

5 The engine can only be started with the gearbox in neutral.

2 Component access

Operations possible with the engine in the frame

1 The components and assemblies listed below can be removed without having to remove the engine from the frame. Note however that removal of the engine is fairly straightforward and it is recommended if a number of items require attention, or if the bike cannot be raised up to a convenient working height on a ramp or platform.
a) *Cylinder head, camshaft, rockers and valves*
b) *Cylinder barrel and piston*
c) *Clutch*
d) *Oil pump and oil strainer*
e) *Primary gears*
f) *Gearchange mechanism*
g) *Generator rotor and stator plate*
h) *Cam chain, tensioner and guides*
i) *Kickstart return spring*

Operations requiring engine removal

2 It is necessary to remove the engine from the frame and split the crankcases to gain access to the following components.
a) *Crankshaft and connecting rod*
b) *Gearshafts and bearings*
c) *Selector drum and forks*
d) *Kickstart shaft, drive gear and ratchet*

3.4a Select the correct adapter (10 x 1.0 mm) to match the spark plug threads

3.4b Thread the gauge hose into the adaptor

3 Compression test

Note: *Special tool: A compression gauge and 10 x 1.0 mm threaded adaptor are required to perform this test.*

1 Poor engine performance may be caused by leaking valves, incorrect valve clearances, a leaking head gasket, a worn piston, worn piston rings or worn cylinder walls. A cylinder compression check will highlight these conditions.

2 Make sure the valve clearances are correctly set (see Chapter 1, Section 12).

3 Run the engine until it is at normal operating temperature. Remove the spark plug (see Chapter 1, Section 10).

4 Screw the threaded adaptor into the spark plug hole making sure that it seats securely and there are no air leaks **(see illustration)**. Connect the compression gauge to the adaptor **(see illustration)**.

5 With the kill switch OFF, kick the engine over for about 4 or 5 kicks until the gauge reading has built up and stabilised **(see illustration)**.

6 A reading of around 150psi is good. If the reading is low, it could be due to a worn cylinder bore, piston or rings, failure of the head gasket, or worn valve seats. To determine which is the cause, pour a small quantity of engine oil into the spark plug hole to seal the rings, then repeat the compression test. If the figures are noticeably higher the cause is a worn cylinder, piston or rings. If there is no change the cause is a leaking head gasket or worn valve seats.

7 Although unlikely, if the reading is high there could be a build-up of carbon deposits in the combustion chamber. Remove the cylinder head and scrape all deposits off the piston and the cylinder head.

4 Engine removal and installation

Caution: The engine is not particularly heavy (around 18 kg), but the aid of an assistant is handy to install the mounting bolts when manoeuvring it back into the frame.

Removal

1 Support the bike on a rear paddock stand, making sure it is on level ground. Work can be made easier by raising the machine to a suitable working height on an hydraulic ramp or a suitable platform. Make sure the motorcycle is secure and will not topple over, and tie the front brake lever to the handlebar to prevent it rolling forwards.

2 Remove the bodywork complete (see Chapter 5, Section 2).

3 If the engine is dirty, particularly around its mountings, wash it thoroughly. This makes work much easier and rules out the possibility of caked on lumps of dirt falling into some vital component.

4 Drain the engine oil (see Chapter 1, Section 4).

5 Remove the exhaust pipe (see Chapter 3, Section 10).

6 Remove the carburettor (see Chapter 3, Section 5). Keep the insulator with the carburettor.

7 Pull the spark plug cap off the plug and secure it clear of the engine **(see illustration)**. Trace the wiring from the generator and disconnect it at the bullet connectors under the tank on the left side.

3.5 Read the compression figure on the gauge

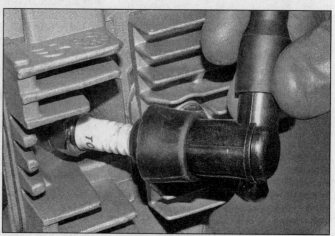

4.7 Pull the cap off the spark plug

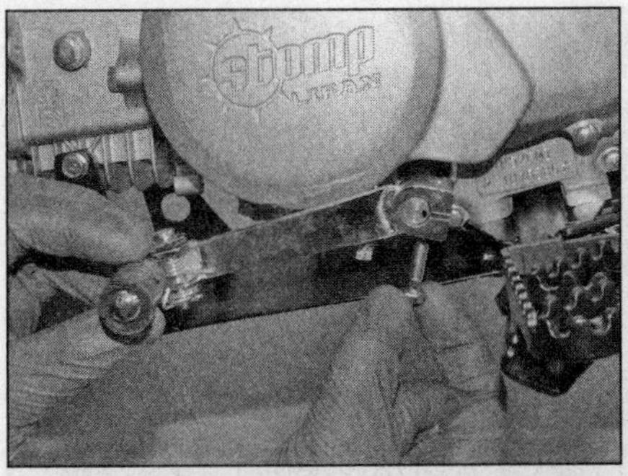
4.8a Make an alignment mark then unscrew the bolt and slide the gear lever off

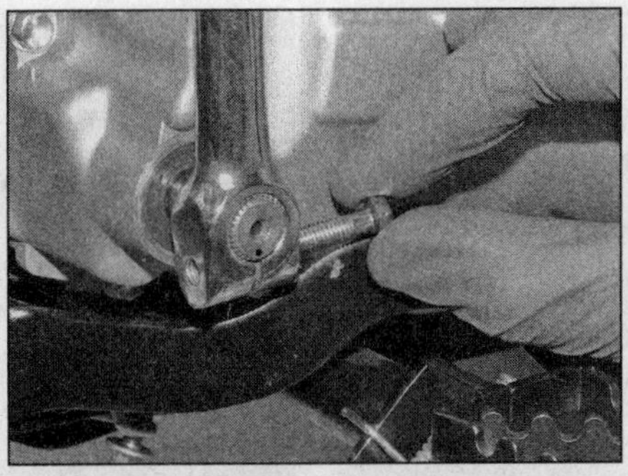
4.8b Mark the end of the shaft where it aligns with the slot in the kickstart lever then remove the pinch bolt

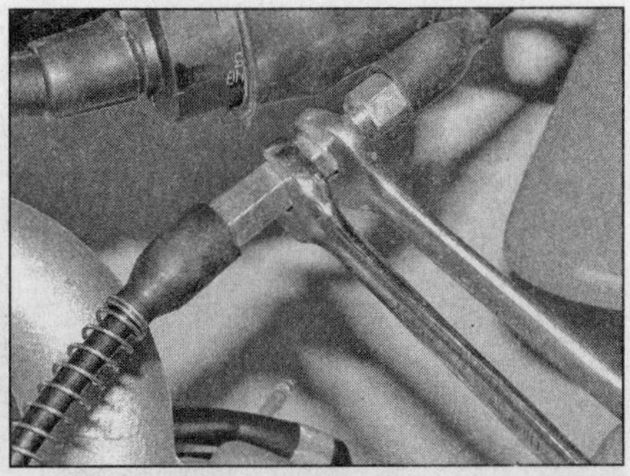
4.9a Increase clutch cable slack at the in-line adjuster

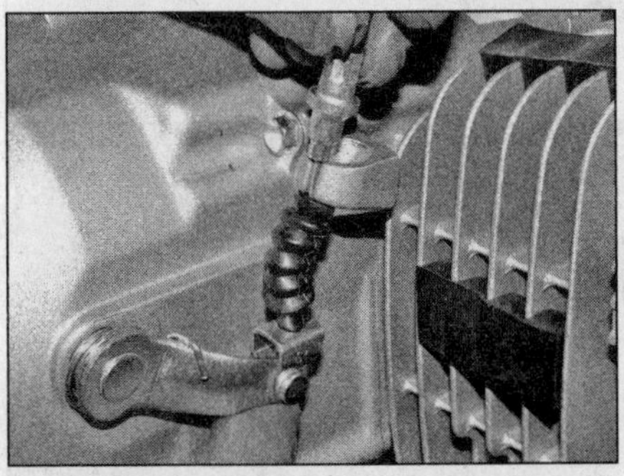
4.9b Pull the cable out of its bracket...

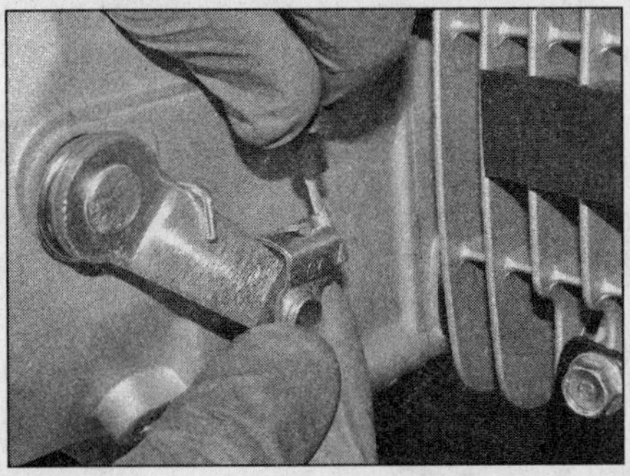
4.9c ...and disconnect its end from the arm

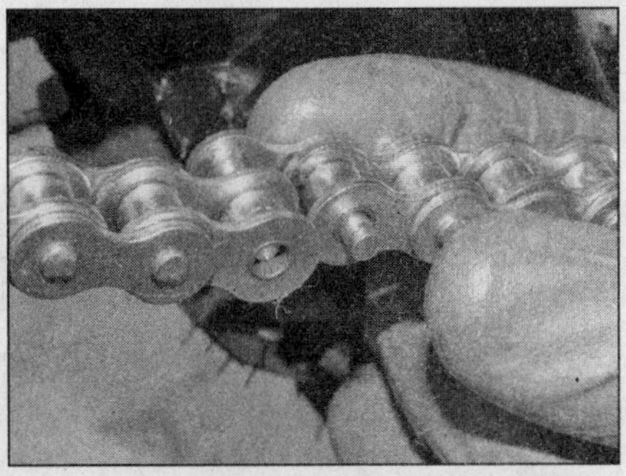
4.10 Disconnecting the drive chain

8 Make a mark where the slot in the gear lever aligns with the shaft **(see illustration)**. Unscrew the pinch bolt and slide the lever off the shaft. Mark its position and remove the kickstart lever in the same way **(see illustration)**.

9 Create some slack in the clutch cable at the in-line adjuster, then push the clutch operating arm up and disconnect the cable end from the slot in the arm **(see illustrations)**.

10 Disconnect the drive chain at the joining link and thread the chain off the engine sprocket **(see illustration)**.

11 Remove the engine bashplate bolts from each side of the cylinder barrel and the two bolts at the rear of the bashplate; these pass through the footrest bracket **(see illustrations)**. Remove the bashplate **(see illustration)**. Remove the two Allen-headed bolts which thread through the footrest bracket and directly into the crankcase, then take the weight of the engine and withdraw the footrest bracket out from between the engine and frame **(see illustrations)**.

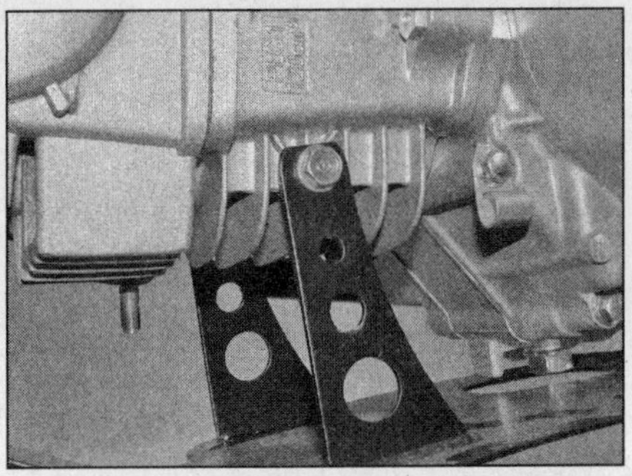
4.11a One bolt on each side secures the bashplate to the barrel...

4.11b ...and two retain it at the back (arrowed)

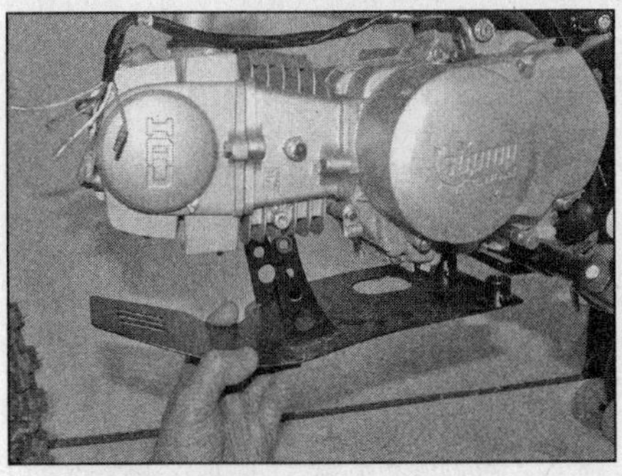
4.11c Lift the bashplate free

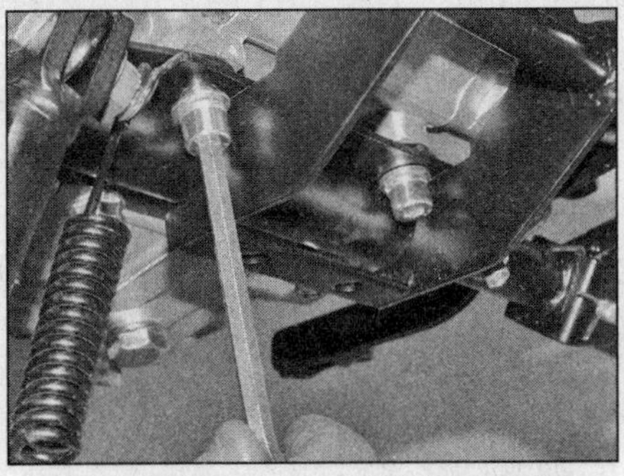
4.11d Remove the two Allen-head bolts...

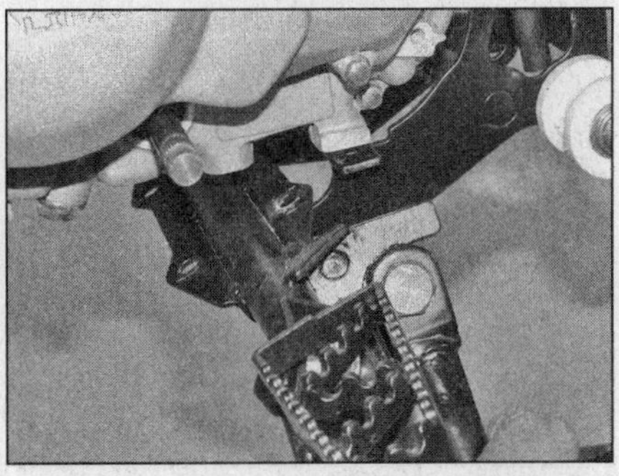
4.11e ...to free the footrest bracket

4.12a Top mounting bracket nuts (arrowed)

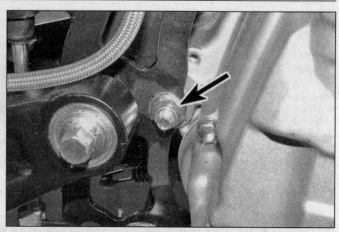

4.12b Rear mounting bolt nut (arrowed)

4.12c Chain slider is retained by two screws

4.13 Engine is easily lifted by one person

12 Remove the nuts from the engine mounting bolts. That's all three bolts on the top mounting bracket and the single through-bolt at the rear **(see illustrations)**. On the model shown it was necessary to remove the chain slider piece to allow the rear mounting bolt to be removed **(see illustration)**.
13 Withdraw the three bolts from the top mounting and remove the brackets. Hold the engine and remove the rear through-bolt. The engine can now be lifted out **(see illustration)**.

Installation

Note: *It is advised to smear copper grease onto the engine mounting bolt shafts, not the threads, to prevent the possibility of them seizing in the engine or frame due to corrosion.*
14 Lift the engine into position, aligning its rear mounting lug with the frame's bolt location, and have an assistant install the engine rear mounting bolt **(see illustration)**; thread its nut lightly into place. Next install the footrest bracket and sidestand assembly,

fitting its rear mounting points between the engine and frame. Thread all four mounting bolts into position and tighten them lightly (note that the front bolts will have to come out later to install the bashplate **(see illustration)**.
15 Insert the top mounting brackets and the three bolts **(see illustration)**. Now that all mountings are in place tighten them, starting with the two rearmost bolts on the footrest bracket, then the rear mounting bolt nut, and finally the three nuts on the top mounting bracket bolts.

4.14a Slide the rear mounting bolt in first

4.14b Fit the footrest bracket without the bashplate at this stage

4.15 Top mounting bracket bolts

16 The remainder of the installation procedure is the reverse of removal, noting the following points:

Note that the bashplate was found to be under considerable tension – take care to align its mounting holes fully when threading the bolts into the cylinder barrel and crankcase.

● When fitting the gear lever and kickstart levers, align the slit in the arm with the mark you made on the shaft.
● Adjust the clutch cable freeplay (Chapter 1, Section 6).
● Remake the drive chain noting that the closed end of the clip faces in the normal direction of chain rotation. Check drive chain slack (see Chapter 1, Section 2).
● Refill the engine with oil to the correct level (see Chapter 1, Section 4). You'll need just under 1 litre of oil.
● Start the engine and check that there are no oil or fuel leaks. Check the valve clearances (see Chapter 1, Section 12) and idle speed (see Chapter 1, Section 13). After the engine has been run and the oil circulated, recheck the oil level and top up if necessary.

5 Engine overhaul –
general information

1 Before beginning the engine overhaul, read through the related procedures to familiarise yourself with the scope and requirements of the job. Overhauling an engine is not difficult, but you will need a set a gaskets and a couple of special tools. Two essential tools are a rotor puller and a peg spanner for slackening the clutch nut; these are cheap to buy and can be obtained from pit bike parts specialists **(see illustrations)**.

2 Most work can be done with a decent set of typical workshop hand tools.

3 To ensure maximum life and minimum trouble from a rebuilt engine, everything must be assembled with care in a spotlessly clean environment.

Disassembly

4 Before disassembling the engine, thoroughly clean and degrease its external surfaces. This will prevent contamination of the engine internals, and will also make the job a lot easier and cleaner. A high flash-point solvent, such as paraffin (kerosene) can be used, or better still, a proprietary engine degreaser such as Gunk. Use old paintbrushes and toothbrushes to work the solvent into the various recesses of the casings. Take care to exclude solvent or water from the electrical components and intake and exhaust ports.

 Warning: The use of petrol (gasoline) as a cleaning agent should be avoided because of the risk of fire.

5 When clean and dry, position the engine on the workbench, leaving suitable clear

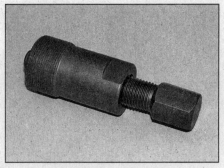
5.1a Rotor puller tool

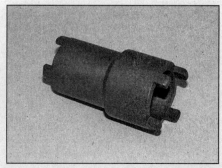
5.1b Peg spanner tool with 20/24 mm ends

area for working. Gather a selection of small containers, plastic bags and some labels so that parts can be grouped together in an easily identifiable manner. Also record component positions with photos or by taking notes. You will also need a supply of clean rag, which should be as absorbent as possible.

6 Before commencing work, read through the appropriate section so that some idea of the necessary procedure can be gained. When removing components note that great force is seldom required, unless specified. In many cases, a component's reluctance to be removed is indicative of an incorrect approach or removal method – if in any doubt, re-check with the text.

7 When disassembling the engine, keep 'mated' parts together that have been in contact with each other during engine operation. These 'mated' parts must be reused or replaced as an assembly.

8 A complete engine stripdown should be done in the following general order with reference to the appropriate Sections.

a) *Remove the generator cover (left-hand engine cover)*
b) *Remove the cylinder head*
c) *Remove the cylinder barrel and piston*
d) *Remove the clutch cover (right-hand engine cover)*
e) *Remove the clutch*
f) *Remove the primary gears*
g) *Remove the oil pump*
h) *Remove the gearchange mechanism*
i) *Remove the kickstart return spring*

j) *Remove the generator rotor and stator*
k) *Remove the cam chain*
l) *Separate the crankcase halves*
m) *Remove the selector drum and forks*
n) *Remove the transmission shafts*
o) *Remove the kickstart shaft*
p) *Remove the crankshaft*

Reassembly

9 Reassembly is accomplished by reversing the general disassembly sequence.

6 Cylinder head removal and installation

Removal

1 If the engine is in the frame, remove the bash plate (see Section 4), exhaust (see Chapter 3, Section 10) and carburettor (see Chapter 3, Section 5), and pull the cap off the spark plug **(see illustration 4.7)**. Shift the gearbox into neutral. Drain the engine oil (see Chapter 1, Section 4).

2 Remove the two valve adjustment caps and unscrew the spark plug **(see illustration)**. Remove the long bolt from the right-hand side of the head to free the sprocket cover from the left side **(see illustration)**.

3 Remove the generator cover from the left-hand side of the engine **(see illustration 16.1)**. Turn the generator rotor anti-clockwise by hand to align its TDC mark (line next to

6.2a Intake and exhaust valve caps are retained by two bolts

6.2b Long bolt with washer retains sprocket cover

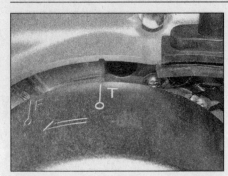

6.3a Line next to T mark on rotor aligns with cut-out in casing

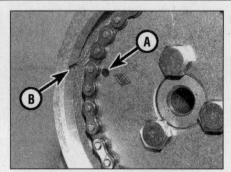

6.3b Punch mark on sprocket (A) and cut-out in head (B)

6.5a Tensioner cap bolt and spring

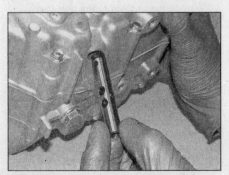

6.5b Tensioner plunger (note black-tipped end goes in first)

6.6 Disengaging the sprocket and cam chain

the T mark) with the cut-out in the top of the casing **(see illustration)**. At this point the punch mark on the cam sprocket should align with the cut-out in the cylinder head at 9 o'clock position **(see illustration)**. You should be able to feel slight play in each valve rocker, indicating that both valves are closed and the engine is on its compression stroke. If one valve is still open, rotate the engine a further 360° and realign the marks.

4 Slacken the three cam sprocket bolts. Hold the rotor if required to stop the engine turning.

5 Now slacken off tension on the cam chain to enable it to be detached from the sprocket. Do this by removing the cam chain tensioner; remove the large tensioner plug from the

lower left side of the crankcase, followed by the spring and tensioner plunger **(see illustrations)**. Note that there is no need to remove the small blanking bolt from the tensioner plunger channel. Be prepared for some oil loss via the tensioner plunger bore.

6 You should be able to see the tension come off the cam chain as the tensioner arm in the crankcase automatically relaxes pressure on the chain. Unscrew the three sprocket bolts and ease the sprocket off the end of the camshaft at the same time as working the chain off the sprocket **(see illustration)**.

7 Remove the single bolt which retains the head to the barrel on the left-hand side **(see illustration)**. Slacken the four domed nuts at

the top of the head evenly and in a diagonal sequence. Remove them with their washers followed by the finned cover **(see illustration)**.

8 Lift off the cylinder head **(see illustration)**. You may need to tap around the head-to-barrel joint with a soft-faced hammer to break the seal between the two components. Remove the old head gasket and retrieve the dowels and seal. Lay the cam chain down across the face of the barrel.

9 Clean all traces of old gasket material from the cylinder head and cylinder barrel. If a scraper is used, take care not to scratch or gouge the soft aluminium. Be careful not to let any of the gasket material fall into the cylinder bore or the oil passages. If there's a build up of corrosion on the studs or dowels, remove it carefully with wire wool. The dowels should come out easily, but if they are stuck in the underside of the head or top of the barrel, use thin-nosed pliers to extract them.

10 Check the cylinder head gasket and the mating surfaces on the cylinder head and cylinder barrel for signs of leakage, which could indicate warpage. Refer to Section 7 and check the cylinder head gasket surface for warpage.

Installation

11 Fit the dowels into the cylinder barrel; the two plain dowels go in the top right and bottom left stub locations and the short dowel with seal goes in the bottom right

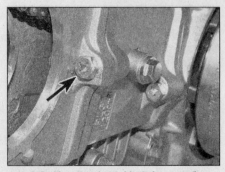

6.7a Head-to-barrel bolt (arrowed)

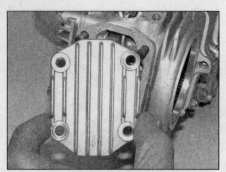

6.7b Removing the finned cover

6.8 Carefully lift the head up off the barrel

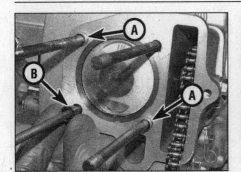

6.11a Fit the plain dowels (A), short dowel and seal (B)...

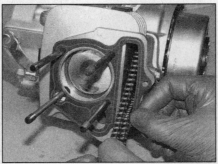

6.11b ...then lay the new gasket on the barrel

6.12 Cam chain located over camshaft shoulder

stud location (see illustration). Place a new head gasket onto the face of the barrel (see illustration).

12 Carefully fit the cylinder head over the studs and feed the cam chain up through the tunnel as you do, and making sure it locates correctly onto the dowels (see illustration 6.8). Ensure the head seats fully against the barrel surface. Position the cam chain over the end of the camshaft (see illustration).

13 Place a new gasket over the studs, following by the finned cover, noting that its cast arrow points downwards. Fit the washers, noting that the copper washer is on the lower right stud, aluminium washers are on the three other studs (see illustration). Fit the four domed nuts and tighten them evenly and in a diagonal sequence. Correct tightening is important – a torque setting of 11 Nm is recommended. Tighten the single bolt down the left side of the head (see illustration).

14 Make sure the generator rotor TDC mark is correctly aligned (see Step 3). Hold the cam chain taut with one finger and fit the cam sprocket so that the punch mark on its outer face aligns with the cut-out in the head, also aligning the bolt holes in the sprocket with those in the camshaft (they are offset slightly). Use a small screwdriver to locate the chain onto the sprocket teeth (see illustration). Seat the sprocket onto the camshaft shoulder

6.13a Fit a new gasket...

6.13b ...the finned cover and the head nuts. Note the copper washer on the lower right stud (arrowed)

and check the alignment of the punch mark and cut-out. Reposition the chain on the sprocket if necessary. Fit the sprocket bolts and tighten them lightly.

15 Now install the chain tensioner plunger (black tipped end first). Locate the shaped end of the spring in the end of the plunger and push both components into position with the cap bolt (see illustration). You'll see the chain tension be taken up as the plunger is installed. Check that the TDC mark on the rotor and the punch mark on the sprocket correctly align with their cut-outs, then tighten the three sprocket bolts and the tensioner plunger cap bolt.

16 Fit a new gasket to the circular end cover on the left side of the head (see illustration). Insert the cover so that its tab aligns with the tab on the head (and the cast CDI is up the right way), then secure with the long bolt from the other side of the head.

17 Clean and refit the spark plug.

18 Check the valve clearances, especially if the head has been worked on and new valves fitted. Fit the valve inspection caps.

19 Refit all other components in a reverse of the removal sequence. Refill the engine with the correct amount of oil (see Chapter 1, Section 4).

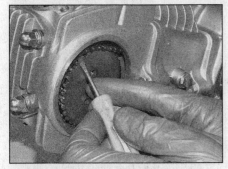

6.14 Feed the chain onto the sprocket as shown

6.15 Locate the tightly coiled end of the spring in the base of the plunger

6.16 Fit a new gasket and align the cover and head tabs (arrowed)

7.3a End cover bolts (arrowed)

7.3b Thread an M8 bolt into the shaft end and pull the shaft out

7.5 Withdraw the camshaft from the head

7   Camshaft, rockers and valves

1 Valve overhaul involves removing the valves and associated components from the cylinder head, cleaning them and checking them for wear. Valve seat re-cutting or valve guide replacement, if necessary, are a job for an engineer, but note that renewal of the head would be the cheaper option.

Rocker arms and camshaft

Removal

2 Removal of the cylinder head is advised. It is possible to work on the camshaft with the head in place, having disconnected the cam chain from the sprocket, but it's much easier to do this on the bench.

3 Remove the two bolts from the right-hand side of the head to free the end cover **(see illustration)**. This will give access to the rocker shaft ends. The shafts are only a slip fit in the head but it's best to thread an M8 bolt into the shaft end and pull it to withdraw the shaft **(see illustration)**. Note which is the intake and which is the exhaust rocker shaft so that they can be returned to their original locations.

4 The rocker shafts also support the decompressor mechanism which rides on the camshaft.

5 Withdraw the camshaft from the cylinder head **(see illustration)**.

Inspection

6 Check the bearing on each end of the camshaft – they must run smoothly, quietly and freely and there should be no excessive play between the inner and outer races or obvious signs of wear between the outer race and the housing in the cylinder head. Also check the cam lobes for heat discoloration (blue appearance), score marks, chipped areas, flat spots and spalling **(see illustration)**. The lobe heights measure 26.4 mm when new.

7 Check the fit of each rocker arm on its shaft. They should move freely with a light fit, but no appreciable freeplay **(see illustration)**. Check the contact pad and contact tip of the valve clearance adjuster; again there should be no sign of wear **(see illustration)**.

Installation

8 Lubricate the camshaft bearings and lobes with engine oil then slide the camshaft into the head.

9 Install the first rocker shaft in the head (intake or exhaust as noted on removal), hold the decompressor in position and push the rocker shaft through **(see illustration)**. Do the same for the other rocker arm **(see illustration)**.

10 Fit a new gasket to the end cover and

7.6 Check the cam lobes (arrowed)

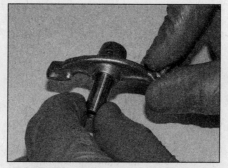

7.7a Feel for play between the shaft and rocker

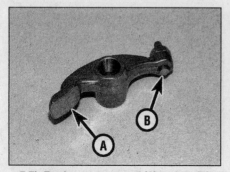

7.7b Rocker contact pad (A) and tip (B)

7.9a Slide the shaft through the exhaust rocker, then the decompressor bracket

7.9b Slide the other shaft through the decompressor bracket and the intake rocker

7.10 Use a new gasket when fitting the end cover

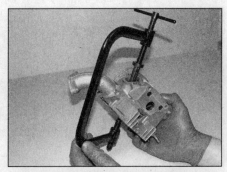

7.12a Compressing the valve springs using a valve spring compressor

7.12b Make sure the compressor locates correctly both on the top of the spring retainer...

install it **(see illustration)**. Tighten its two bolts.

Valves

11 Keep the intake and exhaust valves separate, along with their related components, so that they can be returned to their original locations without getting mixed up.

12 Compress the valve spring on the first valve with a spring compressor, making sure it is correctly located onto each end of the valve assembly **(see illustration)**. On the top of the valve the adaptor needs to be about the same size as the spring retainer – if it is too small it will be difficult to remove and install the collets **(see illustration)**. On the underside of the head make sure the compressor contacts the centre of the valve **(see illustration)**. Do not compress the springs any more than is absolutely necessary.

13 Refer to the valve procedure in Chapter 2C, Section 7. The procedure is the same for all engines.

Cylinder head

14 Inspect the head very carefully for cracks and other damage. If cracks are found, a new head is required.

15 Using a precision straight-edge and a feeler gauge, check the head gasket mating surface for warpage **(see illustration)**. Take six measurements, one along each side and two diagonally across. If the head is warped

7.12c ...and on the bottom of the valve

(beyond 0.05 mm), take it to a specialist repair shop for advice on having the surface skimmed.

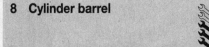

8 Cylinder barrel

Removal

1 Remove the cylinder head (see Section 6).
2 Remove the bolt from the left-hand side of the barrel and hook the cam chain guide wheel out of the tunnel **(see illustration)**. Remove the bolt which retains the barrel to the crankcase on the left-hand side **(see illustration)**.

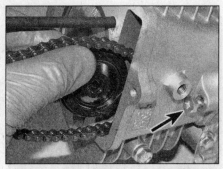

8.2b ...withdraw the guide wheel and remove the barrel-to-crankcase bolt (arrowed)

7.15 Check the gasket face for warpage

3 Hold the cam chain and pull the cylinder barrel off the crankcase, supporting the piston so the connecting rod does not knock against the engine, then pass the cam chain down through the tunnel **(see illustration)**. If the barrel is stuck, tap around the joint faces with a soft-faced mallet. Do not attempt to free it by inserting a screwdriver between the barrel and crankcase mating surfaces – you'll damage them.
4 Remove the base gasket and discard it – a new one must be used. If they are loose, remove the dowels from the crankcase or the underside of the barrel and retrieve the O-ring seal.
5 Stuff clean rag into the cam chain tunnel and around the connecting rod to protect

8.2a Remove the pivot bolt from the side of the barrel...

8.3 Carefully lift the barrel up off the crankcase

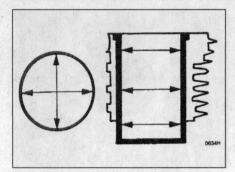

8.9a Measure the cylinder bore in the directions shown

8.9b Use a telescoping gauge to measure the bore…

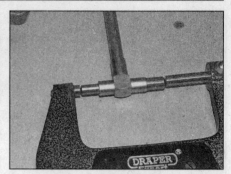

8.9c …then measure the gauge with a mircrometer

and support it and the piston and to prevent anything falling into the engine.

6 Clean all traces of old gasket material from the cylinder barrel and crankcase. If a scraper is used, take care not to scratch or gouge the soft aluminium. Be careful not to let any of the gasket material fall into the engine or to block the oil jet and oil return passage.

Inspection

Note: *Do not attempt to separate the cylinder liner from the cylinder barrel.*

7 Check the cylinder walls carefully for scratches and score marks. No oversizes are available precluding the option of reboring the liner.

8 Using a precision straight-edge and feeler gauges check the barrel top surface for warpage. Take six measurements, one along each side and two diagonally across. If the barrel is warped beyond 0.05 mm take it to an

engineer for an opinion, though be prepared to have to buy a new one.

9 Wear limit figures for the bore are not available, but it is possible to measure the piston diameter (see Section 9) and subtract this from the bore diameter to obtain the piston-to-bore clearance. Generally a clearance of 0.01 to 0.04 mm is acceptable. Using a telescoping bore gauge and a micrometer, check the dimensions of the cylinder to assess the amount of wear, taper and ovality. Measure near the top (but below the level of the top piston ring at TDC), centre and bottom (but above the level of the oil ring at BDC) of the bore, both parallel to and across the crankshaft axis **(see illustrations)**.

10 If the cylinder studs are badly corroded or loose in the crankcase, remove them using one of the stud extraction methods described in *Tools and Workshop Tips* in Reference.

Use a drop of non-permanent thread locking compound on the new or refitted stud and tighten it in the crankcase.

Installation

11 Check that the mating surfaces of the cylinder barrel and crankcase are free from oil or pieces of old gasket.

12 Fit the dowels over the studs and into the crankcase and push them firmly home. Also fit the O-ring seal into its location **(see illustration)**.

13 Remove the rags from around the piston and the cam chain tunnel, taking care not to let the connecting rod fall against the rim of the crankcase, and lay the new base gasket in place, locating it over the dowels on the two left side studs **(see illustration)**. The gasket can only fit one way. Never re-use the old gasket.

14 Ensure the piston ring end gaps are positioned at 120° intervals before fitting the cylinder barrel.

15 Rotate the crankshaft so that the piston is at its highest point (top dead centre). Lubricate the cylinder bore, piston and piston rings with clean engine oil.

16 Carefully lower the barrel over the studs and onto the piston until the crown fits into the bore, holding the underside of the piston to prevent it dropping, and making sure it enters the bore squarely and does not get cocked sideways **(see illustration)**. Feed the cam chain up the tunnel and slip a piece of wire through it to prevent it falling back into the engine.

17 Carefully compress and feed each ring into the bore as the cylinder is lowered. If necessary, use a soft mallet to gently tap the cylinder down, but do not use force if it appears to be stuck as the piston and/or rings will be damaged.

18 When the piston and rings are correctly located in the bore, press the cylinder barrel down onto the base gasket, making sure the dowels locate.

19 Hold the barrel down and turn the crankshaft to check that everything moves as it should. Fit the bolt which retains the barrel to the crankcase on the left-hand side.

20 Insert the guide wheel into the cam chain and hold it in position whilst the retaining bolt is installed **(see illustration)**.

21 Install the cylinder head (see Section 6).

8.12 Dowel locations (A) and O-ring seal (B)

8.13 Lay the new gasket over the dowels and onto the crankcase

8.16 Take care with the rings as they're brittle and easy to break

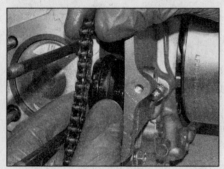

8.20 Insert the guide wheel in through the chain and secure it with the pivot bolt

9.2 Note the piston IN marking

9.3 Grasp the circlip removal tang with long-nose pliers

9.4 Look for ID marks on the ring top surface, in this case DY

9 Piston and rings

Removal

1 Remove the cylinder barrel (see Section 8). Check that the holes into the crankcase and the cam chain tunnel are completely blocked with rag.
2 Note that the piston crown is marked IN (though the mark is likely to be invisible until the piston is cleaned) and this mark faces the intake side of the cylinder **(see illustration)**.
3 Carefully prise out the circlip on one side of the piston using long-nose pliers **(see illustration)**. Push the piston pin out from the other side to free the piston from the connecting rod. Remove the other circlip and discard them as new ones must be used.

HAYNES HiNT *If the piston pin is a tight fit in the piston bosses, heat the piston using a heat gun – this will expand the alloy piston sufficiently to release its grip on the pin. If the piston pin is particularly stubborn, extract it using a drawbolt tool, but be careful to protect the piston's working surfaces.*

Inspection

Note: *Inspection of the piston and rings is described below but you may prefer to purchase a piston and ring kit if the engine is undergoing an overhaul or if there is obvious damage to the components. The expense is minimal.*
4 Using your thumbs, carefully remove the rings from the piston. Do not nick or gouge the piston in the process. Carefully note which way up each ring fits and in which groove as they must be installed in their original positions if being re-used. Look for identification marks on the upper surfaces of the two compression rings **(see illustration)**.
5 Scrape all traces of carbon from the top of the piston. A hand-held wire brush or a piece of fine emery cloth can be used once most of the deposits have been scraped away. Do not, under any circumstances, use a wire brush mounted in a drill motor to remove carbon deposits; the piston material is soft and will be eroded away by the wire brush. Remove any carbon deposits from the ring grooves; a piece broken off an old ring will do the job. Be very careful to remove only the carbon deposits. Do not remove any metal and do not nick or gouge the sides of the ring grooves. Once the deposits have been removed, clean the piston with solvent and dry it thoroughly. Make sure

the oil return holes below the oil ring groove are clear.
6 Carefully inspect the piston for cracks around the skirt, at the pin bosses and at the ring lands. Normal piston wear appears as even, vertical wear on the thrust surfaces. If the skirt is scored or scuffed, the engine may have been suffering from overheating and/or abnormal combustion, which caused excessively high operating temperatures. Also check that the circlip grooves are not damaged.
7 A hole in the top of the piston, in one extreme, or burned areas around the edge of the piston crown, indicate that pre-ignition or knocking under load have occurred. If you find evidence of any problems the cause must be corrected or the damage will occur again (see *Fault Finding* in the Reference section).
8 Check the piston-to-bore clearance by measuring the bore (see Section 8), then measure the piston 8 mm up from the bottom of the skirt and at 90° to the piston pin axis **(see illustration)**. Subtract the piston diameter from the bore diameter to obtain the clearance. If it is greater than 0.04mm, fit a new piston. If the clearance is excessive, fit a new piston and cylinder barrel kit.
9 Apply clean engine oil to the piston pin, insert it into the piston and feel for any freeplay between the two **(see illustration)**.

9.8 Measure the piston diameter with a micrometer 8 mm up from the bottom of the skirt

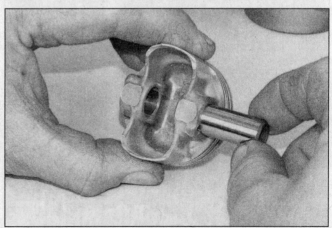

9.9 Feel for play between the ends of the pin and the piston bosses

9.10a Fit the expander into the lower groove...

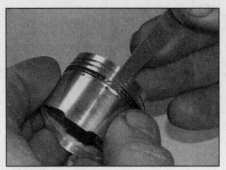

9.10b... and fit a side rail on each side of it

9.11 Fitting the lower of the two compression rings into the middle groove in the piston

Installation

10 Fit the oil control ring (lowest on the piston) first. It is composed of three separate components, namely the expander and the upper and lower side-rails. Slip the expander into the groove, making sure the ends don't overlap, then fit the lower side-rail (see illustrations). Place one end of the side-rail into the groove between the expander and the ring land, hold it firmly in place and slide a finger around the piston while pushing the rail into the groove. Next, fit the upper side-rail in the same manner (see illustration). Check that the ends of the expander have not overlapped.

11 The upper surface of the two compression rings should be marked at one end (see illustration 9.4). Make sure that its identification letters are facing up. Fit the lower compression ring (tapered section) into the middle groove of the piston (see illustration). The rings are brittle – do not expand them any more than is necessary to slide them into their grooves; using feeler gauge blades helps.

12 Check that all rings can be rotated freely in their grooves. Position the ring end gaps

so that none of them align. Spacing of 120° is recommended.

13 Lubricate the piston pin, the piston pin bore and the connecting rod small-end bore with engine oil. When fitting the piston onto the connecting rod make sure the IN mark on the piston crown faces the intake side of the engine (see illustration 9.2).

14 Fit a new circlip into one side of the piston (do not reuse old circlips). Line up the piston on the connecting rod and insert the piston pin from the other side. Secure the pin with the other new circlip. When fitting the circlips, compress them only just enough to fit them in the piston, and make sure they are properly seated in their grooves with the open end away from the removal notch.

15 Install the cylinder barrel (see Section 8).

10 Clutch cable

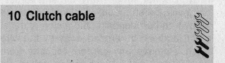

1 Create slack in the cable by adjusting the in-line adjuster at mid position in the cable (see illustration 4.9a).

2 Align the slots in the adjuster and lockring with that in the lever bracket, then pull the outer cable end from the socket in the adjuster and release the inner cable from the lever (see illustrations).

3 Hold the clutch arm up at the lower end of the cable and lift the cable end from the lug on the engine cover (see illustration 4.9b). The inner cable can now be freed from the clutch arm (see illustration 4.9c).

4 Remove the cable from the bike, noting its routing through the guides.

5 Installation is the reverse of removal. Apply grease to the cable ends. Make sure the cable is correctly routed through its guides. Adjust the amount of clutch lever freeplay (see Chapter 1, Section 6).

11 Clutch

Removal

1 Drain the engine oil (see Chapter 1, Section 4).

10.2a Wiggle the cable end out of the lever...

10.2b ...and slip it out through the slot in the adjuster and locknut

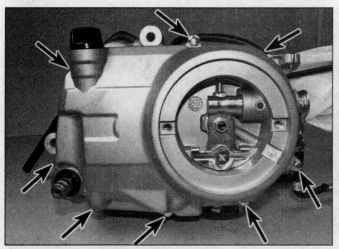

11.4 Clutch cover bolts (arrowed)

11.5 Undo the screws (arrowed) and remove the lifter plate

2 Mark the position of the kickstart lever on its shaft, then remove the pinch bolt and pull the lever off the shaft splines **(see illustration 4.8b)**. If there's signs of oil leakage from the seal obtain a new seal for use on installation. Remove the rear brake pedal (see Chapter 5, Section 3).

3 Disconnect the clutch cable from the operating arm (see Section 10) and position the cable clear of the engine.

4 Working evenly in a criss-cross pattern, unscrew the clutch cover bolts **(see illustration)**. Remove the cover, being prepared to catch any residual oil. If the engine is in the frame you'll have to manoeuvre the cover past the footrest as it clears the end of the kickstart shaft. Remove the gasket and discard it. Remove the two dowels from either the cover or the crankcase if they are loose **(see illustration 11.20)**. Note the short spring and pushrod set in the centre of the

clutch – make sure they do not drop out **(see illustration 11.19d)**.

5 Remove the four countersunk screws from the clutch lifter plate and withdraw the plate with its gasket **(see illustration)**. The plate holds the thrust bearing, insert, spring and short pushrod.

6 Use a small screwdriver to ease the locking tab out of the clutch nut slot **(see illustration)**. Hold the body of the clutch to stop the crankshaft turning, and unscrew the clutch nut using the special tool described in Section 5 **(see illustration)**. You can hold the clutch using a strap wrench as shown, or by removing the generator cover and holding the rotor with a strap wrench or with a socket and extension bar on the generator rotor nut. The clutch nut was found to be very tight so you might find the help of an assistant useful at this point.

7 With the nut slackened, thread it off the

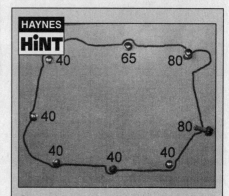

Store the cover bolts in a template of the cover (either draw around the actual cover or produce a sketch) to record the bolt locations. On this engine bolts were of 40, 65 and 80 mm lengths.

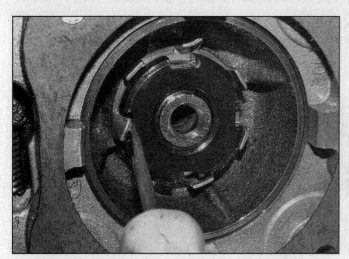

11.6a Work the locking tab out of the slot in the clutch nut

11.6b Hold the clutch as shown and undo the nut using the special tool

11.7 Draw the complete clutch assembly off the crankshaft

11.10a Assemble the puller and tighten to compress the clutch...

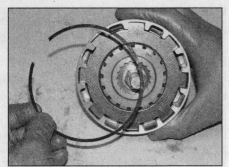

11.10b ...and free the large circlip from its groove

11.11 Friction plate thickness can be measured to check for wear

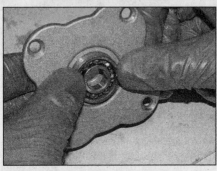

11.12 Check the lifter plate and its bearing

11.13 Use a small screwdriver to free the coil springs

crankshaft followed by the lock washer and tab washer. Grasp the complete clutch assembly and draw it off the crankshaft **(see illustration)**.

Inspection

8 The clutch is sold as a complete unit. It is possible to dismantle it to inspect for wear but check first whether you can purchase individual parts. Also you'll need a means of holding the clutch compressed – hand pressure isn't enough.

9 After an extended period of service the clutch friction plates will wear and promote clutch slip, and the plain plates can distort. The plates can also take on a glazed appearance and smell burnt and the clutch springs will weaken.

10 Assemble the puller across the outer face of the clutch and the inner hub, tightening its

centre bolt to compress the two components sufficiently to allow the large circlip around the periphery to be hooked out of its groove **(see illustrations)**. Remove the puller. The plates and centre can now be removed – there are 3 plain plates and 3 friction plates fitted alternately.

11 Inspect the friction plates for wear between the inner teeth of the plain plates and the slots in the clutch centre. Wear of this nature will cause clutch drag and slow disengagement during gear changes as the plates will snag. The friction material will wear over time, causing the clutch to slip; note that new plates measure 3 mm thick **(see illustration)**.

12 Check the lifter plate and its thrust bearing for signs of wear or damage and roughness **(see illustration)**.

13 To access the clutch springs, first manoeuvre the four small coil springs from

the outer face of the clutch housing **(see illustration)**. Fully remove the puller and separate the backing plate and four clutch springs from the housing. Note that the springs on this engine measured 21.4 mm in length. Springs become sagged in use. All four springs must be of the same length.

14 Removal of the operating mechanism in the clutch cover is necessary if the oil seal needs changing. Note that the oil supply from the pump is fed via the passage in the front of the crankcase, across into the clutch cover and into the crankshaft end for lubrication of the big-end bearing. The passageways which route the oil inside the clutch cover can be clearly seen in the casting. Remove the circular cover from the outside of the casing **(see illustration)**. Remove the single screw to free the 2-piece operating plate with adjuster screw **(see illustrations)**. From the inside of

11.14a Two screws retain the cover

11.14b Remove the single screw...

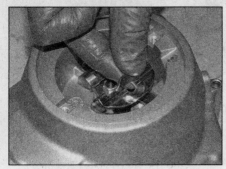

11.14c ...retainer...

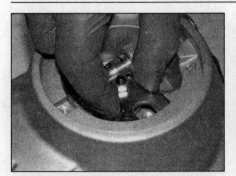

11.14d ...and adjuster screw plate

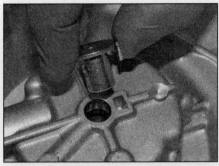

11.14e The pushrod piece is on the inside of the cover. Note its oilways and how its tab locates in the slot

11.14f Lever out the old oil seal

the cover withdraw the pushrod piece (see illustration). Turn the cover over again and use a large flat-bladed screwdriver to prise out the oil seal (see illustration). Note the oil supply passage behind the seal – this must remain clear. Press the new seal into place with its manufacturer's markings facing outwards.

15 To build the clutch back up, start by placing the four clutch springs on their seats in the housing (see illustration). Carefully fit the backing plate taking care to keep the springs in position (see illustration). Assemble the puller and clamp the two components together. Try not to cover the insertion slots for the small backlash springs with the puller arms. Insert the springs using a small screwdriver (see illustration).

16 Keeping the puller in place, install the centre, then the plates in the order: friction, plain, friction, plain, friction, plain (see illustrations). Fit the large circlip, locating one end in its groove and working around the circlip to work it into all slots (see illustration). Make sure it is fully seated, then remove the puller.

Installation

17 Remove all traces of old gasket from the crankcase and cover surfaces.
18 Fit the clutch onto the crankshaft end and engage it over the teeth of the primary gear;

11.15a Fit the four clutch springs on their seats...

11.15b ...and fit the backing plate

11.15c Clamp the backing plate down and fit the four small coil springs

11.16a Install the centre

11.16b The clutch plates are fitted alternately, starting with a friction plate...

11.16c ...then a plain plate, and so on

11.16d Start one end of the large circlip in its slot then work around the entire clip until it is located fully in the slot

11.18a Fit the tab washer...

11.18b ...the lockwasher (OUTSIDE mark faces outwards)

11.18c Tighten the nut whilst holding the clutch body as shown

only the shallow part of the gear sits inside the clutch. Fit the tab washer, the lock washer with its OUTSIDE marking facing outwards, then the clutch nut (see illustrations). Using the method employed on removal to lock

the crankshaft and the tool to fit the nut (see Step 6), tighten the nut (see illustration). A torque setting of 42 Nm is recommended. Bend one of the tab washer tabs into one of the slots in the nut (whichever one aligns)

(see illustration). If none align, tighten the nut fractionally more until it does – never back the nut off for this purpose.

19 Fit the bearing into the lifter plate if removed, and lubricate it with oil (see illustration 11.12). Fit the lifter plate (with its gasket) and secure it to the clutch with the four screws, then install the insert in the bearing and insert the spring and short pushrod into its centre (see illustrations). These components connect with the clutch operating arm shaft set in the clutch cover when assembled. Look inside the cover and check that the push piece is in place in the cover and hasn't dropped out.

20 Fit the two dowels into the crankcase if removed, then fit a new gasket, locating it over the dowels (see illustration).

21 Before fitting the cover, it's a good time to clean the oil filter screen set in the bottom of the crankcase. Use long-nose pliers to pull the screen out. Clean any debris and oil sludge off the screen using a soft brush and solvent. When inserting the screen note that its narrow edge goes in first (see illustration 10.20 in Chapter 2A).

22 Check the kickstart oil seal set in the clutch cover. If it has shown signs of leaking or is obviously damaged, prise it out of the cover and tap a new seal into place (see illustration). Fit the seal with its markings facing outwards.

23 Lubricate the kickstart shaft end with engine oil as this will help protect the seal lips as the splined end of the shaft passes through. Fit the cover and make sure it seats fully onto

11.18d Tab of washer bent into slot of nut (arrowed)

11.19b ...the lifter plate with its screws

11.19a Fit a new gasket...

11.19c Fit the insert into the bearing...

11.19d ...followed by the spring and short pushrod

11.20 Locate a new cover gasket over the two dowels (arrowed)

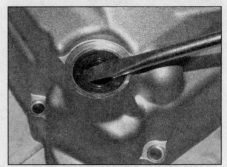

11.22 Prising out the old kickstart shaft oil seal

11.23 Fitting the clutch cover

11.25 Adjusting clutch freeplay

the gasket and dowels **(see illustration)**. There may be resistance around the kickstart shaft – grasp the kickstart shaft end and very gently wiggle it to aid seating of the cover.

24 Return the cover bolts to their original positions and tighten them in a diagonal sequence.

25 It is important that the clutch has a small amount of freeplay in its operating mechanism. Freeplay should be checked at this point, particularly if a new clutch has been fitted. Remove its two screws and remove the circular cover **(see illustration 11.14a)**. Hold the adjuster screw then slacken its locknut off by a couple of turns **(see illustration)**. Now turn the adjuster screw in until light resistance is felt, then back it off a quarter turn. Hold the adjuster in this position whilst the locknut is tightened. Fit the circular cover when adjustment is complete.

26 Engage the clutch cable end in the clutch arm, then locate the cable in its bracket and adjust freeplay (see Chapter 1, Section 6).

27 Fit the kickstart lever back onto its shaft, aligning the marks make on removal to get the lever angle right. Tighten the pinch bolt.

28 Fill the engine with the correct amount of 10W/40 semi-synthetic motorcycle oil (see Chapter 1, Section 4). Just under 1 litre will be required, although check the oil level using the dipstick.

12 Primary drive gears

Removal

1 Remove the clutch (see Section 11). Slide the primary drive gear off the crankshaft followed by its bush **(see illustrations)**.

2 The large primary driven gear is retained to the gearbox input shaft by a circlip. Use circlip pliers to expand the circlip and remove it from its groove **(see illustration)**. Slide the driven gear off the shaft **(see illustration)**.

12.1a Primary gear...

No dismantling of the driven gear is possible. The gear incorporates a shock absorber arrangement which isolates the ring gear from the hub.

Installation

3 Fit the driven gear onto the input shaft making sure it's the correct way round. Install the circlip making sure it locates in its groove **(see illustration)**.

4 Lubricate the drive gear bush and slide it onto the crankshaft. Fit the drive gear so that its shorter toothed section is facing outwards and mesh the drive and driven gears together.

5 Install the clutch (see Section 11).

12.1b ...and its bush can be slipped off the crankshaft

12.2a Use circlip pliers to free the driven gear circlip

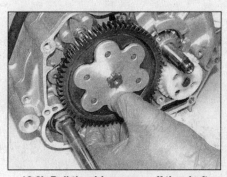

12.2b Pull the driven gear off the shaft splines

12.3 Ensure that the circlip locates fully in the shaft groove

13.2a Ease the E-clip off the oil pump shaft to free the driven gear

13.2b Oil pump mounting bolts (arrowed)

13.4a Two O-rings fit between the pump and crankcase (arrowed)

13 Oil pump

Removal

1 Remove the clutch (see Section 11) and primary drive gear (see Section 12).

2 Use a small screwdriver to work the E-clip off the pump drive shaft and lift off the driven gear (see illustration). Unscrew the three screws and remove the pump from the crankcase (see illustration). Note the two O-rings between the pump and crankcase.

3 The pump can be dismantled to check the rotors but note that spare parts are not available.

Installation

4 Make sure the two O-rings are in place, then fit the pump onto the crankcase, securing it with the three screws (see illustration). Fit the driven gear onto the shaft and mesh its teeth with those of the drive gear on the crankshaft (see illustration). Fit the E-clip to secure it, applying pressure to its closed side.

5 Install the primary drive gear and clutch.

6 Take this opportunity to clean the oil filter screen at the bottom of the casing. Pull it out with long-nose pliers and clean it in solvent. Note that the strainer is installed narrow edge inwards.

13.4b Push the E-clip into place in the shaft groove

14 Gearchange mechanism

Removal

1 Make sure the transmission is in neutral. Remove the clutch (see Section 11) and primary driven gear (see Section 12).

2 Make a mark where the slot in the gear lever aligns with the shaft (see illustration 4.8a). Unscrew the pinch bolt and slide the lever off the shaft.

3 Wrap a single layer of thin insulating tape around the gearchange shaft splines to protect the oil seal lips as the shaft is removed.

4 Note how the stopper arm spring ends locate and how the roller on the arm locates

14.4 Stopper arm pivot bolt (arrowed)

in the neutral detent on the selector drum cam, then unscrew the stopper arm bolt and remove the arm and the spring, noting how they fit (see illustration).

5 Unscrew the camplate bolt, then the camplate itself and the pin retaining plate (see illustration). There are five pins pressed into the drum – they should not be loose but take care just in case (see illustration). There are also two small pins that locate the plate on the end of the selector drum – they should stay in the end of the drum, but again take care as they could drop out. Remove them from the drum for safekeeping.

6 Note how the gearchange shaft centralising spring ends fit on each side of the locating pin in the casing, and how the pawls on the selector arm locate onto the pins on the end of the selector drum. Grasp the end of the

14.5a Remove the bolt and camplate...

14.5b ...and the pin retaining plate

14.6 Lower the arm and withdraw the shaft/arm assembly, noting how it fits

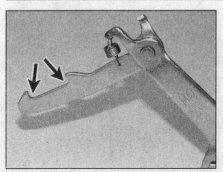

14.7a Check the selector arm pawls where they engage the pins (arrowed)…

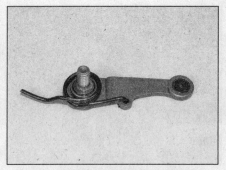

14.7b …and the stopper arm roller and camplate detents

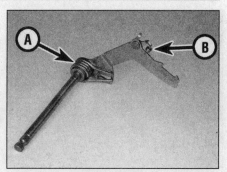

14.8 Shaft centralising spring (A) and pawl return spring (B)

shaft, then push the selector arm down until it clears the pins and withdraw the shaft/arm assembly **(see illustration)**.

Inspection

7 Check the selector arm for cracks, distortion and wear of its pawls, and check for any corresponding wear on the pins set in the end of the selector drum **(see illustration)**. Also check the stopper arm roller and the detents in the camplate for any wear or damage, and make sure the roller turns freely **(see illustration)**. Fit a new selector shaft assembly if wear is found.

8 Inspect the shaft centralising spring, the selector arm spring **(see illustration)** and the stopper arm return spring for fatigue, wear or damage. Also check that the centralising spring locating pin in the crankcase is securely tightened. If it is loose, remove it and apply a

non-permanent thread locking compound to its threads, then tighten it.

9 If the bike has been dropped on its gear lever and there are problems selecting gears, the gearchange shaft may be bent. Fit a new gearchange shaft assembly rather than attempting to straighten it. Also check the condition of the splines on the shaft end, although any damage is more likely to be found on the gear lever splines. Also check the condition of the shaft oil seal in the left-hand side of the crankcase. If it is damaged, deteriorated or shows signs of leakage it must be replaced with a new one – lever out the old seal with a seal hook or screwdriver. Press or drive the new seal squarely into place using your fingers, a seal driver or suitable socket.

Installation

10 Check that the shaft centralising spring

is properly positioned. Apply some grease to the lips of the gearchange shaft oil seal in the left-hand side of the crankcase. Slide the shaft into place and push it all the way through the case until the splined end comes out the other side, and push the selector arm down as its pawls engage the change pins **(see illustration)**. Locate the centralising spring ends onto each side of the locating pin in the crankcase.

11 If removed, fit the five change pins and the two smaller pins into the end of the selector drum **(see illustration)**. Locate the retaining plate onto the pins, followed by the camplate, aligning their holes – note that the pins and holes and offset slightly so the components can only be installed one way **(see illustration)**. Apply a drop of non-permanent thread locking compound to the camplate bolt before tightening it.

12 Fit the stopper arm spring onto its post with the ends facing back and the curved end outermost. Fit the bolt through the stopper arm. Apply a drop of non-permanent thread locking compound to the bolt threads. Install the arm, locating the roller onto the neutral detent on the selector drum and making sure the free end of the spring is positioned correctly against the crankcase **(see illustration)**.

13 Check that all components are correctly positioned **(see illustration)**. Install the primary driven gear (see Section 12) and the clutch (see Section 11).

14 Slide the gear lever onto the shaft, aligning its slit with the punch mark on the shaft. Fit the pinch bolt and tighten it.

14.10 Locate the centralising spring ends over the locating pin and the pawls with the change pins

14.11a Refit the small pins in the end of the drum

14.11b The pin retaining plate and camplate fit over the offset pins

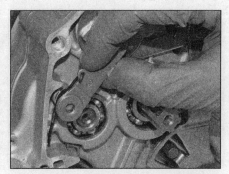

14.12 Locate the stopper arm spring correctly

14.13 Gearchange mechanism correctly installed

15.2 Freeing the circlip from the kickstart shaft

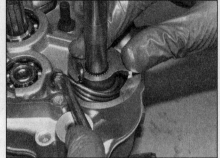

15.3a Free the return spring end...

15.3b ...and withdraw the return spring with its retainer

15 Kickstart

Removal

1 Remove the clutch (see Section 11) and primary driven gear (see Section 12).

2 Use circlip pliers to free the circlip from its groove and withdraw it from the shaft **(see illustration)**.

3 Take a look at how the return spring ends locate on the crankcase lug and on the spring retainer and also check that you can make out the two punch marks which align on the shaft and retainer **(see illustration 15.8b)** – this is crucial to setting the assembly up correctly when refitting. Unhook the long end of the spring from the crankcase and draw the retainer off the shaft splines with the return spring **(see illustrations)**.

4 The remainder of the kickstart components are located inside the crankcase. Separate the cases (see Section 18) and lift out the shaft, ratchet and gear.

Inspection

5 Inspect the kickstart gear and the 4th gear on the output shaft which it drives. If severely worn the kickstart could slip. Also check the condition of the ratchet teeth and the efficiency of the return spring. If any wear or faults are noted, purchase a new shaft; individual parts are not available.

Installation

6 Fit the shaft into its locating hole in the crankcase and mesh the drive gear with the 4th gear on the output shaft **(see illustration)**.

Abut the ratchet stop with the guide plate **(see illustration)**. Make sure the washer is in place on the end of the shaft.

7 Join the crankcase halves (see Section 18).

8 Assemble the return spring on its retainer **(see illustration)**. Fit the retainer over the shaft and as it reaches the splined section align its punch mark with the punch mark on the shaft **(see illustration)**. Push the retainer onto the splines, but before seating it fully hook the long end of the return spring over the crankcase lug **(see illustration)**. Now push the retainer down so that its lug abuts the cast step in the bottom of the case. Push it fully home.

9 Fit the circlip down the shaft and into its groove.

10 Fit the kickstart lever on the shaft and check the kickstart operation **(see illustration)**. If all is well install the primary driven gear and the clutch.

15.6a Installing the kickstart shaft in the crankcase

15.6b Ratchet stop (arrowed)

15.8a Install the return spring on its retainer, hooking the spring end on the lug as shown

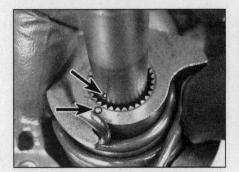

15.8b Align the punch marks (arrowed)

15.8c Return spring end and lug correctly positioned

15.10 Fit the lever and check kickstart operation

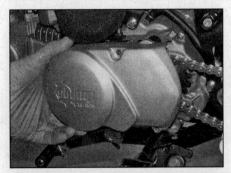

16.1 Three bolts retain the generator cover

16.4a Thread the puller in anti-clockwise

16.4b Operating the centre-bolt puller

16.5 Woodruff key location

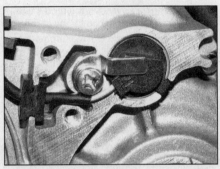

16.7a Plug is retained by a set plate and screw

16.7b Stator plate screws (arrowed)

16 Generator

Removal

1 Remove the engine left-hand cover; it is retained by three bolts (see illustration).
2 Trace the generator wiring from the top of the crankcase to the connectors just beneath the fuel tank and disconnect them. Note that not all wires connect into the loom unless the lighting coil is being utilised.
3 Hold the rotor with a strap wrench (see illustration 16.13c) and undo the rotor nut. Take care not to damage the face of the pick-up coil when fitting the strap – only a thin metal band type will fit into the gap between the coil and rotor. Remove the nut and washer.
4 You'll need a centre-bolt type puller to pull the rotor off its taper on the crankshaft. The type shown can be obtained through pit bike part suppliers and is not expensive (see illustration 5.1a). Back off the puller's centre bolt and thread the body of the puller into the rotor (see illustration). Note that the thread is left-hand, so it must be turned in an anti-clockwise direction. Turn the puller's centre bolt in so that it contacts the end of the crankshaft then hold the body with an open-end spanner and tighten the centre bolt until the rotor comes free of its taper (see illustration).
5 The rotor has a slot in its boss which locates over a key (Woodruff key) set in the crankshaft taper. If the key is loose, remove it and keep in

with the rotor for now (see illustration). The key prevents the rotor attempting to spin on the crankshaft end.
6 Drain the engine oil (see Chapter 1, Section 4).
7 The stator plate and coils comes off as a unit, together with the plug and light green/red wire which is set in the left-hand end of the selector drum; this would serve as a neutral switch on other models. Start by removing the set plate and plug from the selector drum end (see illustration). Remove the two countersunk screws which retain the stator plate and gently pull the assembly out of the crankcase (see illustration).
8 Note the large O-ring around the periphery of the stator plate, the two small O-rings at the screw mounting points and the oil seal set in the centre of the stator plate. All prevent the escape of oil from the cam chain and inner crankcase areas.

9 Refer to Chapter 4 for details of generator coil testing.

Installation

10 Check the condition of the stator plate O-rings and the oil seal set in its centre. If there are signs of oil escaping into the outer cover area, the seals must be renewed. To remove the oil seal prise it out from the back of the stator plate (see illustration) and press a new seal into position; the seal must be fitted so that its spring side faces inwards towards the crankcase.
11 Make sure the two small O-rings are in their recesses in the crankcase then fit the stator plate (see illustration). Press it into position and secure it with the two screws – you should be able to hear it click into place as the large O-ring seats. Position the wiring grommet into the cut-out in the top edge of

16.10 Prising out the stator plate oil seal

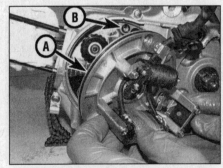

16.11 Stator plate large O-ring (A) and two small O-rings (B – top shown)

16.13a Align the rotor slot with the Woodruff key...

16.13b ...fit the washer and nut...

16.13c ...then hold the rotor and tighten the nut

the casing and insert the plug in the neutral switch location. Secure the set plate with the screw to retain the plug.

12 Refill the engine oil (see Chapter 1, Section 4).

13 If removed, install the Woodruff key back into its slot **(see illustration 16.5)**. Install the rotor so that its cut-out fits over the key, noting that the pull of its magnets will be felt as it passes over the coils **(see illustration)**. Fit the washer and rotor nut and tighten the nut **(see illustration)**. Hold the rotor using a strap wrench to enable the nut to be fully tightened **(see illustration)**. A torque setting of 41 Nm is recommended.

14 Reconnect the generator wiring and fit the left-hand engine cover. On the model shown, the front bolt retained a clip for the carburettor drain hose.

17 Cam chain, tensioner and guides

Cam chain tensioner

1 The tensioner is automatic in operation **(see illustration)**. Note that earlier generations of this engine had a manually adjustable tensioner and you'll see evidence of this in the drilling in the side of the tensioner plunger bore (now blanked off with a plain bolt).

2 The tensioner plunger and spring can be accessed easily from the lower left side of the engine although first the engine must be set to TDC compression as described in the cylinder head removal procedure (see Section 6). This procedure covers removal of the engine bashplate, then the tensioner cap bolt, spring and plunger. Note that valve timing must be checked after refitting the plunger particularly if the crankshaft has been rotated with tension off the chain.

Tensioner arm and lower guide wheel

3 Remove the generator and its stator plate to access the tensioner arm (see Section 16).

4 Set the engine to TDC and remove the tensioner cap, plunger and spring as described in the cylinder head removal procedure (see Section 6); this procedure will relax tension on the cam chain.

5 Lift the wheel off the tensioner arm **(see illustration)**. The tensioner arm is retained to the crankcase by a single pivot bolt. The guide wheel can be removed from its pivot if required.

6 Installation is a reverse of the removal procedure. Note that the valve timing must be checked after refitting the tensioner plunger, particularly if the crankshaft has been rotated with tension off the chain.

Cam chain guide wheel in cylinder barrel

7 Remove the cylinder head (see Section 6). Refer to the first part of the cylinder barrel removal procedure and remove the guide wheel from the cam chain tunnel (see Section 8).

8 Installation is a reverse of the removal procedure.

Cam chain

9 Remove the cylinder head (see Section 6). Refer to the first part of the cylinder barrel removal procedure and remove the guide wheel from the cam chain tunnel (see Section 8).

10 Remove the generator and its stator plate (see Section 16).

11 Remove the wheel from the tensioner arm **(see illustration 17.5)**. Withdraw the cam chain from its sprocket on the crankshaft **(see illustration)**.

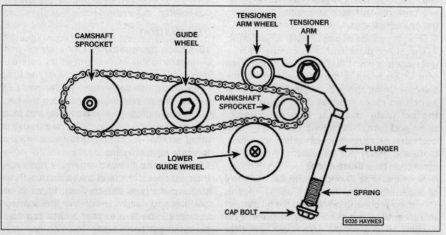

CAMSHAFT SPROCKET

GUIDE WHEEL

TENSIONER ARM WHEEL

TENSIONER ARM

CRANKSHAFT SPROCKET

LOWER GUIDE WHEEL

PLUNGER

SPRING

CAP BOLT

6035 HAYNES

17.1 Cam chain tensioner components

17.5 Tensioner wheel can be slipped off its pivot

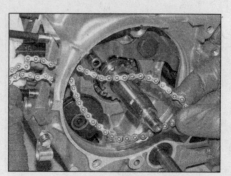

17.11 Lift the cam chain off its sprocket and out of the engine

18.3 Bolt and switch contact plate must be removed prior to crankcase separation

18.4 Crankcase bolts (arrowed). Clips at bolts marked A

12 Check the chain for binding, kinks and any obvious damage and replace it with a new one if necessary.
13 Installation is a reverse of the removal procedure.

18 Crankcase separation and reassembly

Separation

1 To access the crankshaft and connecting rod assembly, kickstart shaft, gear shafts, selector drum and forks, and their bearings, the crankcase halves must be separated. Remove the engine from the frame (see Section 4).
2 Before the crankcases can be separated the following components must be removed:
a) Cylinder head (Section 6)
b) Cylinder barrel (Section 8). The piston can remain attached to the rod, but wrap rag around it to protect the rings.
c) Generator (Section 16)
d) Drive sprocket (Chapter 6, Section 17)
e) Clutch (Section 11)
f) Primary drive gears (Section 12)
g) Gearchange mechanism (Section 14)
h) Oil pump (Section 13)

i) Kickstart shaft external components (return spring and retainer) (Section 15)
j) Cam chain and tensioner arm wheel (Section 17)
3 Remove the bolt and switch contact plate from the left-hand end of the selector drum (see illustration).
4 Slacken the seven bolts in the left-hand side of the crankcase evenly and in a diagonal sequence (see illustration). Remove the bolts and record their positions as an aid to refitting (see Hint). All bolts on the engine shown were of 65 mm in length except for the 50 mm bolt next to the rear engine mounting point.

HAYNES HINT *As each bolt is removed, store it in its relative position in a cardboard template of the crankcase halves. This will ensure all bolts and any washers/guides with them are returned to their original locations on reassembly.*

5 Turn the engine over so that it is resting on its left-hand side. Support it using blocks of wood to prevent the shaft ends contacting the bench.
6 Using a heat gun, warm the area around the main bearing for a few minutes. Use of heat here will expand the aluminium housing enough to release its grip on the main bearing. Immediately lift off the right crankcase half,

if necessary using a soft-faced mallet to tap around the gasket joint. If the halves do not separate easily, make sure all fasteners have been removed. Do not try and separate the halves by levering against the crankcase mating surfaces as they are easily scored and will leak oil in the future if damaged. The right-hand crankcase half will come away leaving the crankshaft, kickstart shaft, transmission shafts and selector drum and forks in the left-hand half.
7 Remove the kickstart shaft, then grasp the gear shafts and selector drum and remove them as an assembly. Turn the engine over. Heat the area around the main bearing then lift or lightly tap the crankshaft out.

Reassembly

8 Remove all traces of old gasket material from both crankcase mating surfaces.
9 Use the heat gun to warm the main bearing housing in the left case, then support the piston and con-rod with one hand and fit the crankshaft into the crankcase with the other (see illustration). The crankshaft is fitted with its tapered end downwards (see illustration).
10 Generously lubricate the transmission shaft bearings and the bore for the selector drum end. Mesh the gear shafts together and insert the two selector forks in their gear grooves (see illustration). Hold the assembly

18.9a Warm the main bearing housing area...

18.9b ...and fit the crankshaft

18.10 Fitting the gearshafts and drum as a unit

18.12a Crankcase dowel positions

18.12b Lay a new gasket on the left crankcase

18.13a Warm the main bearing housing area...

18.13b ...and fit the half over the left-hand crankcase

18.14 Don't forget to install clips on two of the bolts

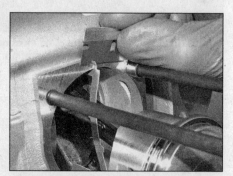

18.16 Use a sharp blade to trim off the excess gasket from the crankcase mouth

together and fit the shafts into the left-hand half.

11 Fit the kickstart shaft into the left-hand crankcase half, meshing its gear with the output shaft 4th gear (see illustration 15.6a). The stop on the ratchet abuts the plate in the casing (see illustration 15.6b). Check that the thrust washer is in place on the kickstart shaft end,

12 Apply engine oil to the gearshaft ends. Wipe the crankcase mating surface over with solvent. Ensure the two dowels are in position in the left-hand half (see illustration). Place a new gasket in position (see illustration). Note that there's no need for any sealant.

13 Use the heat gun to warm the bearing housing of the right-hand crankcase half (see illustration). Immediately fit the right half down over the crankshaft main bearing (see illustration). Check that the crankcase halves are fully seated. Clean the threads of all the crankcase bolts. Turn the engine over.

Caution: The crankcase halves should fit together without being forced. If the casings are not correctly seated, remove the right-hand crankcase half and investigate the problem. Do not attempt to pull them together using the crankcase bolts as the casing will crack and be ruined.

14 Install the seven crankcase bolts including the two clips (see illustration and 18.4). Secure the bolts finger-tight at first, then tighten them evenly and a little at a time in a criss-cross sequence – no torque setting is specified, but bolts of that size should be tightened to 12 Nm.

15 With all crankcase fasteners tightened, check that the crankshaft and gear shafts rotate smoothly and easily. Check that the gear shafts rotate freely and independently in neutral, then rotate the selector drum by hand and select each gear in turn whilst rotating the input shaft. If there are any signs of undue stiffness, tight or rough spots, or of any other problem, the fault must be rectified before proceeding further.

16 Trim off the section of gasket from the mouth of the crankcase (see illustration).

17 Install all other removed assemblies in a reverse of the sequence given in Step 2.

19 Crankcases and bearings

Crankcases

1 After the crankcases have been separated, remove the gear shafts, selector drum, kickstart shaft and crankshaft.

2 Clean the crankcases thoroughly with new solvent and dry them with compressed air. Blow out all oil passages with compressed air. Clean up minor damage to the surfaces with a fine sharpening stone or grindstone.

Caution: Be very careful not to nick or gouge the crankcase mating surfaces or oil leaks will result. Check both crankcase halves very carefully for cracks and other damage.

3 Small cracks or holes in aluminium castings

can be repaired with an epoxy resin adhesive as a temporary measure or with one of the low temperature welding kits. Permanent repairs can only be done by TIG (tungsten inert gas or heli-arc) welding, and only a specialist in this process is in a position to advise on the economy or practical aspect of such a repair. If any damage is found that can't be repaired, replace the crankcase halves as a set.

4 Damaged threads can be economically reclaimed using a diamond section wire insert, for example of the Heli-Coil type (though there are other makes), which are easily fitted after drilling and re-tapping the affected thread.

5 If the cylinder studs are badly corroded or loose in the crankcase, remove them using one of the stud extraction methods described in *Tools and Workshop Tips* in Reference. Use a drop of non-permanent thread locking compound on the new or refitted stud and tighten it in the crankcase.

6 Sheared studs or screws can usually be removed with extractors, which consist of a tapered, left-hand thread screw of very hard steel. These are inserted into a pre-drilled hole in the stud, and usually succeed in dislodging the most stubborn stud or screw. If a stud has sheared above its bore line, it can be removed using a conventional stud extractor which avoids the need for drilling.

7 Install all components and assemblies, referring to the relevant Sections of this and the other Chapters, before reassembling the crankcase halves.

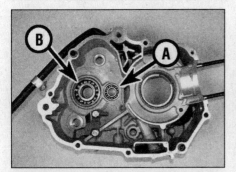

19.10a Input shaft (A) and output shaft (B) bearings in the left-hand crankcase half

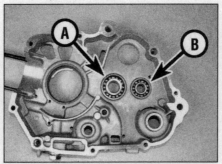

19.10b Input shaft (A) and output shaft (B) bearings in the right-hand crankcase half

Bearings

8 Dirt and other foreign particles get into the engine in a variety of ways. They may be left in the engine during assembly or they may pass through the filter screen, then get into the oil and from there into the bearings. Metal chips from machining operations and normal engine wear are often present. Abrasives are sometimes left in engine components after reconditioning operations, especially when parts are not thoroughly cleaned afterwards. The best prevention for this cause of bearing failure is to clean all parts thoroughly and keep everything spotlessly clean during engine reassembly. Regular oil changes are also recommended.

Gear shaft bearings

9 If the gear shaft bearings have failed, excessive rumbling and vibration will be felt when the engine is running.They should rotate smoothly, freely and quietly, there should be no rough spots or excessive play between the inner and outer races, or between the inner race and the shaft it fits on, or between the outer race and its housing in the crankcase.

10 The output shaft bearings and input shaft right-hand bearing can be removed by tapping them out from the outside of the casing, although prise out the output shaft oil seal first (see illustrations). Heat the bearing housing with a hot air gun, then tap the bearing out from the outside of the crankcase using a bearing driver or a suitable socket.

11 Smear the outside of the new bearing with clean oil and fit it with its marked side towards the inside of the engine, then heat the housing again and drive the bearing squarely in until it seats using a driver or socket that bears only on the bearing's outer race.

12 To remove the input shaft left-hand bearing from its blind hole, an expanding knife-edge bearing puller with slide-hammer attachment is required. Heat the bearing housing with a hot air gun, then fit the expanding end of the puller behind the bearing, then turn the puller to expand it and lock it in position. Attach the slide-hammer to the puller, then hold the crankcase firmly down and operate the slide-hammer to jar the bearing out. Refer to the procedure and photos in Reference 7 for more information. Drive the new bearing in as described above.

Crankshaft bearings

13 Refer to Section 20.

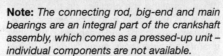

20 Crankshaft and connecting rod

Note: *The connecting rod, big-end and main bearings are an integral part of the crankshaft assembly, which comes as a pressed-up unit – individual components are not available.*

1 Remove the engine from the frame (see Section 4) and separate the crankcase halves (see Section 18).

2 Clean the crankshaft with solvent. If available, blow the crank dry with compressed air. Check the cam chain sprocket and oil pump drive gear for wear or damage (see illustrations). If any of the sprocket/gear teeth are excessively worn, chipped or broken, the crankshaft must be renewed. Also check the condition of the Woodruff key slot in the left-hand end of the shaft; if there is evidence of the key attempting to twist out of the slot and the slot being distorted, renew the crankshaft.

3 Measure the connecting rod side clearance (the gap between the connecting rod big-end and the crankshaft web) with a feeler gauge (see illustration). No figures are available from the manufacturer, but a clearance of 0.1 to 0.3 mm is normal. Anything greater than 0.8 mm should be considered worn.

4 Hold the crankshaft still and check for any radial (up and down) play in the big-end bearing by pushing and pulling the con-rod against the crank. Also remove the piston and check for excessive play between the piston pin and small-end. If the connecting rod (big-end) bearing has failed, there will be a pronounced knocking noise when the engine is running, particularly under load and increasing with engine speed.

5 The main bearings are a press-fit on the crankshaft. If they have failed, excessive rumbling and vibration will be felt when the engine is running.

6 If you're in doubt about the condition of the crankshaft or bearings, seek advice from an automotive engineer.

21 Gear shafts and selector drum

Gear shafts

1 Remove the transmission shafts from the crankcase (see Section 18).

2 If the gear pinions show signs of stripped or chipped teeth or excessive wear, e.g. from

20.2a Crankshaft right-hand end showing oil pump drive gear

20.2b Crankshaft left-hand end showing cam chain sprocket

20.3 Measuring con-rod side clearance

21.2 Input shaft (A) and output shaft (B) – gear positions numbered

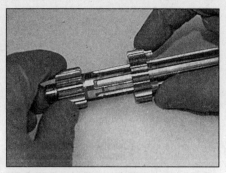

21.5a Input shaft – second gear dogs face away from first gear...

21.5b ...washer and circlip retain second gear

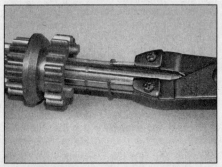

21.5c Fit the third gear with its fork groove towards the second gear, then slide on the circlip...

21.5d ...and fit it into the shaft groove

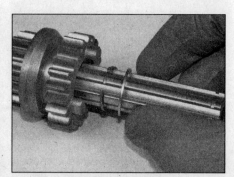

21.5e Install the washer...

missing a gear, it's best to renew them (see illustration). A complete pair of shafts can be purchased very cheaply. If you wish to strip the shafts it's a straightforward operation. Use the appropriate circlips pliers when removing circlips and take care not to strain or distort them.

3 Inspect the dogs and the dog holes in the gears for cracks, chips, and excessive wear especially in the form of rounded edges. Make sure mating gears engage properly.

HAYNES HINT *When disassembling the transmission shafts, place the parts on a long rod or thread a wire through them to keep them in order and facing the proper direction.*

Input shaft

4 Slide the 4th gear (largest gear) off the shaft followed by the thrust washer. Use circlip pliers to remove the circlip from its groove in the shaft, then slide off the 3rd gear. Remove the circlip and thrust washer and slide off the 2nd gear. First gear is part of the shaft.

5 Build up the gears according to the photo sequence (see illustrations). During reassembly, apply engine oil to the mating surfaces of the shaft, pinions and bushes. When installing the circlips, do not expand their ends any further than is necessary. Install the stamped circlips and washers so that their chamfered side faces away from the thrust side.

Output shaft

6 Remove the thrust washer, 1st gear (largest gear) and its bush from the shaft end. From the opposite end of the shaft, remove the thrust washer, 4th gear (smallest gear), thrust washer, 3rd gear and thrust washer. Use circlip pliers to remove the circlip from the shaft groove and slide the 2nd gear off. Free the remaining circlip from the shaft and slide off the thrust washer.

7 Build up the gears according to the photo sequence (see illustrations). During reassembly, apply engine oil to the mating surfaces of the shaft, pinions and bushes. When installing the circlips, do not expand their ends any further than is necessary. Install the stamped circlips and washers so that their

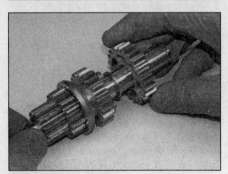

21.5f ...before fitting the fourth gear (dog holes towards third gear)

21.7a Output shaft – Fit the washer and circlip over the shaft right-hand end...

21.7b ...then fit the second gear with its dogs facing outwards and install the circlip in the shaft groove...

21.7c ...and fit the washer

21.7d Fit the third gear with its dog holes facing the second gear...

21.7e ....followed by the washer...

21.7f ...and the fourth gear with its chamfered edge facing the third gear...

21.7g ...and the washer

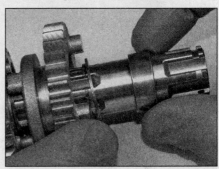

21.7h On the opposite end of the shaft fit the bush...

21.7i ...first gear...

21.7j ...and washer

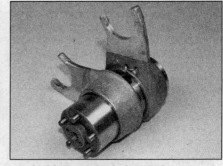

21.8 Inspect the fork ends for wear

chamfered side faces away from the thrust side.

Selector drum and forks

8 Inspect the selector forks for any signs of wear or damage, especially around the fork ends where they engage with the groove in the gear pinion (see illustration). The fork ends (tips) will wear rapidly if you do clutchless gearchanges – always use the clutch when changing gear.
9 Check that each fork fits correctly in its pinion groove. Check closely to see if the forks are bent. If the forks are in any way damaged the complete selector drum and fork assembly must be renewed.

22 Running-in procedure

1 Make sure the engine oil level is correct (see Chapter 1, Section 3). Make sure there is fuel in the tank.
2 Turn the engine kill switch to the RUN position and shift the gearbox into neutral. Set the choke to ON.
3 Start the engine and allow it to run until it reaches operating temperature.
4 Check carefully that there are no oil or fuel leaks and make sure the gearbox and

controls, especially the brakes, function properly.
5 Treat the bike gently to make sure oil has circulated throughout the engine and any new parts installed have started to seat.
6 Even greater care is necessary if a new piston and rings have been fitted; the bike will have to be run in as when new. This means not over-revving the engine, change up a gear instead, and not running it at more than two thirds throttle. Apply this running-in period for the first two hours of the bike's use. After that, change the engine oil, check the valve clearances and the idle speed, and check the tightness of all nuts and bolts.

Chapter 2 Part C
Engine – Lifan 1P56FMJ (YX140)

Contents

Degrees of difficulty

Easy, suitable for novice with little experience	**Fairly easy,** suitable for beginner with some experience	**Fairly difficult,** suitable for competent DIY mechanic	**Difficult,** suitable for experienced DIY mechanic	**Very difficult,** suitable for expert DIY or professional

1 General Information

1 The horizontal engine/transmission unit is an air-cooled single cylinder of unit construction (see illustrations opposite). The two valves are operated by rocker arms actuated by a single overhead camshaft that is chain driven off the left-hand end of the crankshaft. The crankcase divides vertically.

2 The crankcase incorporates a wet sump, pressure-fed lubrication system that uses a single rotor trochoidal oil pump that is gear-driven off a separate gear on the right-hand end of the crankshaft. Oil is filtered by a screen in the bottom of the crankcase and there's a centrifugal filter (oil spinner) on the right-hand end of the crankshaft. The oil is cooled by a radiator mounted on the frame.

3 The generator is on the left-hand end of the crankshaft. The ignition timing trigger is on the outside of the generator rotor, and the

pick-up coil is mounted on the stator plate.

4 Power from the crankshaft is routed to the transmission via the primary gears. The clutch is of the wet multi-plate type and is mounted directly to the right-hand end of the gearbox input shaft. The clutch is operated by cable. The transmission is a four-speed constant-mesh unit. Final drive to the rear wheel is by chain and sprockets.

5 This is a 'start in gear' engine; the engine can be started in gear if the clutch lever is held in.

2 Component access

Operations possible with the engine in the frame

1 The components and assemblies listed below can be removed without having to remove the engine from the frame. Note however that removal of the engine is fairly

straightforward and it is recommended if a number of items require attention, or if the bike cannot be raised up to a convenient working height on a ramp or platform.
a) Cylinder head, camshaft, rockers and valves
b) Cylinder barrel and piston
c) Clutch
d) Oil pump, paper filter, oil screen and centrifugal filter (oil spinner)
e) Primary drive gear
f) Gearchange mechanism
g) Generator rotor and stator plate
h) Cam chain, tensioner and guides
i) Kickstart drive gears

Operations requiring engine removal

2 It is necessary to remove the engine from the frame and split the crankcases to gain access to the following components.
a) Crankshaft and connecting rod
b) Gearshafts and bearings
c) Selector drum and forks
d) Kickstart shaft and return spring

3.4a Select the correct adapter (10 x 1.0 mm) to match the spark plug threads

3.4b Thread the gauge hose into the adaptor

3 Compression test

Note: *Special tool: A compression gauge and 10 x 1.0 mm threaded adaptor are required to perform this test.*

1 Poor engine performance may be caused by leaking valves, incorrect valve clearances, a leaking head gasket, a worn piston, worn piston rings or worn cylinder walls. A cylinder compression check will highlight these conditions.

2 Make sure the valve clearances are correctly set (see Chapter 1, Section 12).

3 Run the engine until it is at normal operating temperature. Remove the spark plug (see Chapter 1, Section 10).

4 Screw the threaded adaptor into the spark plug hole making sure that it seats securely and there are no air leaks (see illustration). Connect the compression gauge to the adaptor (see illustration).

5 With the kill switch OFF, kick the engine over for about 4 or 5 kicks until the gauge reading has built up and stabilised (see illustration).

6 A reading of around 150psi is good. If the reading is low, it could be due to a worn cylinder bore, piston or rings, failure of the head gasket, or worn valve seats. To determine which is the cause, pour a small quantity of engine oil into the spark plug hole to seal the rings, then repeat the compression test. If the figures are noticeably higher the cause is a worn cylinder, piston or rings. If there is no change the cause is a leaking head gasket or worn valve seats.

7 Although unlikely, if the reading is high there could be a build-up of carbon deposits in the combustion chamber. Remove the cylinder head and scrape all deposits off the piston and the cylinder head.

4 Engine removal and installation

Caution: The engine is not particularly heavy (around 18 kg), but the aid of an assistant is handy to install the mounting bolts when manoeuvring it back into the frame.

Removal

1 Support the bike on a rear paddock stand, making sure it is on level ground. Work can be made easier by raising the machine to a suitable working height on an hydraulic ramp or a suitable platform. Make sure the motorcycle is secure and will not topple over, and tie the front brake lever to the handlebar to prevent it rolling forwards.

2 If the engine is dirty, particularly around its mountings, wash it thoroughly. This makes work much easier and rules out the possibility of caked on lumps of dirt falling into some vital component.

3 Drain the engine oil (see Chapter 1, Section 4). Remove the two union bolts which retain the oil cooler pipes to the right side of the cylinder head (see illustration). Keep the copper washers with the bolts and pipes and tie both pipes out the way of the engine area.

4 Remove the exhaust pipe (see Chapter 3, Section 10).

5 Remove the carburettor (see Chapter 3, Section 5). Keep the insulator with the carburettor.

6 Pull the spark plug cap off the plug and secure it clear of the engine (see illustration). Trace the

3.5 Read the compression figure on the gauge

4.3 Disconnect the oil cooler pipes

4.6a Pull the cap off the spark plug

4.6b Generator wire connectors are on the left side of the frame

4.7a Make an alignment mark then unscrew the bolt and slide the gear lever off

4.7b Use a flat-bladed screwdriver to open up the slot if necessary

4.7c Mark the end of the shaft where it aligns with the slot in the kickstart lever then remove the pinch bolt

4.8a Increase clutch cable slack at the in-line adjuster at the top of the engine cover

wiring from the generator and disconnect it at the bullet connectors (see illustration).

7 Make a mark where the slot in the gear lever aligns with the shaft then unscrew the pinch bolt and slide the lever off the shaft (see illustration). You may need to open up the slot in the lever slightly (see illustration). Mark its position and remove the kickstart lever in the same way (see illustration).

8 Create some slack in the clutch cable at the adjuster, then push the clutch operating arm forwards and disconnect the cable end from the slot in the arm (see illustrations). Slide the cable out of the bracket on the clutch cover (see illustration).

9 Disconnect the drive chain at the joining link and thread the chain off the engine sprocket (see illustration).

10 Remove the bodywork complete (see Chapter 5, Section 2).

11 Remove the engine bashplate bolts from each side of the cylinder barrel and the two bolts at the rear of the bashplate; these pass through the footrest bracket (see

4.8b Pull the cable end out of the arm...

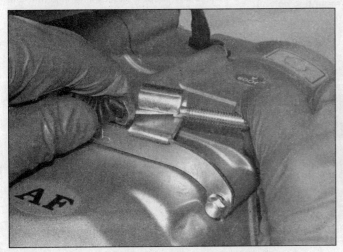

4.8c ...and slip the cable out of the bracket

4.9 Drive chain can be threaded off the engine sprocket

4.11a One bolt on each side secures the bashplate to the barrel…

4.11b …and two retain it at the back (arrowed)

4.11c Lift the bashplate free

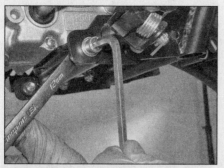

4.12a Remove the two Allen-head bolts on each side…

4.12b …and the two which thread into the crankcase…

4.12c …then remove the footrest bracket

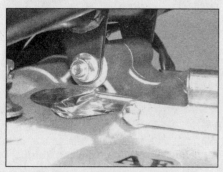

4.13a Top engine mounting bolt nut

4.13b Rear engine mounting bolt nut (arrowed)

illustrations). Remove the bashplate (see illustration).

12 Remove the four Allen-headed bolts which thread through the footrest bracket to the frame (see illustration). Remove the two Allen-headed bolts which bolt through the footrest bracket and into the crankcase (see illustrations).

13 Remove the nuts from the top and rear mounting bolts (see illustrations). On the model shown the rear mounting bolt couldn't be removed because its flange wouldn't clear the swingarm lug on the left side (see illustration). If this is the case on your model, move any support under the swingarm to the frame (see illustration), then remove the pivot bolt nut and withdraw the swingarm pivot bolt (see illustration); the link arm will drop down

4.13c Rear mounting bolt can't be removed with the swingarm in situ (chain slider removed for clarity)

4.13d Locate the axle stands under the frame

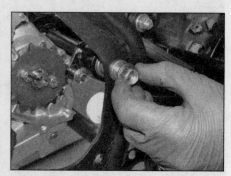

4.13e Remove the swingarm pivot nut…

4.13f ...then note how the link drops clear as the swingarm pivot bolt is withdrawn

4.14a Take the weight of the engine and withdrawn the top mounting bolt

4.14b Remove the engine complete with the link plate

from the swingarm pivot at this point (see illustration).

14 Remove the top mounting bolt and lower the engine out of the frame (see illustrations).

Installation

Note: *It is advised to smear copper grease onto the engine mounting bolt shafts, not the threads, to prevent the possibility of them seizing in the engine or frame due to corrosion.*

15 Insert the rear mounting bolt through the link plate and thread the nut lightly onto its end (see illustration). Lift the engine into position and insert the top mounting bolt (see illustration 4.14a). Move the swingarm into positon and rotate the link plate so that their centres aline, then insert the pivot bolt from the right side noting that it must also pass through the headed spacers in each side of the frame (see illustration). Thread the swingarm pivot bolt nut on and tighten it lightly at this stage (see illustration 4.13e). Also tighten the engine rear mounting bolt nut lightly, then install and tighten the top mounting nut lightly.

16 Install the footrest bracket, making sure that it's the correct way around, and thread the two Allen bolts into the crankcase (see illustration 4.12b). Assemble the four bracket-to-frame nuts and bolts (see illustration) and tighten them finger-tight.

17 Now go round all engine and footrest bracket mountings tightening them securely: Top mounting bolt nut, rear mounting bolt nut, swingarm pivot bolt nut, footrest bracket-to-

4.15a Assemble the link plate are rear mounting bolt before fitting the engine in the frame

4.15b Swingarm pivot bolt must pass through the headed spacer on each side

crankcase bolts, footrest bracket-to-frame bolts/nuts.

18 The remainder of the installation procedure is the reverse of removal, noting the following points:
Note that the bashplate was found to be under considerable tension – take care to align its mounting holes fully when threading the bolts into the cylinder barrel and crankcase.

● The engine breather hose should locate in the guide on the link plate.
● When fitting the gear lever and kickstart levers, align the slit in the arm with the mark you made on the shaft.
● Adjust the clutch cable freeplay (Chapter 1, Section 6).
● Remake the drive chain noting that the closed end of the clip faces in the normal

direction of chain rotation. Check drive chain slack (see Chapter 1, Section 2).
● Make sure the copper sealing washers are positioned each side of the union when fitting the oil cooler hoses (see illustration). If the washers are flattened or distorted, fit new ones.
● Refill the engine with oil to the correct level (see Chapter 1, Section 4). You'll need just under 1 litre of oil.
● Start the engine and check that there are no oil or fuel leaks. Check the valve clearances (see Chapter 1, Section 12) and idle speed (see Chapter 1, Section 13). After the engine has been run and the oil circulated, recheck the oil level and top up if necessary.

4.16 Make sure any washers are correctly positioned on the footrest bracket bolts

4.18a Engine breather hose guide (arrowed)

4.18b Oil cooler copper sealing washers (arrowed)

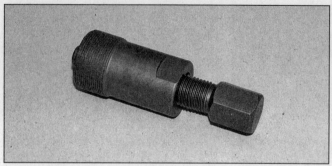

5.1a Rotor puller tool

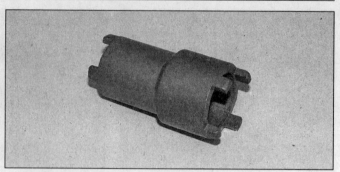

5.1b Double-ended peg spanner tool with 20/24 mm ends

5 Engine overhaul – general information

1 Before beginning the engine overhaul, read through the related procedures to familiarise yourself with the scope and requirements of the job. Overhauling an engine is not difficult, but you will need a set a gaskets and a couple of special tools. Two essential tools are a rotor puller and a peg spanner for slackening the clutch nut and primary drive nut; these are cheap to buy and can be obtained from pit bike parts specialists (see illustrations).

2 Most work can be done with a decent set of typical workshop hand tools.

3 To ensure maximum life and minimum trouble from a rebuilt engine, everything must be assembled with care in a spotlessly clean environment.

Disassembly

4 Before disassembling the engine, thoroughly clean and degrease its external surfaces. This will prevent contamination of the engine internals, and will also make the job a lot easier and cleaner. A high flash-point solvent, such as paraffin (kerosene) can be used, or better still, a proprietary engine degreaser such as Gunk. Use old paintbrushes and toothbrushes to work the solvent into the various recesses of the casings. Take care to exclude solvent or water from the electrical components and intake and exhaust ports.

 Warning: The use of petrol (gasoline) as a cleaning agent should be avoided because of the risk of fire.

5 When clean and dry, position the engine on the workbench, leaving suitable clear area for working. Gather a selection of small containers, plastic bags and some labels so that parts can be grouped together in an easily identifiable manner. Also record component positions with photos or by taking notes.

6 Before commencing work, read through the appropriate section so that some idea of the necessary procedure can be gained. When removing components note that great force is seldom required, unless specified. In many cases, a component's reluctance to be removed is indicative of an incorrect approach or removal method – if in any doubt, re-check with the text.

7 When disassembling the engine, keep 'mated' parts together that have been in contact with each other during engine operation. These 'mated' parts must be reused or replaced as an assembly.

8 A complete engine stripdown should be done in the following general order with reference to the appropriate Sections.

a) Remove the generator cover (left-hand engine cover)
b) Remove the cylinder head
c) Remove the cylinder barrel and piston
d) Remove the clutch cover (right-hand engine cover)
e) Remove the centrifugal oil filter (oil spinner)
f) Remove the oil pump
g) Remove the clutch

h) Remove the primary drive gear
i) Remove the kickstart gears
j) Remove the gearchange mechanism
k) Remove the generator rotor and stator
l) Remove the cam chain
m) Separate the crankcase halves
n) Remove the selector drum and forks
o) Remove the transmission shafts
p) Remove the kickstart shaft
q) Remove the crankshaft

Reassembly

9 Reassembly is accomplished by reversing the general disassembly sequence.

6 Cylinder head removal and installation

Removal

1 If the engine is in the frame, remove the bashplate (see Section 4), exhaust (see Chapter 3, Section 10) and carburettor (see Chapter 3, Section 5). Drain the engine oil (see Chapter 1, Section 4). Disconnect the oil cooler hoses from the right-hand side of the cylinder head and catch the small amount of oil which will drain from the cooler. Pull the cap off the spark plug. Shift the gearbox into neutral.

2 Remove the two valve adjustment caps and unscrew the spark plug (see illustrations). Remove the long bolt from the right-hand side of the head to free the sprocket cover from the left side (see illustration).

6.2a Intake and exhaust valve caps are retained by two bolts

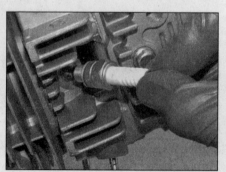

6.2b Unscrew the spark plug

6.2c Long bolt with washer retains sprocket cover

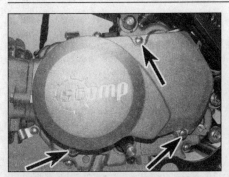

6.3a Generator cover bolts (arrowed)

6.3b Line next to T mark on rotor aligns with cut-out in casing

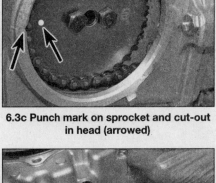

6.3c Punch mark on sprocket and cut-out in head (arrowed)

3 Remove the generator cover from the left-hand side of the engine **(see illustration)**. Turn the generator rotor anti-clockwise by hand to align its TDC mark (line next to the T mark) with the cut-out in the top of the casing **(see illustration)**. At this point the punch mark on the cam sprocket should align with the cut-out in the cylinder head at 9 o'clock position **(see illustration)**. You should be able to feel slight play in each valve rocker, indicating that both valves are closed and the engine is on its compression stroke. If one valve is open, rotate the engine a further 360° and realign the marks.

4 Slacken the two cam sprocket bolts. Hold the rotor if required to stop the engine turning.

5 Now slacken off tension on the cam chain to enable it to be detached from the sprocket. Do this by removing the cam chain tensioner; remove the large cap bolt from the lower left side of the crankcase, followed by the spring and tensioner plunger **(see illustrations)**.

6 You should be able to see the tension come off the cam chain as the tensioner arm in the crankcase automatically relaxes pressure on the chain. Unscrew the two sprocket bolts and ease the sprocket off the end of the camshaft at the same time as working the chain off the sprocket **(see illustration)**.

7 Remove the single bolt which retains the head to the barrel on the left-hand side **(see illustration)**. Slacken the four domed nuts at the top of the head evenly and in a diagonal sequence. Remove them with their washers followed by the finned cover **(see illustration)**.

8 Lift off the cylinder head **(see illustration)**.

6.5a Unscrew the tensioner cap bolt...

6.5c ...followed by the tensioner plunger

6.5b ...removing it and the long spring...

6.6 Disengaging the sprocket and cam chain

You may need to tap around the head-to-barrel joint with a soft-faced hammer to break the seal between the two components. Remove the old head gasket and retrieve the

dowels if they are loose. Lay the cam chain down across the face of the barrel.

9 Peel off the old head gasket and clean any remaining traces of old gasket material

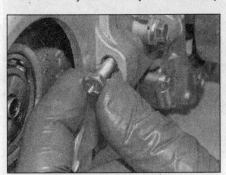

6.7a Head-to-barrel bolt

6.7b Domed nuts retain the finned cover

6.8 Carefully lift the head up off the barrel

6.11 Dowel locations (arrowed)

6.12 Fit the head onto the new cylinder head gasket

from the cylinder head and cylinder barrel. If a scraper is used, take care not to scratch or gouge the soft aluminium. Be careful not to let any of the gasket material fall into the cylinder bore or the oil passages. If there's a build up of corrosion on the studs or dowels, remove it carefully with wire wool. The dowels should come out easily, but if they are stuck in the underside of the head or top of the barrel, use thin-nose pliers to extract them.

10 Check the cylinder head gasket and the mating surfaces on the cylinder head and cylinder barrel for signs of leakage, which could indicate warpage. Refer to Chapter 2B,

Section 7 and check the cylinder head gasket surface for warpage.

Installation

11 Fit the dowels into the cylinder barrel; they fit into the top right and bottom left stub locations **(see illustration)**. Place a new head gasket onto the face of the barrel.

12 Carefully fit the cylinder head over the studs and feed the cam chain up through the tunnel as you do, making sure it locates correctly onto the dowels **(see illustration)**. Ensure the head seats fully against the barrel surface. Position the cam chain over the end of the camshaft.

13 Place a new gasket over the studs, following by the finned cover, noting that its cast diamond shape points upwards **(see illustration)**. Fit the washers, noting that the copper washer is on the lower right stud, aluminium washers are on the three other studs **(see illustration)**. Fit the four domed nuts and tighten them evenly and in a diagonal sequence. Correct tightening is important – a torque setting of 11 Nm is recommended. Tighten the single bolt down the left side of the head **(see illustration 6.7a)**.

14 Make sure the generator rotor TDC mark is correctly aligned (see Step 3). Bring the camchain up into the head aperture, then position the camshaft so that the reference hole is in the 6 o'clock position and fit the sprocket so that its punch mark aligns with the cut-out in the head in the 9 o'clock position **(see illustration)**. Use a small screwdriver to locate the chain onto the sprocket teeth **(see illustration 6.6)**. Seat the sprocket onto the camshaft shoulder and check the alignment of the punch mark and cut-out **(see illustrations)**. Reposition the chain on the sprocket if necessary. Fit the sprocket bolts and tighten them lightly **(see illustration 6.3c)**.

15 Now install the chain tensioner plunger

6.13a Fit a new gasket and the finned cover

6.13b The copper washer goes on the lower right stud (arrowed)

6.14a Positioning the camshaft and lining up the sprocket

6.14b Press the sprocket onto the camshaft shoulder

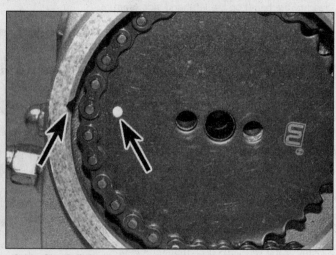

6.14c Check holes in sprocket align with those in camshaft and that timing marks align (arrowed)

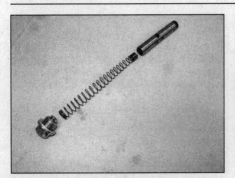

6.15a Cam chain tensioner components

6.15b Push the tensioner plunger into its bore…

6.15c …fit the narrow end of the spring into the end of the plunger…

(black tipped end first). Locate the shaped end of the spring in the end of the plunger and push both components into position with the the large bolt **(see illustrations)**. You'll see chain tension be taken up as the plunger is installed. Check that the TDC mark on the rotor and the punch mark on the sprocket correctly align with their cut-outs, then tighten the sprocket bolts and the tensioner plunger cap bolt.

16 Fit a new gasket to the circular end cover on the left side of the head **(see illustration)**. Insert the cover so that its tab aligns with the tab on the head, then secure with the long bolt from the other side of the head **(see illustrations)**.

17 Clean and refit the spark plug. Reconnect the oil cooler pipes **(see illustration 4.18b)**.

18 Check the valve clearances, especially if the head has been worked on and new valves fitted (see Chapter 1, Section 12). Fit the valve inspection caps. Refill the engine with oil to the correct level (see Chapter 1, Section 4).

19 Refit all other components in a reverse of the removal sequence.

6.15d …and secure them with the cap bolt

6.16a Fit a new gasket…

---

7 Camshaft, rockers and valves

1 Valve overhaul involves removing the valves and associated components from the cylinder head, cleaning them and checking them for wear. Valve seat re-cutting or valve guide replacement, if necessary, is a job for an engineer, but note that renewal of the head would be the cheaper option.

Rocker arms and camshaft

Removal

2 Removal of the cylinder head is advised. It is possible to work on the camshaft with the head in place, having disconnected the cam chain from the sprocket, but it's much easier to do this on the bench.

3 Remove the two bolts from the right-hand side of the head to free the end cover **(see illustration)**. This will give access to the

6.16b …align the tabs (arrowed)…

6.16c …and tighten the long bolt (arrowed)

rocker shaft ends. The shafts are only a slip fit in the head but it's best to thread an M8 bolt into the shaft end and pull it to withdraw the shaft **(see illustration)**. Note which is the

intake and which is the exhaust rocker shaft so that they can be returned to their original locations.

4 The rocker shafts also support the

7.3a End cover bolts (arrowed)

7.3b Thread an M8 bolt into the shaft end and pull the shaft out

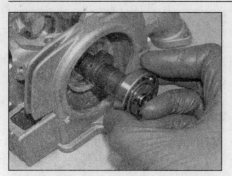

7.5 Withdraw the camshaft from the head

7.6a Check the cam lobes (arrowed)

7.6b Measuring cam lobe height with a micrometer

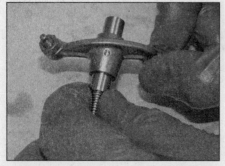

7.7 Feel for play between the shaft and rocker

7.9a Insert the exhaust rocker arm…

7.9b …and the decompressor bracket, then slide the shaft through them

decompressor mechanism which rides on the camshaft.

5 Withdraw the camshaft from the cylinder head **(see illustration)**.

Inspection

6 Check the bearing on each end of the camshaft – they must run smoothly, quietly and freely and there should be no excessive play between the inner and outer races or obvious signs of wear between the outer race and the housing in the cylinder head. Also check the cam lobes for heat discoloration (blue appearance), score marks, chipped areas, flat spots and spalling **(see illustration)**. Cam lobe height can be measured as shown **(see illustration)**; the measurement being from the tip of the cam base circle to the tip of

the lobe. On this engine the intake valve lobe height measured 27.8 mm and the exhaust 27.7 mm.

7 Check the fit of each rocker arm on its shaft. They should move freely with a light fit, but no appreciable freeplay **(see illustration)**. Check the contact pad and contact tip of the valve clearance adjuster; again there should be no sign of wear.

Installation

8 Lubricate the camshaft bearings and lobes with engine oil then slide the camshaft into the head.

9 Install the first rocker shaft in the head (intake or exhaust as noted on removal), hold the decompressor in position and push the rocker shaft through **(see illustrations)**.

Do the same for the other rocker arm **(see illustration)**.

10 Fit a new gasket to the end cover and install it **(see illustration)**. Tighten its two bolts.

Valves

Removal

11 Keep the intake and exhaust valves separate, along with their related components, so that they can be returned to their original locations without getting mixed up.

12 Compress the valve spring on the first valve with a spring compressor, making sure it is correctly located onto each end of the valve assembly **(see illustration)**. On the top of the valve the adaptor needs to be about the same

7.9c Install the intake valve rocker in the same way

7.10 Use a new gasket when fitting the end cover

7.12a Compressing the valve springs using a valve spring compressor

7.12b Make sure the compressor locates correctly both on the top of the spring retainer...

7.12c ...and on the bottom of the valve

7.13a Remove the collets

size as the spring retainer – if it is too small it will be difficult to remove and install the collets **(see illustration)**. On the underside of the head make sure the compressor contacts the centre of the valve **(see illustration)**. Do not compress the springs any more than is absolutely necessary.

13 Pick out the two collets; a magnet is good for this **(see illustration)**. Unscrew and remove the valve spring compressor, then lift out the spring retainer and the two springs **(see illustrations)**. Slide the valve out **(see illustration)**. Use a magnet or small screwdriver to remove the spring seat then prise off the valve stem seal **(see illustrations)**. Note that it's important to renew the seal every time the valve is disturbed. Repeat the procedure for the other valve but keep the components separate.

Inspection

14 Clean the cylinder head with solvent and dry it thoroughly. Clean carbon deposits from the combustion chamber using a kitchen scouring pad, then polish using steel wool. There should be no obvious signs of gas leakage from the combustion chamber itself. Examine the valve seats – light damage to the valve seats can be corrected by lapping the valves **(see illustration)**.

7.13b Remove the spring retainer...

7.13c ...inner and outer springs...

7.13d ...slide out the valve...

7.13e ...and remove the spring seat

7.13f Prise the valve stem seal off the top of the valve guide

7.14 Valve seats must be free from pitting, cracking and signs of burning

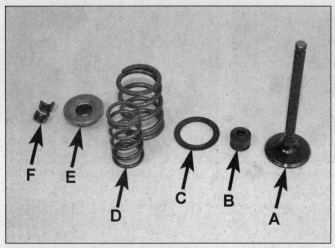

7.15a Valve assembly: valve (A), seal (B), spring seat (C), inner and outer springs (D), spring retainer (E), collets (F)

7.15b The valve face should be a continuous grey ring and be free from pitting, cracks and burning

15 Clean both valves and their springs, seats and retainers in solvent (see illustration). Scrape off carbon deposits which have formed on the valves, then use the scouring pad and steel wool to clean the valve heads. Inspect the valve face (see illustration). Slight imperfections can be corrected by lapping.

16 Service limits aren't available for measuring and determining wear. Following carbon removal and cleaning all that can be done is a visual check for wear and lapping of the valve face and seat contact faces. If renewing the head, valve and camshaft assembly also consider fitting a race head.

17 Before reassembling the valves in the head, lap them lightly to ensure a good seal between the valve face and seat. You'll need a valve grinding tool (either hand-held or drill driven) and some valve grinding compound.

18 Apply a small amount of fine or light grinding compound to the valve face (see illustration). Don't use coarse grinding compound. Smear engine oil on the valve stem, then slip the valve into the guide (see illustration 7.13d). Note: *Make sure the valve is installed in its correct guide and be careful not to get any grinding compound on the valve stem.*

19 Attach the grinding tool to the valve and rotate the tool between the palms of your hands (see illustration). Use a back-and-forth motion (as though rubbing your hands together) rather than a circular motion (i.e. so that the valve rotates alternately clockwise and anti-clockwise rather than in one direction only). If a motorised tool is being used, take note of the correct drive speed for it – if your drill runs too fast and is not variable, use a hand tool instead. Lift the valve off the seat and turn it at regular intervals to distribute the grinding compound properly. Continue the grinding procedure until the valve face and seat contact area is of uniform width, and unbroken around the entire circumference.

20 Carefully remove the valve and wipe off all traces of grinding compound, making sure none gets in the guide. Use solvent to clean the valve and wipe the seat area thoroughly with a solvent soaked cloth.

Installation

21 Working on one valve at a time, fit a new valve stem seal onto the guide, using finger pressure, a stem seal fitting tool or an appropriate size deep socket, to push the seal squarely onto the top of the valve guide until it is felt to clip into place (see illustrations).

22 Coat the valve stem with engine oil and slide it into its guide (see illustration 7.13d). Check that the valve moves up-and-down freely in the guide.

23 Lay the spring seat in place in the cylinder head (see illustration 7.13e).

24 Next fit the inner and outer springs (see illustration 7.13c). If the springs on your bike have dabs of paint at the top of the coils fit them so that this end faces upwards. Similarly if the valve springs have tighter coils at one end fit them so that the the tighter coils face down into the cylinder head. Fit the spring retainer, with its shouldered side facing down so that it fits into the top of the spring (see illustration 7.13b).

7.18 Apply small dabs of the paste around the circumference of the valve

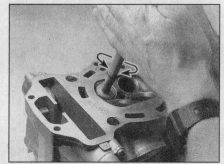

7.19 Valve lapping

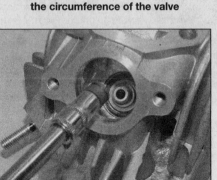

7.21a Load the new valve stem seal into a socket...

7.21b ...and press it squarely into place on the top of the guide

7.25 Collets correctly located

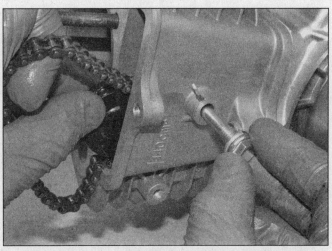

8.2a Remove the pivot bolt from the side of the barrel and withdraw the guide wheel

8.2b Remove the barrel-to-crankcase bolt

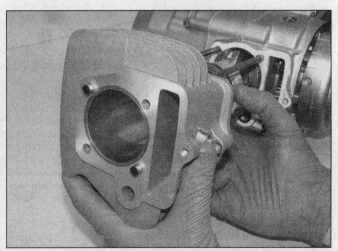

8.3 Carefully lift the barrel up off the crankcase

25 Apply a small amount of grease to the collets to help hold them in place. Compress the valve springs with the spring compressor, making sure it is correctly located onto each end of the valve assembly (see Step 12). Do not compress the springs any more than is necessary to slip the collets into place. Locate each collet in turn into the groove in the valve stem using a screwdriver with a dab of grease on it. Carefully release the compressor, making sure the collets seat and lock in the retaining groove (see illustration).

26 Repeat the procedure for the other valve.

27 Support the cylinder head on blocks so the valves can't contact the work surface, then tap the end of each valve stem lightly to make sure the collets have seated in their grooves.

28 After the camshaft and cylinder head have been installed, check the valve clearances and adjust as required (see Chapter 1, Section 12).

 HAYNES HiNT *Check for proper sealing of the valves by pouring a small amount of solvent into each of the valve ports. If the solvent leaks past either valve into the combustion chamber the valve lapping operation on that valve should be repeated.*

Cylinder head

29 Check the cylinder head for warpage as described for the 1P52FMI engine (see Chapter 2B, Section 7).

8 Cylinder barrel

Removal

1 Remove the cylinder head (see Section 6).

2 Remove the bolt from the left-hand side

of the barrel and hook the cam chain guide wheel out of the tunnel (see illustration). Remove the bolt which retains the barrel to the crankcase on the left-hand side (see illustration).

3 Pull the cylinder barrel off the crankcase, supporting the piston so the connecting rod does not knock against the engine (see illustration). If the barrel is stuck, tap around the joint faces with a soft-faced mallet. Do not attempt to free it by inserting a screwdriver between the barrel and crankcase mating surfaces – you'll damage them.

4 Remove the base gasket and discard it – a new one must be used. If they are loose, remove the dowels from the crankcase or the underside of the barrel and retrieve the O-ring seal.

5 Stuff clean rag into the cam chain tunnel and around the connecting rod to protect and support it and the piston and to prevent anything falling into the engine.

6 Clean all traces of old gasket material from

8.12a Always use a new cylinder base gasket

8.12b Dowel locations and O-ring seal on the right side

8.12c There are no dowels on the left side but check the oil feed jet (arrowed) is clean and unobstructed

the cylinder barrel and crankcase. If a scraper is used, take care not to scratch or gouge the soft aluminium. Be careful not to let any of the gasket material fall into the engine or to block the oil feed jet (see illustration 8.12c) and return passage (see illustration 8.12b).

Inspection

7 Check the cylinder walls carefully for scratches and score marks. The cylinder bore surface is plated with a hard wearing material and apart from catastrophic damage, say from a seizure, it shouldn't sustain excessive wear. There is no cylinder liner.

8 Using a precision straight-edge and feeler gauges check the barrel top surface for warpage. Take six measurements, one along each side and two diagonally across. If the barrel is warped beyond 0.05 mm take it to an engineer for an opinion, though be prepared to have to buy a new one.

9 Wear limit figures for the bore are not available, but it is possible to measure the piston diameter and subtract this from the bore diameter to obtain the piston-to-bore clearance. Generally a clearance of 0.01 to 0.04 mm is acceptable. Using a telescoping bore gauge and a micrometer, check the dimensions of the cylinder to assess the amount of wear, taper and ovality. Using a telescoping bore gauge and a micrometer, measure near the top (but below the level of the top piston ring at TDC), centre and bottom (but above the level of the oil ring at BDC)

of the bore, both parallel to and across the crankshaft axis (see Chapter 2B, Section 8).

10 If the cylinder studs are badly corroded or loose in the crankcase, remove them using one of the stud extraction methods described in Tools and Workshop Tips in Reference. Use a drop of non-permanent thread locking compound on the new or refitted stud and tighten it in the crankcase.

Installation

11 Check that the mating surfaces of the cylinder barrel and crankcase are free from oil or pieces of old gasket.

12 Remove any rag from around the piston and the cam chain tunnel. Fit the dowels over the studs and into the crankcase and push them firmly home, then fit a new base gasket (see illustration). Also fit the O-ring seal into its location (see illustrations).

13 Ensure the piston ring end gaps are positioned at 120° intervals before fitting the cylinder barrel.

14 Rotate the crankshaft so that the piston is at its highest point (top dead centre). Lubricate the cylinder bore, piston and piston rings with clean engine oil.

15 Carefully lower the barrel over the studs and onto the piston until the crown fits into the bore, holding the underside of the piston to prevent it dropping, and making sure it enters the bore squarely and does not get cocked sideways (see illustration). Feed the cam chain up the tunnel and slip a piece of

wire through it to prevent it falling back into the engine (see illustration).

16 Carefully compress and feed each ring into the bore as the cylinder is lowered. If necessary, use a soft-faced mallet to gently tap the cylinder down, but do not use force if it appears to be stuck as the piston and/or rings will be damaged.

17 When the piston and rings are correctly located in the bore, press the cylinder barrel down onto the base gasket, making sure the dowels locate.

18 Hold the barrel down and turn the crankshaft to check that everything moves as it should. Fit the bolt which retains the barrel to the crankcase on the left-hand side (see illustration 8.2b).

19 Insert the guide wheel into the cam chain and hold it in position whilst the retaining bolt is installed (see illustration).

20 Install the cylinder head (see Section 6).

9 Piston and rings

Removal

1 Remove the cylinder barrel (see Section 8). Check that the holes into the crankcase and the cam chain tunnel are completely blocked with rag.

8.15a Feed the rings into the barrel carefully as they're brittle and easy to break

8.15b Pull the cam chain up through its tunnel as the barrel is lowered onto the crankcase

8.19 Insert the guide wheel in through the chain and secure it with the pivot bolt

9.2 Note the piston IN marking

9.3 Use a small screwdriver to hook the circlip out of its groove

9.4 Look for markings near to the end gap of each compression ring, denoting their top surface

2 Note that the piston crown is marked IN (though the mark is likely to be invisible until the piston is cleaned) and this mark faces the intake side of the cylinder **(see illustration)**.

3 Carefully prise out the circlip on one side of the piston **(see illustration)**. Push the piston pin out from the other side to free the piston from the connecting rod. Remove the other circlip and discard them as new ones must be used.

 HAYNES HiNT *If the piston pin is a tight fit in the piston bosses, heat the piston using a heat gun – this will expand the alloy piston sufficiently to release its grip on the pin. If the piston pin is particularly stubborn, extract it using a drawbolt tool, but be careful to protect the piston's working surfaces.*

Inspection and installation

4 Refer to Chapter 2B, Section 9 for inspection procedures **(see illustration)**.

10 Clutch cable

1 Slacken the locknuts on the adjuster at the lower end of the cable and reposition the

adjuster in its bracket to give more freeplay in the cable **(see illustration)**.

2 Align the slots in the adjuster and lockring with that in the lever bracket, then pull the outer cable end from the socket in the adjuster and release the inner cable from the lever **(see illustrations)**. If needed, you can thread the adjuster fully into the lever bracket to create more freeplay in the cable.

3 Push the clutch operating arm forwards and disconnect the cable end from the slot in the arm **(see illustration)**. Slide the cable out of the bracket on the clutch cover **(see illustration)**.

4 Remove the cable from the bike, noting its routing through the guides.

5 Installation is the reverse of removal. Apply grease to the cable ends. Make sure the cable is correctly routed through its guides. Adjust the amount of clutch lever freeplay (see Chapter 1, Section 6).

11 Clutch, oil filter and primary drive gear

Removal

1 Drain the engine oil (see Chapter 1, Section 4).

2 Mark the position of the kickstart lever on its

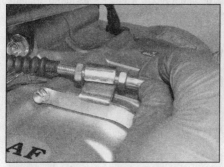

10.1 Create freeplay in the cable using the adjuster at its lower end

10.2a Wiggle the cable end out of the lever...

10.2b ...and slip it out through the slot in the adjuster and locknut

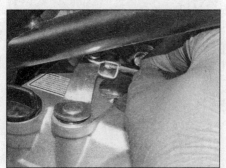

10.3a Disconnect the cable from the slot in the arm...

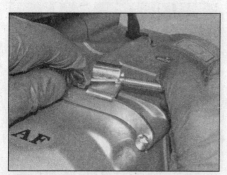

10.3b ...then slip the inner cable out of the bracket

11.2 Removing the kickstart lever from its splines. Check the oil seal (arrowed) for oil leaks

11.4 Clutch cover bolts (arrowed)

shaft, then remove the pinch bolt and pull the lever off the shaft splines **(see illustration)**. If there's signs of oil leakage from the seal obtain a new seal for use on installation.

3 Disconnect the clutch cable from the operating arm (see Section 10) and position the cable clear of the engine.

4 Working evenly in a criss-cross pattern, unscrew the clutch cover bolts **(see**

illustration). Remove the cover, being prepared to catch any residual oil. Remove the gasket and discard it. Remove the two dowels from either the cover or the crankcase if they are loose. Note also the headed pushrod inside the cover and the washer on the end of the kickstart shaft – both may drop free as the cover is removed.

5 Remove the four screws to free the cover from the centrifugal oil filter (oil spinner) **(see illustration)**. Use the larger end of the peg spanner (see Section) to free the slotted filter retaining nut **(see illustration)**. Note that a large aluminium washer was used to jam

the primary and secondary gears at the top to prevent crankshaft rotation; the use of an aluminium washer is important because it is softer that the gear teeth **(see illustration)**. Pick the washer out of the gears once nut has been slackened. Remove the nut, its lock washer and slide the filter unit off the end of the crankshaft.

6 Remove the four bolts from the clutch spring plate, slackening them evenly rather than one at a time **(see illustration)**. Lift off the spring plate together with the thrust bearing in its centre, then remove the four coil springs **(see illustration)**.

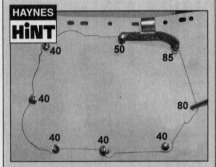

HAYNES HiNT

Store the cover bolts in a template of the cover (either draw around the actual cover or produce a sketch) to record the bolt locations. On this engine bolts were of 40, 50, 80 and 85 mm lengths.

11.5a Undo the screws and remove the filter cover (clean any deposits from inside the filter)

11.5b Tools for slackening the filter's slotted nut

11.5c Aluminium washer jammed between gear teeth to lock them

11.6a Remove the four bolts and spring retaining plate...

11.6b ...lift out the four coil springs

11.7a Slackening the clutch nut

11.7b Locking grips being used to hold the sprocket

11.7c Once slackened, thread the clutch nut off by hand

7 Now use the smaller end of the peg spanner to slacken the slotted clutch nut **(see illustration)**. To prevent the gearshaft rotating whilst slackening the nut, select a gear then hold the sprocket as shown – the round pegs on the back of this tool are held clamped into the wells of the sprocket teeth **(see illustration)**. If the engine is in the frame, put the bike into top gear and have someone sit on the bike with the rear brake held on whilst you undo the clutch nut. Whichever method you choose, note the clutch nut was found to be very tight. Thread the clutch nut off followed by the lockwasher, then grasp the set of clutch plates, together with the pressure plate and clutch centre, and withdraw it from the gearshaft as an assembly **(see illustrations)**.

8 To remove the clutch housing (basket), slide off the locking washer then rotate the splined washer in the shaft groove so that it can be withdrawn **(see illustrations)**. Slide the housing off the gearshaft followed by the kickstart driven gear sleeve **(see illustration)**.

9 The spacer, primary drive gear and oil pump drive gear can now be slid off the end of the crankshaft; it's not possible to remove them with the clutch housing/basket in place **(see illustration)**. Take note of any markings on the gears. On the bike photographed the primary gear was fitted with its part number marking facing inwards and the oil pump gear with its part number marking facing outwards.

11.7d Grab the plate assembly as a set

11.8a Lockwasher's three internal tangs locate under the splined washer

11.8b Once rotated so that internal splines align with the shaft grooves the splined washer can be removed

11.8c Removing the clutch housing from the gear shaft

11.9a Slide the spacer...

11.9b ...primary drive gear...

11.9c ...and oil pump drive gear off the crankshaft

11.13a Headed pushrod (arrowed)

11.13b Free the return spring from the shaft (it's inner end locates in a drilling in the shaft)…

11.13c …and withdraw the shaft from the cover taking care not to tear the oil seal

11.15a Alternate clutch plates, friction…

11.15b …then plain

11.15c Finish with the pressure plate

Inspection

10 The clutch is sold as a complete unit (housing, plates, pressure plate, springs and spring retaining plate with its bearing).

11 The friction material on the clutch friction plates will wear and promote clutch slip, and the plain plates can distort. Note that friction plate material thickness measures 3 mm when new. The plates can also take on a glazed appearance and smell burnt and the clutch springs will weaken and sag – new springs measure 24 mm. Inspect the friction plates for wear between the inner teeth of the plain plates and the slots in the clutch centre. Wear of this nature will cause clutch drag and slow disengagement during gear changes as the plates will snag.

12 Check the thrust bearing set in the spring retaining plate for signs of wear or damage and roughness (see illustration 11.6a).

13 To remove the clutch operating shaft from the cover, lift out the headed pushrod and free the return spring as the shaft is removed (see illustrations).

Installation

14 Fit the oil pump drive gear, primary gear and spacer on the crankshaft.

15 If the clutch plates need to be built back up start with a friction plate, then a plain plate, and build them up alternately on the clutch centre (see illustrations). Align the outer tabs of the friction plates and then fit the pressure plate, engaging it with the clutch centre splines (see illustration).

16 Fit the kickstart driven gear sleeve through the clutch housing (see illustration). Insert it on the gearshaft (see illustration 11.8c) meshing the kickstart driven gear with its idler gear and meshing the secondary gear around the outside of the housing with the primary drive gear on the crankshaft. Slide the splined washer on and rotate it in the shaft groove so that its tabs locate with the raised splines (see illustration). Slide the lockwasher on so that its tangs locate under the splined washer (see illustration).

11.16a Kickstart driven gear locates in back of clutch housing

11.16b Position the splined washer as shown…

11.16c …then fit the lockwasher (two of its tangs arrowed)

11.17a The lockwasher OUTSIDE mark faces outwards

11.17b Tighten the nut whilst holding the sprocket as shown

17 Hold the assembled clutch plate unit and fit it into the housing, aligning the friction plate tangs with the housing slots **(see illustration 11.7d)**. Fit the lockwasher and clutch nut, then with the transmission in gear and the sprocket held, tighten the clutch nut **(see illustrations)**. A torque setting of 42 Nm is recommended.

18 Install the four coil springs over their posts and fit the lifter plate, having applied a drop of engine oil to its bearing **(see illustration)**. Tighten the four bolts down evenly.

19 Clean all oil residue from the inside the centrifugal filter housing (oil spinner) and

insert it on the end of the crankshaft **(see illustration)**. Fit the lockwasher and nut and tighten them with the peg spanner **(see illustrations)**. Lock the primary gears at the bottom this time **(see illustration)**.

20 Before fitting the filter (spinner) cover check its oil seal and fit a new gasket **(see illustration)**. A good seal on the filter cover is vital to maintain a supply of oil into the crankshaft end and from there to the big-end bearing.

21 Before fitting the clutch cover, it's a good time to clean the oil filter screen set in the

11.18 Installing the springs and lifter plate

11.19a Install the cleaned centrifugal filter over the splines

11.19b Lockwasher OUTSIDE marking faces outwards

11.19c Fit the slotted nut...

11.19d ...and tighten as shown...

11.19e ...then remove the aluminium washer from between the gear teeth

11.20 Filter cover oil seal and new gasket

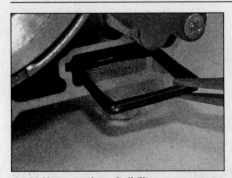

11.21 Narrow edge of oil filter screen goes in first

11.22a Prise out the old oil seal

11.22b Press the new seal in using thumb pressure

11.23 Locate a new cover gasket over the two dowels (arrowed)

bottom of the crankcase **(see illustration)**. Use long-nose pliers to pull the screen out. Clean any debris and oil sludge off the screen using a soft brush and solvent.

22 Also check the kickstart shaft oil seal. If it show signs of leaking prise it out with a flat-bladed screwdriver and press a new seal into place **(see illustrations)**. The spring side of the seal faces inwards and the side with the seal size number and other markings faces outwards. Apply a smear of engine oil to the seal lips to protect them when the cover is fitted over the splined end of the kickstart shaft.

23 Make sure the washer is in place on the kickstart shaft **(see illustration 14.3a)** and that the headed pushrod is located inside the cover **(see illustration 11.13a)**. Remove any traces of old gasket from the crankcase and the clutch cover surfaces, then fit a new gasket over the two dowels **(see illustration)**.

24 Install the clutch cover noting that you may need to wiggle the kickstart shaft slight to get the cover to seat. Return the cover bolts to their original positions and tighten them in a diagonal sequence.

25 Engage the clutch cable through the bracket and its end in the arm. Adjust cable freeplay (see Chapter 1, Section 6).

26 Fit the kickstart lever back onto its shaft, aligning the marks make on removal to get the lever angle right. Tighten the pinch bolt.

27 Fill the engine with the correct amount of 10W/40 semi-synthetic motorcycle oil (see Chapter 1, Section 4). Just under 1 litre will be required, although check the oil level using the dipstick.

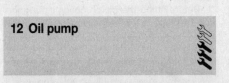

12 Oil pump

Removal

1 Remove the clutch cover and the centrifugal oil filter (oil spinner) (see Section 11).

2 Unscrew the three screws and remove the pump from the crankcase complete with its nylon driven gear **(see illustration)**. Note the two dowels and gasket between the pump and crankcase.

3 The pump can be dismantled to check the rotors but note that spare parts are not available **(see illustration)**.

4 Remove the oil filter screen from its housing

beneath the oil pump and clean it. Also check that the oilways are clear. Clean the inside of the centrifugal filter and inspect the oil in the filter cover (see Section 11).

Installation

5 Fit a new gasket over the two dowels then fit the pump onto the crankcase, meshing its gear with the drive gear on the crankshaft **(see illustration)**.

6 Install the centrifugal oil filter and clutch cover.

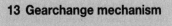

13 Gearchange mechanism

Removal

1 Make sure the transmission is in neutral. Remove the clutch (see Section 11). Remove the kickstart idler gear **(see illustrations 14.2a and b)**.

2 Make a mark where the slot in the gear lever aligns with the shaft **(see illustration 4.7a)**. Unscrew the pinch bolt and slide the lever off the shaft.

3 Wrap a single layer of thin insulating tape around the gearchange shaft splines to protect the oil seal lips as the shaft is removed.

4 Note how the stopper arm spring ends locate and how the roller on the arm locates in the neutral detent on the selector drum cam, then unscrew the stopper arm bolt and

12.2 Oil pump retaining screws (arrowed)

12.3 Check the teeth of the pump's nylon gear

12.5 Clean the filter screen (arrowed) and fit a new gasket

13.4 Stopper arm pivot bolt (arrowed)

13.5a Spring ends locate on each side of the post

13.5b Hold the selector arm down to clear the pins...

13.5c ...then withdraw the gearchange shaft

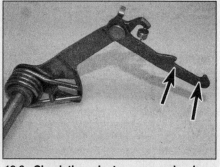

13.6a Check the selector arm pawls where they engage the pins (arrowed)...

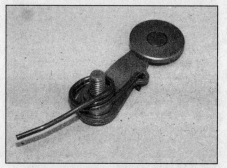

13.6b ...and the stopper arm roller

remove the arm and the spring, noting how they fit (see illustration).

5 Note how the gearchange shaft centralising spring ends fit on each side of the locating pin in the casing (see illustration), and how the pawls on the selector arm locate onto the pins in the end of the selector drum. Grasp the end of the shaft, then push the selector arm down until it clears the pins and withdraw the shaft/ arm assembly (see illustrations).

Inspection

6 Check the selector arm for cracks, distortion and wear of its pawls, and check for any corresponding wear on the five pins set in the end of the selector drum (see illustration). Also check the stopper arm roller and the detents in the camplate for any wear or damage, and make sure the roller turns

freely (see illustration). Fit a new selector shaft assembly if wear is found.

7 Inspect the shaft centralising spring, the selector arm spring and the stopper arm return spring for fatigue, wear or damage. Also check that the centralising spring locating pin in the crankcase is securely tightened. If it is loose, remove it and apply a non-permanent thread locking compound to its threads, then tighten it.

8 If the bike has been dropped on its gear lever and there are problems selecting gears, the gearchange shaft may be bent. Fit a new selector fork shaft assembly rather than attempting to straighten it. Also check the condition of the splines on the shaft end, although any damage is more likely to be found on the gear lever splines. Check the condition of the shaft oil seal in the left-hand side of the crankcase (see illustration). If it is damaged, deteriorated or shows signs

of leakage it must be replaced with a new one – lever out the old seal with a seal hook or screwdriver. Press or drive the new seal squarely into place using your fingers, a seal driver or suitable socket.

Installation

9 Check that the shaft centralising spring is properly positioned. Apply some grease to the lips of the gearchange shaft oil seal in the left-hand side of the crankcase. Slide the shaft into place and push it all the way through the case until the splined end comes out the other side, and push the selector arm down as its pawls engage the change pins (see illustration 13.5b). Locate the centralising spring ends onto each side of the locating pin in the crankcase (see illustration 13.5a).

10 Assemble the spring and washer on the stopper arm and its bolt (see illustration).

13.8 Check the gearchange shaft seal (arrowed)

13.9 Gearchange shaft/arm correctly installed

13.10 The hooked end of the spring goes through the hole in the stopper arm

Apply a drop of non-permanent thread locking compound to the bolt threads. Install the arm, locating the roller onto the neutral detent on the selector drum cam, and making sure the free end of the spring is positioned correctly against the crankcase (see illustration 13.4).

11 Check that all components are correctly positioned. Install the clutch (see Section 11). Install the kickstart idler gear.

12 Slide the gear lever onto the shaft, aligning its slit with the punch mark on the shaft. Fit the pinch bolt and tighten it.

14 Kickstart

Removal

1 Remove the clutch (see Section 11). The kickstart driven gear sleeve can be separated from the clutch housing/basket if required.

2 Use circlip pliers to free the idler gear circlip, then draw the gear and washer off the output shaft (see illustrations).

3 From the kickstart shaft, remove the washer, circlip, washer and kickstart drive gear (see illustrations).

4 The remainder of the kickstart components are located inside the crankcase. Separate the crankcases (see Section 17) and remove the gearshafts and selector drum. Disengage the kickstart return spring and remove the entire shaft from the left-hand crankcase half (see illustrations).

Inspection

5 Inspect the gear teeth on drive, idler and driven gears. If severely worn the kickstart could slip. If any wear or faults are noted, purchase a new set of gears. Note that the idler gear is available in two different size 'steps' – 6.5 mm and 9 mm. That shown in the photographs measures 6.5 mm

6 Individual parts aren't available for the kickstart shaft – it is sold as an assembly (see illustration). The shaft can be dismantled if required (see illustrations). When rebuilding note that the spring guide and ratchet have punch marks which must align with those on the shaft. All circlips must locate in their shaft grooves.

Installation

7 Insert the left end of the kickstart shaft into the crankcase. With the inner end of the return spring hooked onto the spring guide, force the free end over the crankcase lug with a screwdriver (see illustration). When fitted the stop on the guide will butt against the crankcase and the spring end will be over the lug (see illustration). This may take a couple of attempts!

8 Reassemble the crankcase halves (see Section 17). The drive gears can be fitted once the gearchange components are in place.

9 Install the drive gear components in a reverse of the removal sequence.

14.2a Free the circlip...

14.2b ...kickstart idler gear and washer (arrowed)

14.3a Remove the washer...

14.3b ...circlip...

14.3c ...washer...

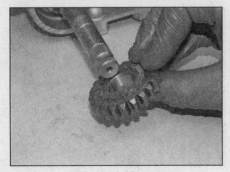

14.3d ...and drive gear

14.4 Removing the kickstart shaft from the crankcase

14.6a Kickstart shaft assembly

14.6b From the left end of the shaft remove the washer...

14.6c ...the circlip...

14.6d ...washer...

14.6e ...spring seat...

14.6f ...return spring...

14.6g ...and spring guide (punch marks align it on the shaft)

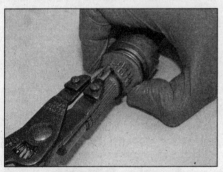

14.6h Free the circlip...

14.6i ...to release the splined washer and ratchet spring...

14.6j ...and the ratchet (punch marks align it on the shaft)

14.6k Lastly remove the circlip from its groove in the shaft

14.7a Hook the free end of the return spring over the lug

14.7b Components fully fitted in crankcase

15.3a Undoing the rotor nut

15.3b Detail of the rotor holding tool

15.4 Operating the centre-bolt puller

15 Generator

Removal

1 Remove the gearchange lever **(see illustration 4.7a)**. Remove the engine left-hand cover; it is retained by three bolts.
2 Trace the generator wiring from the top of the crankcase to the connectors just beneath the fuel tank and disconnect them **(see illustration 4.6b)**.
3 Hold the rotor and undo the rotor nut **(see illustration)**. Note the rotor holding tool made from two pieces of steel strap with bolts to engage the holes in the rotor **(see illustration)**. Remove the nut.
4 You'll need a centre-bolt type puller to pull the rotor off its taper on the crankshaft. The type shown can be obtained through pit bike part suppliers and is not expensive **(see illustration 5.1a)**. Back off the puller's centre bolt and thread the body of the puller into the rotor. Note that the thread is left-hand, so it must be turned in an anti-clockwise direction. Turn the puller's centre bolt in so that it contacts the end of the crankshaft then hold the body with an open-end spanner and tighten the centre bolt until the rotor comes free of its taper **(see illustration)**.

15.5 Woodruff key location

5 The rotor has a slot in its boss which locates over a key (Woodruff key) set in the crankshaft taper. If the key is loose, remove it and keep it with the rotor for now **(see illustration)**. The key prevents the rotor attempting to spin on the crankshaft end.
6 Drain the engine oil (see Chapter 1, Section 4).
7 Remove the two countersunk screws which retain the stator plate and gently pull the assembly out of the crankcase **(see illustration)**.
8 Note the large O-ring around the periphery of the stator plate, the two small O-rings at the screw mounting points and the oil seal set in the centre of the stator plate. All prevent the escape of oil from the cam chain and inner crankcase areas.

15.7 Startor plate screws (arrowed)

9 Refer to Chapter 4 for details of generator coil testing.

Installation

10 Check the condition of the stator plate O-rings and the oil seal set in its centre. If there are signs of oil escaping into the outer cover area, the seals must be renewed. To remove the oil seal prise it out from the back of the stator plate **(see illustration)** and press a new seal into position; the seal must be fitted so that its spring side faces inwards towards the crankcase.
11 Make sure the two small O-rings are in their recesses in the crankcase then fit the stator plate **(see illustration)**. Press it into position

15.10 Prise out the stator plate oil seal from the back of the plate if it needs changing

15.11 Stator plate large O-ring (A) and two small O-rings (B – top shown)

15.13a Align the rotor slot with the Woodruff key...

15.13b ...fit the nut...

15.13c ...then hold the rotor and tighten the nut

and secure it with the two screws – you should be able to hear it click into place as the large O-ring seats. Position the wiring grommet into the cut-out in the top edge of the casing.

12 Refill the engine oil to the correct level (see Chapter 1, Section 4).

13 If removed, install the Woodruff key back into its slot **(see illustration 15.5)**. Install the rotor so that its cut-out fits over the key, noting that the pull of its magnets will be felt as it passes over the coils **(see illustration)**. Fit the rotor nut and tighten it **(see illustrations)**. A torque setting of 41 Nm is recommended.

14 Reconnect the generator wiring and fit the left-hand engine cover.

15 Slide the gear lever onto the shaft, aligning its slit with the punch mark on the shaft. Fit the pinch bolt and tighten it.

16 Cam chain, tensioner and guides

Cam chain tensioner

1 The tensioner is automatic in operation **(see illustration)**.

2 The tensioner plunger and spring can be accessed easily from the lower left side of the engine although first the engine must be set to TDC compression as described in the cylinder head removal procedure (see Section 6). This procedure covers removal of the engine bashplate, then the tensioner cap bolt, spring and plunger. Note that valve timing must be checked after refitting the plunger particularly if the crankshaft has been rotated with tension off the chain.

Tensioner arm and lower guide wheel

3 Remove the generator and its stator plate to access the tensioner arm (see Section 15).

4 Set the engine to TDC and remove the tensioner cap, plunger and spring as described in the cylinder head removal procedure (see Section 6); this will relax tension on the cam chain.

5 Lift the wheel off the tensioner arm **(see illustration)**. The tensioner arm is retained to the crankcase by a single pivot bolt. The guide wheel can be removed from its pivot if required.

6 Installation is a reverse of the removal

procedure. Note that the valve timing must be checked after refitting the tensioner plunger particularly if the crankshaft has been rotated with tension off the chain.

Cam chain guide wheel in cylinder barrel

7 Remove the cylinder head (see Section 6). Refer to the first part of the cylinder barrel removal procedure and remove the guide wheel from the cam chain tunnel (see Section 8).

8 Installation is a reverse of the removal procedure.

Cam chain

9 Remove the cylinder head (see Section 6).

Refer to the first part of the cylinder barrel removal procedure and remove the guide wheel from the cam chain tunnel (see Section 8).

10 Remove the generator and its stator plate (see Section 15).

11 Remove the wheel from the tensioner arm **(see illustration 16.5)**. Withdraw the cam chain from its sprocket on the crankshaft **(see illustration)**.

12 Check the chain for binding, kinks and any obvious damage and replace it with a new one if necessary.

13 Installation is a reverse of the removal procedure.

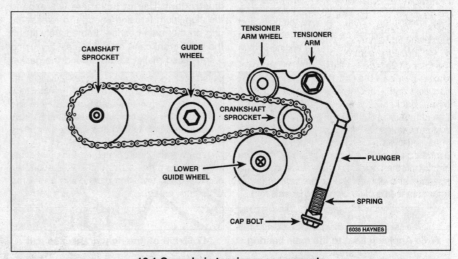

16.1 Cam chain tensioner components

16.5 Tensioner wheel can be slipped off its pivot

16.11 Lift the cam chain off its sprocket and out of the engine

17 Crankcase separation and reassembly

Separation

1 To access the crankshaft and connecting rod assembly, kickstart shaft, gear shafts, selector drum and forks, and their bearings, the crankcase halves must be separated. Remove the engine from the frame (see Section 4).

2 Before the crankcases can be separated the following components must be removed:

a) *Cylinder head (Section 6)*
b) *Cylinder barrel (Section 8). The piston can remain attached to the rod, but wrap rag around it to protect the rings.*
c) *Generator (Section 15)*
d) *Drive sprocket (Chapter 6, Section 17)*
e) *Clutch and primary drive gear (Section 11)*
f) *Kickstart drive gears (Section 14)*
g) *Gearchange mechanism (Section 13)*
h) *Oil pump (Section 12)*
i) *Cam chain and tensioner arm wheel (Section 16)*

3 Remove the bolt and washer from the left-hand end of the selector drum **(see illustrations)**.

4 Slacken the seven bolts in the left-hand side of the crankcase evenly and in a diagonal sequence **(see illustration 17.14)**. Remove the bolts and record their positions as an aid to refitting (see **Haynes Hint**). The bolts on the engine shown were of 50, 60 and 65 mm in length.

17.3a Prise out the bung at the top of the left crankcase half...

HAYNES HINT *As each bolt is removed, store it in its relative position in a cardboard template of the crankcase halves. This will ensure all bolts and any washers/guides with them are returned to their original locations on reassembly.*

5 Turn the engine over so that it is resting on its left-hand side. Support it using blocks of wood to prevent the shaft ends contacting the bench.

6 Using a heat gun, warm the area around the main bearing for a few minutes **(see illustration)**. Use of heat here will expand the aluminium housing enough to release its grip on the main bearing. Immediately lift off the right crankcase half, if necessary using a soft-faced mallet to tap around the gasket

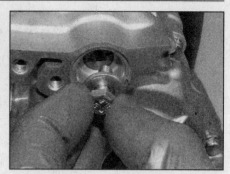

17.3b ...and remove the bolt and washer from the end of the selector drum

joint **(see illustration)**. If the halves do not separate easily, make sure all fasteners have been removed. Do not try and separate the halves by levering against the crankcase mating surfaces as they are easily scored and will leak oil in the future if damaged. The right-hand crankcase half will come away leaving the crankshaft, kickstart shaft, transmission shafts and selector drum and forks in the left-hand half.

7 Hold the kickstart return spring away from the lower gear pinion on the output shaft, then grasp the gear shafts and selector drum and remove them as an assembly **(see illustrations)**. Disengage the kickstart return spring from the crankcase lug and lift it out complete with the washer **(see illustrations)**. Turn the engine over. Heat the area around the main bearing then lift or lightly tap the crankshaft out **(see illustration)**.

17.6a Applying heat to the main bearing area

17.6b Lift off the right crankcase half

17.7a The lower gear on the output shaft won't clear the kickstart return spring unless the spring is held out of the way

17.7b Remove the gear shafts and selector drum as a unit

17.7c Unhook the end of the kickstart return spring and remove the kickstart shaft

17.7d Applying heat to ease removal of the crankshaft

17.9a Warm the main bearing housing area…

17.9b …and fit the crankshaft

17.11a Mesh the gearshafts and drum together…

17.11b …and fit as a unit locating their ends in the bearings

Reassembly

8 Remove all traces of old gasket material from both crankcase mating surfaces.
9 Use the heat gun to warm the main bearing housing in the left case, then support the piston and con-rod with one hand and fit the crankshaft into the crankcase with the other **(see illustration)**. The crankshaft is fitted with its tapered end downwards **(see illustration)**.
10 Install the kickstart shaft (see Section 14).
11 Generously lubricate the transmission

shaft bearings and the bore for the selector drum end. Mesh the gear shafts together and insert the two selector forks in their gear grooves **(see illustration)**. Hold the assembly together and fit the shafts into the left-hand half **(see illustration)**.
12 Apply engine oil to the gearshaft ends. Wipe the crankcase mating surface over with solvent. Ensure the two dowels are in position in the left-hand half and place a new gasket in position **(see illustration)**. Note that there's no need for any sealant.

13 Use the heat gun to warm the bearing housing of the right-hand crankcase half **(see illustration)**. Immediately fit the right half down over the crankshaft main bearing **(see illustration 17.6b)**. Check that the crankcase halves are correctly seated, noting that you may need to install the kickstart lever and rotate the shaft slightly to enable the cases to seat **(see illustration)**. Clean the threads of all the crankcase bolts. Turn the engine over.
Caution: The crankcase halves should fit together without being forced. If the

17.12 Lay a new gasket on the left crankcase. Dowels (arrowed)

17.13a Warm the main bearing housing area

17.13b Fitting the kickstart lever helps to hold the shaft aligned when getting the cases to seat

17.14 Crankcase bolt lengths

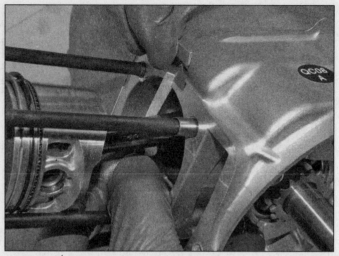

17.15 Use a sharp blade to trim off the excess gasket from the crankcase mouth

casings are not correctly seated, remove the right-hand crankcase half and investigate the problem. Do not attempt to pull them together using the crankcase bolts as the casing will crack and be ruined.

14 Install the seven crankcase bolts including the clip on the front bolt (**see illustration**). Secure the bolts finger-tight at first, then tighten them evenly and a little at a time in a criss-cross sequence – no torque setting is specified, but bolts of that size should be tightened to 12 Nm.

15 With all crankcase fasteners tightened, check that the crankshaft and gear shafts rotate smoothly and easily. Check that the gear shafts rotate freely and independently in neutral, then rotate the selector drum by hand and select each gear in turn whilst rotating the input shaft. If there are any signs of undue stiffness, tight or rough spots, or of any other problem, the fault must be rectified before proceeding further.

16 Trim off the section of gasket from the mouth of the crankcase (**see illustration**). Install all other removed assemblies in a reverse of the sequence given in Step 2.

18 Crankcases and bearings

1 Refer to Chapter 2B, Section 19 noting that the output shaft right-hand bearing is a needle-roller type on this engine (**see illustrations**).

19 Crankshaft and connecting rod

1 Refer to Chapter 2B, Section 20 for details (**see illustrations**).

20 Gear shafts and selector drum

Gear shafts

1 Remove the transmission shafts from the crankcase (see Section 20).

2 If the gear pinions show signs of stripped or chipped teeth or excessive wear, e.g. from missing a gear, it's best to renew them (**see illustrations**). A complete pair of shafts can be purchased very cheaply. If you wish to strip the shafts it's a straightforward operation. Use the appropriate circlips pliers when removing circlips and take care not to strain or distort them.

3 Inspect the dogs and the dog holes in the gears for cracks, chips, and excessive wear especially in the form of rounded edges. Make sure mating gears engage properly.

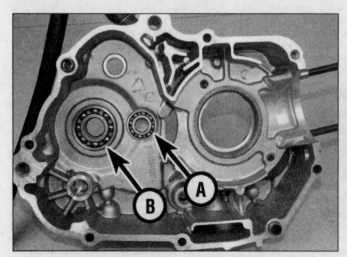

18.1a Input shaft (A) and output shaft (B) bearings in left-hand crankcase half

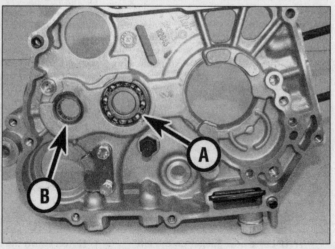

18.1b Input shaft (A) and output shaft (B) bearings in right-hand crankcase half

19.1a Crankshaft right-hand end

19.1b Crankshaft left-hand end showing cam chain sprocket

HAYNES HiNT *When disassembling the transmission shafts, place the parts on a long rod or thread a wire through them to keep them in order and facing the proper direction.*

Input shaft

4 Slide the 4th gear (largest gear) off the shaft followed by the thrust washer. Use circlip pliers to remove the circlip from its groove in the shaft, then slide off the 3rd gear. Remove the circlip and thrust washer and slide off the 2nd gear. First gear is part of the shaft.
5 Build up the gears according to the photo sequence **(see illustrations)**. During reassembly, apply engine oil to the mating surfaces of the shaft, pinions and bushes. When installing the circlips, do not expand their ends any further than is necessary. Install the stamped circlips and washers so that their chamfered side faces away from the thrust side.

20.2a Input shaft gear positions

Output shaft

6 Remove the thrust washer and 4th gear (smallest gear) from the shaft end. Remove the thrust washer, 3rd gear and thrust washer. Use circlip pliers to remove the circlip from the shaft groove and slide the 2nd gear off. Free the remaining circlip from the shaft and slide off the washer and first gear.

20.5a Input shaft – second gear dogs face away from first gear...

20.2b Output shaft gear positions

20.5b ...washer and cirlip retain second gear

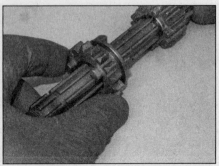

20.5c Fit the third gear with its fork groove towards the second gear...

20.5d ...then slide on the circlip and fit it into the shaft groove

20.5e Install the washer...

20.5f ...before fitting the fourth gear (with its holes towards the third gear)

20.7a The bare output shaft

20.7b Fit the first gear with its dog holes facing away from the shaft shoulder, followed by the washer...

20.7c ...and secure the gear with the circlip making sure it locates in its groove

20.7d Second gear is fitted with its selector groove facing away from the first gear

20.7e Fit the circlip into its groove then fit the washer

20.7f Install the third gear with its dogs facing the second gear...

20.7g ...then fit the washer...

20.7h ...first gear (with its chamfered edge towards the third gear)...

20.7i ...and finally the washer

20.8 Inspect the fork ends for wear

7 Build up the gears according to the photo sequence **(see illustrations)**. During reassembly, apply engine oil to the mating surfaces of the shaft, pinions and bushes. When installing the circlips, do not expand their ends any further than is necessary. Install the stamped circlips and washers so that their chamfered side faces away from the thrust side.

Selector drum and forks

8 Inspect the selector forks for any signs of wear or damage, especially around the fork ends where they engage with the groove in the gear pinion **(see illustration)**. The fork ends (tips) will wear rapidly if you do clutchless gearchanges – always use the clutch when changing gear.

9 Check that each fork fits correctly in its pinion groove. Check closely to see if the forks are bent. If the forks are in any way damaged the complete selector drum and fork assembly must be renewed.

21 Running-in procedure

1 Make sure the engine oil level is correct (see Chapter 1, Section 3). Make sure there is fuel in the tank.
2 Turn the engine kill switch to the RUN position and shift the gearbox into neutral. Set the choke to ON.
3 Start the engine and allow it to run until it reaches operating temperature.

4 Check carefully that there are no oil or fuel leaks and make sure the gearbox and controls, especially the brakes, function properly.
5 Treat the bike gently to make sure oil has circulated throughout the engine and any new parts installed have started to seat.
6 Even greater care is necessary if a new piston and rings have been fitted; the bike will have to be run in as when new. This means not over-revving the engine, change up a gear instead, and not running it at more than two thirds throttle. Apply this running-in period for the first two hours of the bike's use. After that, change the engine oil, check the valve clearances and the idle speed and check the tightness of all nuts and bolts.

Chapter 2 Part D
Engine – Zongshen 1P60YMJ (ZS155)

Contents

Degrees of difficulty

Easy, suitable for novice with little experience	**Fairly easy,** suitable for beginner with some experience	**Fairly difficult,** suitable for competent DIY mechanic	**Difficult,** suitable for experienced DIY mechanic	**Very difficult,** suitable for expert DIY or professional 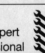

1 General Information

1 The 155cc horizontal engine/transmission unit is an air-cooled single cylinder of unit construction **(see illustrations opposite)**. The two valves are operated by rocker arms actuated by a single overhead camshaft that is chain driven off the left-hand end of the crankshaft. The crankcase divides vertically.

2 The crankcase incorporates a wet sump, pressure-fed lubrication system that uses a single rotor trochoidal oil pump that is gear-driven off a separate gear on the right-hand end of the crankshaft. Oil is filtered by a screen in the bottom of the crankcase and also by a paper element filter. The oil is cooled by a radiator mounted on the frame.

3 The generator is on the left-hand end of the crankshaft. The ignition timing trigger is on the outside of the generator rotor, and the pick-up coil is mounted on the stator plate.

4 Power from the crankshaft is routed to the transmission via the primary gears. The clutch is of the wet multi-plate type and is mounted directly to the right-hand end of the gearbox input shaft. The clutch is operated by cable. The transmission is a four-speed constant-mesh unit. Final drive to the rear wheel is by chain and sprockets.

5 This is a 'start in gear' engine; the engine can be started in gear if the clutch lever is held in.

2 Component access

Operations possible with the engine in the frame

1 The components and assemblies listed below can be removed without having to remove the engine from the frame. Note however that removal of the engine is fairly straightforward and it is recommended if a number of items require attention, or if the bike cannot be raised up to a convenient working height on a ramp or platform.

a) Cylinder head, camshaft, rockers and valves
b) Cylinder barrel and piston
c) Clutch
d) Oil pump, oil screen and paper filter
e) Primary drive gear
f) Gearchange mechanism
g) Generator rotor and stator plate
h) Cam chain, tensioner and guides
i) Kickstart drive gears

Operations requiring engine removal

2 It is necessary to remove the engine from the frame and split the crankcases to gain access to the following components.

a) Crankshaft and connecting rod
b) Gearshafts and bearings
c) Selector drum and forks
d) Kickstart shaft and return spring

3 Compression test

1 Refer to the procedure for the YX140 engine (see Chapter 2C, Section 3).

4 Engine removal and installation

1 Refer to the procedure for the YX140 engine (Chapter 2C, Section 4).

5 Engine overhaul – general information

1 Refer to the procedure for the YX140 engine (see Chapter 2C, Section 5), noting the following.
2 A complete engine stripdown should be done in the following general order with reference to the appropriate Sections.
a) Remove the generator cover (left-hand engine cover)
b) Remove the cylinder head
c) Remove the cylinder barrel and piston
d) Remove the clutch cover (right-hand engine cover)
e) Remove the oil pump
f) Remove the clutch
g) Remove the primary drive gear
h) Remove the kickstart gears
i) Remove the gearchange mechanism
j) Remove the generator rotor and stator
k) Remove the cam chain and tensioner blade
l) Separate the crankcase halves
m) Remove the selector drum and forks
n) Remove the transmission shafts
o) Remove the kickstart shaft
p) Remove the crankshaft

6 Cylinder head removal and installation

Removal

1 If the engine is in the frame, remove the bashplate, exhaust (see Chapter 3, Section 10) and carburettor (see Chapter 3, Section 5). Drain the engine oil (see Chapter 1, Section 4). Disconnect the oil cooler hoses from the cooler and catch the small amount of oil which will drain from them (the hoses don't prevent head removal but the working area is improved with them disconnected and tied out of the way). Pull the cap off the spark plug. Shift the gearbox into neutral.
2 Remove the spark plug (see illustration). Remove the union bolt from each end of the metal oil delivery pipe and detach the pipe with its copper washers from the head and crankcase (see illustration).
3 Remove the two valve adjustment caps (see illustration). Remove the camshaft sprocket cover from the left-hand side of the head (see illustration).
4 Remove the generator cover from the left-hand side of the engine (see illustration 15.1). Turn the generator rotor anti-clockwise by hand to align its TDC mark (line next to the T mark) with the cut-out in the top of the casing (see illustration). At this point the scribed line on the cam sprocket should align with the cast pointer in the cylinder head in the 9 o'clock position (see illustration). You should be able to feel slight play in each valve rocker, indicating that both valves are closed and the engine is on its compression stroke. If one valve is open, rotate the engine a further 360° and realign the marks.
5 Slacken the two cam sprocket bolts. Hold the rotor if required to stop the engine turning.
6 Now slacken off tension on the cam chain to enable it to be detached from the sprocket. Do this by removing the cam chain tensioner; remove the cap bolt from the centre of the tensioner body and withdraw the long spring. Remove the two mounting bolts

6.2a Unscrew the spark plug

6.2b Remove the metal oil delivery pipe

6.3a Intake and exhaust valve caps are retained by two bolts

6.3b Sprocket cover is retained by four bolts

6.4a Line next to T mark on rotor aligns with cut-out in casing

6.4b Sprocket mark and cast pointer correctly aligned

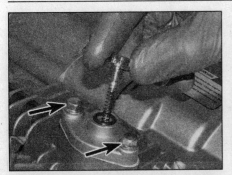

6.6 Remove the tensioner cap bolt and spring, then the two mounting bolts (arrowed)

6.7 Sprocket tooth and camshaft marked with paint (arrowed) to aid refitting

6.8a The head-to-barrel bolts are inside the head casting

and lift the tensioner out from the top of the cylinder barrel together with its gasket (see illustrations).

7 You should be able to see the tension come off the cam chain as the tensioner blade relaxes its pressure on the chain. Unscrew the two sprocket bolts (see illustration 6.4b) and ease the sprocket off the end of the camshaft at the same time as working the chain off the sprocket (see illustration 6.15a). Note how we applied a dab of paint to the sprocket tooth level with the alignment mark and to the end of the camshaft in the same position – this ensured correct reassembly (see illustration).

8 Remove the two long bolts which retain the head to the barrel on the left-hand side (see illustration). Slacken the four domed nuts at the top of the head evenly and in a diagonal sequence (see illustration). Retrieve the washers from the studs.

9 Lift off the cylinder head (see illustration). You may need to tap around the head-to-barrel joint with a soft-faced hammer to break the seal between the two components. Remove the old head gasket and retrieve the dowels if they are loose.

10 Peel off the old head gasket and clean any remaining traces of old gasket material from the cylinder head and cylinder barrel. If

6.8b Cylinder head nuts

6.9 Carefully lift the head up off the barrel

a scraper is used, take care not to scratch or gouge the soft aluminium. Be careful not to let any of the gasket material fall into the cylinder bore or the oil passages. If there's a build up of corrosion on the studs or dowels, remove it carefully with wire wool. The dowels should come out easily, but if they are stuck in the underside of the head or top of the barrel, use thin-nosed pliers to extract them.

11 Check the cylinder head gasket and the mating surfaces on the cylinder head and cylinder barrel for signs of leakage, which could indicate warpage. Refer to Chapter 2B,

Section 7 and check the cylinder head gasket surface for warpage.

Installation

12 Fit the dowels into the cylinder barrel; they fit into the top left and bottom right stud locations (see illustration). Place a new head gasket onto the face of the barrel (see illustration). Check that the cam chain guide blade, tensioner blade and cam chain are correctly in place.

13 Carefully fit the cylinder head over the studs and feed the cam chain up through

6.12a Dowel locations (arrowed)

6.12b Always use a new base gasket

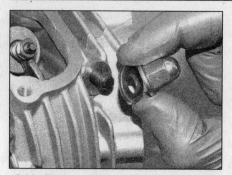

6.14a Fit the copper washers and domed head nuts

6.14b Install the two bolts down the left side of the head

6.15a Positioning the camshaft and lining up the sprocket

6.15b Check sprocket marks align...

6.15c ...before fitting the bolts

the tunnel as you do, and making sure the head locates correctly onto the dowels (see illustration 6.9). Ensure the head seats fully against the barrel surface.

14 Place a copper washer over the studs followed by the domed nuts securing them finger-tight (see illustration). Thread the two long bolts into their locations in the left-hand side of the head and secure them lightly (see illustration). Tighten the four head nuts evenly and in a diagonal sequence (see illustration 6.8b). Correct tightening is important – a torque setting of 11 Nm is recommended. Tighten the two bolts down the left side of the head.

15 Make sure the generator rotor TDC mark is correctly aligned (see Step 4). Draw the cam chain up into the head aperture, then position the camshaft so that its bolt holes will align with those in the sprocket (use the paint mark made previously to position it correctly (see illustration 6.7). Fit the sprocket into the chain, aligning the marks with the cast lug in the head (see illustration). Seat the sprocket onto the camshaft shoulder and check the alignment marks (see illustrations). Reposition the chain on the sprocket if necessary. Fit the sprocket bolts and tighten them lightly (see illustration).

16 Hold the catch on the cam chain tensioner back and push the plunger into the tensioner to retract it fully, then release the catch (see illustrations). Install the tensioner with a new gasket and secure it with the two bolts (see illustration). Fit the spring and cap bolt into the tensioner body and screw them into place (see illustration and 6.6). You should hear the tensioner automatically release as the bolt is tightened and be able to feel the tension in the chain. Now tighten the two sprocket bolts, if necessary holding the generator rotor to prevent the camshaft turning.

17 Fit the circular cover on the left side of the head, checking that its large O-ring is seated in the groove (see illustration). Secure the cover with the four bolts.

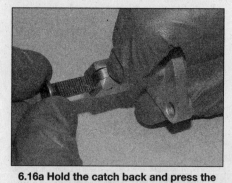

6.16a Hold the catch back and press the plunger inwards...

6.16b ...to retract it into the tensioner body

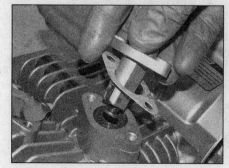

6.16c Insert the tensioner using a new gasket

6.16d Secure the tensioner with the two bolts and fit the spring and cap bolt

6.17 Check the cover O-ring

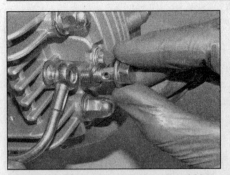

6.18 A copper sealing washer should be located each side of the union bolt

6.19 Check the O-ring on the valve inspection covers

7.3a Retaining plate bolts (arrowed)

7.3b Thread an M8 bolt into the shaft end and pull the shaft out...

7.3c ...to free the intake rocker...

7.3d ...and the exhaust rocker

18 Clean and refit the spark plug. Reconnect the oil delivery pipe (see illustration).
19 Check the valve clearances, especially if the head has been worked on and new valves fitted. Fit the valve inspection covers (see illustration).
20 Refit all other components in a reverse of the removal sequence. Refill the engine with oil up to the level mark on the dipstick (see Chapter 1, Section 4).

7 Camshaft, rockers and valves

1 Valve overhaul involves removing the valves and associated components from the cylinder head, cleaning them and checking them for wear. Valve seat re-cutting or valve guide replacement, if necessary, is a job for an engineer, but note that renewal of the head may be the cheaper option.

Rocker arms and camshaft

Removal

2 Removal of the cylinder head is advised. It is possible to work on the camshaft with the head in place, having disconnected the cam chain from the sprocket, but it's much easier to do this on the bench.
3 Remove the two screws from the left-hand side of the head to free the rocker shaft retaining plate (see illustration). Note how the tangs on the plate bear on the shaft ends and how the plate locates behind the shoulder of the camshaft. The shafts are only a slip fit in the head but it's best to thread an M8 bolt into the shaft end and pull it to withdraw the shaft (see illustrations). Note which is the intake and which is the exhaust rocker shaft so that they can be returned to their original locations.
4 Remove the decompressor detent bolt, with its spring and plunger, from the top of the head (see illustrations).
5 The camshaft is a tight fit in the head. We threaded two bolts into the sprocket bolt holes in the end of the cam to help pull it out (see illustration). Cut-outs are cast into the

7.4a Detent bolt and washer...

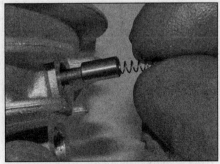

7.4b ...followed by spring and plunger

7.5a Grasp the camshaft and pull it from the head...

7.5b ...noting the cut-outs for the lobes to pass through

7.6a Check the cam lobes (arrowed)

7.6b Measuring cam lobe height with a micrometer

7.7 Feel for play between the shaft and rocker

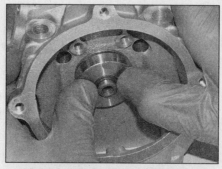

7.8 Apply thumb pressure to seat the camshaft in the head

7.9 Decompressor detent components

head to allow the cam lobes to pass through **(see illustration)**.

Inspection

6 Check the bearing on each end of the camshaft – they must run smoothly, quietly and freely and there should be no excessive play between the inner and outer races or obvious signs of wear between the outer race and the housing in the cylinder head. Also check the cam lobes for heat discoloration (blue appearance), score marks, chipped areas, flat spots and spalling **(see illustration)**. Cam lobe height can be measured as shown **(see illustration)**; the measurement being from the tip of the cam base circle to the tip of the lobe. On this engine the intake valve lobe height measured 30.44 mm and the exhaust 29.78 mm.

7 Check the fit of each rocker arm on its shaft. They should move freely with a light fit, but no appreciable freeplay **(see illustration)**. Check the contact pad and contact tip of the valve clearance adjuster; again there should be no sign of wear.

Installation

8 Lubricate the camshaft bearings and lobes with engine oil then slide the camshaft into the head. Press it fully in with your thumbs **(see illustration)**.
9 Insert the decompressor detent plunger and spring followed by the bolt with its washer **(see illustration)**. Tighten the bolt.
10 Install the first rocker shaft in the head (intake or exhaust as noted on removal) and push the rocker shaft through **(see illustration 7.3c)**. Do the same for the other rocker arm

(see illustration 7.3d). Undo the M8 bolt from the rocker shaft end. Locate the retaining plate against the shaft ends and tighten its two screws **(see illustration)**.

Valves

11 Keep the intake and exhaust valves separate, along with their related components, so that they can be returned to their original locations without getting mixed up.
12 Compress the valve spring on the first valve with a spring compressor, making sure it is correctly located onto each end of the valve assembly **(see illustration)**. On the top of the valve the adaptor needs to be about the same size as the spring retainer – if it is too small it will be difficult to remove and install the collets **(see illustration)**. On the underside of the head make sure the compressor contacts

7.10 Rocker shaft retaining plate correctly located

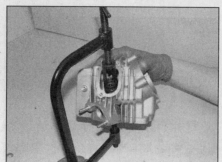

7.12a Compressing the valve springs using a valve spring compressor

7.12b Make sure the compressor locates correctly both on the top of the spring retainer...

7.12c ...and on the bottom of the valve

8.2 The cam chain guide blade is a push fit

8.3 Carefully lift the barrel up off the crankcase

the centre of the valve **(see illustration)**. Do not compress the springs any more than is absolutely necessary.

13 Refer to the valve procedure in Chapter 2C Section 7. The procedure is the same for all engines.

Cylinder head

14 Check the cylinder head for warpage as described for the 1P52FMI engine (see Chapter 2B, Section 7).

8 Cylinder barrel

Removal

1 Remove the cylinder head (see Section 6).

2 Remove the cam chain guide blade from the barrel **(see illustration)**. The tensioner blade remains in place.

3 Pull the cylinder barrel off the crankcase, supporting the piston so the connecting rod does not knock against the engine **(see illustration)**. If the barrel is stuck, tap around the joint faces with a soft-faced mallet. Do not attempt to free it by inserting a screwdriver between the barrel and crankcase mating surfaces – you'll damage them.

4 Remove the base gasket and discard it –

a new one must be used. If they are loose, remove the dowels from the crankcase or the underside of the barrel.

5 Stuff clean rag into the cam chain tunnel and around the connecting rod to protect and support it and the piston and to prevent anything falling into the engine.

6 Clean all traces of old gasket material from the cylinder barrel and crankcase. If a scraper is used, take care not to scratch or gouge the soft aluminium. Be careful not to let any of the gasket material fall into the engine.

Inspection

7 Check the cylinder walls carefully for scratches and score marks. The cylinder bore surface is plated with a Nikasil hard wearing material and apart from catastrophic damage, say from a seizure, it shouldn't sustain excessive wear. There is no cylinder liner.

8 Using a precision straight-edge and feeler gauges check the barrel top surface for warpage. Take six measurements, one along each side and two diagonally across. If the barrel is warped beyond 0.05 mm take it to an engineer for an opinion, though be prepared to have to buy a new one.

9 Wear limit figures for the bore are not available, but it is possible to measure the piston diameter and subtract this from the bore diameter to obtain the piston-to-bore

clearance. Generally a clearance of 0.01 to 0.04 mm is acceptable. Using a telescoping bore gauge and a micrometer, check the dimensions of the cylinder to assess the amount of wear, taper and ovality. Using a telescoping bore gauge and a micrometer, measure near the top (but below the level of the top piston ring at TDC), centre and bottom (but above the level of the oil ring at BDC) of the bore, both parallel to and across the crankshaft axis (see Chapter 2B, Section 8).

10 If the cylinder studs are badly corroded or loose in the crankcase, remove them using one of the stud extraction methods described in *Tools and Workshop Tips* in Reference. Use a drop of non-permanent thread locking compound on the new or refitted stud and tighten it in the crankcase.

Installation

11 Check that the mating surfaces of the cylinder barrel and crankcase are free from oil or pieces of old gasket.

12 Remove any rag from around the piston and the cam chain tunnel. Fit the dowels over the studs and into the crankcase and push them firmly home, then fit a new base gasket **(see illustration)**.

13 Ensure the piston ring end gaps are positioned at 120° intervals before fitting the cylinder barrel **(see illustration)**.

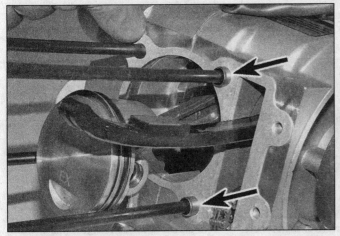

8.12 Fitting the new base gasket. Dowel positions (arrowed)

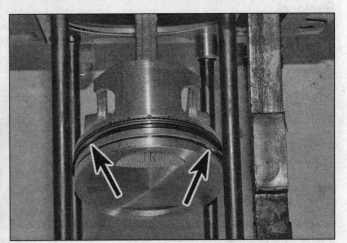

8.13 Check the ring end gap positions before fitting the barrel

8.15a Carefully compress and feed each ring into the bore as the cylinder is lowered

8.15b Pull the cam chain up through its tunnel

8.17 Cam chain guide blade lugs correctly located

14 Rotate the crankshaft so that the piston is at its highest point (top dead centre). Lubricate the cylinder bore, piston and piston rings with clean engine oil.
15 Carefully lower the barrel over the studs and onto the piston until the crown fits into the bore, holding the underside of the piston to prevent it dropping, and making sure it enters the bore squarely and does not get cocked sideways **(see illustration)**. Feed the cam chain up the tunnel **(see illustration)**.
16 When the piston and rings are correctly located in the bore, press the cylinder barrel down onto the base gasket, making sure the dowels locate. Hold the barrel down and turn the crankshaft to check that everything moves as it should.
17 Hold the cam chain taut and insert the cam chain guide into the tunnel **(see illustration 8.2)**. Its lower end will locate in the cast slot in the crankcase **(see illustration 16.3)** and the two lugs locate in the top of the barrel **(see illustration)**.
18 Install the cylinder head (see, Section 6).

9 Piston and rings

Removal

1 Remove the cylinder barrel (see Section 8). Check that the holes into the crankcase and

the cam chain tunnel are completely blocked with rag.
2 Note that the piston crown is marked IN and EX (though the marks are likely to be invisible until the piston is cleaned) **(see illustration)**.
3 Carefully prise out the circlip on one side of the piston **(see illustration)**. Push the piston pin out from the other side to free the piston from the connecting rod. Remove the other circlip and discard them as new ones must be used.

> **HAYNES HiNT** *If the piston pin is a tight fit in the piston bosses, heat the piston using a heat gun – this will expand the alloy piston sufficiently to release its grip on the pin. If the piston pin is particularly stubborn, extract it using a drawbolt tool, but be careful to protect the piston's working surfaces.*

Inspection and installation

4 Refer to Chapter 2B, Section 9 for inspection procedures.

10 Clutch cable

1 Refer to the procedure for the YX140 in Chapter 2C, Section 10.

11 Clutch, oil filter and primary drive gear

Removal

1 Drain the engine oil (see Chapter 1, Section 4).
2 Mark the position of the kickstart lever on its shaft, then remove the pinch bolt and pull the lever off the shaft splines. If there's signs of oil leakage from the seal obtain a new seal for use on installation.
3 Disconnect the clutch cable from the operating arm (see Chapter 2C, Section 10) and position the cable clear of the engine.
4 Note that removal of the clutch cover provides access for a clutch plate change, and removal of the oil filter cover enables the filter element to be changed. These covers can be left in place and the entire engine right-hand cover removed, but the long cover bolt(s) must be removed beforehand.
5 Working evenly in a criss-cross pattern, unscrew the five clutch cover bolts **(see illustration)**. Remove the cover taking care as the oil seal passes over the splines of the kickstart shaft. There's a headed pushrod set in its bore inside the cover – make sure this doesn't drop free.
6 Remove the three bolts from the oil filter cover noting their locations and different

9.2 Note the piston IN (intake side) and EX (exhaust side) markings

9.3 Use a small screwdriver to hook the circlip out of its groove

11.5 Clutch cover bolt lengths (millimeters)

11.6 Three bolts retain the filter cover (long bolt arrowed)

11.7 Remaining engine cover bolts (long bolt A)

lengths **(see illustration)**. Withdraw the oil filter and its spring.

7 To remove the engine right-hand cover, remove the remaining five bolts **(see illustration)**. Withdraw the cover catching the residual oil which will be released and peel off the old gasket. There are two dowels; if loose, remove them from the cover or crankcase for safekeeping.

8 Remove the four bolts to free the clutch lifter plate, slackening them evenly rather than one at a time **(see illustration)**. If required, use one of the methods in the following step to prevent clutch rotation. Remove the four springs.

9 Prise the locking tab of the lockwasher out of the slot in the clutch nut **(see illustration)**. Use the smaller end of the peg spanner to slacken the slotted clutch nut. To prevent the gearshaft rotating whilst slackening the nut, select a gear then hold the sprocket as shown – the round pegs on the back of this tool are held clamped into the wells of the sprocket teeth **(see illustration)**. Alternatively the tool can be used to hold the cast webs in the clutch centre, although take care not to place pressure on the spring posts as they are easy to break off **(see illustration)**. If the engine is in the frame, put the bike into top gear and have someone sit on the bike with the rear brake held on whilst you undo the clutch nut. Thread the clutch nut off followed by the lockwasher and tab washer **(see illustrations 11.20d, c and b)**, then grasp the set of clutch plates, together with the pressure plate and clutch centre, and withdraw it from the gearshaft as an assembly **(see illustration)**.

10 To remove the clutch housing (basket), slide off the locking washer then rotate the splined washer in the shaft groove so that it can be withdrawn **(see illustrations 11.19c, b and a)**. Slide the housing off the gearshaft followed by the kickstart driven gear sleeve **(see illustration)**.

11.8 Unscrew the lifter plate bolts, remove the plate with thrust bearing and the four springs

11.9a Prising the locking tab out of the clutch nut

11.9b Locking grips can be used to hold the sprocket...

11.9c ...or the clutch centre webs

11.9d Grab the plate assembly as a set

11.10 The clutch housing and kickstart driven gear will come off the gearshaft together

11.11a Take the oil nozzle and spring out of the crankshaft end

11.11b Unscrewing the primary drive gear nut

11.12 Primary drive gear nut, spacer, drive gear and oil pump drive gear

11 The primary drive gear and oil pump drive gear can removed once the clutch housing has been removed. First withdraw the oil nozzle and spring from the end of the crankshaft (see illustration). Use the larger end of the peg spanner to undo the primary drive gear nut, preventing the crankshaft from rotating by holding the generator rotor via the holes in its outer face or with a strap wrench around its periphery (see illustration).

12 Once slackened, unscrew the primary drive gear nut and remove the lockwasher, spacer (note which was round it is fitted), primary drive gear and oil pump drive gear from the crankshaft (see illustration).

Inspection

13 The clutch is sold as a complete unit (housing, pressure plate, plates, centre, springs and spring retaining plate).

14 The friction material on the clutch friction plates will wear and promote clutch slip, and the plain plates can distort. Note that friction plate material thickness measures 3 mm when new (see illustration). The plates can also take on a glazed appearance and smell burnt and the clutch springs will weaken and sag – new springs measure 30 mm. Inspect the friction plates for wear between their tabs and the slots in the clutch housing, and the plain plates between their inner teeth and the slots in the clutch centre. Wear of this nature will cause clutch drag and slow disengagement during gear changes as the plates will snag.

15 Check the thrust bearing set in the lifter plate for signs of wear or damage and roughness (see illustration 11.8).

16 To remove the clutch operating shaft from the cover, lift out the headed pushrod and free the return spring as the shaft is removed (see illustrations).

Installation

17 Fit the oil pump drive gear, primary gear and spacer on the crankshaft; on the engine photographed the spacer was fitted with its recessed face inwards and its chamferred outside edge facing outwards

11.14 Measuring the clutch friction plate material thickness

11.16a Headed pushrod (arrowed)

11.16b Free the return spring from the shaft (it's inner end locates in a drilling in the shaft)...

11.16c ...and withdraw the shaft from the cover taking care not to tear the oil seal

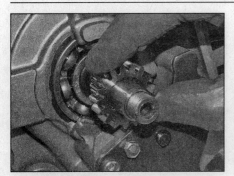

11.17a Install the oil pump drive gear (stamped side faced inwards on this engine)…

11.17b …the primary drive gear…

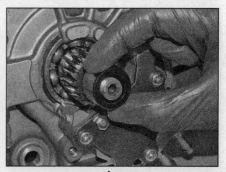

11.17c …the spacer (chamfered outer edge outwards)

11.17d Note the OUTSIDE marking on the lock washer

11.17e Thread the slotted nut on…

11.17f …and tighten it as shown

(see illustration). Fit the lockwasher with its OUTSIDE face outwards and thread on the slotted nut (see illustration). Lock the crankshaft as on removal and tighten the primary drive gear nut securely (see illustration).

18 If the clutch plates need to be built back up start with a friction plate, then a plain plate, and build them up alternately on the clutch centre; there are 6 friction and 5 plain plates (see illustration). Fit the pressure plate, engaging it with the clutch centre splines (see illustration).

19 Fit the kickstart driven gear sleeve into the back of the clutch housing. Insert it on the gearshaft (see illustration 11.10) meshing the kickstart driven gear with its idler gear and meshing the secondary gear around the outside of the housing with the primary drive

gear on the crankshaft. Slide the splined washer on and rotate it in the shaft groove so that its tabs locate with the raised splines (see

illustrations). Slide the lockwasher on so that its tangs locate under the splined washer (see illustration).

11.18a Build up the plates on the centre, alternating friction, plain etc. and finishing with a friction plate…

11.18b …before fitting the pressure plate

11.19a Slide on the splined washer…

11.19b …rotate it in the shaft groove as shown…

11.19c …then install the lockwasher so that its tangs face inwards

11.20a Friction plate tabs aligned for insertion into the clutch housing

11.20b Fit the tab washer with its tabs facing outwards…

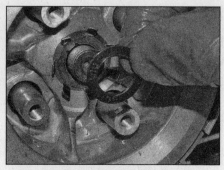

11.20c …followed by the lockwasher (OUTSIDE mark faces outwards)…

11.20d …and clutch nut

11.20e Tighten the nut whilst holding the sprocket as shown

11.20f Bend one of the tab washer tabs up into a nut slot as shown

11.21 Locate a clutch spring over each post

HAYNES HiNT

You can use an aluminium washer between the primary gear teeth at the top to lock the clutch whilst the lifter plate bolts are tightened. Remember to remove the washer afterwards of course.

20 Hold the assembled clutch plate unit and fit it into the housing, aligning the friction plate tabs with the housing slots (see illustration). Fit the tab washer, lockwasher and clutch nut, then with the transmission in gear and the sprocket held, tighten the clutch nut (see illustrations). A torque setting of 42 Nm is recommended. Bend one of the tab washer tabs into a slot in the nut to secure it (see illustration).

21 Install the four coil springs over their posts and fit the lifter plate, having applied a drop of engine oil to its bearing (see illustration). Tighten the four bolts down evenly.

22 Fit the oil nozzle and its spring into the end of the crankshaft (see illustration 11.11a).

23 Before fitting the cover, it's a good time to clean the oil filter screen set in the bottom of the crankcase (see illustration). Use long-nose pliers to pull the screen out. Clean any debris and oil sludge off the screen using a soft brush and solvent.

24 Ensure the cover gasket surface and crankcase gasket surface is clean and that all traces of old gasket have been removed. The

11.23 Narrow edge of oil filter screen goes in first

11.24a Fit the new gasket over the dowels (arrowed)

11.24b Fitting the engine right-hand cover

11.24c Check here that the nozzle has remained in place

11.26 Clutch cover O-ring and seal

11.27a Fit the spring and new filter…

11.27b …check the O-rings and fit the cover

two dowels must be in position and a new gasket placed over them **(see illustration)**. Off up the cover and guide it over the kickstart shaft **(see illustration)**. As the cover seats on its dowels check that the oil nozzle is still in place; this part is critical to the supply of filtered oil to the crankshaft big-end bearing **(see illustration)**.

25 Fit the five cover retaining bolts, with the long bolt at the top retaining the clutch cable bracket **(see illustration 11.7)**.

26 Check the O-ring around the inside of the clutch cover and the oil seal set in the kickstart shaft bore in the cover **(see illustration)**. Any sign of oil leakage indicates a failed seal. Make sure the pushrod is in place inside the cover then fit the cover, locating it over the kickstart shaft and dowel; note that a smear of grease over the seal lips will prevent the shaft splines damaging the seal. Fit the five cover bolts and tighten them.

27 Fit the spring and new filter element into their housing; the filter goes in with its closed end inwards **(see illustration)**. Check the O-rings around the oil filter cover periphery and inner boss, and also the small O-ring at the feed into the crankshaft; all must be in good condition **(see illustration)**. Fit the cover and its three retaining bolts **(see illustration 11.6)**.

28 Engage the clutch cable through the bracket and its end in the arm. Adjust cable freeplay (see Chapter 1, Section 6).

29 Fit the kickstart lever back onto its shaft, aligning the marks make on removal to get the lever angle right. Tighten the pinch bolt.

30 Fill the engine with the correct amount of 10W/40 semi-synthetic motorcycle oil (see

Chapter 1, Section 4). Just under 1 litre will be required, although check the oil level using the dipstick.

12 Oil pump

Removal

1 Remove the engine right-hand cover (see Section 11).

2 Unscrew the three screws and remove the pump from the crankcase manoeuvring its nylon driven gear out from behind the primary gear **(see illustration)**. Note the two dowels and gasket between the pump and crankcase.

3 The pump can be dismantled to check the rotors but note that spare parts are not available.

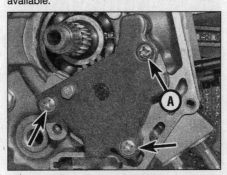

12.2 Oil pump retaining screws (short screw arrowed)

4 Remove the oil filter screen from its housing beneath the oil pump and clean it. Also check that the oilways are clear. Renew the pleated paper oil filter whenever it is disturbed (see Section 11).

Installation

5 Fit a new gasket over the two dowels then fit the pump onto the crankcase, meshing its gear with the drive gear on the crankshaft **(see illustration)**.

6 Install the engine cover.

13 Gearchange mechanism

1 Remove the clutch (see Section 11), then refer to the procedure for the YX140 engine (see Chapter 2C, Section 13).

12.5 Fitting a new pump gasket

15.1 Generator cover is retained by three bolts (arrowed)

15.3 Undoing the rotor nut

15.4 Operating the centre-bolt puller

14 Kickstart

1 Refer to the procedure for the YX140 (see Chapter 2C, Section 14).

15 Generator

Removal

1 Remove the gearchange lever. Remove the engine left-hand cover **(see illustration)**.
2 Trace the generator wiring from the top of the crankcase to the connectors just beneath the fuel tank and disconnect them.

3 Hold the rotor and undo the rotor nut **(see illustration)**. The pegs on the reverse face of these self-locking grips engage the holes in the rotor. Remove the nut.
4 You'll need a centre-bolt type puller to pull the rotor off its taper on the crankshaft. The type shown can be obtained through pit bike part suppliers and is not expensive (see Chapter 2C, Section 5). Back off the puller's centre bolt and thread the body of the puller into the rotor. Note that the thread is left-hand, so it must be turned in an anti-clockwise direction. Turn the puller's centre bolt in so that it contacts the end of the crankshaft then hold the body with an open-end spanner and tighten the centre bolt until the rotor comes free of its taper **(see illustration)**.
5 The rotor has a slot in its boss which locates over a key (Woodruff key) set in the crankshaft taper. If the key is loose, remove it and keep in

with the rotor for now **(see illustration)**. The key prevents the rotor attempting to spin on the crankshaft end.
6 Drain the engine oil (see Chapter 1, Section 4).
7 The stator plate and coils comes off as a unit, together with the plug and light green/red wire which is set in the left-hand end of the selector drum; this would serve as a neutral switch on other models. Remove the two countersunk screws which retain the stator plate and gently pull the assembly out of the crankcase **(see illustrations)**.
8 Note the large O-ring around the periphery of the stator plate, the two small O-rings at the screw mounting points and the oil seal set in the centre of the stator plate. All prevent the escape of oil from the cam chain and inner crankcase areas.
9 Refer to Chapter 4 for details of generator coil testing.

Installation

10 Check the condition of the stator plate O-rings and the oil seal set in its centre. If there are signs of oil escaping into the outer cover area, the seals must be renewed. To remove the oil seal prise it out from the back of the stator plate **(see illustration)** and press a new seal into position; the seal must be fitted so that its spring side faces inwards towards the crankcase.
11 Make sure the two small O-rings are in their recesses in the crankcase then fit the stator plate **(see illustration)**. Press it into position and secure it with the two screws –

15.5 Woodruff key location

15.7a Stator plate screws (arrowed)

15.7b Prise out the plug from the end of the selector drum

15.10 Prise out the stator plate oil seal from the back of the plate if it needs changing

15.11 Stator plate large O-ring and two small O-rings (top arrowed)

15.13 Fit the rotor nut

16.3 Guide blade seats in crankcase recess

16.4 Remove the pivot bolt to free the tensioner blade

you should be able to hear it click into place as the large O-ring seats. Position the wiring grommet into the cut-out in the top edge of the casing and insert the plug in the neutral switch location. Secure the set plate with the screw to retain the plug.

12 Refill the engine oil (see Chapter 1, Section 4).

13 If removed, install the Woodruff key back into its slot **(see illustration 15.5)**. Instal the rotor so that its cut-out fits over the key, noting that the pull of its magnets will be felt as it passes over the coils **(see illustration 15.5)**. Fit the washer and rotor nut and tighten the nut **(see illustration)**. Hold the rotor to enable the nut to be fully tightened. A torque setting of 41 Nm is recommended.

14 Reconnect the generator wiring and fit the left-hand engine cover.

15 Slide the gear lever onto the shaft, aligning its slit with the punch mark on the shaft. Fit the pinch bolt and tighten it.

16 Cam chain, tensioner and blades

Cam chain tensioner

1 The tensioner is automatic in operation.

2 The tensioner plunger and spring can be accessed easily from the top surface of the cylinder barrel although first the engine must be set to TDC compression as described in the

cylinder head removal procedure (see Section 6). This procedure covers removal, resetting and refitting of the tensioner. Note that valve timing must be checked after refitting the plunger particularly if the crankshaft has been rotated with tension off the chain.

Blades

3 Remove the cylinder head to access the guide blade. The blade is a push fit into its recess in the crankcase left-hand half **(see illustration)** and also locates in the top surface of the cylinder barrel **(see illustration 8.17)**.

4 Remove the cylinder head (see Section 6) and barrel (see Section 8), and the generator stator plate (see Section 15) to access the tensioner blade **(see illustration)**.

5 Check the working surfaces of the guide and tensioner blades for deep grooves denoting extreme wear **(see illustration)**.

Cam chain

6 Remove the cylinder head (see Section 6), barrel and guide blade (see Section 8).

7 Remove the generator and its stator plate (see Section 15).

8 Withdraw the cam chain from its sprocket on the crankshaft **(see illustration)**.

9 Check the chain for binding, kinks and any obvious damage and replace it with a new one if necessary.

10 Installation is a reverse of the removal procedure.

17 Crankcase separation and reassembly

Separation

1 To access the crankshaft and connecting rod assembly, kickstart shaft, gear shafts, selector drum and forks, and their bearings, the crankcase halves must be separated. Remove the engine from the frame (see Chapter 2C, Section 4).

2 Before the crankcases can be separated the following components must be removed:

a) *Cylinder head and cam chain tensioner (Section 6)*

b) *Cylinder barrel and cam chain guide blade (Section 8). The piston can remain attached to the rod, but wrap rag around it to protect the rings.*

c) *Generator (Section 15)*

d) *Drive sprocket (see Chapter 6, Section 17)*

e) *Clutch and primary drive gear (Section 11)*

f) *Kickstart drive gears (Section 14)*

g) *Gearchange mechanism (Section 13)*

h) *Oil pump (Section 12)*

i) *Cam chain and tensioner blade (Section 16)*

3 Remove the bolt and neutral switch contact from the left-hand end of the selector drum **(see illustration)**.

4 Remove the kickstart ratchet plate from

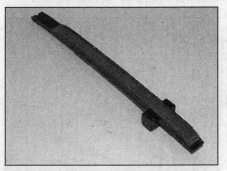

16.5 This guide blade is new. A worn blade will have worn a deep groove where it has been in contact with the chain

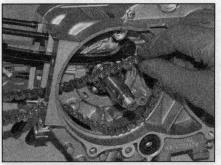

16.8 Lift the cam chain off its sprocket and out of the engine

17.3 Note how the pin on the back of the neutral switch contact locates in the cut-out in the end of the drum

17.4 Ratchet plate is retained by two bolts

17.5 Crankcase bolt locations and lengths

the right-hand side of the crankcase (see illustration).

5 Slacken the seven bolts in the left-hand side of the crankcase evenly and in a diagonal sequence (see illustration). Remove the bolts and record their positions as an aid to refitting

HAYNES HiNT *As each bolt is removed, store it in its relative position in a cardboard template of the crankcase halves. This will ensure all bolts and any washers/ guides with them are returned to their original locations on reassembly.*

(see **Haynes Hint**). The bolts on the engine shown are of 45, 60 and 65 and 85 mm in length.

6 Turn the engine over so that it is resting on its left-hand side. Support it using blocks of wood to prevent the shaft ends contacting the bench.

7 Using a heat gun, warm the area around the main bearing for a few minutes. Use of heat here will expand the aluminium housing enough to release its grip on the main bearing. Immediately lift off the right crankcase half, if necessary using a soft-faced mallet to tap around the gasket joint. If the halves do not

separate easily, make sure all fasteners have been removed. Do not try and separate the halves by levering against the crankcase mating surfaces as they are easily scored and will leak oil in the future if damaged. The right-hand crankcase half will come away leaving the crankshaft, kickstart shaft, transmission shafts and selector drum and forks in the left-hand half. Note that it is necessary to rotate the kickshaft shaft so that the lug on the ratchet can pass through the cut-out in the casing (see illustrations).

8 Grasp the gear shafts and selector drum and remove them as an assembly (see illustration). Disengage the kickstart return spring from the crankcase lug and lift it out complete with the washer (see illustrations). Turn the engine over. Heat the area around the main bearing then lift or lightly tap the crankshaft out.

Reassembly

9 Remove all traces of old gasket material from both crankcase mating surfaces.

10 Use the heat gun to warm the main bearing housing in the left case, then support the piston and con-rod with one hand and fit the crankshaft into the crankcase with the other (see illustrations). The crankshaft is fitted with its tapered end downwards.

17.7a Grasp the kickshaft shaft and rotate to allow its ratchet lug...

17.7b ...to pass through the cut-out in the casing

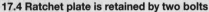

17.8a Lifting out the gear shafts and drum

17.8b Disengage its return spring and lift out the kickstart shaft

17.10a Warm the main bearing housing area...

17.10b ...and fit the crankshaft

17.11a Use a screwdriver to manoeuvre the end of the return spring...

17.11b ...over the casing lug

17.12a Mesh the gear shafts and drum together...

17.12b ...and fit as a unit locating their ends in the bearings

17.13 Lay a new gasket on the left crankcase. Dowels (arrowed)

11 Install the kickstart shaft **(see illustrations).**

12 Generously lubricate the transmission shaft bearings and the bore for the selector drum end. Mesh the gear shafts together and insert the two selector forks in their gear grooves **(see illustration)**. Hold the assembly together and fit the shafts into the left-hand half **(see illustration)**.

13 Apply engine oil to the gearshaft ends. Wipe the crankcase mating surface over with solvent. Ensure the two dowels are in position in the left-hand half and place a new gasket in position **(see illustration)**. Note that there's no need for any sealant.

14 Use the heat gun to warm the bearing housing of the right-hand crankcase half. Immediately fit the right half down over the

crankshaft main bearing **(see illustration)**. You need to rotate the kickstart shaft to enable the ratchet lug to fit through the cut-out **(see illustration)**. Check that the crankcase halves seat fully. Clean the threads of all the crankcase bolts and turn the engine over onto its right-hand side.

Caution: The crankcase halves should fit together without being forced. If the casings are not correctly seated, remove the right-hand crankcase half and investigate the problem. Do not attempt to pull them together using the crankcase bolts as the casing will crack and be ruined.

15 Install the seven crankcase bolts including the clip on the front bolt **(see illustration 17.5)**. Secure the bolts finger-tight at first, then tighten them evenly and a little at

a time in a criss-cross sequence – no torque setting is specified, but bolts of that size should be tightened to 12 Nm.

16 With all crankcase fasteners tightened, check that the crankshaft and gear shafts rotate smoothly and easily. Check that the gear shafts rotate freely and independently in neutral, then rotate the selector drum by hand and select each gear in turn whilst rotating the input shaft. If there are any signs of undue stiffness, tight or rough spots, or of any other problem, the fault must be rectified before proceeding further.

17 Trim off the section of gasket from the mouth of the crankcase **(see illustration)**. Install all other removed assemblies in a reverse of the sequence given in Step 2.

17.14a Fit the right-hand half...

17.14b ...noting that you need to rotate the kickstart shaft to allow the ratchet lug to pass through the cut-out

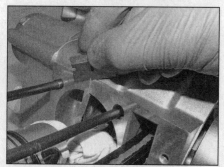

17.16 Use a sharp blade to trim off the excess gasket from the crankcase mouth

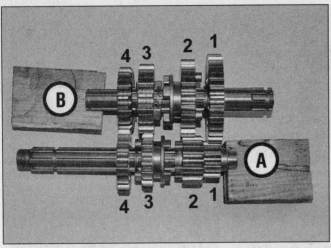

20.2 Input shaft (A) and output shaft (B) – gear positions numbered

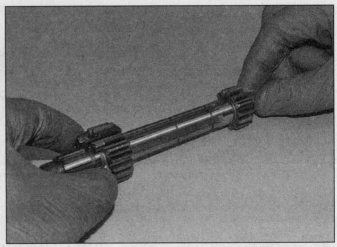

20.5a Input shaft – second gear dogs face away from first gear

18 Crankcases and bearings

1 Refer to Chapter 2B, Section 19 and Chapter 2C, Section 18.

19 Crankshaft and connecting rod

1 Refer to Chapter 2B, Section 20 and Chapter 2C, Section 19 for details.

20 Gear shafts and selector drum

Gear shafts

1 Remove the transmission shafts from the crankcase (see Section 17).
2 If the gear pinions show signs of stripped or chipped teeth or excessive wear, e.g. from missing a gear, it's best to renew them (see illustrations). A complete pair of shafts can be purchased very cheaply. If you wish to strip the shafts it's a straightforward operation. Use the appropriate circlips pliers when removing circlips and take care not to strain or distort them.
3 Inspect the dogs and the dog holes in the

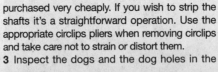

HAYNES HINT *When disassembling the transmission shafts, place the parts on a long rod or thread a wire through them to keep them in order and facing the proper direction.*

gears for cracks, chips, and excessive wear especially in the form of rounded edges. Make sure mating gears engage properly.

Input shaft

4 Slide the plain washer and 4th gear (largest gear) off the shaft followed by the thrust washer. Use circlip pliers to remove the circlip from its groove in the shaft, then slide off the 3rd gear. Remove the circlip and thrust washer and slide off the 2nd gear. First gear is part of the shaft.
5 Build up the gears according to the photo sequence (see illustrations). During

20.5b Thrust washer and circlip retain second gear

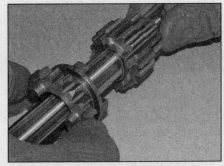

20.5c Fit the third gear with its fork groove towards the second gear...

20.5d ...slide on the circlip and fit it into the shaft groove

20.5e Install the thrust washer...

20.5f ...before fitting the fourth gear (with its holes towards the third gear)

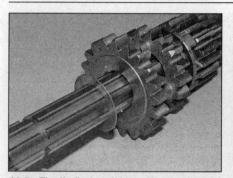

20.5g Finally fit the plain washer to the end of the shaft

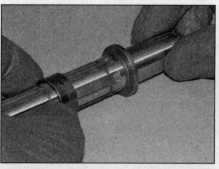

20.7a Slide the bush onto the bare output shaft...

20.7b ...and install the first gear over it (dog holes face away from the shaft shoulder)

reassembly, apply engine oil to the mating surfaces of the shaft, pinions and bushes. When installing the circlips, do not expand their ends any further than is necessary. Install the stamped circlips and washers so that their chamfered side faces away from the thrust side.

Output shaft

6 Remove the washer and 4th gear (smallest gear) from the shaft end. Remove the thrust washer, 3rd gear and thrust washer. Use circlip pliers to remove the circlip from the shaft groove and slide the 2nd gear off. Free the remaining circlip from the shaft and slide off the washer, 1st gear and its bush.

7 Build up the gears according to the photo sequence (see illustrations). During reassembly, apply engine oil to the mating surfaces of the shaft, pinions and bushes. When installing the circlips, do not expand their ends any further than is necessary. Install the stamped circlips and washers so that their chamfered side faces away from the thrust side.

20.7c Install the washer...

20.7d ...and secure the gear with the circlip

20.7e Second gear is fitted with its selector groove facing away from the first gear

20.7f Fit the circlip into its groove then fit the washer

20.7g Install the third gear with its dogs facing the second gear...

20.7h ...then fit the thrust washer...

20.7i ...fourth gear (with its chamfered edge towards the third gear)...

20.7j ...and finally the washer

20.8 Inspect the fork ends for wear

Selector drum and forks

8 Inspect the selector forks for any signs of wear or damage, especially around the fork ends where they engage with the groove in the gear pinion **(see illustration)**. The fork ends (tips) will wear rapidly if you do clutchless gearchanges – always use the clutch when changing gear.

9 Check that each fork fits correctly in its pinion groove. Check closely to see if the forks are bent. If the forks are in any way damaged the complete selector drum and fork assembly must be renewed.

21 Running-in procedure

1 Make sure the engine oil level is correct (see Chapter 1, Section 3). Make sure there is fuel in the tank.

2 Turn the engine kill switch to the RUN position and shift the gearbox into neutral. Set the choke to ON.

3 Start the engine and allow it to run until it reaches operating temperature.

4 Check carefully that there are no oil or fuel leaks and make sure the gearbox and controls, especially the brakes, function properly.

5 Treat the bike gently to make sure oil has circulated throughout the engine and any new parts installed have started to seat.

6 Even greater care is necessary if a new piston and rings have been fitted; the bike will have to be run in as when new. This means not over-revving the engine, change up a gear instead, and not running it at more than two thirds throttle. Apply this running-in period for the first two hours of the bike's use. After that, change the engine oil, check the valve clearances and the idle speed, and check that all nuts and bolts are tight.

Chapter 3
Fuel and exhaust systems

Contents

Degrees of difficulty

Easy, suitable for novice with little experience	Fairly easy, suitable for beginner with some experience	Fairly difficult, suitable for competent DIY mechanic	Difficult, suitable for experienced DIY mechanic	Very difficult, suitable for expert DIY or professional

1 General information and precautions

General information

1 The fuel supply system consists of the fuel tank, tap and filter, the fuel hose and carburettor. A slide type carburettor is fitted to all models. Changes to the engine idle speed and mixture are made via adjuster screws on the carburettor body. Filtered air is drawn into the carburettor via a two-piece foam element on the left-hand side.
2 Fuel system routine checks are covered in Chapter 1.

Precautions

 Warning: Petrol (gasoline) is extremely flammable, so take extra precautions when you work on any part of the fuel system.

Don't smoke or allow open flames or bare light bulbs near the work area, and don't work in a garage where a natural gas-type appliance is present. If you spill any fuel on your skin, rinse it off immediately with soap and water. When you perform any kind of work on the fuel system, wear safety glasses and have a fire extinguisher suitable for a class B type fire (flammable liquids) on hand.
3 Always perform service procedures in a well-ventilated area to prevent a build-up of fumes.
4 Never work in a building containing a gas appliance with a pilot light, or any other form of naked flame. Ensure that there are no naked light bulbs or any sources of flame or sparks nearby.
5 Do not smoke (or allow anyone else to smoke) while in the vicinity of petrol (gasoline) or of components containing it. Remember the possible presence of vapour from these sources and move well clear before smoking.
6 Check all electrical equipment belonging

to the house, garage or workshop where work is being undertaken (see the *Safety first!* section of this beginning of this manual). Remember that certain electrical appliances such as drills, cutters etc, create sparks in the normal course of operation and must not be used near petrol (gasoline) or any component containing it. Again, remember the possible presence of fumes before using electrical equipment.
7 Always mop up any spilt fuel and safely dispose of the rag used.
8 Any stored fuel that is drained off during servicing work must be kept in sealed containers that are suitable for holding petrol (gasoline), and clearly marked as such; the containers themselves should be kept in a safe place. Note that this last point applies equally to the fuel tank if it is removed from the machine; also remember to keep its filler cap closed at all times.
9 Read the *Safety first!* section of this beginning of this manual carefully before starting work.

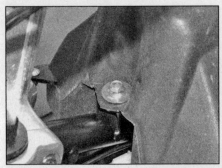

2.3a Fuel tank front mounting bolt...

2.3b ...and rear mounting bolt

2.7a Tap is retained by a nut...

2.7b ...or two bolts

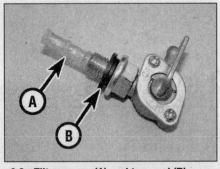

2.8a Filter gauze (A) and tap seal (B) on a simple ON/OFF fuel tap

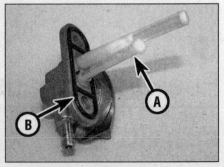

2.8b Filter gauze (A) and tap seal (B) on a tap with ON, OFF and RES positions

2 Fuel tank and tap

 Warning: Refer to the precautions given in Section 1 before starting work.

Removal

1 Remove the bodywork.

2 Turn the fuel tap to OFF. Ease the wire pipe clip back off the fuel tap stub, then hold some rag under the stub to catch any drops of fuel and pull the hose off.

3 Remove the mounting bolts at the front and rear of the tank and lift it off the frame **(see illustrations)**.

4 If the tank is leaking or has been damaged, renew it. The expense is minimal.

5 Check that the breather tube in the fuel filler cap is clear. A blockage here due to mud if the bike has been dropped or even a build-up of dust and dirt can cause the engine to cutout due to a vacuum being created in the tank.

Fuel tap

6 Drain any fuel from the tank into a container suitable for storing petrol (gasoline).

7 Depending on the type of tap fitted, use an open-ended spanner on the tap hex to screw it from the tank, or remove the two bolts **(see illustrations)**. Withdraw the tap carefully to avoid damaging the filter.

8 The gauze filter will pick up particles of dirt in the fuel **(see illustrations)**. Use a fine

soft-bristled brush to remove any particles caught in the gauze. If the filter is torn or is not a good fit on the tap buy a new tap. Also check the condition of the tap seal – a deteriorated seal will allow fuel to leak out at the tap-to-tank joint.

9 If fuel has been leaking from the tap lever area you can try tightening the two screws which retain the cover plate. The tap lever can be removed to access the main seal inside the tap, but note that no spare parts are available.

10 Make sure the tap seal is in place, then insert the filter end of the tap into the tank and hold it in position whilst the nut is tightened or the two bolts are tightened.

Installation

11 Fit the tank onto the frame and fit the two mounting bolts. Reconnect the fuel hose and

hold it in place by easing the clip back over the tap stub **(see illustration)**. Turn the tap ON and check there are no leaks.

12 Refit the bodywork.

3 Air filter

1 Refer to Chapter 1 for filter cleaning techniques.

2 Before purchasing a new filter measure the inlet stub diameter to make sure the filter will fit **(see illustration)**. The filter clamp will also have a range marking, e.g. 35 to 51 mm.

3 The important consideration is that the joint between the filter and carburettor stub is airtight otherwise unfiltered air will enter the carb.

2.11 Fuel hose hose correctly fitted and secured by wire clip

3.2 Measuring the stub diameter

4.4 Idle speed screw on JingKe PD carb

4.8a Mixture screw (A) and idle screw (B) on JingKe PZ19 carb

4.8b Mixture screw on JingKe PD carb

4.8c Mixture screw (A) and idle screw (B) on Molkt carb

4 Carburettor adjustments

Idle speed

1 The engine should tick over evenly in neutral. If it keeps cutting out or races use the idle speed adjuster to get the tickover right.

2 When setting the idle speed the engine should be warmed up to normal operating temperature and the choke should be OFF.

3 Check that there's a small amount of freeplay in the throttle cable – 2 to 3 mm at the twistgrip flange is good. You'll find how to measure and adjust the setting in Routine maintenance (see Chapter 1, Section 13).

4 The adjuster screw is set in the body of the carburettor and will be either a knurled screw head which you can turn by hand or a screw which you can turn with a flat-blade screwdriver **(see illustration)**. See also illustrations 4.8a and 4.8c for idle screw locations. The inner end of the screw locates in the throttle slide and adjustment effects a raising or lowering of the slide.

5 With the engine in neutral and idling and the twistgrip closed, turn the screw in to increase idle speed or out to reduce it. Only a small adjustment will be necessary. Blip the throttle a couple of times and check that you are happy with the idle speed.

6 If you cannot achieve a steady idle speed, check that the valve clearances are set correctly and that there isn't an air leak between carburettor and intake stub (check the bolts/nuts are tight). Also check the air screw adjustment.

Mixture screw adjustment

7 If a steady idle speed cannot be obtained by adjusting the idle speed, try adjusting the air screw.

8 The air screw is located in the side of the carburettor **(see illustrations)**. It's position is set at the factory and recorded as the number of turns out from seated, e.g. 1 1/2 turns out.

9 Before disturbing the screw, check that the valve clearances are correct, and that there isn't an air leak at either end of the intake stub between the engine and carburettor. Leaks here will affect the air/fuel mixture.

4.9 Loose bolts at the carb-to-intake stub joint will affect the air/fuel mixture – check they're tight

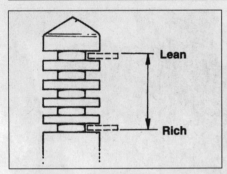

4.14 Effect of changing the jet needle clip position

5.1a Free the fuel hose from the tap

5.1b Direct the end of the drain hose into a container, then slacken the drain screw (arrowed)

10 With the engine idling and choke OFF, turn the screw in by a small amount (1/4 turn) and note the effect on the idle speed, then take it back out 1/4 turn and back out a further 1/4 turn and note the effect. What you are looking for is the position which will give the fastest consistant tickover. The engine speed can then be reduced to normal using the idle speed screw.

11 Blip the throttle a couple of times and if necessary readjust.

Float height adjustment

12 The float height setting determines the fuel level in the carburettor float bowl. If flooding of the carb has been experienced, apart the bike being dropped, the float height could need adjustment.

13 You need to dismantle the carburettor to check the float height. Refer to the appropriate section of this chapter.

Jet needle setting

14 The height of the jet needle in the slide will affect the amount of fuel being passed into the venturi. Raising the clip position will allow the jet needle to sit lower down in the slide and produce a lean mixture, whereas lowering the clip position on the jet needle will richen the mixture (see illustration).

---

5 Carburettor removal and installation

> ⚠ **Warning: Refer to the precautions given in Section 1 before starting work.**

Removal

1 Turn the fuel tap to OFF. Pull back the clip off the fuel tap stub and pull off the fuel pipe (see illustration). You can drain the fuel from the float chamber at this stage or have some rag ready to mop up fuel from the float chamber when the carburettor is moved to the bench (see illustration).

2 On models where the air filter connects to the carburettor through the frame, loosen off its clamp and pull the air filter off. On other designs the air filter can stay attached, but if you're going to strip the carb it's easier to do it with the filter out of the way.

5.3 Free the carb drain or overflow hoses from the guide

3 Slip the drain and overflow pipes out of their guides (see illustration).

4 Remove the two bolts (with nuts on some models) which retain the carburettor to the intake stub and lift the carb free (see illustrations). Check the locations of the O-rings and insulator at the carb-to-stub joint.

5 Unscrew the carburettor top and withdraw the slide and jet needle (see illustration). Tie the cable and slide out of the way to prevent damaging the delicate jet needle.

Installation

6 Refit components in a reverse of the removal procedure whilst noting the following.

● It's important to get an air-tight seal at the joint with the intake stub. Check the surfaces are good and that the O-rings each side of the insulator are intact and not broken or deteriorated (see illustrations).

5.4 Remove the two bolts which retain the carb to the stub. Nuts secure the bolts on this model but on others the bolts thread into the carb body

5.5 Carburettor top can be unscrewed by hand

5.6a Check the O-rings are in place between the stub, insulator and carburettor...

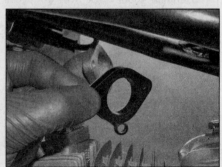

5.6b ... noting that some models may have a paper gasket between the stub and insulator

5.6c Install the slide so that its cutout is facing the rear (air filter side)…

5.6d ,..and check that the jet needle inserts correctly into the needle jet (arrowed)

6.1a Remove the float chamber screws (arrowed)…

● Be careful when inserting the throttle slide back into the carburettor not to bend or damage the jet needle **(see illustrations)**.
● Turn the fuel tap ON and check that there are no fuel leaks from the pipe.

6   JingKe carburettor (PZ19)

 Warning: Refer to the precautions given in Section 1 before starting work.

1 Remove the two screws from the base of the carb and withdraw the float chamber **(see illustration)**. The O-ring seal should stay set in the groove of the float bowl – peel it off carefully if part of it has stuck to the carb body **(see illustration)**. Access is now possible to the main jet, needle jet and pilot jet, or the float assembly – all can be removed individually.
2 Push out the float pivot pin and lift the plastic float out together with its hinge and float valve **(see illustration)**.
3 Use close-fitting screwdrivers to remove the brass jets as their soft material is easily damaged **(see illustrations)**.
4 Hold the throttle spring compressed against the carburettor top and slip the cable end out of its location in the base of the throttle slide and through the slot in the side of the slide **(see illustration)**. The jet needle can

6.1b …and lift off the chamber

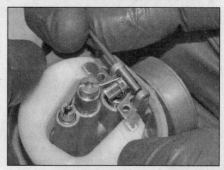

6.2 Pin retains float assembly

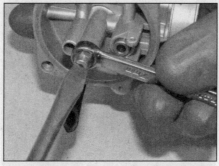

6.3a Hold the needle holder with a spanner and unscrew the main jet from its top…

6.3b …then unscrew the needle jet holder…

6.3c …to free the needle jet

6.3d The pilot jet can be unscrewed from its bore

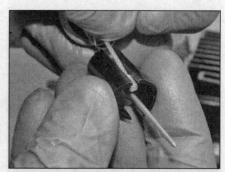

6.4a Hold the spring compressed against the carb top and slip the cable end out of the slide

6.4b Use a small screwdriver to extract the spring clip

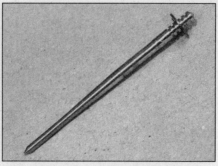

6.4c Clip set in the third groove from the top of the jet needle

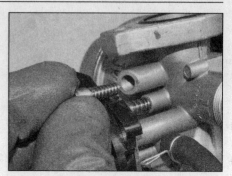

6.6 Mixture screw and its spring

be separated from the slide by removing the spring clip from the top of the slide **(see illustration)**. The needle has five grooves and on the model shown the clip (which determines needle height) was in the middle groove, expressed as third groove from top **(see illustration)**.

5 It is not recommended to disturb the choke butterfly valve or the choke operating lever. None of these parts are available separately.

6 The mixture adjustment screw can be removed if required, but you should record its position first. Doing so will make setting up after refitting much easier. Turn the screw in until it seats lightly, counting the number of turns required to do so. On the carb photographed 1 3/4 turns were recorded. Now fully unscrew the mixture screw and its spring **(see illustration)**. To fit a new mixture screw, screw it in until it seats lightly, then unscrew it the number of turns recorded.

7 Use an aerosol carb cleaner to clean fuel gum and residue from the jets and castings. Don't be tempted to poke wire or similar metal items though the jets as their metering rates could be affected. Allow the jets to soak in the cleaner if necessary. Note that the jets are marked in some cases to indicate their flow rate.

8 The float determines the fuel height in the float chamber. Problems such as dirt between the float valve face and its seat or a leaking float can cause carburettor flooding. The float height can be checked by taking a measurement between the gasket face of the carburettor and the top of the float; on the model shown it measured 11 mm **(see illustration)**. If flooding from the carburettor has been experienced and the float height is incorrect, it is possible to bend the metal tang which the float valve hangs from by a very small amount to effect a change **(see illustration 6.9)**.

9 Make sure the carb body is clean and dry before refitting the jets. Take care not to overtighten them. Hook the float valve onto its tang and guide the valve into its seat as the float is positioned **(see illustration)**. Push the pivot pin through both posts to secure it.

10 Insert the jet needle into the slide so that its clips seats in the base of the slide **(see illustration)**. Insert the spring clip to hold it in place **(see illustration 6.4b)**. Fit the top and spring over the cable **(see illustration)**. Thread the throttle cable through the groove in the slide **(see illustration 6.4a)** and locate its end in the base of the slide **(see illustration)**.

11 Refit the carburettor (see Section 5).

7 JingKe carburettor (PD)

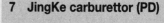

Warning: Refer to the precautions given in Section 1 before starting work.

6.8 Measuring the float height

6.9 Float valve hangs from the metal tang on the float pivot

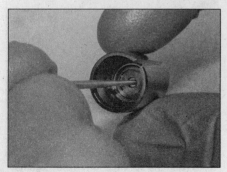

6.10a Insert the jet needle into the slide

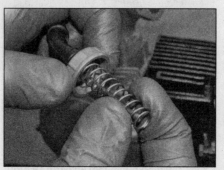

6.10b Fit the top and spring over the cable end

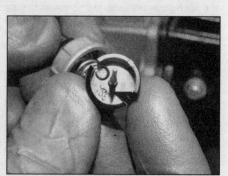

6.10c Cable end correctly engaged in base of slide

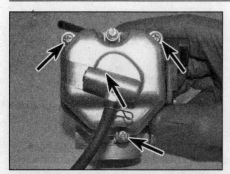

7.1a Remove the screws (arrowed)...

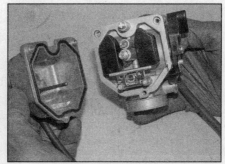

7.1b ...to free the float chamber

7.2 Pivot pin passes through the each support post and the float hinge

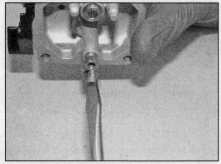

7.3a Unscrew the main jet from the needle jet

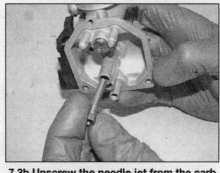

7.3b Unscrew the needle jet from the carb body

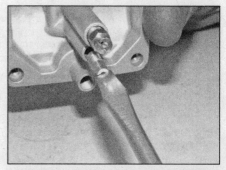

7.3c Pilot jet can be unscrewed from its bore

1 Remove the three screws from the base of the carb and withdraw the float chamber **(see illustrations)**. The O-ring seal should stay set in the groove of the float bowl – peel it off carefully if part of it has stuck to the carb body. Access is now possible to the main jet, needle jet and pilot jet, or the float assembly – all can be removed individually.

2 Push out the float pivot pin and lift the plastic float out together with its hinge and float valve **(see illustration)**.

3 Use close-fitting screwdrivers to remove the brass jets as their soft material is easily damaged **(see illustrations)**.

4 Hold the throttle spring compressed against the carburettor top and slip the cable end out of its location in the base of the throttle slide and through the slot in the side of the slide **(see illustration)**. The jet needle can be separated from the slide by removing the spring clip from the top of the slide **(see illustration)**. The needle has five grooves and on the model shown the clip (which determines needle height) was in the fourth groove from top **(see illustration)**.

5 It is not recommended to disturb the choke butterfly valve or the choke operating lever. None of these parts are available separately.

6 The mixture adjustment screw can be removed if required, but you should record its position first. Doing so will make setting up after refitting so much easier. Turn the screw in until it seats lightly, counting the number of turns required to do so. On the carb photographed 1 3/4 turns were recorded. Now fully unscrew the mixture screw and its

spring **(see illustration)**. To fit a new mixture screw, screw it in until it seats lightly, then unscrew it the number of turns recorded.

7 Use an aerosol carb cleaner to clean fuel

7.4a Hold the spring compressed against the carb top and slip the cable out of the slide

7.4c Jet needle clip in 4th groove from the top

gum and residue from the jets and castings. Don't be tempted to poke wire or similar metal items though the jets as their metering rates could be affected. Allow the jets to soak in

7.4b Withdraw the spring clip to free the jet needle from the slide

7.6 The mixture screw can be unscrewed from its location in the base of the carb body

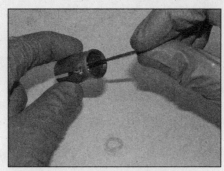

7.8 Measuring the float height

7.10a Insert the jet needle into the slide

7.10b Fit the cap and spring over the cable end

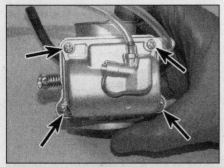

7.10c Cable end correctly located in the base of the slide

float height is incorrect, it is possible to bend the metal tang which the float valve hangs from by a very small amount to effect a change.

9 Make sure the carb body is clean and dry before refitting the jets. Take care not to overtighten them. Hook the float valve onto its tang and guide the valve into its seat as the float is positioned. Push the pivot pin through both posts to secure it.

10 Insert the jet needle into the slide so that its clips seats in the base of the slide **(see illustration)**. Insert the spring clip to hold it in place **(see illustration 7.4b)**. If removed, fit the top over the cable and fit the spring. Thread the throttle cable through the groove in the slide **(see illustration 7.4a)** and locate its end in the base of the slide **(see illustration)**.

11 Refer the carburettor (see Section 5).

---

8 Molkt carburettor

Note: *The Molkt carburettor described here is fitted to the YX140 and ZS155 engines.*

⚠ *Warning: Refer to the precautions given in Section 1 before starting work.*

1 Remove the four screws from the base of the carb and withdraw the float chamber **(see illustration)**. The gasket should stay stuck to the float bowl – peel it off carefully if part of it has stuck to the carb body **(see illustration)**. Access is now possible to the main jet, needle jet and pilot jet, or the float assembly – all can be removed individually.

2 Push out the float pivot pin and lift the plastic float out together with its hinge and float valve **(see illustration)**.

3 Use close-fitting screwdrivers to remove

the cleaner if necessary. Note that the jets are marked in some cases to indicate their flow rate.

8 The float determines the fuel height in the float chamber. Problems such as dirt between the float valve face and its seat or a leaking float can cause carburettor flooding. The float height can be checked by taking a measurement between the gasket face of the carburettor and the top of the float; on the model shown it measured 13.5 mm **(see illustration)**. If flooding from the carburettor has been experienced and the

8.1a Four screws retain the float chamber (arrowed)

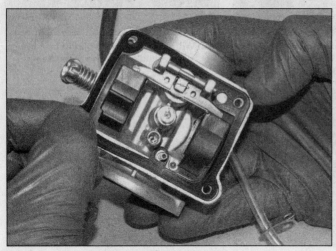

8.1b Carefully peel off the gasket

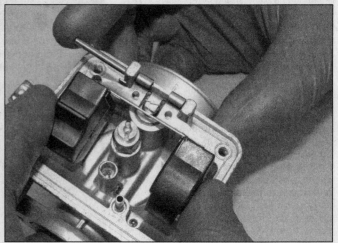

8.2 Pivot pin passes through the support posts and the float hinge

the brass jets as their soft material is easily damaged (see illustrations).

4 Hold the throttle spring compressed against the carburettor top and dislodge the retaining plate from inside the top of the slide (see illustration). Slip the cable end out of its location in the base of the throttle slide (see illustration). The jet needle can now be withdrawn from the slide (see illustration). The needle has five grooves and on the model shown the clip (which determines needle height) was in the middle groove, expressed as third groove from top (see illustration).

5 The two-stage choke operating plunger can be unscrewed from the carburettor body using an open-ended spanner on its flats (see illustration). There's little to go wrong with the plunger itself. Clean the end of the plunger and spray carburettor cleaner into its bore in the carb body if there are signs of dirt.

6 The mixture adjustment screw can be removed if required, but you should record its position first (see illustration). Doing so will make setting up after refitting much easier. Turn the screw in until it seats lightly, counting the number of turns required to do so. On the carb photographed 1/2 a turn was recorded. Now fully unscrew the mixture screw and its spring. To fit a new mixture screw, screw it in until it seats lightly, then unscrew it the number of turns recorded.

7 Use an aerosol carb cleaner to clean fuel gum and residue from the jets and castings. Don't be tempted to poke wire or similar metal items though the jets as their metering rates could be affected. Allow the jets to soak in

8.3a Unscrew the main jet from the needle jet holder…

8.3c …to free the needle jet

8.3b …then unscrew the holder…

8.3d The pilot jet screws into a bore next to the main and needle jets

the cleaner if necessary. Note that the jets are marked in some cases to indicate their flow rate.

8 The float determines the fuel height in the float chamber. Problems such as dirt

between the float valve face and its seat or a leaking float can cause carburettor flooding. The float height can be checked by taking a measurement between the gasket face of the carburettor (gasket peeled off) and the top of

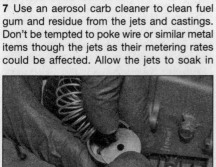
8.4a Dislodge the retaining plate from the top of the slide…

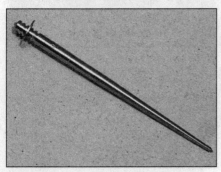
8.4d …and note its clip position

8.4b …move the cable end across to the larger hole in the slide to free it

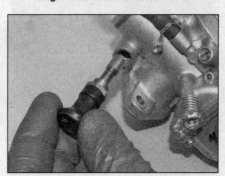
8.5 The choke plunger can be removed for inspection and renewal

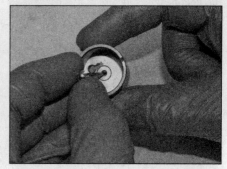
8.4c Lift the jet needle from the slide…

8.6 Mixture screw and its spring

8.8 Measuring the float height

8.9 Hook the float valve over the tang

8.10a Insert the spring over the cable end...

8.10b ...and hold it compressed whilst the cable end is slipped through the large hole and then across

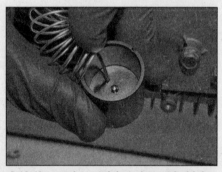

8.10c Insert the retaining plate to hold the cable in the slide

9.1 Unscrew the carburettor top (arrowed) and withdraw the slide assembly

the float; on the model shown it measured 22 mm **(see illustration)**. If flooding from the carburettor has been experienced and the float height is incorrect, it is possible to bend the metal tang which the float valve hangs from by a very small amount to effect a change.

9 Make sure the carb body is clean and dry before refitting the jets. Take care not to overtighten them. Hook the float valve onto its tang and guide the valve into its seat as the float is positioned **(see illustration)**. Push the pivot pin through both posts to secure it.

10 Insert the jet needle into the slide so that its clip seats in the base of the slide. If removed insert the top over the cable end and fit the spring. Hold the spring compressed

against the carburettor top and pass the end of the throttle cable through the large opening in the slide then move it across to lock it under the base of the slide **(see illustrations)**. Insert the retaining plate to secure the cable in the slide then allow the spring to extend back into place inside the slide **(see illustration)**.

11 Refit the carburettor (see Section 5).

9 Throttle cable

Removal

1 Unscrew the top from the carburettor and

withdraw the throttle valve **(see illustration)**. Disconnect the cable from the slide either by slipping its end out of the slot in the slide **(see illustration 6.4a)** or by removing the retaining plate and freeing the cable from its slot in the slide **(see illustrations 8.4a and b)**. Draw the cable out of the carburettor top.

2 Remove the two screws which retain the rear half of the throttle pulley housing at the handlebar and remove the housing half **(see illustrations)**. Use a small screwdriver to push the cable trunnion out of the pulley then remove the front half of the housing as the cable is freed from the pulley groove **(see illustration)**.

3 Use a small screwdriver to ease the guide out of the housing front half **(see illustration)**.

9.2a Remove the two screws (arrowed)...

9.2b ...and pull off the rear part of the housing

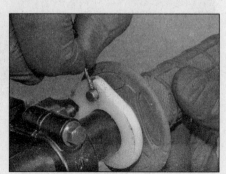

9.2c Wiggle the cable end out of the throttle grip

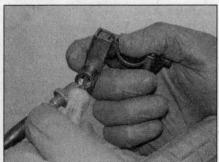

9.3a Pop the guide block out as shown

9.3b Unscrew the knurled nut to free the cable from the housing

9.6 Fit guide so that the cable locates in its channel

9.7 Make sure the cable is fully located in the twistgrip flange before joining the housing halves

Unscrew the cable knurled nut to allow the outer cable to be separated from the front half of the pulley **(see illustration)**.

4 Draw the cable out, noting its routing through any guides on the frame and around the handlebar and numberboard.

5 When buying a new cable, take the old cable with you to enable it to be matched up exactly for length and fitting design. If buying on-line or by telephone measure the length of the outer and inner parts of the cable and specify whether it has an angled or straight end where it joins the twistgrip, also whether an in-line adjuster is fitted. Colour of the outer cable is sometimes an option.

Installation

6 Thread the throttle cable nut into the front housing without it becoming tight **(see illustration 9.3b)** – where an elbowed fitting is used note that it must stay loose so that it aligns itself. Press the guide into place so that the cable locates in its channel **(see illustration)**.

7 Lubricate the cable trunnion with multi-purpose grease and fit it into the throttle pulley **(see illustration 9.2c)**. Assemble the front and rear housings onto the handlebar, and tighten the two screws **(see illustration)**. Tighten the knurled nut securing the metal end to the front housing. Slacken the locknut on the adjuster and thread the adjuster into

the housing – this will create freeplay in the cable.

8 Ensure the new cable is routed correctly through its guides and is not kinked or bent sharply at any point. Correct routing is important.

9 Thread the lower end of the cable through the carburettor top and fit the spring **(see illustration 8.10a)**. Hold the spring compressed against the top and reconnect the lower end of the cable to the throttle slide **(see illustrations 7.10b and c)**. Locate the slide into the carburettor so that the cutout at the base of the slide is towards the rear (air filter) side, being careful as the jet needle is inserted into its jet. Thread the top onto the carburettor.

10 Operate the throttle to check that it opens and closes freely and snaps shut when the twistgrip is released.

11 Turn the handlebars back-and-forth to make sure the cable doesn't cause the steering to bind.

12 Reset the adjuster at the upper end of the cable so that there is 2 to 3 mm of freeplay at the twistgrip flange (see Chapter 1, Section 9).

13 Start the engine and check that the idle speed does not rise as the handlebars are turned. If it does, the throttle cable is routed incorrectly. Correct the problem before riding.

10 Exhaust system

 Warning: If the engine has been running the exhaust system will be very hot. Allow the system to cool before carrying out any work.

Removal

1 The exhaust will come off as one-piece, except on models where it passes through the frame. Remove the bodywork to gain access to the silencer mounting.

2 Remove the two domed nuts at the cylinder head **(see illustrations)**. If they are hard to shift spray them with penetrating oil and wait

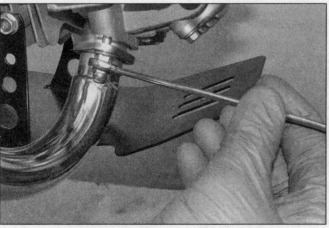

10.2a Unscrew the domed nuts...

10.2b ...and withdraw the flange plate from the studs

10.3a Unbolt the rear mounting from the frame, noting the exact location of the spacer

10.3b Pull off the silencer on models where the exhaust pipe is routed inside the frame

Installation

4 If the studs in the cylinder head are damaged, refer to the stud extractor methods in Section 2 of *Tools and Workshop Tips* in the Reference Section at the end of the manual. New studs and domed nuts can be purchased.

5 Replacement exhausts aren't expensive. Choose a system which has the correct pipe size external and internal to match the bike. Note that you may need to buy the rear mounting clamp/bracket separately.

6 If there was a copper washer fitted at the exhaust port it's best to renew it as they normally become squashed in use. If no washer is fitted, check that the mating surfaces of the pipe and seating area inside the head are clean and even – scrape them if necessary.

7 When you've installed the exhaust run the engine and check there are no leaks.

a while for it to work. Thread the nuts and flange plate off the studs.

3 At the silencer end, remove the clamp bolt and nut with its spacer **(see illustrations)**. Remove the complete system from the bike **(see illustration)**. On certain models there'll be a copper washer at the exhaust port joint with the pipe and on others the pipe contacts the face of the exhaust port directly.

10.3c Support the system at each end as it's lifted away from the bike

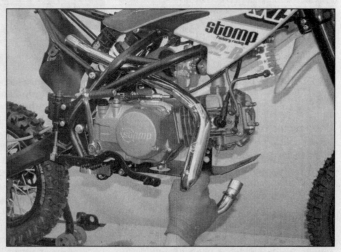

10.3d On this model the system has to removed forwards from behind the frame tubes

Chapter 4
Ignition system

Contents

Degrees of difficulty

Easy, suitable for novice with little experience	Fairly easy, suitable for beginner with some experience	Fairly difficult, suitable for competent DIY mechanic	Difficult, suitable for experienced DIY mechanic	Very difficult, suitable for expert DIY or professional

1 General Information

1 A magneto type generator powers the electronic ignition system. The generator source coil provides power to the CDI unit and the pick-up coil provides the CDI with crankshaft position information.
2 The output side of the CDI unit supplies a low tension current to the primary winding of the HT coil. This induces a high tension in the coil's secondary winding which is supplied to the spark plug via the HT lead and suppressor cap. Timing of the spark is governed by the pick-up coil's signal and pre-programmed values in the CDI unit.
3 The kill switch is fitted to isolate the ignition system and to stop the engine.

2 Ignition system check

1 As no means of adjustment is available, any failure of the system can be traced to failure of a system component or a simple wiring fault. Of the two possibilities, the latter is by far the most likely. In the event of failure, check the system in a logical fashion, as described below.
2 Remove the spark plug and fit it back into the cap **(see illustration)**. Lay the plug against the cylinder head with the threads contacting it, but away from the plug hole **(see illustration)**.

⚠ *Warning: Always cover the open plug hole because otherwise atomised fuel being pumped out of the spark plug hole could ignite, causing severe injury! Make sure the plug is securely held against the engine – if it is not earthed when the engine is turned over, the CDI unit could be damaged.*
3 Check that the transmission is in neutral, then set the kill switch to RUN and kick the engine over a couple of times. If the system is in good condition a regular, fat blue spark should be evident at the plug electrodes. If the spark appears thin or yellowish, or is non-existent, further investigation will be necessary.
4 Ignition faults can be divided into two categories, namely those where the ignition system has failed completely, and those that are due to a partial failure. The likely faults are listed below, starting with the most probable source of failure. Work through the list systematically and also check the wiring between components.

a) Faulty spark plug, dirty, worn or corroded plug electrodes. Fit a new plug (see Chapter 1).
b) Loose or faulty HT lead or spark plug cap (see Section 4).
c) Faulty kill switch (see Section 3).
d) Faulty pick-up coil or damaged trigger (see Section 5).
e) Faulty ignition HT coil (see Section 4).
f) Faulty ignition source coil (see Section 5).
g) Faulty CDI unit (see Section 6).

3 Kill switch

Note: *A rocker type kill switch is described. Push button switches are also used for cutting the ignition.*
1 The kill switch isolates the ignition system, bridging its contacts between the green and black/white (or black) wires to earth the

2.2a Unscrew the plug from the cylinder head

2.2b Fit the plug into the cap and rest it against the cylinder head

3.3a Remove the two screws…

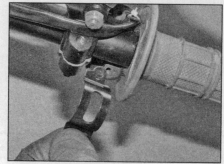

3.3b …remove the handlebar clamp…

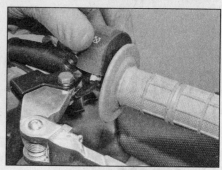

3.3c …and lift the switch clear

ignition signal when in the OFF position. To test, disconnect the two-pin wire connector under the fuel tank **(see illustration 6.2b)** and connect a multimeter between the pins on the switch side; with the switch OFF continuity should be shown, and with the switch ON there should be no continuity, i.e. infinite resistance.

2 Problems with the kill switch are likely to be caused by water getting into the switch and corroding the contacts.

3 To access the switch contacts remove the two screws from underneath the switch, then remove the clamp retaining the switch to handlebar **(see illustrations)**. Take the switch off the handlebar and spray its contacts with a water-dispersant contact cleaner **(see illustrations)**.

4 If you are renewing the switch remove if from the handlebar as described, then cut the cable-ties securing it to the handlebar **(see illustration)** and disconnect its 2-pin

3.3d Spray the switch contacts if they are damp or corroded

connector into the wiring loom under the fuel tank **(see illustration 6.2b)**.

5 On refitting, position the switch at a convenient angle before tightening its clamp screws. Reconnect the wiring and fix it to the handlebar with new cable-ties.

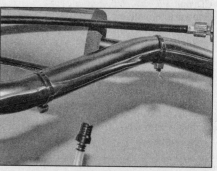

3.4 Cable-ties secure the kill switch wiring to the handlebar. Trim their ends once in place

4 Ignition coil, HT lead and cap

Removal

1 Remove the fuel tank.
2 Disconnect the cap from the spark plug **(see illustration)**. Pull back the protective cover and disconnect the primary wires from the coil terminals **(see illustration)**.
3 Remove its mounting bolt and remove the coil from the frame **(see illustration 4.2b)**.

Coil checks

4 Check the coil and its wiring visually for loose or damaged connectors and terminals, cracks and other damage.
5 To check the condition of the primary windings, set a multimeter to the ohms x 1 scale. Connect the meter probes to the primary terminals on the coil and measure the resistance **(see illustration)**. There is no specific value, but the reading obtained should be around 0.5 ohm; this was the figure recorded across 4 coils tested. A primary reading showing very high or infinite resistance indicates a defective coil.
6 To check the resistance of the secondary windings, set the meter to the K-ohm scale. Connect one meter probe to the end of the HT (unscrew the cap from the lead to make this test) and the other to one of the primary circuit terminals and measure the resistance **(see illustration)**.

4.2a Pull the cap off the spark plug

4.2b Coil wire terminals and mounting bolt

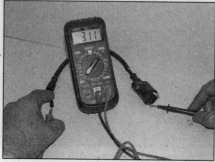

4.5 Primary winding test

4.6 Secondary winding test

The reading obtained obtained on 4 coils tested was found to be 3.1 K-ohms.

7 Note that it is possible for the plug cap to fail. Unscrew it from the HT lead and test it by connecting the meter across the terminals as shown. A sound plug cap should give a reading of 4.5 to 5.0 K-ohms **(see illustration)**. Examine the HT lead; if cracked or damaged in any way it should be renewed. Note that the coil, HT lead and cap are sold as a unit and are relatively inexpensive.

Installation

8 Installation is the reverse of removal. Note that the black/yellow wire connects to the coil terminal with the black tab and the green wire to the coil's green tab. Fit the protective cover back over the coil **(see illustration)**.

5 Generator

Coil check

1 All engines have an ignition source coil and a pick-up coil. Some may also have a lighting coil (two additional wires – yellow and white).

2 All coils are sold complete with the stator plate. There are many different types so take the old one with you for direct part comparison **(see illustrations)**. Variations are available for 3 or 5 wire stator plates. Note also to specify that it's a kickstart-only engine; the charging coil arrangement will differ for electric-start engines.

3 In the following tests, trace the wiring from the generator and disconnect the appropriate wire connectors **(see illustration)**. Make the tests on the generator side of the wires. How easy it is to access the connectors varies according to model; on some you can release them from the clip under the bodywork, whereas on others it is necessary to remove the bodywork and possibly also the fuel tank.

Source coil voltage test

4 The source could provides power for the ignition system. You can check it by connecting a multimeter set to the ac volts range between the black/red wire (positive

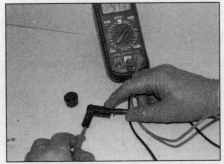

4.7 Testing the plug cap

probe) and green wire or bike frame (negative probe) **(see illustration)**. Remove the spark plug, fit the plug back into the cap and earth the plug firing end against the head **(see illustration 2.2b)**. Kick the engine over several times and note whether there's a reading on the meter. The exact reading will fluctuate (we found anything up to 19acV was shown, but if there's no reading the coil has failed.

5 The source could provides power for the ignition system. You can check it by connecting a multimeter set to the ac volts range between the black/red wire (positive probe) and green wire or bike frame (negative probe). Remove the spark plug, fit the plug back into the cap and earth the plug firing end against the head **(see illustration 2.2b)**. Kick the engine over several times and note whether there's a reading on the meter. The exact reading will fluctuate (we found anything

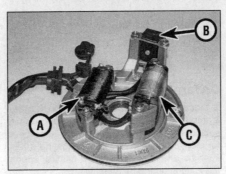

5.2a Two coil stator: source (A), pick-up (B) and lighting (C)

4.8 Cover protects the terminals from water and dust

up to 19acV was shown), but if there's no reading the coil has failed.

Source coil resistance test

6 Trace the wiring from the generator and disconnect the black/red and green wire connectors. Use a multimeter set to the ohms x 100 scale connect its probes across these two wires on the generator side of the connectors. The test results we obtained were 360 to 380 ohms.

7 On the ZS155 engine fitted with the multi-coil stator, trace the wiring from the generator and disconnect the black/red and red/white wire connectors. The test result obtained was 11 ohms.

Pick-up coil

8 Disconnect the generator wiring at the blue/white and green (or green/white) wire connectors. Use a multimeter set to the

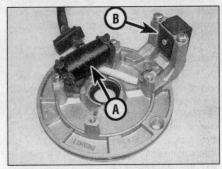

5.2b Single coil stator: source (A), pick-up (B)

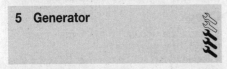

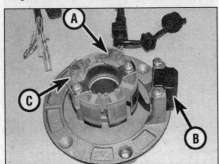

5.2c Multi-coil stator: source (A), pick-up (B), lighting (C)

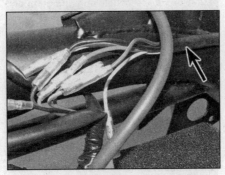

5.3 Wire harness from the generator (arrowed)

5.4 Use crocodile clips to connect the meter (ac volts) to the source coil wires

6.2a CDI can be found on top...

6.2b ...below the main frame tube...

6.2c ...or attached to the side of the frame

ohms x 100 scale connect its probles across these two wires on the generator side of the connectors. The test results we obtained were 115 to 140 ohms.

Lighting coil

9 Disconnect the generator wiring at the yellow and white wire connectors. Use a multimeter set to the ohms x 100 scale connect its probles across these two wires on the generator side of the connectors. The test result we obtained was 1.0 ohm.

Test conclusions

10 As no coil resistance values are specified by the manufacturer our findings can only be used as a guide but the values you obtain should be around the same. If a very high or infinite resistance is measured this indicates no continuity in the circuit and failure of the coil. Check first though that the fault is not caused by a broken wire or poor connection between the connector and the stator plate.

Removal and installation

11 The generator is mounted to the left-hand end of the crankshaft. It can be removed with the engine in the frame.
12 Refer to Chapter 2, according to the engine type fitted. Note that you'll need a rotor holding tool and puller, and that if the stator plate is to be removed, you'll need to first drain the engine oil.

6 CDI unit

1 The CDI (capacitor discharge ignition) unit supplies the low tension signal to the HT coil using a signal from the pick-up coil. It is powered by the generator's source coil. The CDI contains pre-programmed values to advance the ignition in accordance with engine speed.
2 The CDI unit is either mounted directly to the frame by two bolts or set in a rubber holder to reduce vibration **(see illustrations)**. Release its clip to free the wire connector.
3 Testing of the CDI unit is not possible. If an ignition problem exists and testing of all other system components has failed to trace the cause, the CDI unit can be assumed faulty.

7 Ignition timing

General information

1 Since no provision exists for adjusting the ignition timing and since no component is subject to mechanical wear, there is no need for regular checks: only if investigating a fault such as a loss of power or a misfire, should the ignition timing be checked.

2 The ignition timing is checked dynamically (engine running) using a stroboscopic lamp.

Check

3 Warm the engine up to normal operating temperature, then stop it.
4 Remove the left-hand cover from the side of the engine **(see illustration)**. Connect the strobe to the HT lead and connect its power source **(see illustration)**.
5 The mark on the timing rotor that indicates the firing point at idle speed is an 'F'. The static timing mark with which this should align is the notch in the inspection hole **(see illustration)**. Start the engine and aim the light at the timing marks. With the machine idling at the specified speed, the 'F' mark should align with the static timing mark.
6 Slowly increase the engine speed whilst observing the 'F' mark. The mark should appear to move, increasing in relation to the engine speed until it reaches full advance; on some engines the full advance mark is identified by two parallel scribed lines but on others no mark is provided.
7 As already stated, there is no means of adjustment of the ignition timing. If the ignition timing is incorrect, or suspected of being incorrect, one of the ignition system components is at fault, and the system must be tested as described in the preceding Sections of this Chapter.
8 Refit the engine cover when the test is complete.

7.4a Engine left cover is retained by two or three bolts (gear lever can usually remain in place)

7.4b Inductive pickup of strobe light clips around HT lead

7.5 Line next to the F mark should align with the notch at idle speed

Chapter 5
Suspension, controls and body panels

Contents

Degrees of difficulty

| **Easy,** suitable for novice with little experience | | **Fairly easy,** suitable for beginner with some experience | | **Fairly difficult,** suitable for competent DIY mechanic | | **Difficult,** suitable for experienced DIY mechanic | | **Very difficult,** suitable for expert DIY or professional | |

1 General information

1 The backbone style frame is of welded steel construction, with detachable rear sub-frame on certain models. More exotic aftermarket frames can be of trellis design or of aluminium construction.

2 Front suspension is by a pair of oil-damped USD (upside-down) telescopic forks on most models. Higher end models have adjustable damping. Conventional right way up forks are fitted to small pit bikes.

3 At the rear, a swingarm acts on a single shock absorber. Most shocks have preload adjustment, high spec shocks provide preload, rebound and compression damping adjustment.

2 Bodywork and frame

Bodywork

Bodywork and seat – one-piece type

1 The bodypanels and seat are removed as one. At the front remove the two screws which thread into the fuel tank and the screw and the screw and nut which mount through the fuel tank tabs on each side **(see illustrations)**.

2 From the rear underside, remove the two nuts and throughbolts which retain the rear bodywork to the frame **(see illustration)**. Lift at the rear and pull the bodywork and seat assembly off the bike so that its two prongs release from the loops on the frame **(see illustration)**.

3 The plastic bodypanels are fixed to the seat **(see illustrations)**.

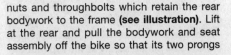

2.1a Bodywork mounts to top of tank on each side...

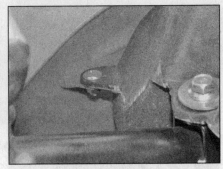
2.1b ...and on the inner front edge on each side

2.2a Bodywork fixings to the frame at the rear

2.2b Prongs fit through loops on the frame

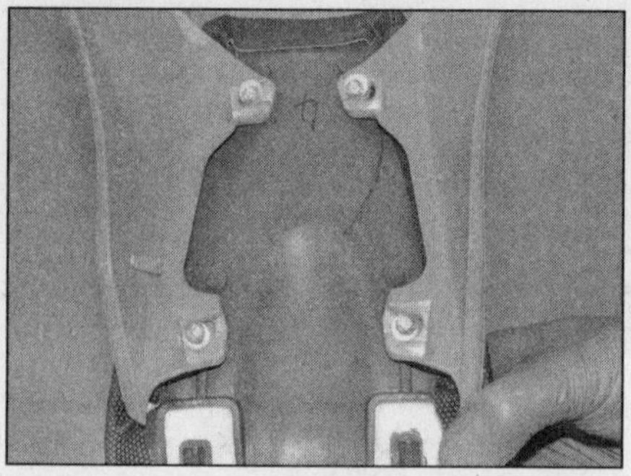

2.3a Screws secure the front bodywork (fuel tank panels)...

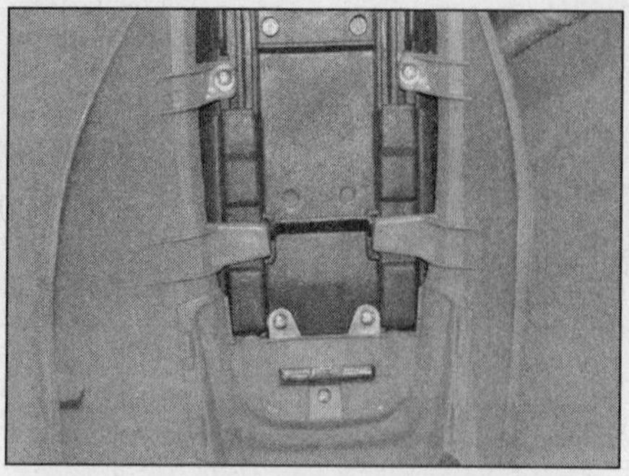

2.3b ...and rear bodywork to the seat

Bodywork and seat – two piece type

4 The front and rear bodywork can be removed individually. To remove the rear section and seat, remove the two nuts and through-bolts which retain it to the sub-frame **(see illustration)**. Remove the single screw from the top and two screws from each side **(see illustrations)**. Pull the seat and rear bodywork back to disengage its two prongs from the loops on the frame **(see illustration)**. The front of the seat also locates over a post set in the fuel tank **(see illustration)**.

5 To remove the front section, remove the single screw into the tank at the top, and the screw and nut securing it to the tank tab at the front **(see illustration)**. Move the panel rearwards off the peg at the rear of the tank and manoeuvre its top edge out from under the seat **(see illustration)**.

Front mudguard

6 Two or three bolts secure the mudguard to the lower yoke on most models **(see illustrations)**.

Frame

7 The frame should not require attention unless accident damage has occurred. In most cases, fitting a new frame is the only satisfactory remedy for such damage. A few frame specialists have the jigs and other

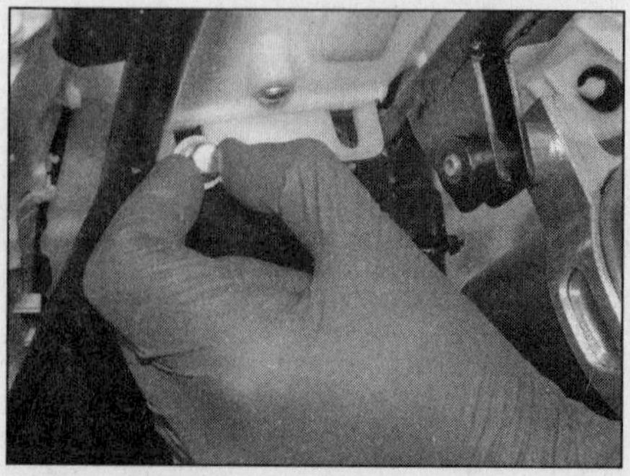

2.4a Remove the two throughbolts...

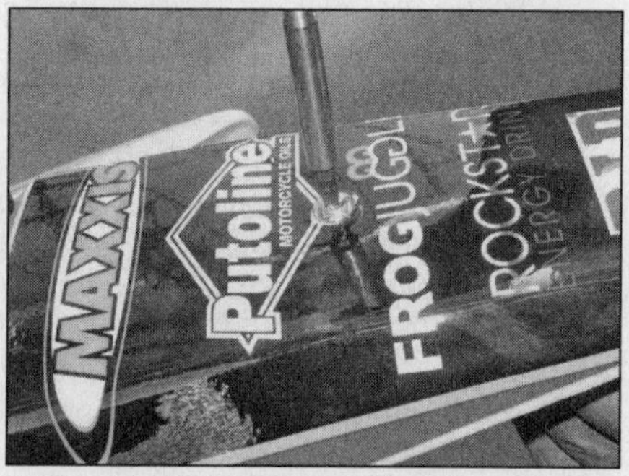

2.4b ...the single screw at the top (nut on underside)...

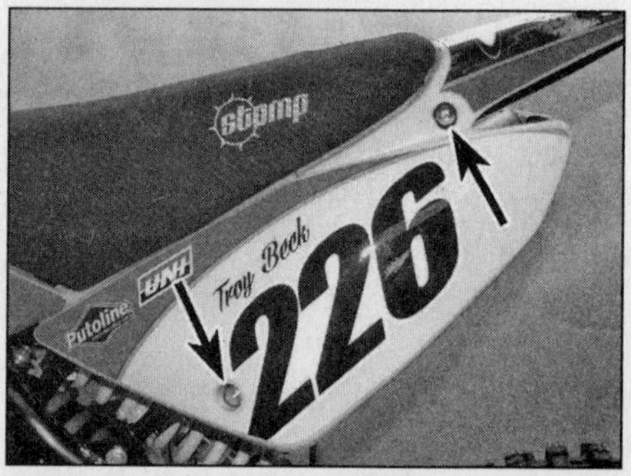

2.4c ...and the two screws on each side

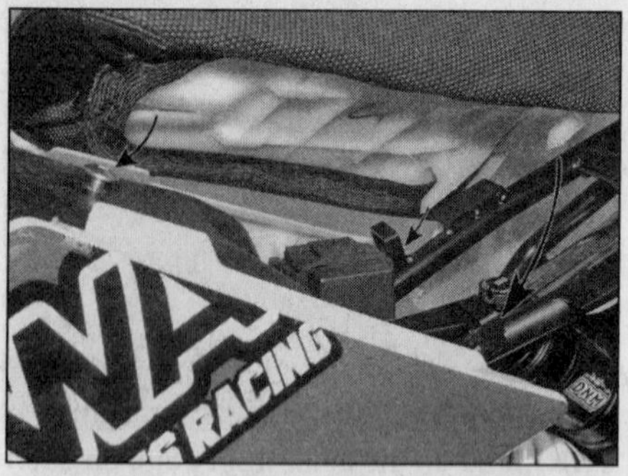

2.4d Free the two prongs from the frame and the channel from the post

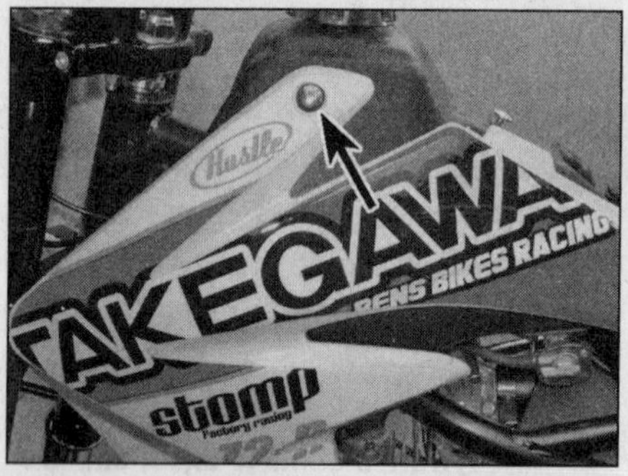

2.5a Front bodywork is secured to the tank at the top...

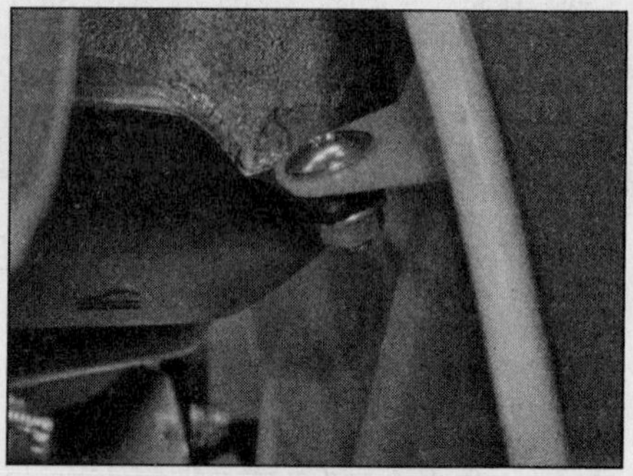

2.5b ...on the inside front...

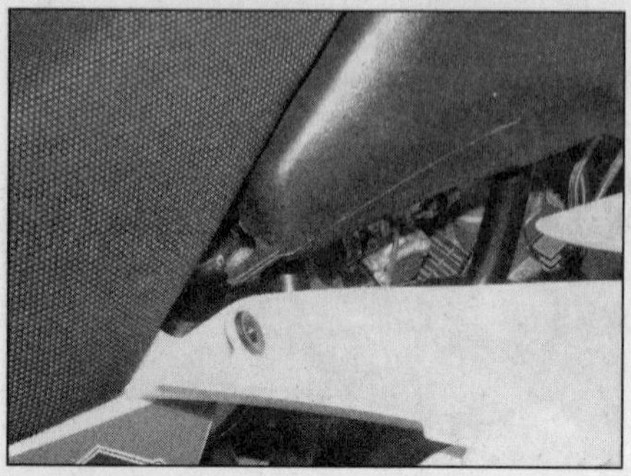

2.5c ...and by a peg and grommet at the rear

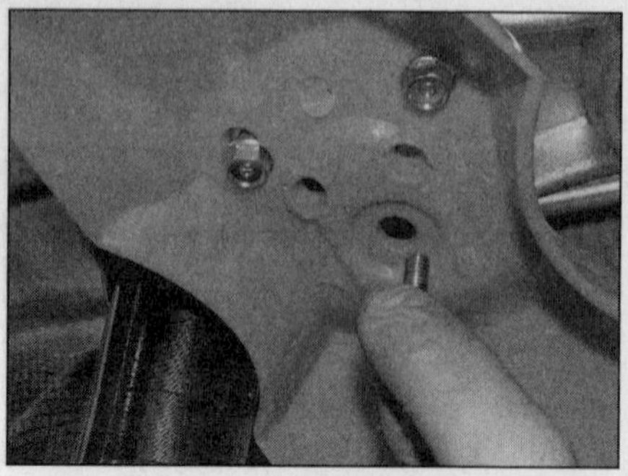

2.6a Bolts pass through mudguard and thread directly into the yoke...

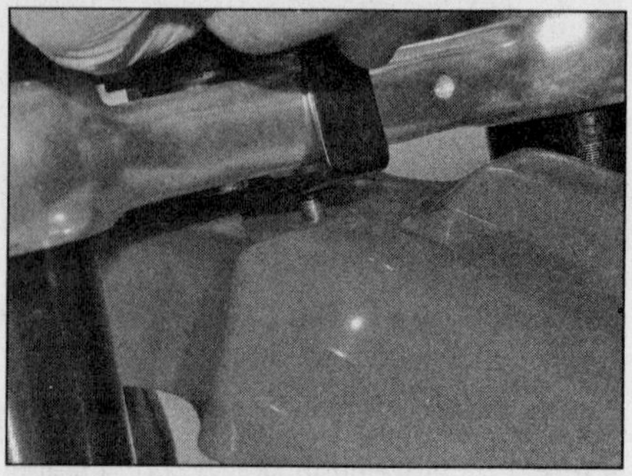

2.6b ...and may also secure the number board bracket

3.1 Split pin passes through a hole in the pivot pin end

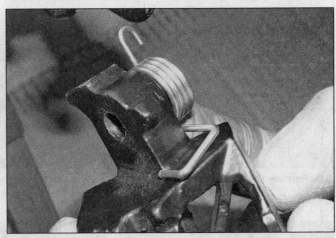

3.2a One end of the return spring locates on the footrest and the other over the footrest bracket

equipment necessary for straightening frames to the required standard of accuracy, but even then there is no simple way of assessing to what extent the frame may have been over stressed. On some models the rear sub-frame can be unbolted and replaced separately.

8 The frame should be examined closely for signs of cracking or splitting at the welded joints, and for signs of penetrating rust. Loose engine mounting bolts can cause ovaling or fracturing of the mounting points. Minor damage can often be repaired by welding, depending on the extent and nature of the damage.

9 Remember that a frame that is out of alignment will cause handling problems. If, as the result of an accident, misalignment is suspected, it will be necessary to strip the machine completely so the frame can be thoroughly checked.

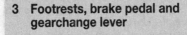

| 3 | Footrests, brake pedal and gearchange lever |

Footrests

1 Remove the split pin from the footrest pivot pin, then withdraw the pivot pin and remove the footrest and return spring **(see illustration)**.

2 Position the return spring ends correctly when fitting the footrest and secure it with the pivot pin (having applied a smear of grease) and a new split pin **(see illustrations)**. Bend the split pin ends around the pivot pin to lock the pin in place. Check that the footrest can fold back rearwards and that it springs back to its 'at rest' position when released.

Brake pedal – drum brake

3 Unhook the pedal return spring end from the end of the engine mounting bolt **(see illustration)**. Straighten the split pin ends and remove the pin and its washer from the ends

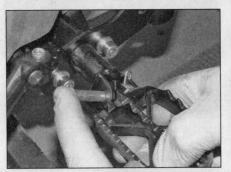

3.2b Holes in footrest and bracket must line up to insert the pivot pin

of the brake rod link and pedal shaft **(see illustration)**. Withdraw the brake pedal/shaft from its bore in the frame. **(see illustration)**.

4 Refit the pedal in a reverse of the removal procedure.

● Grease the pedal shaft before inserting it into its bore in the frame.
● Use new split pins to secure the pedal and link rod joints **(see illustration)**.

Brake pedal – disc brake

5 Disconnect the pedal from the master cylinder pushrod (see Chapter 6, Section 5).

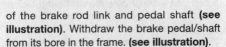

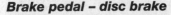

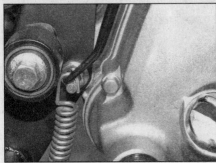

3.3a Using a spring hook to disconnect the pedal return spring from the engine bolt

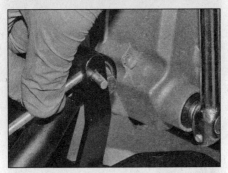

3.3b Having removed their split pins and washers, disconnect the brake rod from the pedal...

3.3c ...and slide the pedal out of the frame

3.4 Bend the split pin ends as shown to secure it

3.6a Remove the split pin and washer from the pivot…

3.6b …note how the return spring ends locate (arrowed)…

3.6c …press down on the pedal at the rear then unhook the spring before sliding the pedal off its shaft

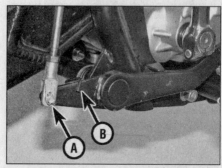

3.6d Disconnect the link at the master cylinder (A) and disconnect the spring end (B)…

3.6e …remove the pivot bolt…

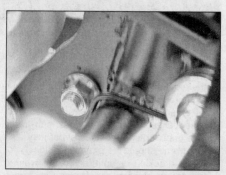

3.6f …the other end of the spring locates around the frame on this model

3.8a Make a dot on the shaft end level with the slot (A) then remove the pinch bolt (B)…

6 The pedal will either be secured by a washer and split pin **(see illustrations)** or by a bolt and washer **(see illustrations)**. Before disturbing the pedal, note how the return spring ends locate.

7 Refitting is a reverse of removal whlist noting the following:

● Note that refitting is trickly because of the tension of the return spring. There are some tips in 'Building a bike from the crate' in the Reference 7 section at the end of this manual.

● Apply grease to the pedal pivot before assembly and use a new split pin where applicable.

● The height of the rear brake pedal can be adjusted to suit rider preference by adjusting the clevis position on the master cylinder pushrod before reconnecting the pedal (see Chapter 6, Section 5).

Gearchange lever

8 Remove the pinch bolt from the gearchange lever and pull the lever off the splined shaft **(see illustrations)**. If necessary open up the clamp slightly if the lever is a tight fit on its splines **(see illustration)**.

9 On refitting, line up the lever slot with the mark made previously to preserve the same lever position relative to the footrest.

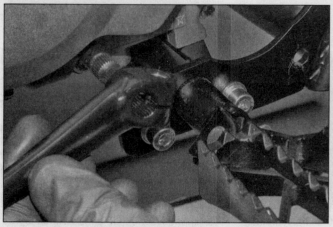

3.8b …then pull the lever off the gearshaft splines

3.8c Use a flat-bladed screwdriver to open up the slot if needed

4 Kickstart lever and sidestand

Kickstart lever

1 Remove the pinch bolt from the kickstart lever and pull the lever off the splined shaft **(see illustrations)**. If necessary open up the clamp slightly if the lever is a tight fit on its splines **(see illustration)**.
2 When refitting, align the lever slot with the shaft mark and push the lever onto the splines. Secure with the pinch bolt.

Sidestand (where fitted)

3 Prop the bike against a wall or pull it on a rear paddock stand.
4 Carefully unhook and remove the stand return spring **(see illustration)**.
5 Unscrew the nut from the pivot bolt. Unscrew the pivot bolt and remove the stand **(see illustration)**.
6 Apply grease to the pivot bolt shank and tighten the bolt.
7 Fit the nut, then counter-hold the bolt and tighten the nut.
8 Reconnect the spring.
9 Check the operation of the stand. Make sure it remains fully retracted when flipped back up.

5 Handlebars

Removal

1 Release the cable-ties securing the wiring to the handlebar **(see illustration)**. Take note (or a photo) of how the cables and wiring and brake hose are routed from the handlebar, e.g. whether in front or behind the numberboard and whether they pass through any guides or clamps on the frame.
2 Remove the two screws securing the kill switch clamp and remove the switch from the handlebar **(see illustrations)**. If required, the old grip rubber can be removed from the left-hand end of the bar as described in Step 5.

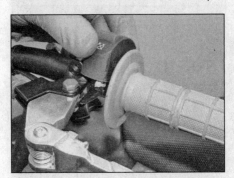
5.2b Free the switch from the handlebar

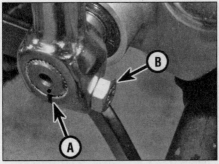
4.1a Mark the end of the kickstart shaft level with the slot (A) and remove the pinch bolt (B)...

4.4 A spring hook tool is useful for stretching the spring to get it off and back on the hook

3 Remove the two clamp bolts and separate the clutch lever bracket from the handlebar **(see illustration)**; there's no need to disconnect the cable.

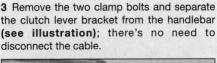
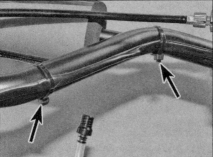
5.1 Cut the cable-ties (arrowed) to free the wiring from the bars

5.3 Two bolts retain the clutch bracket clamp

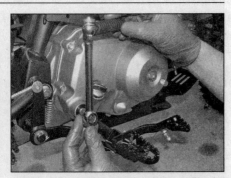
4.1b ...then pull the lever off the splines

4.5 Stand pivot bolt and nut arrangement

4 Remove the two clamp bolts and separate the brake master cylinder clamp and bracket from the handlebar **(see illustration)**. Keep the master cylinder upright if possible to

5.2a Kill switch bracket is retained by two screws

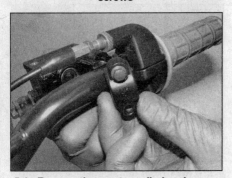
5.4a Remove the master cylinder clamp...

5.4b …or the brake lever bracket clamp (drum brake)

5.5a Withdraw the twistgrip from the right-hand end of the bar

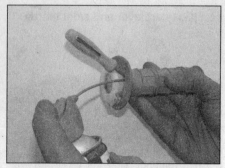

5.5b Method of removing old grip rubbers

prevent fluid loss. For a cable-operated drum front brake, remove the clamp bracket from the handlebar – there's no need to disconnect the brake cable **(see illustration)**.

5 Disconnect the throttle cable from the twistgrip (see Chapter 3, Section 9). Slip the twistgrip off the bar end **(see illustration)**. If you're going to change the grips, work a thin screwdriver between the grip rubber and twistgrip sleeve then insert the nozzle of WD40 or similar and squirt a small amount of lubricant in enable the old grip to be twisted off the sleeve **(see illustration)** – otherwise cut the old grip off using a sharp knife.

⚠️ *Warning: Avoid spray-back when using spray lubricant in this way by wearing eye protection or looking away.*

6 Before unscrewing the handlebar clamp bolts, scribe a line on the middle section of the handlebar where it aligns with the joint surface of the clamp **(see illustration 5.8a)**; this will allow you to return the bar to exactly the same position on installation.

7 Slacken all handlebar bolts evenly, noting that on some models you'll have to counterhold a nut on the base of the top yoke **(see illustration)**. Lift the clamps and handlebar off the top yoke **(see illustration)**.

Installation

8 Installation is the reverse of removal, noting the following.
● If you're fitting new grip rubbers, make sure their inner surface and bar end are dry. Use an adhesive to bond the right grip

to the throttle twistgrip and the left grip to the bar end. Allow the glue dry fully before riding the bike.
● Smear some grease onto the throttle twistgrip inner sliding surface and bar right-hand end.
● Align any mark you made on removal to position the handlebar back to its original angle in the lower clamp. Fit the top clamp and the two bolts. Whilst holding the handlebar in position start by tightening the front bolts down fully, then the rear bolts – the gap should be at the rear **(see illustration 5.8a)**.
● When you're fitting the master cylinder and clutch lever bracket clamps, tighten the top bolt fully first, then the lower bolt **(see illustration 5.8b)**. The gap at the bottom

5.7a Handlebar clamp bolts being slackened with retaining nuts underneath yoke being held

5.7b Bridge-type handlebar clamp…

5.7c …with each long bolt through-bolt secured by a nut under the top yoke

5.7d Handlebar bolts thread directly into threaded clamps on some models

5.8a Handlebar front bolts must be tightened down first. The gap at the rear of the clamp is intentional

5.8b Take note of the UP markings on the clamps where they have them

6.1 Removing the brake lever on a disc brake model

6.2a Grease the pivot bolt shank and surfaces of the lever where it engages the bracket

6.2b Secure the pivot bolt with the nut and tighten securely

of the clamp is intentional. Note that the clamps must be positioned so that lever access is comfortable when riding.
● Secure the wiring to the handlebars with new cable-ties.
● Check the operation of the throttle and clutch, and adjust cable freeplay as required (see Chapter 1). Check front brake operation.

6 Handlebar levers (brake and clutch)

Brake lever – disc brake model

1 Hold the pivot bolt nut from underneath the

master cylinder and unscrew the pivot bolt to free the lever **(see illustration)**.
2 On refitting, apply a smear of grease to the working surfaces of the lever and pivot bolt before securing them in place **(see illustrations)**. If fitting a new lever set the span adjustment to suit your hand size **(see illustration)**. If fitting a different brand of lever, check that there's clearance between the lever and master cylinder piston with the lever 'at rest'.

Brake lever – drum brake model

3 Slacken the cable adjuster locknut and thread the adjuster into the bracket to create freeplay in the cable. Align the removal slots and disconnect the cable end from its location

in the lever **(see illustration)**. Unscrew the pivot bolt and remove the lever **(see illustration)**.
4 On installation apply a smear of grease to the surfaces of the lever where it engages the bracket and to the plain shank of the pivot bolt. Tighten the pivot bolt to secure the lever.

Clutch lever

5 Slacken the cable adjuster locknut and thread the adjuster into the bracket to create freeplay in the cable **(see illustration)**. Align the removal slots and disconnect the cable end from its location in the lever **(see illustration)**.
6 Hold the pivot bolt nut underneath and

6.2c Brake lever correctly fitted and aligned with master cylinder piston. Span adjuster (arrowed)

6.3a Disconnecting the brake cable from the lever

6.3b Remove the lever pivot bolt (no nut is fitted on this type)

6.5a Thread the adjuster into the bracket and align its slots...

6.5b ...slip the cable end out of the lever...

6.5c ...and out through the slots

6.6 Hold the pivot bolt nut from underneath the bracket with a ring spanner

unscrew the pivot bolt to free the lever **(see illustration)**.
7 On installation apply a smear of grease to the surfaces of the lever where it engages the

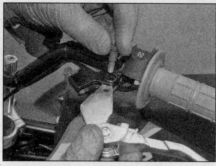

6.7 Apply grease to the shank of the pivot and lever working faces.

bracket and to the plain shank of the pivot bolt **(see illustration)**. Thread the pivot bolt into place and tighten the nut.
8 Reconnect the cable and set clutch lever

freeplay (see Chapter 1). If fitting a new lever with span adjustment, set it to fit your hand size.

7 Fork removal and installation

Removal

1 On models with a disc brake, unbolt the front brake caliper from the fork leg **(see illustration)**. Tie the caliper back so that it is out of the way. On models with a drum brake, remove the brake adjuster nut from the cable end, then unscrew the lower nut from the cable support bracket and slip the cable out of the bracket **(see illustrations)**.
2 Remove the front wheel (see Chapter 6).
3 If required remove the fork shields **(see illustration)**. Note the position and routing of any hoses and cables which pass around or alongside the forks.
4 Make note of the fork position above the top yoke. They will either be fitted flush **(see illustration 7.9)** or above for reduced ride height, in which case measure the distance so that you can return the forks to the same position **(see illustration)**.
5 Working on one fork at a time, slacken the fork clamp bolt(s) in the top and bottom yokes **(see illustrations)**. On the USD fork, if the fork is to be disassembled, or if the fork oil is being changed, slacken the fork top bolt now **(see illustration)**.

7.1a Slide the caliper off the disc

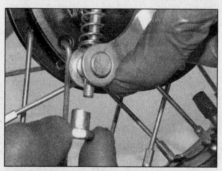

7.1b Remove the brake adjuster nut

7.1c Free the cable from the support bracket on the fork

7.3 Fork shields are mounted to the fork lower section

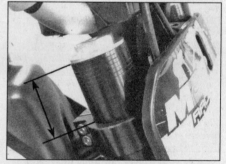

7.4 Fork protrusion above top yoke

7.5a Slacken the clamp bolts in the top yoke...

7.5b ...and lower yoke

7.5c It's a good idea to slacken the top bolt whilst it is clamped in place. Note the use of masking tape to protect its finish

7.6a Remove the mounting bolt...

7.6b ...slacken the clamp bolt (arrowed)...

7.6c ...and slip the fork out of the yokes

6 On some smaller models, the forks are secured through the top yoke with a bolt rather than a clamp arrangement. Remove the mounting bolt from the top yoke and slacken the bolt in the lower yoke clamp, then slide the fork down and out of the yokes **(see illustrations)**.

7 Remove each fork by twisting it and pulling it downwards. If the forks are seized in the yokes, spray the area with penetrating oil and allow time for it to soak in before trying again.

Installation

8 Remove any dirt or corrosion from the fork tube and in the yokes. Slide the fork up through the bottom yoke and into the top yoke.

9 On models where the fork is clamped in the top yoke, set the fork so the joint between the tube and the top bolt is level with the upper surface of the top yoke or as noted on removal **(see illustration)**.

10 Tighten the fork clamp bolts (and fork mounting bolt, where applicable). On USD forks, if the fork has been dismantled or if the fork oil was changed, tighten the fork top bolt.

11 Install the front wheel, and where applicable, the front brake caliper.

12 Install all remaining components in a reverse of removal. Check the operation of the front forks and brake before riding.

8   Fork oil change

Conventional (right-way up) forks

1 Remove the fork legs (see Section 7).

2 With the fork fully extended remove the top bolt from the inner tube **(see illustration)**. Keep downwards pressure on the top bolt as the last threads are released as it will be under tension from the spring. Have a measuring vessel ready and remove the spring from the fork **(see illustration 8.3a)** and leave it to drain in the vessel. Tip the old oil from the fork into the vessel, pumping the fork to help it drain **(see illustration)**.

3 Note down the amount of oil drained (70 ml from the fork shown), then measure out the same quantity of new fork oil (5W to 10W is recommended). Extend the fork fully, refit the spring and slowly pour the new oil into the fork, pumping the fork gently to distribute it **(see illustrations)**.

4 Draw the inner tube back up to the top bolt and thread the top bolt into the tube **(see illustration 8.2a)**. Repeat the procedure on the other fork and put in the same amount of oil. Install the forks (see Section 7).

USD (upside-down) non-adjustable forks

5 With the fork fully extended unscrew the top

7.9 Top of fork tube set level with the surface of the yoke

8.2a Unscrew the fork top bolt

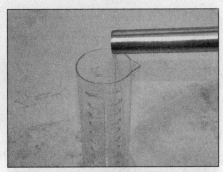

8.2b Drain the old oil from the fork

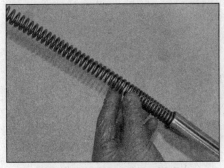

8.3a Install the spring with its closer-wound coils towards the bottom...

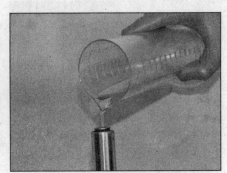

8.3b ...and pour in the new fork oil

8.5a Use an open-ended spanner on the top bolt flats

8.5b Move the outer tube down to expose the spring

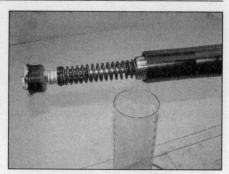

8.6 Draining the fork oil

bolt from the outer tube **(see illustrations)**. If you can't hold the fork tight enough by hand clamp it back into the yokes whilst it is slackened. Keep downwards pressure on the

top bolt as the last threads are released as it will be under tension from the spring.
6 Drain the old fork oil into a measuring vessel so that its volume can be recorded **(see**

illustration). Pump the fork to assist draining and leave it for a minute or two to drain fully.
7 Note down the amount of oil drained (200 ml on the fork shown), then measure out the same quantity of new fork oil (5W or 10W fork oil is recommended) **(see illustration)**.
8 Slowly pour the new oil into the fork, letting it run down the coils of the spring **(see illustration)**. Stop every now and then to gently pump the fork so that the new oil doesn't spill over the sides **(see illustration)**.
9 Draw the outer tube back up to the top bolt and thread the top bolt into the tube **(see illustration 8.5a)**. Repeat the procedure on the other fork and put in the same amount of oil. Install the forks (see Section 7).

USD (upside-down) adjustable forks

10 With the fork fully extended unscrew the top bolt from the outer tube **(see illustration)**. Keep downwards pressure on the top bolt as the last threads are released as it will be under tension from the spring. Drain the old fork oil into a measuring vessel **(see illustration)**.
11 Slide the outer tube down over the inner tube to give full access to the top bolt and spring. Counterhold the nut under the top bolt and unscrew the top bolt via its hex section **(see illustration)**. Fully unscrew the top bolt from the damper rod **(see illustration)**. Keep the thick rubber damper with the top bolt and take note of which way round it is fitted.
12 Lift out the upper spring followed by the damping adjustment rod **(see illustrations)**;

8.7 Measure out the exact quantity of new fork oil...

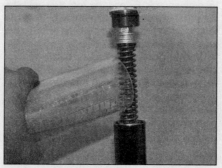

8.8a ...and pour it slowly into the fork...

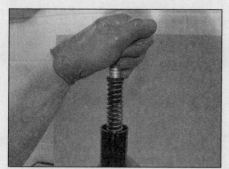

8.8b ...pumping the fork gently to distribute it

8.10a Thread the top bolt out...

8.10b ...and drain the oil

8.11a Hold the nut using the lower spanner and unscrew the top bolt via its hex section

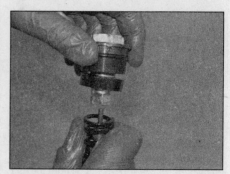

8.11b Detach the top bolt from the damper rod

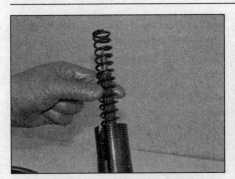

8.12a Remove the upper fork spring

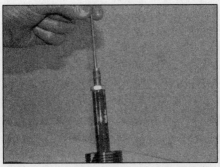

8.12b Remove the adjuster rod from the damper rod

8.12c Drain out the remaining oil from the damper assembly

the damping valve and its spring may well follow it **(see illustration 8.14a)**. Drain out the remaining oil **(see illustration)** into the measuring vessel and remove the spring seat and lower spring **(see illustrations 8.14b and c)**.

13 Note the amount of oil drained (we measured 300 ml from the fork shown) and measure out the same quantity of new fork oil (5W to 10W fork oil is recommended). Extend the damper assembly, then add the new oil slowly to the fork **(see illustration)**. Pump the damper assembly to distribute the oil **(see illustration)**.

14 Insert the damping valve with its spring **(see illustration)**, followed by the adjuster rod **(see illustration 8.12b)**. Install the lower spring over the damper assembly and into the fork tube **(see illustration)**. Fit the spring seat **(see illustration)** and the upper spring **(see illustration 8.12a)**.

15 Check that the damper is in place on the top bolt and is the correct way round, then thread it onto the threaded end of the damper rod **(see illustrations)**. Hold the locknut

8.13a Pour in the fresh fork oil

8.13b Pump the damper to distribute the oil

through the coils of the spring and tighten the top bolt down to meet the locknut **(see illustration)**.

16 Extend the fork, and thread the top bolt

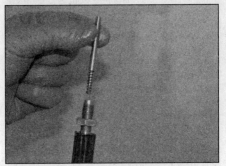

8.14a Reinsert the valve and spring into the damper rod before fitting the adjuster rod

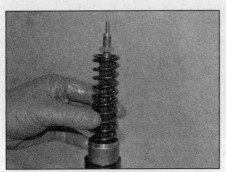

8.14b Refit the lower spring...

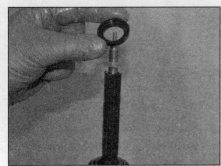

8.14c ...and the seat for the upper spring

8.15a Damper (arrowed) is fitted with its open side away from the top bolt

8.15b Thread the top bolt onto the damper rod...

8.15c ...holding the nut whilst the top bolt is tightened down against it

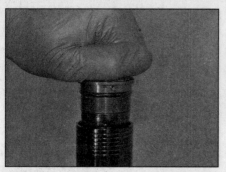

8.16 Thread the top bolt into the outer tube

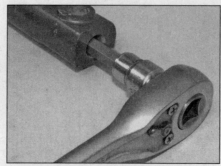

9.3a Slacken the damper rod bolt

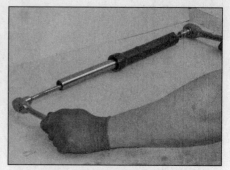

9.3b If required, locate a tool in the recessed head of the damper rod and slacken the bolt

fully into the outer tube **(see illustration)**. Final tightening of the top bolt can be left until the fork is back in the yokes and firmly clamped in place.

17 Repeat the procedure on the other fork and put in the same amount of oil. Install the forks in the yokes.

18 On models with an air bleed screw set in the top bolts **(see illustration 13.1)**, release any air from the forks.

9 Fork oil seal change

Note: *If the bike has accident damage and bent forks you might consider fitting an entire new front end – kits are available. New oil*

seals can be obtained but check first about the availability of other spare parts.

1 Always dismantle the fork legs separately to avoid interchanging parts and thus causing an accelerated rate of wear. Store all components in separate, clearly marked containers.

Conventional (right way up) forks

Disassembly

2 Remove the forks (see Section 7) and drain the fork oil (see Section 8).
3 Lay the fork flat on the bench. Hold the fork down and remove the damper rod bolt in the base of the fork **(see illustration)**. If the damper rod rotates inside the fork whilst attempting to unscrew the bolt, refit the spring and top bolt then compress the fork so that the spring exerts pressure on the rod whilst

the bolt is unscrewed. If the damper rod bolt is tight even this method may not work, in which case try locating a tool in the recessed head of the damper rod to stop it turning; on the fork shown a 12mm length of hex bar located exactly **(see illustration)**.
4 Use a flat-bladed screwdriver to ease the dust seal out of the outer tube **(see illustration)**.
5 Pull the inner and outer tubes apart and take the damper rod out of the outer tube **(see illustrations)**.
6 Prise the oil seal retaining clip out of its groove **(see illustration)**, then prise out the oil seal **(see illustration)**.

Inspection

7 Clean up the fork components. If you're stripping the forks to renew the seal check whether pitting or chipping of the plated inner tubes has ripped the lips of the seal.
8 If the bike has sustained front end damage you can check whether the inner tubes are bent by rotating them in vee-blocks with a dial gauge to measure runout, or simply by rotating them across a perfectly flat surface.
9 The spring should be in one-piece and not cracked or otherwise damaged. Fork springs will sag in use but the only means of checking this is to compare the spring with a new one.

Reassembly

10 Clean up the fork components and fit a new oil seal, making sure it's fitted the correct way up. Select a socket which will just fit inside the seal housing and tap the seal into place until the groove for its retaining clip is

9.4 Removing the dust seal

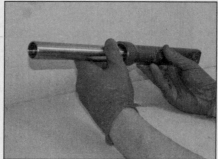

9.5a Fork tubes will now pull apart...

9.5b ...and the damper rod can be removed

9.6a The seal retaining clip is shaped to allow a removal tool to be inserted

9.6b A large flat-bladed screwdriver is ideal for removing the oil seal

9.10 Use of a socket ensures the new seal is driven in squarely

9.11 Fit the seal retaining clip into its groove

9.12a Fit a 12 mm hex bit into the damper rod head...

9.12b ...pass the components down through the inner tube...

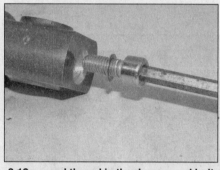

9.12c ...and thread in the damper rod bolt with its sealing washer

9.13 Dust seal will seat with finger pressure

exposed **(see illustration)**. Smear the lips of the new seal with fork oil.

HAYNES HiNT *Place the old oil seal on top of the new one to protect it when driving the seal into place.*

11   Once the seal is correctly seated, fit the retaining clip, making sure it is correctly located in its groove **(see illustration)**.
12   Slide the inner tube into the outer tube **(see illustration 9.5a)**. If you have access to a section of 12mm (across flats) bar such as an Allen key bit, fit this into the head of the damper rod and attached a socket and extension to the other end. Pass the assembly down the inner tube and thread the damper rod bolt into the end of the outer tube **(see illustrations)**. Hold the socket extension whilst the bolt is tightened.

13   Fit the dust seal back down over the inner tube and press it into the top of the outer tube **(see illustration)**.
14   Refer to Section 8and fill the fork with the recorded amount of oil and finish reassembly, then install the fork.
15   If the damper rod bolt requires tightening, place the fork upside down on the floor, using a rag to protect it, then have an assistant compress the fork so that maximum spring pressure is placed on the damper rod head while tightening the bolt.

USD (upside-down) forks

Note: *This procedure describes oil seal renewal on a fork fitted with rebound damping and compression damping adjustment. If working on a USD fork without adjustment, the fork damper bolt in the base of the fork leg will require removal in order to separate the inner and outer tubes.*

Disassembly

16   Remove the fork (see Section 7) and drain the fork oil (see Section 8). This procedure involves removal of the fork top bolt and springs, and additional on adjustable forks, also the damping adjustment components.
17   Extend the fork fully and prise the dust seal from the bottom of the outer tube, then use circlip pliers to free the seal retaining circlip from its groove in the outer tube **(see illustrations)**.
18   To separate the inner and outer tubes it is necessary to displace the bush and oil seal from the top of the outer tube. The bush on the inner tube will not pass through the bush set in the outer tube, and this can be used to good effect. Grasp the inner tube in one hand and the outer tube in the other and compress them slightly, then pull them apart so that one bush strikes the other **(see illustration)**.

9.17a Prise out the dust seal using a flat-bladed screwdriver

9.17b Circlip pliers with angled ends are best for removing the circlip

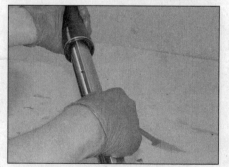

9.18a To separate the tubes pull them apart firmly several times...

9.18b ...the slide-hammer effect will displace the oil seal and bush from the outer tube

9.19a Carefully lever the bush ends apart to expand it

9.19b Slide off the outer tube bush...

9.19c ...the washer...

9.19d ...the oil seal...

9.19e ...the circlip...

Repeat this operation until the bush and oil seal are freed from the outer tube **(see illustration)**.

19 Prise the bush apart just enough for it to be slid off the end of the inner tube, then remove the other bush, washer, oil seal, circlip and dust seal **(see illustrations)**. Take note of which way around these components are fitted as a guide to reassembly.

Inspection

20 Clean up the fork components. If you're stripping the forks to renew the seal check whether pitting or chipping of the plated inner tubes has ripped the lips of the seal.

21 Examine the grey Teflon working surfaces of the two bushes (i.e. the outer surface of the bush from the inner tube and the inner surface of the bush from the outer tube). Bushes are usually considered worn if this coating has been worn away to reveal the copper inner surface over more than 75% of the surface area, or if the bushes are scored or badly scuffed **(see illustration)**.

22 Bent, worn or damaged fork tubes or a failed damper cartridge require complete renewal of the forks. Never attempt to straighten bent forks.

23 Check the springs for cracks and other damage. No wear length figures are available with which to check the springs for sagging.

Reassembly

24 Obtain a set of new fork seals. Sets usually come with new dust seals **(see illustration)**. If you cannot obtain seals from your usual parts supplier note that oil seals can be obtained from a seal supplier – all you need to supply are the size and type codes as marked on the top surface of the old seal.

25 Wrap a single layer of insulating tape over the step at the end of the inner tube and smear the lips of the dust seal and oil seal with fork oil; these measures will help prevent damage to the seal lips during assembly. Taking note of their correct orientation, install the new dust seal, circlip, new oil seal, washer and bush

9.19f ...and the dust seal

9.21 Check the working surfaces (arrowed) of each bush for wear

9.24 New oil seal and dust seal for the remaining fork leg

9.25 Components installed on the inner tube ready for reassembly. Note the tape (arrowed)

9.27a Start the oil seal into its housing with finger pressure

over the inner tube (see illustration). Remove the tape from the inner tube.

26 Fit the bush back into its groove in the inner tube (see illustration 9.19a) and apply fork oil to its surface. Insert the inner tube into the outer tube and slide the other bush down into its recess in the outer tube. The bush is an interference fit so will need to be driven into place. It is possible to use a punch to carefully tap the seal into place, but extreme care must be taken not to score the inner tube

surface and to keep the bush square to its housing at all times. A better method is to use a seal driver (see illustration 9.27c) to install the bush. Note that you'll hear when the bush has seated in its housing.

27 Fit the washer, followed by the oil seal (see illustration). Start the seal off by pressing it in by hand, then use either a punch or preferably the seal driver described above to drive it into place (see illustrations). Note that the old oil seal cut in two halves is a good

interface between the new seal and the driver as it will protect the surface of the new seal (see Tool Tip).

28 When the oil seal has seated and the retaining clip groove is exposed, use circlip pliers to fit the retaining clip (see illustration).

29 Press the dust seal into the top of the outer tube (see illustration).

30 Fill the fork with fresh oil and finish reassembly (see Section 8).

31 Install the fork (see Section 7).

9.27b Either tap the seal in with a punch...

9.27c ...or better still, use a seal driver

HAYNES HiNT

The oil seal was found to be an extremely tight fit on the fork shown. It will help to position the fork upright so that maximum effort is available when operating the seal driver. Tape the circlip and dust seal up against the wheel spindle mounting to prevent them interfering with the operation.

Cut the old oil seal in half and seat the halves on top of the new seal. Drive against the face of the two halves thus protecting the new seal below it. Pick the halves out with a small screwdriver once the job is done.

9.28 Check that the circlip locates fully into its groove

9.29 The dust seal should seat using finger pressure

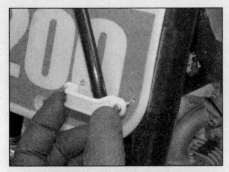

10.1a Unscrew any hose clamps

10.1b Remove the mounting screws...

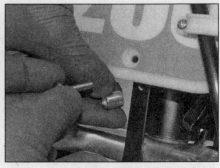

10.1c ...noting the location of any spacers

10.5a Remove the steering stem bolt (nut on some models)...

10.5b ...and move the whole unit back to rest on the fuel tank

10.6a Thread the adjuster nut off the steering stem...

10 Steering yokes and bearings

Removal

1 Remove the numberboard (see illustrations) and the front mudgard (see illustrations 2.6a and b).

2 Slacken the steering stem nut (or bolt) (see illustration 10.5a). Do not remove it at this stage.

3 Support the bike on a crate underneath the engine or on a rear paddock stand so that the front wheel is raised off the ground.

4 Remove the front wheel (see Chapter 6, Section 12) and front forks (see Section 7).

5 Remove the steering stem nut (or bolt) and lift the complete handlebar/top yoke assembly back off the frame headstock, resting it on some rag placed on the tank (see illustrations).

6 Using a C-spanner, slacken the steering adjuster nut and thread it completely off the steering stem whilst holding the lower yoke to prevent it dropping free (see illustration). Lift off the dust cover (on some models it may be fixed to the adjuster nut) and lower the stem out of the frame headstock (see illustrations).

Bearings – tapered roller type

7 The top bearing is simply lifted out of the headstock (see illustration).

8 The lower bearing is pressed onto the steering stem and requires some effort to remove it (see illustration). Removal will

10.6b ...followed by the dust cover...

10.7 Lift the top bearing out of the headstock

almost certainly damage the bearing so don't disturb it unless you are fitting new bearings.

9 Clean all old grease from the bearings and

10.6c ...and guide the stem and lower yoke out

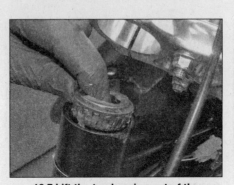

10.8 The lower bearing is a tight fit on the base of the stem

10.9 Outer races must be polished and free from dents (lower race shown)

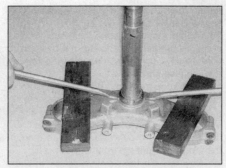

10.10 Work the bearing off the stem as shown

10.11a Driving the lower race...

10.11b ...and upper race out of the headstock

10.13a Remove the inner race...

10.13b ...then the bearing from the outer race in the top of the headstock

examine them and their outer races set in each end of the headstock **(see illustration)**. If the rollers are dented or loose in their cage or the outer races are scored, dented or obviously worn, renew the steering head bearings as a set.

10 Removal of the lower bearing from the stem will require either two large flat-bladed screwdrivers inserted between the yoke and bearing to work it evenly off the stem **(see illustration)**. To fit the new lower bearing, use a length of tubing which locates over the stem and bears against the top edge of the cage NOT THE ROLLERS to drive the bearing down into place.

11 Drive the outer races from the headstock using a drift passed down through the opposite end of the headstock. Work the drift

around the back of the race so that it leaves the headstock squarely **(see illustrations)**. Alternatively, remove the races using a slide-hammer type bearing extractor.

12 Press the new outer races into the headstock using a drawbolt arrangement (see *Tools and Workshop Tips* in Reference), or drive them in using a large diameter tubular drift (to do this the bike must be solidly supported as all the force needs to be transmitted to the race). Make sure that the drawbolt washer or drift (as applicable) bears only on the outer edge of the race and does not contact the working surface.

Bearings – caged ball type

13 The top bearing is simply lifted out of the headstock **(see illustrations)**.

14 The lower bearing can be lifted off the steering stem, but its inner race is pressed in place and requires some effort to remove it **(see illustrations)**. Only disturb the race if you are fitting new bearings and use the method shown in illustration 10.10.

15 Clean all old grease from the bearings and examine them and their outer races set in each end of the headstock**(see illustration)**. If the balls are dented or loose in their cage or the outer races are stored, dented or obviously worn, renew the steering head bearings as a set.

16 Refer to Steps 11 and 12 for removal of the old races and fitting the new ones.

Installation

17 Smear a liberal quantity of multi-purpose

10.14a Lift the lower bearing off the stem

10.14b Lower bearing inner race is pressed in place on the stem

10.15 Outer races must be polished and be free of dents (top race)

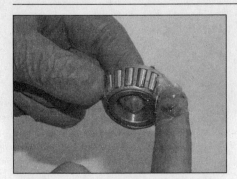

10.17 Apply fresh grease to the bearings

grease onto the bearing rollers/balls and the races (see illustration). With the lower bearing installed on the stem, pass the stem up through the headstock and hold it there whilst fitting the upper bearing (tapered-roller) or upper bearing and inner race (caged ball). Fit the dust cap, and thread the adjuster

nut on to hold all components in place (only secure it finger-tight at this stage).

18 Rotate the lower yoke from side to side and again tighten the adjuster nut by hand to take up any play yet still enable side-to-side rotation (see illustration).

19 Fit the top yoke and handlebar assembly back onto the stem and install the steering stem nut or bolt. Tighten it only lightly at this stage. Fit the forks back into the yokes and nip up their top mountings to secure them in the top yoke. Refit the front wheel.

20 Now that the forks and wheel are in place and the top and lower yokes aligned, the steering head bearing play can be properly adjusted. Grasp the forks at the bottom and attempt to push and pull them back and forwards, feeling for any looseness or play in the head bearings (see illustration). Also rotate the steering from side to side and check that the action is smooth and not notchy or tight.

21 To re-adjust the bearings, use a C-spanner in the slots of the adjuster nut to turn it (see

illustration). Only a small adjustment is likely to be necessary. Recheck for bearing play afterwards and check that the steering is able to move freely. When correctly set, tighten the steering stem nut or bolt (see illustration).

Caution: Take great care not to apply excessive pressure because this will cause premature failure of the bearings.

22 Tighten the fork clamp mountings and install all other components. Take the bike off the crate or stand and check the steering action before riding.

11 Rear shock absorber

⚠ *Warning: Do not attempt to disassemble the shock absorber – attempts could result in serious injury. No individual components are available for it.*

10.18 Tighten the adjuster nut to eliminate freeplay

10.20 Checking the steering head bearing freeplay

10.21a Use a slim C-spanner to access the adjuster nut

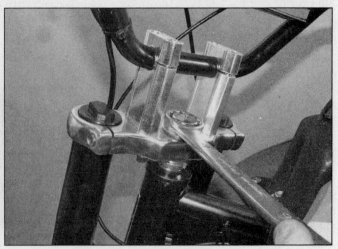

10.21b Tightening the steering stem nut (or bolt)

11.2 Dirt deflector is retained by bolt and tab (arrowed)

11.3a Through-bolt and flanged nut retain the shock at its lower…

11.3b …and upper mounting points

11.4a Check the shock for oil leakage from a failed damper seal, broken spring and bent rod

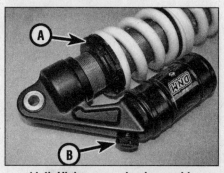

11.4b Higher spec shocks provide adjustment for spring pre-load (A), compression damping (B)…

11.4c …and rebound damping

1 Support the bike on a stand or crate so that the rear wheel is off the ground. Remove the bodywork to give access to the shock upper mounting (see Section 2). If the bike particularly dirty, give it a good wash around the shock and swingarm area.

2 If a dirt deflector is fitted, remove its bolt and position it out of the way of the lower mounting point **(see illustration)**.

3 Remove the shock lower mounting bolt and nut and allow the swingarm to pivot down under the weight of the rear wheel **(see illustration)**. Remove the upper mounting nut and bolt and withdraw the shock from the frame **(see illustration)**.

4 If the shock has obviously failed, simply fit a new one. Unless a high spec aftermarket shock has been fitted, rebuilds are not cost effective. The rear shock is one of the most

likely components to fail on a pit bike. Failure of the shock is likely to be blown damper unit seals which will be apparent through oil loss, a cracked or broken spring or a bent damper rod **(see illustrations)**.

5 Install the shock in a reverse of the removal procedure, tightening its mountings securely. If fitting a new shock with adjustment take some time to get the setting right for you (see Section 13).

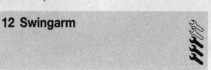

12 Swingarm

Removal

1 Support the bike on a crate or stand

so that the rear wheel is off the ground. If the bike particularly dirty, give it a good wash around the shock and swingarm area.

2 Unbolt the brake hose guides from the right-hand side of the swingarm **(see illustration)**.

3 Remove the rear wheel (see Chapter 6, Section 13).

4 Where fitted, unbolt the chainguard **(see illustration)**.

5 Remove the nut from the rear shock lower mounting and withdraw the pivot bolt to separate the shock from the swingarm **(see illustration)**. On some models you may need to first detach the mud deflector **(see illustration 11.2)**.

6 Remove the nut from the end of the swingarm pivot bolt, support the arm

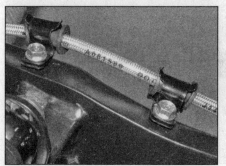

12.2 Unbolt the brake hose guides from the swingarm

12.4 Two bolts retain the chainguard on this model

12.5 Remove the nut and pivot bolt to free the shock from the swingarm

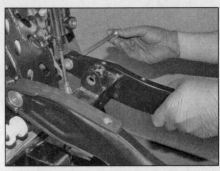

12.6 Withdrawing the swingarm pivot bolt

12.7a Chain guide bolts to underside of the left-hand arm

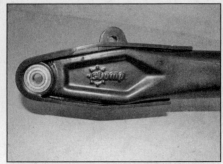

12.7b Chain slider will be secured around the left-hand pivot and can be moulded plastic, nylon strips or rubber composition

12.8a Typical swingarm

12.8b A-frame swingarm structure

12.9a Remove the spacer...

12.9b ...to access the bearing

12.9c Alternative bearing fitting

12.11a Align the swingarm with its mounting points...

12.11b ...insert the pivot bolt...

and withdraw the pivot bolt **(see illustration)**.

Inspection

7 Remove the chain guide, and the chain slider strip or rubber from the swingarm **(see illustrations)**. Give the swingarm a thorough clean to remove all dirt and chain lube. Also clean the lugs on the frame or separate bracket which the pivot bolt passes through.

8 Inspect the swingarm looking for cracks in the welded sections and dents or distortion of the steel or aluminium structure **(see illustrations)**.

9 Check the mounting point for the shock. There are no bearings here but the mounting should be solid and the pivot bolt hole not worn oval. The pivot bearings should be checked for smooth action and no sign of radial (up/down and front/back) or axial (side-to-side) play **(see illustrations)**. Check the swingarm pivot bolt is straight by rolling it on a flat surface (first wipe off all old grease and remove any corrosion using wire wool); fit a new pivot bolt and nut if necessary.

Installation

10 Install the chain slider, chain guide etc and all fittings to the swingarm. If the chain slider is worn through, fit a new one.

11 Offer up the swingarm and slide the pivot bolt into place having smeared its surface with grease **(see illustrations)**.

12.12 ...and thread the nut onto its end

12.13 Reconnect the shock

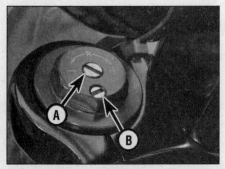

13.1 Damping adjustment (A) and air bleed screw (B)

12 Thread the nut on the other end of the pivot bolt and tighten it securely **(see illustration)**. Check that the swingarm pivots smoothly without binding.
13 Reconnect the shock lower mounting and tighten its bolt/nut securely **(see illustration)**.
14 Install all other components in a reverse of the removal procedure. Check chain adjustment (Chapter 1 Section 2) afterwards.

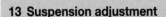

13 Suspension adjustment

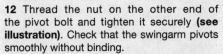
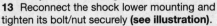

13.3 Markings on the bottom of the fork indicate direction of turning for compression damping adjustment

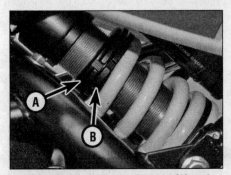

13.5a Preload adjuster locking (A) and adjuster ring (B) – remove bodywork for full access when adjusting

Front forks

Note: *Where adjusters are fitted, make sure you set them to the same position on each fork otherwise uneven damping will result.*
1 Rebound damping is adjusted via the screw in the centre of the fork top bolts **(see illustration)**. Turn the screw clockwise to increase damping and anti-clockwise to reduce it.
2 The screw to the side of the damping adjuster is an air bleed screw. It is there to periodically release any build up of pressure inside the fork, which could lead to seal failure. From time to time, slacken the bleed screw and check for the hiss of air as you do. Tighten the screw afterwards.
3 Forks may also be fitted with compression damping adjustment. In the example shown the adjuster screw is set in the base of the fork **(see illustration)**.

Rear shock

4 Basic shocks will have a cam type preload adjuster **(see illustration)**. Ensure the setting locates in the detent, not on the top of the cam.

13.5b Rebound damping adjuster

13.4 Use a C-spanner to rotate the preload collar

5 Higher spec shocks have a preload adjuster which consists of a lockring and adjuster ring. Using a slim C-spanner slacken off the lockring and rotate the adjuster ring to adjust preload **(see illustration)**. Where fitted, a rebound damping adjuster is set in the base of the shock and a compression damping adjuster in the remote reservoir **(see illustrations)**.
6 There are no standard adjustment positions.

13.5c Compression damping adjuster

Chapter 6
Brakes, wheels, tyres and chain

Contents

Degrees of difficulty

Easy, suitable for novice with little experience	**Fairly easy,** suitable for beginner with some experience	**Fairly difficult,** suitable for competent DIY mechanic	**Difficult,** suitable for experienced DIY mechanic	**Very difficult,** suitable for expert DIY or professional

---

1 General Information

1 Braking is by hydraulic disc on most models, with a drum brake at the front (or front and rear) on lower end pit bikes. Disc brake calipers are either single or two-piston types.
2 Wheels are wire spoked and steel rimmed on most production models, with alloy rimmed wheels on high end models and as aftermarket fitment. Wheel diameter is 10 inch or 12 inch on most bikes, with options of 14 inch front wheels on certain models. Tyres are tubed MX style for off-road use only.

2 Front brake pads

⚠ *Warning: The dust created by the brake system may be harmful to your health. Never blow it out with compressed air and don't inhale any of it. An approved filtering mask should be worn when working on the brakes.*
Note: *Do not operate the brake lever while the caliper is off the disc.*

Single piston caliper

1 Remove the two caliper mounting bolts and slide the caliper off the disc **(see illustration).** Slide the bracket and caliper apart and remove the two pads **(see illustration).**
2 Brush road dirt off the pads and check the depth of friction material **(see illustration).** When new the pads measure 3 mm so if yours have worn down to 1 mm or less renew them. Also renew them if they are badly scored (in which case check the disc too) or contaminated with hydraulic fluid from a leaking caliper seal.
3 If the pads are in good condition clean them carefully, using a fine wire brush that is completely free of oil and grease to remove all traces of road dirt and corrosion. Using a pointed instrument, dig out any embedded particles of grit.

2.1a Unscrew the two bolts and slide the caliper off the disc

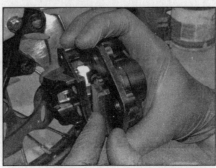

2.1b Slide the caliper and bracket apart and remove the pads

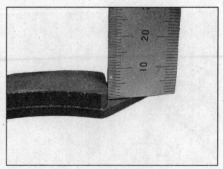

2.2 Measure the friction material on both pads

2.4 Press the piston in as described to make clearance for new pads

2.6a Pull the bracket out of the caliper so you can check the slider pins...

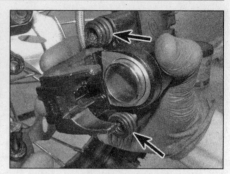

2.6b ...and rubber boots (arrowed)

4 Remove the pad spring from the caliper if required, noting which way round it fits (see illustration 2.7). Clean around the exposed section of the piston to remove any dirt or debris that could cause the seals to be damaged. If new pads are being fitted, now push the piston back into the caliper to create room for them; if the old pads are still serviceable push the piston in a little way (see illustration). To push the piston back use finger pressure or a piece of wood or metal as leverage, or place the old pads back in the caliper and use a metal bar or a screwdriver inserted between them (do not use this method if the pads are being re-used). It may be necessary to remove the master cylinder reservoir cover, plate and diaphragm and siphon out some fluid (see Chapter 1 Section 17). If the piston is difficult to push back, remove the bleed valve cap, then attach a length of clear hose to the bleed valve and place the open end suitable container, then open the valve and try again (see Section 8). Take great care not to draw any air into the system. If in doubt, bleed the brake afterwards.

5 If the piston is seized, apply the brake lever and check whether the piston moves at all. If it moves out but can't be pushed back in the chances are there is some hidden corrosion stopping it. If it doesn't move at all fit a new caliper (see Section 4).

6 Separate the caliper and bracket (see illustration). Clean off all traces of corrosion and hardened grease from the slider pins on the bracket and the rubber boots in the caliper. Replace the boots with new ones if they are damaged, deformed or deteriorated (see illustration). Smear silicone grease over the slider pins and insert the bracket into the caliper.

7 Clean the pad spring and fit it into the caliper, making sure it locates correctly (see illustration).

8 Lightly smear the back of the pad backing material with copper-based grease, making sure that none gets on the friction material.

9 Fit the pads into the caliper making sure the tangs on the piston-side pad locate correctly, and that the holes in the larger pad locate over the bracket posts (see illustrations). Check that there's enough space between the pads to fit over the disc, then slide the caliper over the disc, making sure the pads locate correctly on each side (see illustration). Clean the threads of the caliper bolts and apply fresh thread locking compound, then tighten them.

10 Pump the brake lever until the pads contact the disc. Check the level of fluid in the reservoir and top-up if necessary (see Chapter 1, Section 17).

11 Test the brake before riding.

Two piston front caliper

12 Slacken the two pad pins, then remove the two mounting bolts and slide the caliper

2.7 Fit the pad spring

2.9a Fit the large (inner) pad over the posts...

2.9b ...and the smaller (outer) pad against the piston

2.9c Check there's space for the disc to fit between the pads...

2.9d ...and slide the caliper into place

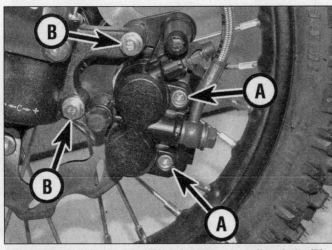

2.12a Slacken the pad pins (A) and remove the caliper bolts (B)

2.12b Slide the caliper off the disc

off the disc (see illustrations). Now unscrew the pad pins and withdraw the pads from the caliper.

13 Brush road dirt off the pads and check them for wear (see illustration). If they are worn down to the base of the grooves or if there's less than 1 mm material remaining, renew them.

14 Slide the caliper bracket out of the caliper. Clean old hardened grease off the pins and check the rubber boots set in the caliper. Smear silicone grease over the slider pins before inserting the bracket back into the caliper (see illustration). Make sure the pad spring is fixed inside the caliper (see illustration).

15 Clean around the exposed section of each piston to remove any dirt or debris that could cause the seals to be damaged. If new pads are being fitted, now push the pistons back into the caliper to create room for them; if the old pads are still serviceable push the pistons in a little way (see illustration). To push the pistons back use finger pressure or a piece

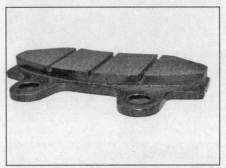

2.13 Check the depth of friction material remaining

2.14a Smear silicone grease over the slider pins before inserting the bracket into the caliper

of wood or metal as leverage, or place the old pads back in the caliper and use a metal bar or a screwdriver inserted between them (do not use this method if the pads are being re-used). It may be necessary to remove the master cylinder reservoir cover, plate and diaphragm and siphon out some fluid. If the

pistons are difficult to push back, remove the bleed valve cap, then attach a length of clear hose to the bleed valve and place the open end suitable container, then open the valve and try again (see Section 8). Take great care not to draw any air into the system. If in doubt, bleed the brake afterwards.

2.14b Pad spring in place in the caliper

2.15 Push the pistons back into their bores

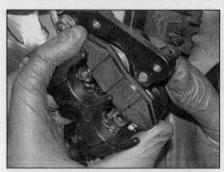

2.16a Locate the outer pad against the piston…

2.16b …and the inner pad against the bracket

2.16c Secure the pads with the pins

2.17 Check there's space between the pads then slide the caliper over the disc

3.2 The caliper fits over slider pins on the bracket

16 Fit the outer pad against the piston and the inner pad against the bracket so that their friction side will be against the disc **(see illustrations)**. Fit the two pad pins making sure the pins pass through the holes in each pad **(see illustration)**.

17 Fit the caliper back over the disc **(see illustration)**. Clean old locking compound off the threads of the caliper mounting bolts, then apply a drop of non-permanent locking compound to each bolt and thread them into place. Tighten the bolts. Make sure that the pad pins are tight.

18 Pump the brake lever until the pads contact the disc. Check the level of fluid in the reservoir and top-up if necessary (see Chapter 1, Section 17).

19 Test the brake before riding.

3   Rear brake pads

⚠ *Warning: The dust created by the brake system may be harmful to your health. Never blow it out with compressed air and don't inhale any of it. An approved filtering mask should be worn when working on the brakes.*

Note: *The photos which accompany this section show a single piston rear caliper. A two-piston type (as described in Section 2) may be fitted at the rear on certain models.*

1 Remove the rear wheel (see Section 13).

Note: *Do not operate the brake pedal while the pads are out.*

2 Slide the caliper off the mounting bracket **(see illustration)**.

3 Unscrew the two pad pins to free the pads from the caliper **(see illustration)**. Brush road dirt off the pads and check the depth of the friction material. If the material has worn down to the base of the groove or if there's less than 1 mm material remaining, renew the pads.

4 Remove the pad spring from the caliper if required, noting which way round it fits **(see illustration)**. Clean around the exposed section of the piston to remove any dirt or debris that could cause the seals to be damaged. If new pads are being fitted, now push the piston back into the caliper to create room for them **(see illustration)**; if the old pads are still serviceable push the piston in a little way. To push the piston back use finger pressure or a piece of wood or metal as leverage, or place the old pads back in the caliper and use a metal bar or a screwdriver inserted between them (do not use this method if the pads are being re-used). It may be necessary to remove the master cylinder reservoir cover, plate and diaphragm and siphon out some fluid. If the piston is difficult to push back, remove the bleed valve cap, then attach a length of clear hose to the bleed valve and place the open end suitable container, then open the valve and try again (see Section 8). Take great care not to draw any air into the system. If in doubt, bleed the brake afterwards.

5 If the piston is seized, apply the brake pedal and check whether the piston moves at all. If

3.3 Two pins retain the pads (arrowed)

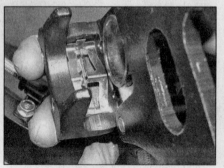

3.4a Pad spring locates in the caliper recess

3.4b Piston pushed back into the caliper bore

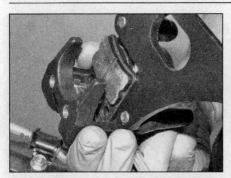

3.7a Fit the outer pad against the piston...

3.7b ...then fit the inner pad and install the two pad pins

it moves out but can't be pushed back in the chances are there is some hidden corrosion stopping it. If it doesn't move at all fit a new caliper (see Section 5).

6 Clean off all traces of corrosion and hardened grease from the slider pins on the bracket and the rubber boots in the caliper. The boots should be free from splits otherwise road dirt will enter and affect caliper movement **(see illustration 3.2)**.

7 Clean the pad spring and fit it into the caliper, making sure it locates correctly. Fit the pads into the caliper so that the friction material will be facing the disc when installed **(see illustrations)**. Apply a smear of silicone grease to the pad pins, insert the pins making sure they pass through the pad holes, and then tighten them.

8 Smear silicone grease over the slider pins

on the bracket, then insert the caliper over the pins **(see illustration 3.2)**.

9 Install the rear wheel (see Section 13). Operate the brake pedal to bring the pads back into contact with the disc. Check the fluid level in the rear brake master cylinder (see Chapter 1, Section 17).

10 Test the brake before riding the motorcycle.

4 Front brake caliper and master cylinder

Removal

Note: *Parts and seals are not available for the caliper and master cylinder, although you can*

fit a new hose and renew the master cylinder or caliper individually, or obtain the complete front brake system.

Caution: Do not operate the brake lever while the caliper is off the disc.

1 If you're going to fit a new system, it's a good idea to drain the brake fluid before disposal (see Section 8).

2 Free the brake hose from its guides on the numberboard and fork leg **(see illustrations)**.

3 Unbolt the caliper from the fork leg and slide it off the disc **(see illustration)**. Unbolt the master cylinder clamp from the handlebar and remove the entire assembly **(see illustration)**.

4 When ordering a new front brake assembly make sure it is suitable for your model. In addition, provide the supplier with disc diameter, distance between mounting holes for the caliper and whether the caliper is mounted on the left or right side fork leg. Consider also fitting a new disc.

Installation

5 If fitting a complete front brake system, check for plastic spacers between the brake pads and in the lever pivot – they are there to prevent operation of the brake whilst off the bike. Remove any found **(see illustration)**.

6 Fit the master cylinder to the handlebar, align it so that the lever is in the desired position, then tighten the clamp bolts **(see illustration)**. Note that the gap between the clamp and handlebar is intentional and should be at the bottom, i.e. tighten the top bolt fully then the bottom bolt.

4.2a Hose guides on the numberboard...

4.2b ...and fork leg

4.3a Unbolt the caliper from the fork leg...

4.3b ...and the master cylinder from the handlebar

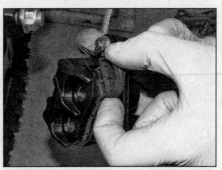

4.5 Plastic spacers are sometimes fitted between the pads when the parts are in transit

4.6 Note the UP mark on the master cylinder clamp

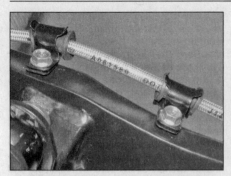

5.3 Unbolt the hose guides from the swingarm

5.4 Remove the split pin and push the clevis pin out to free the rod and pedal

5.5 Master cylinder mounting bolts (arrowed)

7 Check that there is sufficient space between the pads for the disc then slide the caliper into place. Fit the two mounting bolts having applied a drop of thread-locking compound to their threads, and tighten them. Secure the brake hose with the clamp on the numberboard and the clamp on the fork leg.

8 Note that it's best to let the fluid in the system settle for a few hours and enable any bubbles to find their way to the top of the master cylinder. Remove the cover from the master cylinder and check the fluid level. Top up if necessary with new DOT 4 brake fluid.

9 Check brake action and efficiency. If the brake lever feels spongy there will be air in the system, in which case bleed the brake (see Section 8). Check that the hydraulic hose banjo bolts are tight and that there's no sign of fluid leakage from any part of the brake.

10 Check the brake works correctly before riding the bike.

5	Rear brake caliper and master cylinder

Removal

Note: *Parts and seals are not available for the caliper and master cylinder, although you can fit a new hose, caliper and master cylinder. Note that parts suppliers can supply the entire caliper, hose and master cylinder at*

low cost although it's important to match hose length, pushrod length, disc diameter and the distance (centre-to-centre) between the master cylinder mounting holes to ensure the new assembly will fit. Additionally if the caliper bracket is mounted on the wheel axle you'll need to supply the axle diameter as well.
Caution: Do not operate the brake lever while the caliper is off the disc.

1 If you're going to fit a new system, it's a good idea to drain the brake fluid before disposal (see Section 8).

2 Remove the rear wheel to free the brake caliper and its bracket (see Section 13).

3 Free the brake hose from its guides along the swingarm **(see illustration)**.

4 Disconnect the brake pedal from the master cylinder pushrod. Straighten the ends of the split pin then slide it out of the hole in the clevis pin and pull the clevis pin out to free the pushrod from the pedal **(see illustration)**.

5 Remove the two bolts which retain the master cylinder to the frame **(see illustration)**, then lift the entire rear brake assembly off the bike.

Installation

6 If fitting a complete rear brake system, check for a plastic spacer between the brake pads – there to prevent operation of the brake whilst off the bike. Remove any found.

7 Before fitting the new master cylinder, adjust the length of the pushrod to match that the old part – doing this will give you the

same pedal height. To adjust, slacken the locknut and turn the end of the rod to change its length; tighten the locknut against the end piece to lock the position **(see illustration)**. Fit the master cylinder to the frame and align the pushrod end each side of the brake pedal. Insert the clevis pin through the joint **(see illustration)** and secure the pin with a new split pin **(see illustration)**, bending its ends securely **(see illustration 5.4)**.

8 Check that the brake pads are securely fitted inside the caliper and that the pad pins are tight. Also check that the caliper is able to slide on its bracket pins. Refit the rear wheel, caliper bracket and caliper (see Section 13).

9 Secure the brake hose through its guides on the swingarm and make sure the hose is routed clear of the wheel and suspension.

10 Note that it's best to let the fluid in the system settle for a few hours and enable any bubbles to find their way to the top of the master cylinder. Look through the window in the master cyinder to check the fluid level. Top up if necessary with new DOT 4 brake fluid by removing the cap and diaphragm.

11 Check brake action and efficiency. If the brake pedal feels spongy there will be air in the system, in which case bleed the brake (see Section 8). Check that the hydraulic hose banjo bolts are tight and that there's no sign of fluid leakage from any part of the brake.

12 Check that the brake works before riding the bike.

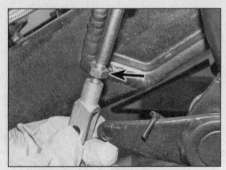

5.7a Pushrod length is adjusted by turning the end piece. Tighten the locknut (arrowed) afterwards

5.7b Clevis pin holds the pushrod end and brake pedal together

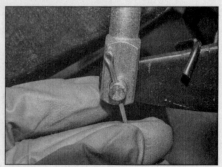

5.7c Secure the clevis pin with a new split pin

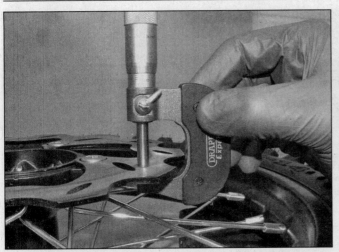

6.2 Ideally use a micrometer to measure disc thickness

6.6 Brake disc is retained to the hub by four bolts

6 Brake disc

Check

1 Inspect the surface of the disc for score marks and other damage. Light scratches are normal after use and won't affect brake operation, but deep grooves and heavy score marks will reduce braking efficiency and accelerate pad wear. If a disc is badly grooved fit a new one and also fit new brake pads.

2 Check for wear of the disc in the middle of the pad contact area **(see illustration)** – use your fingernail to feel for deep ridges or grooves.

3 Make sure you obtain the correct replacement parts; the disc diameter, thickness and mounting hole positions are crucial for its fitting. Also try to obtain new disc bolts.

4 The disc can warp under a lot of heavy braking, and it can also bend if the bike falls against it. It's sometimes possible to feel a warped disc as pulsing through the brake lever, but if in doubt you can measure disc runout with a dial gauge. Position the bike on an auxiliary stand so the wheel is off the ground. Mount a dial gauge to the fork leg (front) or swingarm (rear), with the gauge plunger touching the surface of the disc about 10 mm from its outer edge. Rotate the wheel and note the amount of runout shown on the gauge. Generally if there's more than 0.5 mm runout the disc should be renew although check first that it's not due to worn wheel bearings.

Fitting a new disc

5 Remove the wheel (see Section 13).

6 Slacken the four disc bolts and remove the old disc **(see illustration)**.

7 Make sure the disc mounting surfaces of the wheel flange are completely clean and free of corrosion – any irregularity here will not allow the disc to seat fully. Install the disc making sure it's the correct way round (some discs have a direction of rotation arrow). Apply a drop of non-permanent thread locking compound to the bolt threads, then thread them into place. Tighten the bolts evenly and a little at a time in a criss-cross pattern to avoid distorting the disc.

8 Install the wheel.

9 Operate the brake lever/pedal until the pads contact the disc. Check the level of fluid in the reservoir and top-up if necessary (see Chapter 1, Section 17).

10 Test the brake before riding the bike. Note that the new pads and disc will need to bed in before they're fully efficient.

7 Brake hoses and fittings

1 Drain all old brake fluid from the system (see Section 8).

2 The brake hoses have banjo fittings on each end. Cover the surrounding area with plenty of rags and unscrew the banjo bolt at each end of the hose, noting the alignment of the fitting with the master cylinder or brake caliper **(see illustrations)**. Free the hose from its guides and remove it, noting its routing.

3 Position the new hose, making sure it isn't twisted or otherwise strained, and ensure that it is correctly routed through any clips or guides and is clear of all moving components.

4 Check that the fittings align correctly, then fit the banjo bolts, using a new sealing washer on each side of each fitting.

5 When ordering a new hoses, specify the length and the banjo union size (10 mm is common).

6 Refill the system with new DOT 4 brake fluid (see Chapter 1, Section 17) and bleed the air from it (see Section 8).

7 Check the operation of the brakes before riding the bike.

8 Brake system bleeding and fluid change

Bleeding principles

1 Bleeding a brake is the process of removing aerated brake fluid from the master

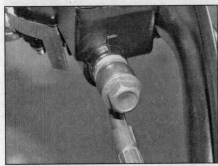

7.2a Take note of the banjo union's fitted angle...

7.2b ...before disturbing it

8.3a Undo the screws...

8.3b ...and remove the cover and diaphragm

8.4a Fit the ring spanner and hose to the bleed valve

8.4b One-man bleeding kit connected to front caliper

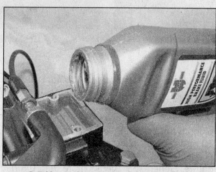

8.5 Keep the reservoir topped up

cylinder, the hose and the caliper. Bleeding is necessary whenever a brake system hydraulic component is renewed or when there is a spongy feel to the lever or pedal and it travels all the way to its stop, and where braking force is less than it should be.

2 To bleed the brakes using the conventional method, you will need some new DOT 4 brake fluid, a length of clear flexible hose, a small container partially filled with clean brake fluid, some rags, and a spanner to fit the brake caliper bleed valve. Bleeding kits that include the hose, a one-way valve and a container are available relatively cheaply from a good auto store, and simplify the task.

Caution: Brake fluid attacks painted finishes and some plastics – to prevent *damage from spilled fluid, always cover paintwork when working on the braking system, and clean up any spills immediately using brake cleaner.*

Bleeding the front brake system

3 Turn the handlebars so the brake fluid reservoir is level. Remove the reservoir cover and diaphragm **(see illustrations)**. Slowly pump the brake lever a few times to dislodge any air bubbles from the holes in the bottom of the reservoir.

4 Pull the dust cap off the bleed valve on the caliper. If using a ring spanner (which is preferable to an open-ended one) fit it onto

the valve **(see illustration)**. Attach one end of the bleed hose to the bleed valve and, if not using a kit, submerge the other end in the clean brake fluid in the container **(see illustration)**.

5 Check the fluid level in the reservoir – keep it topped up and do not allow the level to drop below the bottom of the window during the procedure **(see illustration)**.

6 Slowly pump the brake lever three or four times, then hold it in and open the bleed valve a quarter turn. When the valve is opened, brake fluid will flow out into the clear tubing, and the lever will move toward the handlebar. Tighten the bleed valve, then release the brake lever gradually.

7 If there is air in the system there will be air bubbles visible in the brake fluid, but not necessarily on the first pump. Repeat the process until no air bubbles have been seen for a few pumps, and the lever is firm when applied, topping the reservoir up when necessary.

8 When the system has been successfully bled there should be a good and progressively firm feel as the lever is applied, and the lever should not be able to travel all the way back to the handlebar.

9 On completion remove the equipment and make sure the bleed valve is tight (but do not overtighten it as the threads in the caliper are easily stripped), then fit the dust cap. Top-up the reservoir to the top of the inspection window, then fit the diaphragm and cover. Check that there are no fluid leaks from the system and check the operation of the brake before riding the bike.

Bleeding the rear brake system

10 Undo the screws and remove the reservoir cover and diaphragm **(see illustrations)**.

11 Slowly pump the brake pedal a few times to dislodge any air bubbles from the holes in the bottom of the reservoir.

12 Pull the dust cap off the bleed valve on the caliper. If using a ring spanner (which is preferable to an open-ended one) fit it onto the valve. Attach one end of the bleed hose to the bleed valve and, if not using a kit,

8.10a Undo the screws...

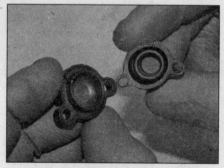

8.10b ...and remove the cover and diaphragm

8.12 One-man bleeding kit connected to rear caliper

8.13 Keep the reservoir topped up

submerge the other end in the clean brake fluid in the container **(see illustration)**.

13 Check the fluid level in the reservoir – keep it topped up and do not allow the level to drop below the bottom of the window during the procedure **(see illustration)**.

14 Slowly pump the brake pedal three or four times, then hold it down and open the bleed valve a quarter turn. When the valve is opened, brake fluid will flow out into the clear tubing, and the pedal will move down. Tighten the bleed valve, then release the brake pedal gradually.

15 If there is air in the system there will be air bubbles visible in the brake fluid, but not necessarily on the first pump. Repeat the process until no air bubbles have been seen for a few pumps, and the pedal is firm when applied, topping the reservoir up when necessary.

16 When the system has been successfully bled there should be a good and progressively firm feel as the pedal is applied.

17 On completion remove the equipment used and make sure the bleed valve is tight (but do not overtighten it as the threads in the caliper are easily stripped), then fit the dust cap. Top-up the reservoir to the top of the window, then fit the diaphragm and cover. Check that there are no fluid leaks from the system and check the operation of the brake before riding the bike.

Bleeding problems

18 If it is not possible to produce a firm feel to the lever or pedal look for any high point in the system in which a pocket of air may become trapped. Displace and move the hose so the bubble can be dislodged – tapping it may help. If necessary displace the master cylinder and/or the caliper, and free the brake hose from its guides and move the parts around to dislodge the air and encourage it towards the bleed valve – refer to the relevant Sections as required to displace components.

19 If you are still having trouble the fluid may

be full of many tiny air bubbles rather than a few big ones. To remedy this apply some pressure to the system, for the front brake by tying the front brake lever lightly back to the handlebar, and for the rear by tying a weight to the brake pedal – do not apply too much pressure or the cup and seals in the master cylinder and caliper may fail. Let the fluid stabilise for a few hours, after which the tiny bubbles should either have risen to the top in the reservoir, or have formed into one or more big bubbles that can be more easily bled out by repeating the bleeding procedure.

Fluid change

20 Changing the brake fluid is a similar process to bleeding the brake and requires the same materials plus a suitable tool (such as a syringe, or alternatively lots of absorbent rag or paper) for siphoning the fluid out of the reservoir.

21 Remove the reservoir cover and diaphragm and siphon the old fluid out of the reservoir. Wipe the reservoir clean. Fill the reservoir with new DOT 4 brake fluid.

22 Connect the brake bleeding hose to the bleed valve. Slowly pump the brake lever or pedal three or four times then hold it in and open the bleed valve. When the valve is opened, brake fluid will flow out of the valve into the clear tubing, and the lever will move toward the handlebar, or the pedal will move down.

23 Tighten the bleed valve, then release the brake lever or pedal gradually. Keep the reservoir topped-up with new fluid at all times or air may enter the system and greatly increase the length of the task. Repeat the process until new fluid can be seen emerging from the caliper bleed valve.

> **HAYNES HINT** *Old brake fluid is invariably much darker in colour than new fluid, making it easy to see when all old fluid has been expelled from the system.*

24 Check the operation of the brakes before riding the bike. If the lever or pedal action is spongy, carry out the bleeding operation as described above.

Draining the system for overhaul

25 Draining the brake fluid is again a similar process to bleeding the brakes. Follow the procedure described above for changing the fluid, but quite simply do not put any new fluid into the reservoir – the system fills itself with air instead.

26 When it comes to refilling the system start by adding new DOT 4 fluid from a sealed container to the reservoir, then perform the bleeding procedure as described above until the fluid comes out of the bleed valve, and keep at it until you are certain there is no more air left in the system.

9 Drum brake

Brake shoes

1 Remove the front (Section 12) or rear wheel (Section 13).

2 Lift the brakeplate and shoe assembly out of the wheel hub **(see illustration)**.

9.2 Remove the wheel and lift out the brake assembly

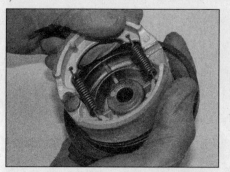

9.3a Fold the shoes inwards into a V to free them from the backplate

9.3b Measure the friction material thickness and check the return springs

9.5 Brake drum surface in perfect condition – no scoring or wear marks

3 Fold the shoes together to free them from the operating cam and pivot post (**see illustration**). Check the amount of friction material remaining on the shoes; it'll be most worn on the leading edge of the shoe (**see illustration**). When new the material measures 3 to 4 mm. If worn down to 1 mm or less, the shoes should be renewed.
4 With the shoes removed from the backplate, use brake cleaner to remove all brake dust. Check the operation of the brake operating arm. If the arm is stiff to operate remove it for greasing of its pivot; mark the position of the arm on its splined shaft (so it can be returned to the same place) and remove the pinch bolt. Push the shaft out of the brakeplate noting the position of any washers or grease seals, then clean old grease the dirt from the shaft and its bore in the brakeplate. Apply a smear of high melting point grease to the pivot area of the shaft then reinsert it with any washers, refit the arm aligning the marks, and tighten its pinch bolt. Also clean off old grease from the show pivot post and apply a smear of high melting point grease.
5 Use brake cleaner to wipe all brake dust from the inside of the drum. Inspect the surface of the shoe contact area in the drum (**see illustration**). A drum which is badly scored, or where the surface has worn through, will require wheel renewal. You may find the drum diameter cast into the wheel – this can be measured with a Vernier caliper.
6 Check the brake shoe return springs; if sagged (worn out), broken or rusty, fit new

springs. Hook the springs onto the shoes when angle the shoes in a V and fit them over the pivot post and operating cam. Work the operating arm by hand to check everything is settled in place and that the shoes return with the force of the springs.
7 Fit the brake assembly back into the wheel, refit the wheel and reconnect the cable or rod (see Section 12 front or Section 13 rear).
8 Check brake lever freeplay (front) or pedal freeplay (rear) and adjust as necessary (Chapter 1, Section 18).

Front brake cable

9 Refer to Chapter 5, Section 6 to disconnect the cable from the handlebar lever and to Section 12 disconnect it from the operating arm on the brake backplate. Free the cable from the stay on the left fork leg (**see illustrations**).
10 Reverse the procedure to fit the new cable, making sure it is routed correctly and does not interfere with steering action. Check brake lever freeplay as adjust as necessary (see Chapter 1, Section 18).

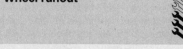

10 Wheel runout

1 Make a general check of the wheels and tyres (see Chapter 1 Section 19).
2 To check axial (side-to-side) runout of the wheel rim attach a dial gauge to the fork or

the swingarm and position its tip against the side of the wheel rim. Spin the wheel slowly and check the amount of run-out (**see illustration**).
3 In order to accurately check radial (out of round) runout with the dial gauge, remove the wheel from the bike, and the tyre from the wheel. With the axle clamped in a vice and the dial gauge positioned on the top of the rim, the wheel can be rotated to check the runout (**see illustration 10.2**).
4 An easier, though slightly less accurate, method is to attach a stiff wire pointer to the fork or the swingarm and position the end a fraction of an inch from the wheel rim where the wheel and tyre join. If the wheel is true, the distance from the pointer to the rim will be constant as the wheel is rotated.
5 Note that poor runout can also be due to worn wheel bearings. If there's excessive play between the bearing inner and outer race, renew the wheel bearings.

9.9a Slacken the locknuts each side of the cable bracket...

9.9b ...thread off the lower nut and slip the cable out of the bracket

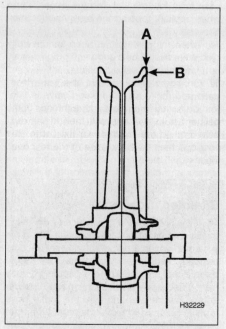

10.2 Check the wheel for radial (out-of-round) runout (A) and axial (side-to-side) runout (B)

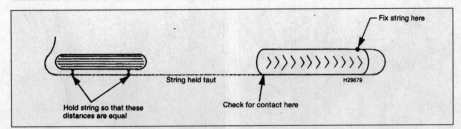

11.5 Wheel alignment check using string

11 Wheel alignment check

1 Misalignment of the wheels can cause serious handling problems and can lead to the chain coming off its sprockets. Poor wheel alignment can be caused by uneven chain adjustment so the rear wheel ends up being skewed to one side in the swingarm, by installing wheels spacers in the wrong position after taking a wheel out or by excessively worn swingarm pivot bearings; all of these are easy to rectify. A more serious problem is if the frame, suspension or rear wheel is bent or buckled after an accident or landing awkwardly after a jump; unless you've access to skilled services for straightening and repair it's best to renew parts in this case.

2 You may be able to see misaligned wheels by eye, simply by sighting along the bike from front to back and vice versa. Measurement can be made using a ruler and either a length of string or two perfectly straight metal bars or lengths of wood.

3 Support the bike on a stand so that it is upright. Measure the width of both tyres at their widest points. Subtract the smaller measurement from the larger measurement, then divide the difference by two. The result is the amount of offset that should exist between the front and rear tyres on both sides of the machine.

4 If the string method is used, have your assistant hold one end of it about halfway between the floor and the rear axle, with the string touching the back edge of the rear tyre tread.

5 Run the other end of the string forward and pull it tight so that it is roughly parallel to the floor (see illustration). Slowly bring the string into contact with the front edge of the rear tyre tread, then turn the front wheel until it is parallel with the string. Measure the distance from the front tyre tread to the string.

6 Repeat the procedure on the other side of the bike. The distance from the front tyre sidewall to the string should be equal on both sides.

7 As previously mentioned, a perfectly straight length of wood or metal bar may be substituted for the string (see illustration).

8 The distance between the string and tyre, or the straight-edge and tyre, should be the same on each side of the bike.

9 A useful tool for checking wheel alignment clamps to the rear sprocket (see illustration). With the bike held upright sight along the bar which extends from the tool's bracket. If the rear sprocket is correctly aligned with the front sprocket the bar should aline with the same part of the chain along its run (see illustration). If the wheel is out of alignment, the bar will be seen to go out of alignment along the chain's run (see illustration).

10 If the front-to-back alignment is correct, the wheels still may be out of alignment vertically.

11 Using a plumb bob or spirit level, check the rear wheel to make sure it is vertical. To do this, hold the string of the plumb bob against

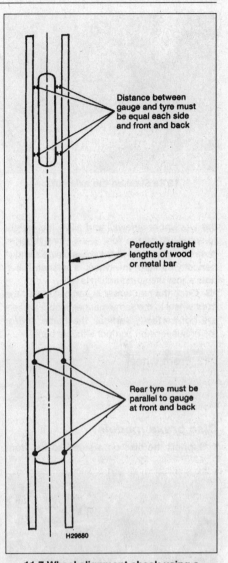

11.7 Wheel alignment check using a straight-edge

11.9a Clamp the tool across the sprocket as shown

11.9b Chain in perfect alignment (bar aligns with inner edge of chain)

11.9c Chain out of alignment (bar out of alignment with chain at tip)

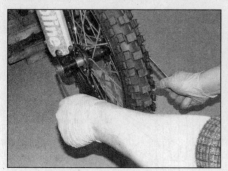

12.2a Slacken the axle nut...

12.2b ...remove it from the end of the axle...

12.2c ...then withdraw the axle and remove the wheel

the tyre upper sidewall and allow the weight to settle just off the floor. If the string touches both the upper and lower tyre sidewalls and is perfectly straight, the wheel is vertical. If it is not, adjust the stand until it is.

12 Once the rear wheel is vertical, check the front wheel in the same manner. If both wheels are not perfectly vertical, the frame and/or major suspension components are bent.

12 Front wheel

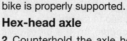

Disc brake models

1 Support the bike on a stand so the front

wheel is off the ground. Always make sure the bike is properly supported.

Hex-head axle

2 Counterhold the axle head and undo the axle nut **(see illustrations)**. Withdraw the axle and lift the wheel free **(see illustration)**, catching the spacers. Make sure you note which spacer fits on the left and which fits on the right – they are often of different lengths.

3 Fit the spacers into the dust seal set in each side of the wheel hub **(see illustrations)**. Offer up the wheel to the forks and guide the disc between the brake pads. Slide the axle into place making sure the spacers don't fall out. Thread on the axle nut and tighten it lightly.

4 Take the bike off the stand and compress the forks whilst applying the front brake a couple of times to bring the pads back into contact with the disc and centre the wheel on the axle. Now tighten the axle nut.

Clamped axle head

5 Remove the two bolts which retain the caliper to the fork and remove the caliper **(see illustration)**. Leave it suspended by its brake hose.

6 Unscrew the axle nut whilst counterholding the axle with large hex-head bit **(see illustration)**. Slacken the clamp bolts at the bottom of the fork leg and withdraw the axle **(see illustrations)**. Lift the wheel free and recover the spacer from the left side.

7 Fit the spacer into the dust seal **(see**

12.3a Spacer lengths are often different on the right...

12.3b ...and left sides

12.5 Unbolt the caliper from the fork leg and slide it off the disc

12.6a Counterhold the axle head while removing the nut

12.6b Slacken the clamp bolts...

12.6c ...then withdraw the axle to free the wheel

12.7 Fit the narrow end of the spacer into the dust seal in the left side of the wheel

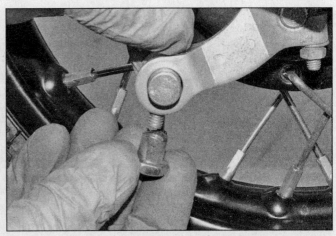

12.11a Unscrew the brake adjuster nut...

illustration). Offer up the wheel to the forks. Slide the axle fully into place making sure the spacer doesn't fall out. Thread the nut onto the end of the axle and tighten it lightly. Leave the clamp bolts loose at this stage.

8 Slide the caliper back over the disc and refit the two caliper bolts.

9 Take the bike off the stand and compress the forks whilst applying the front brake a couple of times to bring the pads back into contact with the disc and centre the wheel on the axle. Now tighten the axle nut (counterholding the axle head with a hex bit), followed by tightening the clamp bolts.

Drum brake models

10 Support the bike on a stand so the front wheel is off the ground. Always make sure the bike is properly supported.

11 Unscrew the brake adjuster nut from the end of the adjuster and withdraw the cable and adjuster from the trunnion in the brake arm **(see illustration)**.

12 Counterhold the axle head and unscrew the nut on the end of the axle **(see illustration)**. Withdraw the axle and lower the wheel from the forks **(see illustration)**.

13 Fit the brakeplate back into the drum and insert the spacer into the dust seal on

the right-hand side **(see illustrations)**. Fit the wheel between the forks so that the lug on the fork fits between the lugs on the brakeplate. Hold it in position whilst the axle is fitted and make sure the spacer doesn't drop free.

14 Fit the axle nut and tighten it lightly at this stage **(see illustration)**.

15 Reconnect the brake cable and adjust it to the correct setting (see Chapter 1 Section 18).

16 Take the bike off the stand and compress the forks whilst applying the front brake a couple of times to centre the wheel on the axle. Now tighten the axle nut whilst counterholding the axle head.

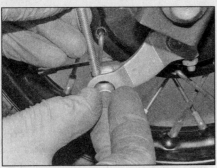

12.11b ...and draw the cable's threaded end out of the trunnion in the brake arm

12.12a Hold the axle head and unscrew the axle nut...

12.12b ...slide out the axle

12.13a Fit the brakeplate into the drum...

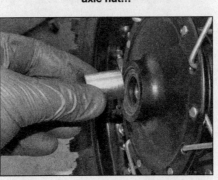

12.13b ...and the spacer into the other side of the hub

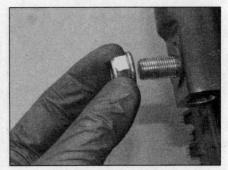

12.14 Thread the axle nut on

13.4b Remove the axle nut and retrieve the chain adjuster block

13.5 Withdraw the axle and lower the wheel

13 Rear wheel

Disc brake models

1 Position the bike on a stand so that the rear wheel is off the ground. Make sure the bike is properly supported.
2 Either disconnect the chain at its split link (see Section 16), or slip the chain off the sprocket as the wheel is removed.
3 Back off the chain adjuster on each side of the swingarm (see Chapter 1, Section 2).
4 Unscrew the axle nut **(see illustration)**.
5 If the chain hasn't already been disconnected at the split link, move the wheel forwards in the swingarm and slip the chain off the sprocket to the left-hand side. Take the weight of the wheel, then withdraw the

axle and lower the wheel to the ground **(see illustration)**. If the axle is difficult to withdraw, drive it out using a soft mallet to prevent damage to the threads.
6 On models where the caliper bracket mounts to the inside of the swingarm, note that the bracket and caliper will drop free once the wheel is removed. Fit the caliper bracket back onto the swingarm if required, and secure it using a cable-tie.
7 Remove the spacer from each side of the wheel, noting which fits where.
8 Clean all dirt and old grease off all components. Remove any corrosion from the axle using wire wool.
9 Check the axle is straight by rolling it on a flat surface.
Caution: Don't lay the wheel down and allow it to rest on the disc or sprocket – they could become warped. Keep it upright, or set the wheel on wood blocks

so the disc doesn't support the weight. Do not operate the brake pedal with the wheel removed.
10 Check the condition of the grease seals and wheel bearings (see Section 14).
11 Apply a smear of grease to the inside of the wheel spacers, and to the lips of the grease seals. Fit the headed spacer into the left-hand side of the wheel and the plain spacer into the right-hand side **(see illustrations)**. Apply a thin coat of grease to the axle. If the caliper bracket is located on the swingarm displace it and support it clear.
12 Fit the axle through the left side chain adjuster (make sure it's the correct way round) and insert it through the spacer, wheel hub, spacer, and the caliper bracket **(see illustrations)**. Fit the right side chain adjuster and the axle nut **(see illustration)**. Check to make sure the disc has located correctly between the brake pads.

13.11a Fit the headed spacer (reduced end first) into the left side...

13.11b ...and the plain spacer (reduced end first) into the right side

13.12a Insert the axle with the chain adjuster in situ...

13.12b ...make sure the adjuster seats correctly (block type shown)

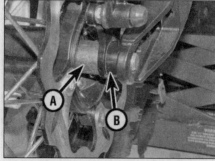

13.12c The axle must pass through the right side spacer (A) and caliper bracket (B)

13.12d Check that the caliper bracket locates over the lug on the inside of the swingarm

13.13 With the wheel pushed forward, route the chain over the sprocket teeth

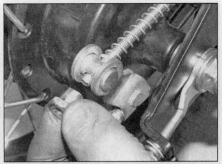

13.18a Remove the adjuster nut and disengage the rod and spring

13.18b Slip the trunnion out of the arm

13 Fit the chain up over the sprocket **(see illustration)** or rejoin the split link (see Section 16).
14 Check and adjust the drive chain slack (see Chapter 1). Tighten the axle nut.
15 Pump the brake pedal to bring the pads into contact with the disc. Test the brake before riding the bike.

Drum brake models

16 Position the bike on a stand so that the rear wheel is off the ground. Make sure the bike is properly supported.
17 Disconnect the chain at the split link (see Section 16).
18 Unscrew the adjuster nut from the end of the brake rod and pull the brake arm back to disengage the rod **(see illustrations)**. Slip the trunnion, spring and adjuster nut back on the rod so they don't get lost.
19 Counterhold the axle head and remove the nut from the axle **(see illustration)**. Pull the axle out from the other side of the wheel **(see illustration)**.
20 Withdraw the wheel and catch the two spacers as they drop free; take note of which side they fit.
21 When installing the wheel fit the brakeplate into the right-hand side, then insert the left-hand wheel spacer **(see illustrations)**.
22 Hold the wheel in position and insert the axle through the swingarm, spacer and wheel hub **(see illustration 13.19b)**. Insert the right-hand spacer as the axle exits the hub **(see illustration)**, then install the nut **(see illustration 13.19a)**. Make sure the chain adjuster brackets have remained in place.
23 Reconnect the drive chain joining link (see Section 16) and adjust chain freeplay (see Chapter 1, Section 2).
24 Reconnect the rear brake and adjust it (see Chapter 1 Section 18).
25 Test the brake before riding the bike.

14 Wheel bearings

Note: *Always renew the wheel bearings in sets, never individually. Avoid using a high pressure cleaner on the wheel bearing area.*

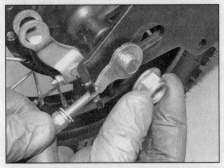

13.19a Remove the axle nut and the chain adjuster…

13.19b …pull the axle out and remove the chain adjuster

13.21a Insert the brakeplate into the drum…

13.21b …and the long spacer into the left side…

13.21c …then move the wheel into position

13.22 Insert the thin spacer between the brakeplate and swingarm on the right-hand side and make sure the post engages the slot in the brakeplate

14.2 Dust seals are easily prised out

14.4 Move the spacer aside and drive the bearing out using a drift as shown

14.7 Using a socket to drive the new bearing into the hub

14.9 Fit the seal, setting it flush with the rim

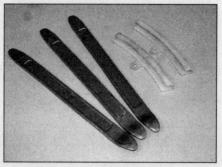

15.1 Good strong tyre levers and a couple of rim protectors will be needed

spacer. Fit the second bearing in the same way as the first until its inner race seats on the spacer.

9 Refit the dust seals using finger pressure or a suitable driver that bears on the outer rim, setting them flush with the hub **(see illustration)**. Smear the seal lips with grease.

10 Install the wheel.

15 Tyres

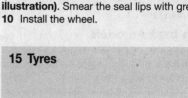

1 Tyre changing is a specialist task. If you attempt it at home you'll need three motorcycle tyre levers and two rim protectors **(see illustration)**. The rim protectors will prevent damage to the rims by the tyre levers and also protect their finish.

Removal

2 Begin by removing the wheel. If the tyre is going to be re-used, mark it next to the valve stem with chalk.

3 Unscrew the dust cap and unscrew the locknut from the tyre valve **(see illustration)**. If a rim lock bolt is fitted (usually only on the rear tyre) remove its nut and spring washer **(see illustration)**.

4 Deflate the tyre by depressing (or unscrewing) the valve core **(see illustration)**.

1 Remove the wheel. Support the wheel rim on wood blocks so that neither the sprocket nor disc is against the surface.

2 Where there's a dust seal fitted, prise it out with a large flat-bladed screwdriver **(see illustration)**.

3 Inspect the bearings – check that the bearing inner race turns smoothly and that the outer race is a tight fit in the hub (see *Tools and Workshop Tips* in the Reference Section). **Note:** *Do not remove the bearings unless they are going to be replaced with new ones.*

4 Move the centre spacer to one side to expose the inner race of the lower bearing, then locate a drift on it and drive the bearing out **(see illustration)**. If you can't move the spacer, or if you can't get sufficient purchase

with the drift, remove the bearings using an internal expanding puller with slide-hammer attachment. Remove the spacer that fits between the bearings.

5 Drive the other bearing out using a suitable drift (such as a socket on an extension) inserted from the opposite side and located on the inner race of the bearing.

6 Thoroughly clean the hub area of the wheel with a suitable solvent and inspect the bearing housing for scoring and wear.

7 Fit the new bearings with the marked side facing out. Drive the bearing in using a bearing driver or suitable socket that bears only on the outer race, and make sure the bearing fits squarely and all the way onto its seat **(see illustration)**.

8 Turn the wheel over and fit the bearing

15.3a Remove the dust cap and locknut from the tyre valve...

15.3b ...and the locknut and washer from the rim bolt

15.4 Deflating the tyre by unscrewing the valve core

15.5 Use firm hand pressure to break the tyre bead from all around the rim

15.6 Insert the rim protectors as shown

15.7 Insert the first tyre lever and hold it in position…

15.8 …as the second lever is inserted…

15.9a …hold both levers and insert a third…

15.9b …until the tyre can be pulled over the rim by hand

5 Push the bead of the tyre away from the rim on both sides **(see illustration)**.

> **HAYNES HiNT** *Dismounting a tyre is easier when the tyre is warm, so an indoor tyre change is recommended in cold climates. The rubber gets very stiff and is difficult to manipulate when cold.*

6 Place the wheel on thick card. This will help protect the disc/sprocket from damage. Fit the rim protectors on one side of the rim **(see illustration)**.
7 Insert one of the tyre levers under the bead of the tyre, then pull it back to lift the bead up over the rim **(see illustration)**. This should

be fairly easy. Take care not to pinch the inner tube as this is done.
8 Hold the tyre lever down with the bead over the rim, then move about 1 or 2 inches to either side and insert the second tyre lever **(see illustration)**. Be careful not to catch or pinch the inner tube as the second tyre lever is levered over. For this reason, tyre levers are recommended over screwdrivers or other implements.
9 With a small section of the bead up over the rim, one of the levers (or an additional lever) can be inserted 1 or 2 inches farther around the rim until about 1/4 of the tyre bead is above the rim edge **(see illustration)**. Make sure that the rest of the bead is in the dropped centre of the rim. At this point, the bead can usually be pulled up over the rim by hand **(see illustration)**.

10 Once all of the first bead is over the rim, the inner tube can be withdrawn from the tyre and rim. Push in on the valve stem, lift up on the tyre next to the stem, reach inside the tyre and carefully pull out the inner tube **(see illustration)**. Also manoeuvre the rim lock bolt out from the opposite side **(see illustration)**. Note that in the case of a puncture it is usually not necessary to completely remove the tyre from the rim to fit a new inner tube, however it is recommended because the item which caused puncture may still be stuck in the tyre.
11 To remove the tyre completely, make sure the bead is broken all the way around on the remaining edge, then insert a rim protector and using a tyre lever work the bead over the rim **(see illustration)**. Continue around the rim

15.10a Pull the inner tube out…

15.10b …and manoeuvre the rim lock bolt out

15.11a Work the bead over the wheel rim…

15.11b ...until the wheel can be pulled free of the tyre

15.12 Inflate the inner tube when checking for the location of the puncture

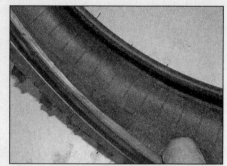

15.14 Feel around the inside of the tyre to check that the source of the puncture isn't still there, ready to puncture the new tube

until you are able to grab the wheel and pull it free **(see illustration)**.

Inspection

12 Fitting a new inner tube is advised when fitting a new tyre and also if the existing inner tube is punctured **(see illustration)**. Puncture repair kits are available, but the expense of a new inner tube is minimal.

13 Check the rim for sharp edges or damage. Make sure the rubber rim tape is in good condition and properly installed before inserting the inner tube.

14 Check the inside of the tyre to make sure the object that caused the puncture is not still inside **(see illustration)**. Also check the outside of the tyre, particularly the tread area, to make sure nothing is projecting through the tyre that may cause another puncture.

Installation

15 Some tyres have directional arrows molded into the sidewall. Look for these marks so that the tyre can be installed properly **(see illustration)**.

16 Lubricate the tyre bead with tyre fitting paste or a silicone spray **(see illustration)**. Use your hands to work the lower bead over the rim **(see illustration)**.

17 If a rim lock bolt is fitted, insert the bolt so that its stem fits through the hole in the rim **(see illustration)**. Thread the retaining nut on to keep it captive inside the rim **(see illustration)**.

18 Inflate the inner tube just enough to make it round. Sprinkle it with talcum powder, which acts as a dry lubricant, then carefully lift up the tyre edge and install the inner tube with the valve stem next to the hole in the rim **(see**

15.15 On this tyre the tread pattern suits different uses – fit accordingly

illustration). Once the inner tube is in place, push the valve stem through the rim and start the locknut on the stem **(see illustration)**.

15.16a Lubrication of the tyre bead will aid fitting

15.16b Work the first bead over the rim by hand

15.17a Work the rim lock bolt inside the tyre and through the rim tape and rim hole

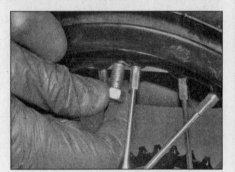

15.17b Thread the nut on the bolt to temporarily hold it in position

15.18a Feed the inner tube into the tyre and insert the valve through the rim hole...

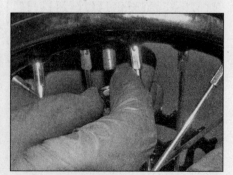

15.18b ...threading the nut on the valve to hold it in place

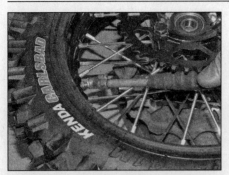

15.19a Partially inflate the inner tube...

15.19b ...then back off the tyre valve nut

15.20a Apply lubricant to the tyre bead...

15.20b ...then work the tyre over the rim...

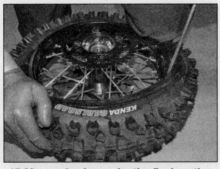

15.20c ...using levers for the final section

15.21 Thread the valve locknut down against the rim. If the valve core was removed, thread it back in using the tool

19 Make sure the inner tube is fully seated on the rim, then partially inflate the tyre **(see illustrations)**. Doing so will ensure the inner tube doesn't become pinched by the tyre levers as the tyre bead is fitted.

20 Lubricate the tyre bead, then push it over the rim edge and into the dropped centre section **(see illustration)**. Work around each side of the rim, carefully pushing the bead over the rim. The last section may have to be levered on with tyre levers. If so, take care not to pinch the inner tube as this is done **(see illustrations)**.

21 Once the bead is over the rim edge, check to see that the inner tube valve stem is pointing to the centre of the hub. If it's angled slightly in either direction, rotate the tyre on the rim to straighten it out. Thread the locknut the rest of the way onto the stem but don't tighten it completely **(see illustration)**.

22 Inflate the inner tube to approximately 40 psi (2.7 Bar) and check to make sure the guidelines on the tyre sidewalls are the same distance from the rim around the circumference of the tyre.

 Warning: Do not overinflate the inner tube or the tyre may burst, causing serious injury.

23 After the tyre bead is correctly seated on the rim, reduce the tyre pressure to 25 psi (1.7 Bar), then tighten the valve stem locknut securely and fit the cap **(see illustration)**. On models with a rim lock bolt, tighten the locknut against the rim **(see illustration)**.

24 Slip the wheel axle through the hub and spin the wheel to check that the tyre is correctly aligned on the rim **(see illustration)**.

25 Refit the wheel to the bike. Adjust the tyre pressure to normal (see Chapter 1, Section 19).

16 Drive chain

Removal

1 Support the bike on a stand so the rear wheel is off the ground. Locate the joining link in a suitable position to work on by rotating the back wheel.

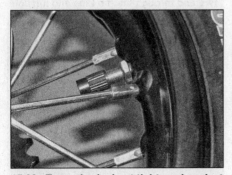

15.23a Tyre valve locknut tightened against the rim and dust cap fitted

15.23b Rim lock bolt plain washer and spring washer fitted and nut tightened against the rim

15.24 Spin the wheel to check tyre alignment

16.2a Slacken the axle nut a couple of turns...

16.2b ...then use the adjuster on each side to create slack in the chain

16.3 Removal of the engine cover gives full access to the front sprocket

2 Slacken the rear axle nut a few turns, then back of the chain adjuster on each side to create some slack in the chain **(see illustrations)**.

3 Remove the front sprocket cover **(see illustration)**; it'll be retained by two or three bolts. This isn't absolutely necessary but doing so will enable you to check the sprocket condition (remember that chain and sprockets are best renewed as a set).

4 Remove the spring clip and outer plate from the joining link and pull the link out from the inner side of the chain **(see illustration)**. Thread the chain off the sprockets, noting how it's routed through the guides.

Caution: If you're fitting a new chain then also fit a new joining link. If you're just disconnecting the chain to remove another component, then take care not to distort the spring clip.

Cleaning and cutting

5 The chain can be cleaned and lubed on the bike easily enough (see Chapter), but for a thorough clean remove the chain and soak it in paraffin (kerosene) for 10 minutes. Put on some rubber gloves and use a brush to scrub all dirt from the chain. Care has to be taken if an O-ring chain has been fitted because the O-rings can be damaged by solvents, but most bikes will be fitted with a standard unsealed chain.

6 Spray aerosol chain cleaner over the sprocket teeth and scrub them clean with a brush. Also clean around the back of the engine sprocket and check the condition of the output shaft seal.

7 Inspect the chain when it's clean and dry. If any links are damaged, kinked or the rollers

show obvious signs of wear, fit a new chain. Remember that the cleaning process will have washed all grease out of the chain so lubricate it thoroughly being riding.

8 If you're fitting a new chain check its number of links against the old chain you've taken off. Chains are often supplied in longer lengths than required. Use a chain link splitting tool to press out the pins of links not required **(see illustration)**.

Installation

9 Route the chain around the sprockets and through the guides leaving the two ends mid-way between the sprockets along the bottom run **(see illustrations)**.

10 Join the two ends together with the split link, inserting it from the inner side of the chain **(see illustration)**. Fit the sideplate and the

16.4 Pliers can be used to squeeze the clips ends against the chain pin so that the clip notches slide over the pin

16.8 Operate the tool to press the pin out of the chain. This is one of many chain splitter tools available

16.9a Fit the chain over the sprockets

16.9b Make sure the chain takes the correct route between the guides

16.10a Fit the split link from the inner side of the chain...

16.10b ...fit the sideplate...

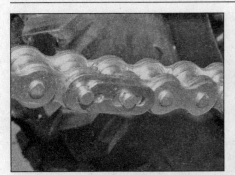

16.10c ...position the spring clip as shown...

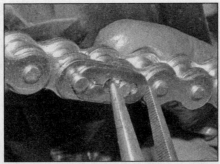

16.10d ...then use pliers to squeeze the clip into position

16.10e Spring clip correctly fitted

spring clip **(see illustrations)**. The closed end of the clip must point in the normal direction of chain travel otherwise there is a danger of its end getting snagged and the link coming apart. Slip the spring clip into the pin grooves and use pliers against the closed end and the pin to squeeze the open end of the clip over the other chain pin **(see illustrations)**.

11 Fit the sprocket cover.

12 Adjust and lubricate the chain following the procedures described in Chapter 1.

17 Sprockets

Front sprocket

1 Remove the front sprocket cover; two or three bolts retain the cover **(see illustration 16.3)**. Before removing the drive chain, slacken each of the sprocket bolts; putting the bike in a high gear and holding the rear brake on with the rear tyre in firm contact with the ground will hold the sprocket whist the bolts are slackened.

2 Split the drive chain at the joining link and thread the chain off the sprockets (see Section 16).

3 Unscrew the sprocket retainer bolts, and rotate the locking plate in the output shaft groove until it can be withdrawn from the shaft splines **(see illustrations)**. Slide the sprocket off the shaft **(see illustration)**.

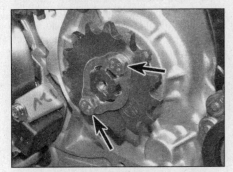

17.3a Unscrew the bolts (arrowed)

17.3b Rotate the plate so that its cutouts align with the shaft splines...

17.3c ...and pull the sprocket off the shaft

A leaking output shaft seal can be changed without splitting the crankcases by using a seal hook or other pointed tool to prise the old seal out. Clean the shaft end, then grease the lip of the new seal and press it in, using a socket to tap it fully into place.

Hook the old seal out

Fit the new seal with its markings outwards...

...and use a socket to tap it squarely into place

17.9 Rear sprocket bolts and tab washers (note the sprocket markings – '420 is the chain size and 41T is chain teeth in this case)

17.10 A through-bolt and nut retain the sprocket on certain models

4 Slide the new sprocket onto the shaft; if the sprocket has any stamped markings such as the number of teeth, install it so the markings face outwards. Slide the retainer plate on until it aligns with the groove, then turn it to align the bolt holes. Fit the bolts and tighten them.

5 If removed, fit the rear sprocket now, and install the wheel (see Section 13). Install the chain and join it with the link, then adjust the chain (see Chapter 1, Section 2).

6 Tighten the sprocket bolts, holding the rear brake on with the gearbox in a high gear to prevent the sprocket turning.

7 Fit the sprocket cover. Lubricate the chain following the procedures described in Chapter 1.

Rear sprocket

8 Remove the rear wheel (see Section 13). Rest it sprocket side up on some blocks of wood.

9 Knock back the tab washer tabs from the flats of the sprocket bolts. Unscrew the sprocket bolts and lift the sprocket off **(see illustration)**.

10 Where the sprocket bolts through the hub flange rather than theads into the hub, counterhold the bolt head and unscrew the nut on the inside to free the sprocket **(see illustration)**.

11 Fit the sprocket onto the hub with the marked side facing out having made sure that the seating surface on the hub is free of corrosion or anything which might not allow the sprocket to seat evenly.

12 Where the sprocket bolts thread directly into the hub check that the washer tabs are good, then tighten the bolts and bend a tab up against the flat of each bolt head. For a through-bolt arrangement, apply a drop of non-permanent thread locking compound the bolt threads then threads the nuts on and tighten them.

13 Install the rear wheel (see Section 13).

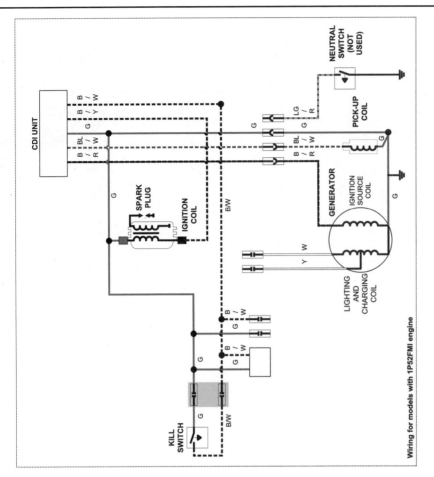

Wiring for models with 1P52FMI engine

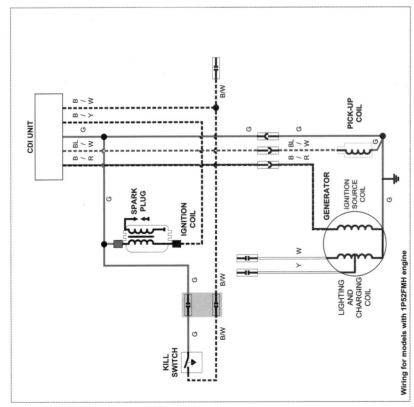

Wiring for models with 1P52FMH engine

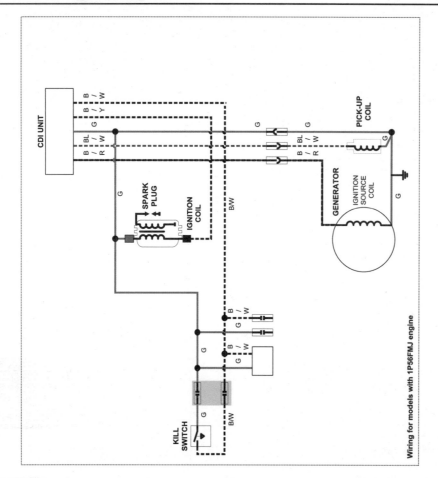

Wiring for models with 1P56FMJ engine

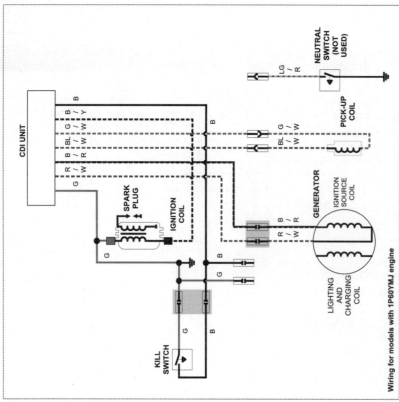

Wiring for models with 1P60YMJ engine

Reference

Tools and Workshop Tips   REF•2

- Building up a tool kit and equipping your workshop ● Using tools ● Understanding bearing, seal, fastener and chain sizes and markings ● Repair techniques

Building a bike from the crate   REF•20

- Uncrating the bike
- Building the bike
- Checking the settings
- Fluids and getting it running

Lubricants and fluids   REF•30

- Engine oils
- Transmission (gear) oils
- Coolant/anti-freeze
- Fork oils and suspension fluids ● Brake/clutch fluids
- Spray lubes, degreasers and solvents

Conversion Factors   REF•33

$$34 \ Nm \times 0.738 = 25 \ lbf \ ft$$

- Formulae for conversion of the metric (SI) units used throughout the manual into Imperial measures

Fault Finding   REF•34

- Common faults and their likely causes ● Links to main chapters for testing and repair procedures

Index   REF•42

Buying tools

A toolkit is a fundamental requirement for servicing and repairing a motorcycle. Although there will be an initial expense in building up enough tools for servicing, this will soon be offset by the savings made by doing the job yourself. As experience and confidence grow, additional tools can be added to enable the repair and overhaul of the motorcycle. Many of the specialist tools are expensive and not often used so it may be preferable to hire them, or for a group of friends or motorcycle club to join in the purchase.

As a rule, it is better to buy more expensive, good quality tools. Cheaper tools are likely to wear out faster and need to be renewed more often, nullifying the original saving.

> ⚠ **Warning: To avoid the risk of a poor quality tool breaking in use, causing injury or damage to the component being worked on, always aim to purchase tools which meet the relevant national safety standards.**

The following lists of tools do not represent the manufacturer's service tools, but serve as a guide to help the owner decide which tools are needed for this level of work. In addition, items such as an electric drill, hacksaw, files, soldering iron and a workbench equipped with a vice, may be needed. Although not classed as tools, a selection of bolts, screws, nuts, washers and pieces of tubing always come in useful.

For more information about tools, refer to the Haynes *Motorcycle Workshop Practice Techbook* (Bk. No. 3470).

Manufacturer's service tools

Inevitably certain tasks require the use of a service tool. Where possible an alternative tool or method of approach is recommended, but sometimes there is no option if personal injury or damage to the component is to be avoided. Where required, service tools are referred to in the relevant procedure.

Service tools can usually only be purchased from a motorcycle dealer and are identified by a part number. Some of the commonly-used tools, such as rotor pullers, are available in aftermarket form from mail-order motorcycle tool and accessory suppliers.

Maintenance and minor repair tools

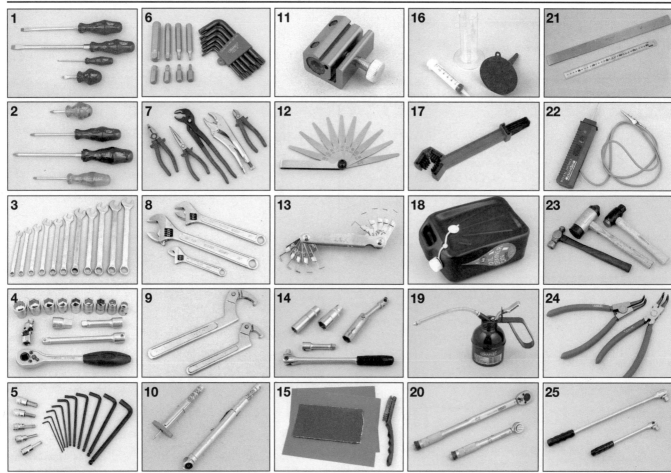

1 Set of flat-bladed screwdrivers
2 Set of Phillips head screwdrivers
3 Combination open-end and ring spanners
4 Socket set (3/8 inch or 1/2 inch drive)
5 Set of Allen keys or bits

6 Set of Torx keys or bits
7 Pliers, cutters and self-locking grips (Mole grips)
8 Adjustable spanners
9 C-spanners
10 Tread depth gauge and tyre pressure gauge

11 Cable oiler clamp
12 Feeler gauges
13 Spark plug gap measuring tool
14 Spark plug spanner or deep plug sockets
15 Wire brush and emery paper

16 Calibrated syringe, measuring vessel and funnel
17 Chain cleaning brush
18 Oil drainer can or tray
19 Pump type oil can
20 Torque wrenches

21 Straight-edge and steel rule
22 Continuity tester
23 Selection of hammers
24 Circlip pliers (internal and external, or combination)
25 Breaker bars

Repair and overhaul tools

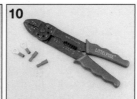

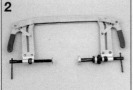

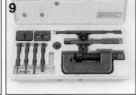

1 *Piston pin drawbolt tool*
2 *Valve spring compressor (4-stroke engines)*
3 *Impact driver set*
4 *Vernier gauge*
5 *Freeze spray and heat gun*
6 *Set of cold chisels and punches*
7 *Flywheel puller*
8 *Peg spanner 20/24mm*
9 *Chain breaking/riveting tool set*
10 *Wire stripper and crimper tool*
11 *Multimeter (measures amps, volts and ohms)*
12 *Stroboscope (for dynamic timing checks)*
13 *Hose clamp (wingnut type shown)*
14 *Clutch holding tool*
15 *One-man brake/clutch bleeder kit*

Specialist tools

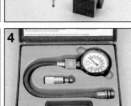

1 *Micrometers (external type)*
2 *Telescoping gauges*
3 *Dial gauge*
4 *Cylinder compression gauge*
5 *Fork seal driver*
6 *Slide-hammer and bearing extractors*
7 *Tap and die set*
8 *Stud extractor*
9 *Screw extractor set*
10 *Bearing driver set*

1 Workshop equipment and facilities

The workbench

● Work is made much easier by raising the bike up on a ramp - components are much more accessible if raised to waist level. The hydraulic or pneumatic types seen in the dealer's workshop are a sound investment if you undertake a lot of repairs or overhauls **(see illustration 1.1)**.

1.1 Hydraulic motorcycle ramp

● If raised off ground level, the bike must be supported on the ramp to avoid it falling. Most ramps incorporate a front wheel locating clamp which can be adjusted to suit different diameter wheels. When tightening the clamp, take care not to mark the wheel rim or damage the tyre - use wood blocks on each side to prevent this.

● Secure the bike to the ramp using tie-downs **(see illustration 1.2)**. If the bike has only a sidestand, and hence leans at a dangerous angle when raised, support the bike on an auxiliary stand.

1.2 Tie-downs are used around the passenger footrests to secure the bike

● Auxiliary (paddock) stands are widely available from mail order companies or motorcycle dealers and attach either to the wheel axle or swingarm pivot **(see illustration 1.3)**. If the motorcycle has a centrestand, you can support it under the crankcase to prevent it toppling whilst either wheel is removed **(see illustration 1.4)**.

1.3 This auxiliary stand attaches to the swingarm pivot

1.4 Always use a block of wood between the engine and jack head when supporting the engine in this way

Fumes and fire

● Refer to the Safety first! page at the beginning of the manual for full details. Make sure your workshop is equipped with a fire extinguisher suitable for fuel-related fires (Class B fire - flammable liquids) - it is not sufficient to have a water-filled extinguisher.

● Always ensure adequate ventilation is available. Unless an exhaust gas extraction system is available for use, ensure that the engine is run outside of the workshop.

● If working on the fuel system, make sure the workshop is ventilated to avoid a build-up of fumes. This applies equally to fume build-up when charging a battery. Do not smoke or allow anyone else to smoke in the workshop.

Fluids

● If you need to drain fuel from the tank, store it in an approved container marked as suitable for the storage of petrol (gasoline) **(see illustration 1.5)**. Do not store fuel in glass jars or bottles.

1.5 Use an approved can only for storing petrol (gasoline)

● Use proprietary engine degreasers or solvents which have a high flash-point, such as paraffin (kerosene), for cleaning off oil, grease and dirt - never use petrol (gasoline) for cleaning. Wear rubber gloves when handling solvent and engine degreaser. The fumes from certain solvents can be dangerous - always work in a well-ventilated area.

Dust, eye and hand protection

● Protect your lungs from inhalation of dust particles by wearing a filtering mask over the nose and mouth. Many frictional materials still contain asbestos which is dangerous to your health. Protect your eyes from spouts of liquid and sprung components by wearing a pair of protective goggles **(see illustration 1.6)**.

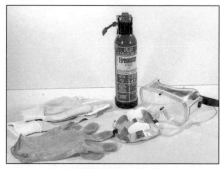

1.6 A fire extinguisher, goggles, mask and protective gloves should be at hand in the workshop

● Protect your hands from contact with solvents, fuel and oils by wearing rubber gloves. Alternatively apply a barrier cream to your hands before starting work. If handling hot components or fluids, wear suitable gloves to protect your hands from scalding and burns.

What to do with old fluids

● Old cleaning solvent, fuel, coolant and oils should not be poured down domestic drains or onto the ground. Package the fluid up in old oil containers, label it accordingly, and take it to a garage or disposal facility. Contact your local authority for location of such sites or ring the oil care hotline.

OIL CARE
FOLLOW THE CODE

Note: It is antisocial and illegal to dump oil down the drain. To find the location of your local oil recycling bank in the UK, call 03708 506 506 or visit www.oilbankline.org.uk

In the USA, note that any oil supplier must accept used oil for recycling.

2 Fasteners -
screws, bolts and nuts

Fastener types and applications

Bolts and screws

● Fastener head types are either of hexagonal, Torx or splined design, with internal and external versions of each type **(see illustrations 2.1 and 2.2)**; splined head fasteners are not in common use on motorcycles. The conventional slotted or Phillips head design is used for certain screws. Bolt or screw length is always measured from the underside of the head to the end of the item **(see illustration 2.11)**.

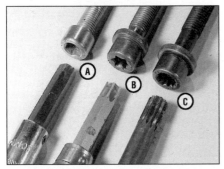

2.1 Internal hexagon/Allen (A), Torx (B) and splined (C) fasteners, with corresponding bits

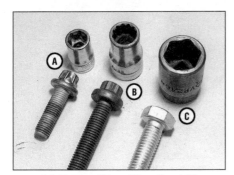

2.2 External Torx (A), splined (B) and hexagon (C) fasteners, with corresponding sockets

● Certain fasteners on the motorcycle have a tensile marking on their heads, the higher the marking the stronger the fastener. High tensile fasteners generally carry a 10 or higher marking. Never replace a high tensile fastener with one of a lower tensile strength.

Washers (see illustration 2.3)

● Plain washers are used between a fastener head and a component to prevent damage to the component or to spread the load when torque is applied. Plain washers can also be used as spacers or shims in certain assemblies. Copper or aluminium plain washers are often used as sealing washers on drain plugs.

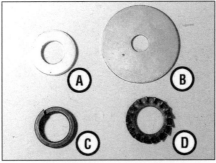

2.3 Plain washer (A), penny washer (B), spring washer (C) and serrated washer (D)

● The split-ring spring washer works by applying axial tension between the fastener head and component. If flattened, it is fatigued and must be renewed. If a plain (flat) washer is used on the fastener, position the spring washer between the fastener and the plain washer.
● Serrated star type washers dig into the fastener and component faces, preventing loosening. They are often used on electrical earth (ground) connections to the frame.
● Cone type washers (sometimes called Belleville) are conical and when tightened apply axial tension between the fastener head and component. They must be installed with the dished side against the component and often carry an OUTSIDE marking on their outer face. If flattened, they are fatigued and must be renewed.
● Tab washers are used to lock plain nuts or bolts on a shaft. A portion of the tab washer is bent up hard against one flat of the nut or bolt to prevent it loosening. Due to the tab washer being deformed in use, a new tab washer should be used every time it is disturbed.
● Wave washers are used to take up endfloat on a shaft. They provide light springing and prevent excessive side-to-side play of a component. Can be found on rocker arm shafts.

Nuts and split pins

● Conventional plain nuts are usually six-sided **(see illustration 2.4)**. They are sized by thread diameter and pitch. High tensile nuts carry a number on one end to denote their tensile strength.

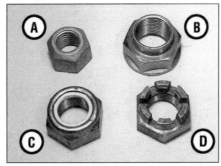

2.4 Plain nut (A), shouldered locknut (B), nylon insert nut (C) and castellated nut (D)

● Self-locking nuts either have a nylon insert, or two spring metal tabs, or a shoulder which is staked into a groove in the shaft - their advantage over conventional plain nuts is a resistance to loosening due to vibration. The nylon insert type can be used a number of times, but must be renewed when the friction of the nylon insert is reduced, ie when the nut spins freely on the shaft. The spring tab type can be reused unless the tabs are damaged. The shouldered type must be renewed every time it is disturbed.
● Split pins (cotter pins) are used to lock a castellated nut to a shaft or to prevent slackening of a plain nut. Common applications are wheel axles and brake torque arms. Because the split pin arms are deformed to lock around the nut a new split pin must always be used on installation - always fit the correct size split pin which will fit snugly in the shaft hole. Make sure the split pin arms are correctly located around the nut **(see illustrations 2.5 and 2.6)**.

2.5 Bend split pin (cotter pin) arms as shown (arrows) to secure a castellated nut

2.6 Bend split pin (cotter pin) arms as shown to secure a plain nut

Caution: If the castellated nut slots do not align with the shaft hole after tightening to the torque setting, tighten the nut until the next slot aligns with the hole - never slacken the nut to align its slot.

● R-pins (shaped like the letter R), or slip pins as they are sometimes called, are sprung and can be reused if they are otherwise in good condition. Always install R-pins with their closed end facing forwards **(see illustration 2.7)**.

2.7 Correct fitting of R-pin. Arrow indicates forward direction

Circlips (see illustration 2.8)

● Circlips (sometimes called snap-rings) are used to retain components on a shaft or in a housing and have corresponding external or internal ears to permit removal. Parallel-sided (machined) circlips can be installed either way round in their groove, whereas stamped circlips (which have a chamfered edge on one face) must be installed with the chamfer facing away from the direction of thrust load **(see illustration 2.9)**.

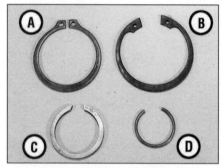

2.8 External stamped circlip (A), internal stamped circlip (B), machined circlip (C) and wire circlip (D)

● Always use circlip pliers to remove and install circlips; expand or compress them just enough to remove them. After installation, rotate the circlip in its groove to ensure it is securely seated. If installing a circlip on a splined shaft, always align its opening with a shaft channel to ensure the circlip ends are well supported and unlikely to catch **(see illustration 2.10)**.

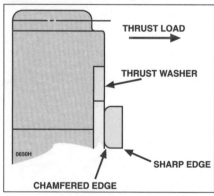

2.9 Correct fitting of a stamped circlip

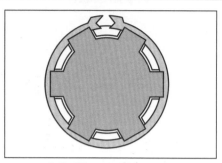

2.10 Align circlip opening with shaft channel

● Circlips can wear due to the thrust of components and become loose in their grooves, with the subsequent danger of becoming dislodged in operation. For this reason, renewal is advised every time a circlip is disturbed.
● Wire circlips are commonly used as piston pin retaining clips. If a removal tang is provided, long-nosed pliers can be used to dislodge them, otherwise careful use of a small flat-bladed screwdriver is necessary. Wire circlips should be renewed every time they are disturbed.

Thread diameter and pitch

● Diameter of a male thread (screw, bolt or stud) is the outside diameter of the threaded portion **(see illustration 2.11)**. Most motorcycle manufacturers use the ISO (International Standards Organisation) metric system expressed in millimetres, eg M6 refers to a 6 mm diameter thread. Sizing is the same for nuts, except that the thread diameter is measured across the valleys of the nut.
● Pitch is the distance between the peaks of the thread **(see illustration 2.11)**. It is expressed in millimetres, thus a common bolt size may be expressed as 6.0 x 1.0 mm (6 mm thread diameter and 1 mm pitch). Generally pitch increases in proportion to thread diameter, although there are always exceptions.
● Thread diameter and pitch are related for conventional fastener applications and the accompanying table can be used as a guide. Additionally, the AF (Across Flats), spanner or socket size dimension of the bolt or nut **(see illustration 2.11)** is linked to thread and pitch specification. Thread pitch can be measured with a thread gauge **(see illustration 2.12)**.

2.12 Using a thread gauge to measure pitch

AF size	Thread diameter x pitch (mm)
8 mm	M5 x 0.8
8 mm	M6 x 1.0
10 mm	M6 x 1.0
12 mm	M8 x 1.25
14 mm	M10 x 1.25
17 mm	M12 x 1.25

● The threads of most fasteners are of the right-hand type, ie they are turned clockwise to tighten and anti-clockwise to loosen. The reverse situation applies to left-hand thread fasteners, which are turned anti-clockwise to tighten and clockwise to loosen. Left-hand threads are used where rotation of a component might loosen a conventional right-hand thread fastener.

Seized fasteners

● Corrosion of external fasteners due to water or reaction between two dissimilar metals can occur over a period of time. It will build up sooner in wet conditions or in countries where salt is used on the roads during the winter. If a fastener is severely corroded it is likely that normal methods of removal will fail and result in its head being ruined. When you attempt removal, the fastener thread should be heard to crack free and unscrew easily - if it doesn't, stop there before damaging something.
● A smart tap on the head of the fastener will often succeed in breaking free corrosion which has occurred in the threads **(see illustration 2.13)**.
● An aerosol penetrating fluid (such as WD-40) applied the night beforehand may work its way down into the thread and ease removal. Depending on the location, you may be able to make up a Plasticine well around the fastener head and fill it with penetrating fluid.

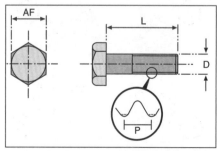

2.11 Fastener length (L), thread diameter (D), thread pitch (P) and head size (AF)

2.13 A sharp tap on the head of a fastener will often break free a corroded thread

● If you are working on an engine internal component, corrosion will most likely not be a problem due to the well lubricated environment. However, components can be very tight and an impact driver is a useful tool in freeing them (see illustration 2.14).

2.14 Using an impact driver to free a fastener

● Where corrosion has occurred between dissimilar metals (eg steel and aluminium alloy), the application of heat to the fastener head will create a disproportionate expansion rate between the two metals and break the seizure caused by the corrosion. Whether heat can be applied depends on the location of the fastener - any surrounding components likely to be damaged must first be removed (see illustration 2.15). Heat can be applied using a paint stripper heat gun or clothes iron, or by immersing the component in boiling water - wear protective gloves to prevent scalding or burns to the hands.

2.15 Using heat to free a seized fastener

● As a last resort, it is possible to use a hammer and cold chisel to work the fastener head unscrewed (see illustration 2.16). This will damage the fastener, but more importantly extreme care must be taken not to damage the surrounding component.

Caution: Remember that the component being secured is generally of more value than the bolt, nut or screw - when the fastener is freed, do not unscrew it with force, instead work the fastener back and forth when resistance is felt to prevent thread damage.

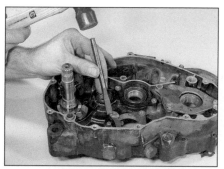

2.16 Using a hammer and chisel to free a seized fastener

Broken fasteners and damaged heads

● If the shank of a broken bolt or screw is accessible you can grip it with self-locking grips. The knurled wheel type stud extractor tool or self-gripping stud puller tool is particularly useful for removing the long studs which screw into the cylinder mouth surface of the crankcase or bolts and screws from which the head has broken off (see illustration 2.17). Studs can also be removed by locking two nuts together on the threaded end of the stud and using a spanner on the lower nut (see illustration 2.18).

2.17 Using a stud extractor tool to remove a broken crankcase stud

2.18 Two nuts can be locked together to unscrew a stud from a component

● A bolt or screw which has broken off below or level with the casing must be extracted using a screw extractor set. Centre punch the fastener to centralise the drill bit, then drill a hole in the fastener (see illustration 2.19). Select a drill bit which is approximately half to three-quarters the diameter of the fastener

2.19 When using a screw extractor, first drill a hole in the fastener . . .

and drill to a depth which will accommodate the extractor. Use the largest size extractor possible, but avoid leaving too small a wall thickness otherwise the extractor will merely force the fastener walls outwards wedging it in the casing thread.

● If a spiral type extractor is used, thread it anti-clockwise into the fastener. As it is screwed in, it will grip the fastener and unscrew it from the casing (see illustration 2.20).

2.20 . . . then thread the extractor anti-clockwise into the fastener

● If a taper type extractor is used, tap it into the fastener so that it is firmly wedged in place. Unscrew the extractor (anti-clockwise) to draw the fastener out.

Warning: Stud extractors are very hard and may break off in the fastener if care is not taken - ask an engineer about spark erosion if this happens.

● Alternatively, the broken bolt/screw can be drilled out and the hole retapped for an oversize bolt/screw or a diamond-section thread insert. It is essential that the drilling is carried out squarely and to the correct depth, otherwise the casing may be ruined - if in doubt, entrust the work to an engineer.

● Bolts and nuts with rounded corners cause the correct size spanner or socket to slip when force is applied. Of the types of spanner/socket available always use a six-point type rather than an eight or twelve-point type - better grip

2.21 Comparison of surface drive ring spanner (left) with 12-point type (right)

is obtained. Surface drive spanners grip the middle of the hex flats, rather than the corners, and are thus good in cases of damaged heads **(see illustration 2.21)**.

● Slotted-head or Phillips-head screws are often damaged by the use of the wrong size screwdriver. Allen-head and Torx-head screws are much less likely to sustain damage. If enough of the screw head is exposed you can use a hacksaw to cut a slot in its head and then use a conventional flat-bladed screwdriver to remove it. Alternatively use a hammer and cold chisel to tap the head of the fastener around to slacken it. Always replace damaged fasteners with new ones, preferably Torx or Allen-head type.

A dab of valve grinding compound between the screw head and screwdriver tip will often give a good grip.

Thread repair

● Threads (particularly those in aluminium alloy components) can be damaged by overtightening, being assembled with dirt in the threads, or from a component working loose and vibrating. Eventually the thread will fail completely, and it will be impossible to tighten the fastener.

● If a thread is damaged or clogged with old locking compound it can be renovated with a thread repair tool (thread chaser) **(see illustrations 2.22 and 2.23)**; special thread

2.22 A thread repair tool being used to correct an internal thread

2.23 A thread repair tool being used to correct an external thread

chasers are available for spark plug hole threads. The tool will not cut a new thread, but clean and true the original thread. Make sure that you use the correct diameter and pitch tool. Similarly, external threads can be cleaned up with a die or a thread restorer file **(see illustration 2.24)**.

2.24 Using a thread restorer file

● It is possible to drill out the old thread and retap the component to the next thread size. This will work where there is enough surrounding material and a new bolt or screw can be obtained. Sometimes, however, this is not possible - such as where the bolt/screw passes through another component which must also be suitably modified, also in cases where a spark plug or oil drain plug cannot be obtained in a larger diameter thread size.

● The diamond-section thread insert (often known by its popular trade name of Heli-Coil) is a simple and effective method of renewing the thread and retaining the original size. A kit can be purchased which contains the tap, insert and installing tool **(see illustration 2.25)**. Drill out the damaged thread with the size drill specified **(see illustration 2.26)**. Carefully retap the thread **(see illustration 2.27)**. Install the

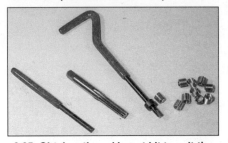

2.25 Obtain a thread insert kit to suit the thread diameter and pitch required

2.26 To install a thread insert, first drill out the original thread . . .

2.27 . . . tap a new thread . . .

2.28 . . . fit insert on the installing tool . . .

2.29 . . . and thread into the component . . .

2.30 . . . break off the tang when complete

insert on the installing tool and thread it slowly into place using a light downward pressure **(see illustrations 2.28 and 2.29)**. When positioned between a 1/4 and 1/2 turn below the surface withdraw the installing tool and use the break-off tool to press down on the tang, breaking it off **(see illustration 2.30)**.

● There are epoxy thread repair kits on the market which can rebuild stripped internal threads, although this repair should not be used on high load-bearing components.

Thread locking and sealing compounds

● Locking compounds are used in locations where the fastener is prone to loosening due to vibration or on important safety-related items which might cause loss of control of the motorcycle if they fail. It is also used where important fasteners cannot be secured by other means such as lockwashers or split pins.

● Before applying locking compound, make sure that the threads (internal and external) are clean and dry with all old compound removed. Select a compound to suit the component being secured - a non-permanent general locking and sealing type is suitable for most applications, but a high strength type is needed for permanent fixing of studs in castings. Apply a drop or two of the compound to the first few threads of the fastener, then thread it into place and tighten to the specified torque. Do not apply excessive thread locking compound otherwise the thread may be damaged on subsequent removal.

● Certain fasteners are impregnated with a dry film type coating of locking compound on their threads. Always renew this type of fastener if disturbed.

● Anti-seize compounds, such as copper-based greases, can be applied to protect threads from seizure due to extreme heat and corrosion. A common instance is spark plug threads and exhaust system fasteners.

3 Measuring tools and gauges

Feeler gauges

● Feeler gauges (or blades) are used for measuring small gaps and clearances (see illustration 3.1). They can also be used to measure endfloat (sideplay) of a component on a shaft where access is not possible with a dial gauge.

● Feeler gauge sets should be treated with care and not bent or damaged. They are etched with their size on one face. Keep them clean and very lightly oiled to prevent corrosion build-up.

3.1 Feeler gauges are used for measuring small gaps and clearances - thickness is marked on one face of gauge

● When measuring a clearance, select a gauge which is a light sliding fit between the two components. You may need to use two gauges together to measure the clearance accurately.

Micrometers

● A micrometer is a precision tool capable of measuring to 0.01 or 0.001 of a millimetre. It should always be stored in its case and not in the general toolbox. It must be kept clean and never dropped, otherwise its frame or measuring anvils could be distorted resulting in inaccurate readings.

● External micrometers are used for measuring outside diameters of components and have many more applications than internal micrometers. Micrometers are available in different size ranges, eg 0 to 25 mm, 25 to 50 mm, and upwards in 25 mm steps; some large micrometers have interchangeable anvils to allow a range of measurements to be taken. Generally the largest precision measurement you are likely to take on a motorcycle is the piston diameter.

● Internal micrometers (or bore micrometers) are used for measuring inside diameters, such as valve guides and cylinder bores. Telescoping gauges and small hole gauges are used in conjunction with an external micrometer, whereas the more expensive internal micrometers have their own measuring device.

External micrometer

Note: *The conventional analogue type instrument is described. Although much easier to read, digital micrometers are considerably more expensive.*

● Always check the calibration of the micrometer before use. With the anvils closed (0 to 25 mm type) or set over a test gauge

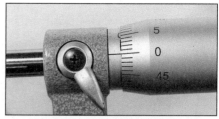

3.2 Check micrometer calibration before use

(for the larger types) the scale should read zero (see illustration 3.2); make sure that the anvils (and test piece) are clean first. Any discrepancy can be adjusted by referring to the instructions supplied with the tool. Remember that the micrometer is a precision measuring tool - don't force the anvils closed, use the ratchet (4) on the end of the micrometer to close it. In this way, a measured force is always applied.

● To use, first make sure that the item being measured is clean. Place the anvil of the micrometer (1) against the item and use the thimble (2) to bring the spindle (3) lightly into contact with the other side of the item (see illustration 3.3). Don't tighten the thimble down because this will damage the micrometer - instead use the ratchet (4) on the end of the micrometer. The ratchet mechanism applies a measured force preventing damage to the instrument.

● The micrometer is read by referring to the linear scale on the sleeve and the annular scale on the thimble. Read off the sleeve first to obtain the base measurement, then add the fine measurement from the thimble to obtain the overall reading. The linear scale on the sleeve represents the measuring range of the micrometer (eg 0 to 25 mm). The annular scale

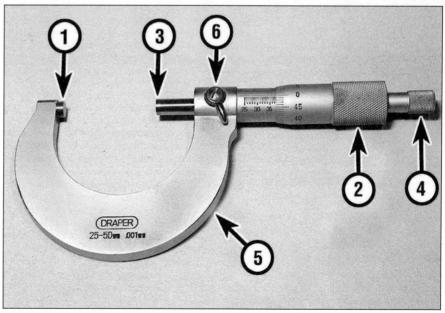

3.3 Micrometer component parts

1	Anvil	3	Spindle	5	Frame
2	Thimble	4	Ratchet	6	Locking lever

on the thimble will be in graduations of 0.01 mm (or as marked on the frame) - one full revolution of the thimble will move 0.5 mm on the linear scale. Take the reading where the datum line on the sleeve intersects the thimble's scale. Always position the eye directly above the scale otherwise an inaccurate reading will result.

In the example shown the item measures 2.95 mm (see illustration 3.4):

Linear scale	2.00 mm
Linear scale	0.50 mm
Annular scale	0.45 mm
Total figure	2.95 mm

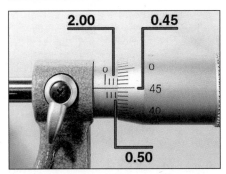

3.4 Micrometer reading of 2.95 mm

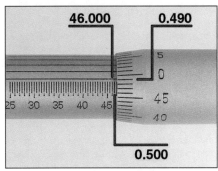

3.5 Micrometer reading of 46.99 mm on linear and annular scales . . .

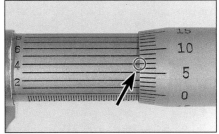
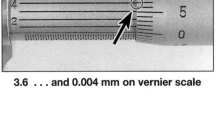

3.6 . . . and 0.004 mm on vernier scale

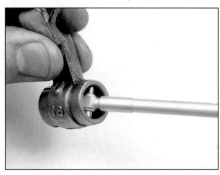

3.7 Expand the telescoping gauge in the bore, lock its position . . .

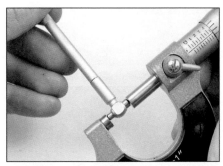

3.8 . . . then measure the gauge with a micrometer

3.9 Expand the small hole gauge in the bore, lock its position . . .

3.10 . . . then measure the gauge with a micrometer

Most micrometers have a locking lever (6) on the frame to hold the setting in place, allowing the item to be removed from the micrometer.
● Some micrometers have a vernier scale on their sleeve, providing an even finer measurement to be taken, in 0.001 increments of a millimetre. Take the sleeve and thimble measurement as described above, then check which graduation on the vernier scale aligns with that of the annular scale on the thimble **Note:** *The eye must be perpendicular to the scale when taking the vernier reading - if necessary rotate the body of the micrometer to ensure this.* Multiply the vernier scale figure by 0.001 and add it to the base and fine measurement figures.

In the example shown the item measures 46.994 mm (see illustrations 3.5 and 3.6):

Linear scale (base)	46.000 mm
Linear scale (base)	00.500 mm
Annular scale (fine)	00.490 mm
Vernier scale	00.004 mm
Total figure	46.994 mm

Internal micrometer

● Internal micrometers are available for measuring bore diameters, but are expensive and unlikely to be available for home use. It is suggested that a set of telescoping gauges and small hole gauges, both of which must be used with an external micrometer, will suffice for taking internal measurements on a motorcycle.
● Telescoping gauges can be used to measure internal diameters of components. Select a gauge with the correct size range, make sure its ends are clean and insert it into the bore. Expand the gauge, then lock its position and withdraw it from the bore **(see illustration 3.7)**. Measure across the gauge ends with a micrometer **(see illustration 3.8)**.
● Very small diameter bores (such as valve guides) are measured with a small hole gauge. Once adjusted to a slip-fit inside the component, its position is locked and the gauge withdrawn for measurement with a micrometer **(see illustrations 3.9 and 3.10)**.

Vernier caliper

Note: *The conventional linear and dial gauge type instruments are described. Digital types are easier to read, but are far more expensive.*
● The vernier caliper does not provide the precision of a micrometer, but is versatile in being able to measure internal and external diameters. Some types also incorporate a depth gauge. It is ideal for measuring clutch plate friction material and spring free lengths.
● To use the conventional linear scale vernier, slacken off the vernier clamp screws (1) and set its jaws over (2), or inside (3), the item to be measured **(see illustration 3.11)**. Slide the jaw into contact, using the thumb-wheel (4) for fine movement of the sliding scale (5) then tighten the clamp screws (1). Read off the main scale (6) where the zero on the sliding scale (5) intersects it, taking the whole number to the left of the zero; this provides the base measurement. View along the sliding scale and select the division which

lines up exactly with any of the divisions on the main scale, noting that the divisions usually represents 0.02 of a millimetre. Add this fine measurement to the base measurement to obtain the total reading.

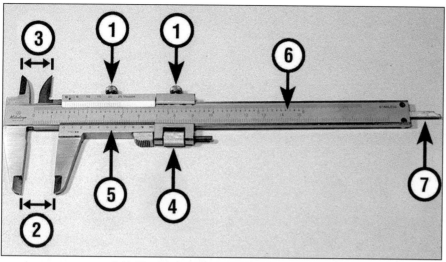

3.11 Vernier component parts (linear gauge)

1 Clamp screws	3 Internal jaws	5 Sliding scale	7 Depth gauge
2 External jaws	4 Thumbwheel	6 Main scale	

In the example shown the item measures 55.92 mm **(see illustration 3.12)**:

Base measurement	55.00 mm
Fine measurement	00.92 mm
Total figure	55.92 mm

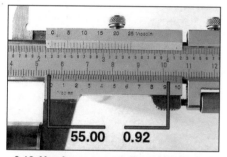

3.12 Vernier gauge reading of 55.92 mm

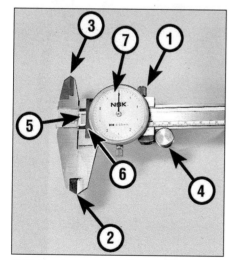

3.13 Vernier component parts (dial gauge)

1 Clamp screw	5 Main scale
2 External jaws	6 Sliding scale
3 Internal jaws	7 Dial gauge
4 Thumbwheel	

● Some vernier calipers are equipped with a dial gauge for fine measurement. Before use, check that the jaws are clean, then close them fully and check that the dial gauge reads zero. If necessary adjust the gauge ring accordingly. Slacken the vernier clamp screw (1) and set its jaws over (2), or inside (3), the item to be measured **(see illustration 3.13)**. Slide the jaws into contact, using the thumbwheel (4) for fine movement. Read off the main scale (5) where the edge of the sliding scale (6) intersects it, taking the whole number to the left of the zero; this provides the base measurement. Read off the needle position on the dial gauge (7) scale to provide the fine measurement; each division represents 0.05 of a millimetre. Add this fine measurement to the base measurement to obtain the total reading.

In the example shown the item measures 55.95 mm **(see illustration 3.14)**:

Base measurement	55.00 mm
Fine measurement	00.95 mm
Total figure	55.95 mm

3.14 Vernier gauge reading of 55.95 mm

Plastigauge

● Plastigauge is a plastic material which can be compressed between two surfaces to measure the oil clearance between them. The width of the compressed Plastigauge is measured against a calibrated scale to determine the clearance.

● Common uses of Plastigauge are for measuring the clearance between crankshaft journal and main bearing inserts, between crankshaft journal and big-end bearing inserts, and between camshaft and bearing surfaces. The following example describes big-end oil clearance measurement.

● Handle the Plastigauge material carefully to prevent distortion. Using a sharp knife, cut a length which corresponds with the width of the bearing being measured and place it carefully across the journal so that it is parallel with the shaft **(see illustration 3.15)**. Carefully install both bearing shells and the connecting rod. Without rotating the rod on the journal tighten its bolts or nuts (as applicable) to the specified torque. The connecting rod and bearings are then disassembled and the crushed Plastigauge examined.

3.15 Plastigauge placed across shaft journal

● Using the scale provided in the Plastigauge kit, measure the width of the material to determine the oil clearance **(see illustration 3.16)**. Always remove all traces of Plastigauge after use using your fingernails.

Caution: Arriving at the correct clearance demands that the assembly is torqued correctly, according to the settings and sequence (where applicable) provided by the motorcycle manufacturer.

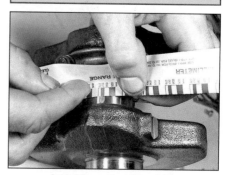

3.16 Measuring the width of the crushed Plastigauge

Dial gauge or DTI (Dial Test Indicator)

● A dial gauge can be used to accurately measure small amounts of movement. Typical uses are measuring shaft runout or shaft endfloat (sideplay) and setting piston position for ignition timing on two-strokes. A dial gauge set usually comes with a range of different probes and adapters and mounting equipment.

● The gauge needle must point to zero when at rest. Rotate the ring around its periphery to zero the gauge.

● Check that the gauge is capable of reading the extent of movement in the work. Most gauges have a small dial set in the face which records whole millimetres of movement as well as the fine scale around the face periphery which is calibrated in 0.01 mm divisions. Read off the small dial first to obtain the base measurement, then add the measurement from the fine scale to obtain the total reading.

In the example shown the gauge reads 1.48 mm (see illustration 3.17):

Base measurement	1.00 mm
Fine measurement	0.48 mm
Total figure	1.48 mm

3.17 Dial gauge reading of 1.48 mm

● If measuring shaft runout, the shaft must be supported in vee-blocks and the gauge mounted on a stand perpendicular to the shaft. Rest the tip of the gauge against the centre of the shaft and rotate the shaft slowly whilst watching the gauge reading (see illustration 3.18). Take several measurements along the length of the shaft and record the

3.18 Using a dial gauge to measure shaft runout

maximum gauge reading as the amount of runout in the shaft. **Note:** *The reading obtained will be total runout at that point - some manufacturers specify that the runout figure is halved to compare with their specified runout limit.*

● Endfloat (sideplay) measurement requires that the gauge is mounted securely to the surrounding component with its probe touching the end of the shaft. Using hand pressure, push and pull on the shaft noting the maximum endfloat recorded on the gauge (see illustration 3.19).

3.19 Using a dial gauge to measure shaft endfloat

● A dial gauge with suitable adapters can be used to determine piston position BTDC on two-stroke engines for the purposes of ignition timing. The gauge, adapter and suitable length probe are installed in the place of the spark plug and the gauge zeroed at TDC. If the piston position is specified as 1.14 mm BTDC, rotate the engine back to 2.00 mm BTDC, then slowly forwards to 1.14 mm BTDC.

Cylinder compression gauges

● A compression gauge is used for measuring cylinder compression. Either the rubber-cone type or the threaded adapter type can be used. The latter is preferred to ensure a perfect seal against the cylinder head. A 0 to 300 psi (0 to 20 Bar) type gauge (for petrol/gasoline engines) will be suitable for motorcycles.

● The spark plug is removed and the gauge either held hard against the cylinder head (cone type) or the gauge adapter screwed into the cylinder head (threaded type) (see illustration 3.20). Cylinder compression is measured with the engine turning over, but not running. The

3.20 Using a rubber-cone type cylinder compression gauge

gauge will hold the reading until manually released.

Oil pressure gauge

● An oil pressure gauge is used for measuring engine oil pressure. Most gauges come with a set of adapters to fit the thread of the take-off point (see illustration 3.21). If the take-off point specified by the motorcycle manufacturer is an external oil pipe union, make sure that the specified replacement union is used to prevent oil starvation.

3.21 Oil pressure gauge and take-off point adapter (arrow)

● Oil pressure is measured with the engine running (at a specific rpm) and often the manufacturer will specify pressure limits for a cold and hot engine.

Straight-edge and surface plate

● If checking the gasket face of a component for warpage, place a steel rule or precision straight-edge across the gasket face and measure any gap between the straight-edge and component with feeler gauges (see illustration 3.22). Check diagonally across the component and between mounting holes (see illustration 3.23).

3.22 Use a straight-edge and feeler gauges to check for warpage

3.23 Check for warpage in these directions

● Checking individual components for warpage, such as clutch plain (metal) plates, requires a perfectly flat plate or piece or plate glass and feeler gauges.

4 Torque and leverage

What is torque?

● Torque describes the twisting force about a shaft. The amount of torque applied is determined by the distance from the centre of the shaft to the end of the lever and the amount of force being applied to the end of the lever; distance multiplied by force equals torque.

● The manufacturer applies a measured torque to a bolt or nut to ensure that it will not slacken in use and to hold two components securely together without movement in the joint. The actual torque setting depends on the thread size, bolt or nut material and the composition of the components being held.

● Too little torque may cause the fastener to loosen due to vibration, whereas too much torque will distort the joint faces of the component or cause the fastener to shear off. Always stick to the specified torque setting.

Using a torque wrench

● Check the calibration of the torque wrench and make sure it has a suitable range for the job. Torque wrenches are available in Nm (Newton-metres), kgf m (kilograms-force metre), lbf ft (pounds-feet), lbf in (inch-pounds). Do not confuse lbf ft with lbf in.

● Adjust the tool to the desired torque on the scale (see illustration 4.1). If your torque wrench is not calibrated in the units specified, carefully convert the figure (see Conversion Factors). A manufacturer sometimes gives a torque setting as a range (8 to 10 Nm) rather than a single figure - in this case set the tool midway between the two settings. The same torque may be expressed as 9 Nm ± 1 Nm. Some torque wrenches have a method of locking the setting so that it isn't inadvertently altered during use.

4.1 Set the torque wrench index mark to the setting required, in this case 12 Nm

● Install the bolts/nuts in their correct location and secure them lightly. Their threads must be clean and free of any old locking compound. Unless specified the threads and flange should be dry - oiled threads are necessary in certain circumstances and the manufacturer will take this into account in the specified torque figure. Similarly, the manufacturer may also specify the application of thread-locking compound.

● Tighten the fasteners in the specified sequence until the torque wrench clicks, indicating that the torque setting has been reached. Apply the torque again to double-check the setting. Where different thread diameter fasteners secure the component, as a rule tighten the larger diameter ones first.

● When the torque wrench has been finished with, release the lock (where applicable) and fully back off its setting to zero - do not leave the torque wrench tensioned. Also, do not use a torque wrench for slackening a fastener.

Angle-tightening

● Manufacturers often specify a figure in degrees for final tightening of a fastener. This usually follows tightening to a specific torque setting.

● A degree disc can be set and attached to the socket (see illustration 4.2) or a protractor can be used to mark the angle of movement on the bolt/nut head and the surrounding casting (see illustration 4.3).

4.2 Angle tightening can be accomplished with a torque-angle gauge . . .

4.3 . . . or by marking the angle on the surrounding component

Loosening sequences

● Where more than one bolt/nut secures a component, loosen each fastener evenly a little at a time. In this way, not all the stress of the joint is held by one fastener and the components are not likely to distort.

● If a tightening sequence is provided, work in the REVERSE of this, but if not, work from the outside in, in a criss-cross sequence (see illustration 4.4).

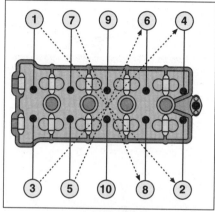

4.4 When slackening, work from the outside inwards

Tightening sequences

● If a component is held by more than one fastener it is important that the retaining bolts/nuts are tightened evenly to prevent uneven stress build-up and distortion of sealing faces. This is especially important on high-compression joints such as the cylinder head.

● A sequence is usually provided by the manufacturer, either in a diagram or actually marked in the casting. If not, always start in the centre and work outwards in a criss-cross pattern (see illustration 4.5). Start off by securing all bolts/nuts finger-tight, then set the torque wrench and tighten each fastener by a small amount in sequence until the final torque is reached. By following this practice,

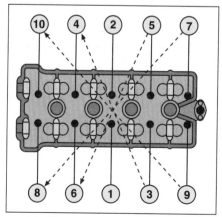

4.5 When tightening, work from the inside outwards

the joint will be held evenly and will not be distorted. Important joints, such as the cylinder head and big-end fasteners often have two- or three-stage torque settings.

Applying leverage

● Use tools at the correct angle. Position a socket wrench or spanner on the bolt/nut so that you pull it towards you when loosening. If this can't be done, push the spanner without curling your fingers around it **(see illustration 4.6)** - the spanner may slip or the fastener loosen suddenly, resulting in your fingers being crushed against a component.

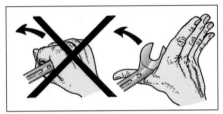

4.6 If you can't pull on the spanner to loosen a fastener, push with your hand open

● Additional leverage is gained by extending the length of the lever. The best way to do this is to use a breaker bar instead of the regular length tool, or to slip a length of tubing over the end of the spanner or socket wrench.
● If additional leverage will not work, the fastener head is either damaged or firmly corroded in place (see Fasteners).

5 Bearings

Bearing removal and installation

Drivers and sockets

● Before removing a bearing, always inspect the casing to see which way it must be driven out - some casings will have retaining plates or a cast step. Also check for any identifying markings on the bearing and if installed to a certain depth, measure this at this stage. Some roller bearings are sealed on one side - take note of the original fitted position.
● Bearings can be driven out of a casing using a bearing driver tool (with the correct size head) or a socket of the correct diameter. Select the driver head or socket so that it contacts the outer race of the bearing, not the balls/rollers or inner race. Always support the casing around the bearing housing with wood blocks, otherwise there is a risk of fracture. The bearing is driven out with a few blows on the driver or socket from a heavy mallet. Unless access is severely restricted (as with wheel bearings), a pin-punch is not recommended unless it is moved around the bearing to keep it square in its housing.

● The same equipment can be used to install bearings. Make sure the bearing housing is supported on wood blocks and line up the bearing in its housing. Fit the bearing as noted on removal - generally they are installed with their marked side facing outwards. Tap the bearing squarely into its housing using a driver or socket which bears only on the bearing's outer race - contact with the bearing balls/rollers or inner race will destroy it **(see illustrations 5.1 and 5.2)**.
● Check that the bearing inner race and balls/rollers rotate freely.

5.1 Using a bearing driver against the bearing's outer race

5.2 Using a large socket against the bearing's outer race

Pullers and slide-hammers

● Where a bearing is pressed on a shaft a puller will be required to extract it **(see illustration 5.3)**. Make sure that the puller clamp or legs fit securely behind the bearing and are unlikely to slip out. If pulling a bearing

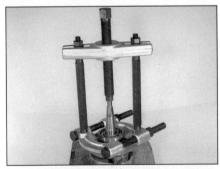

5.3 This bearing puller clamps behind the bearing and pressure is applied to the shaft end to draw the bearing off

off a gear shaft for example, you may have to locate the puller behind a gear pinion if there is no access to the race and draw the gear pinion off the shaft as well **(see illustration 5.4)**.

Caution: Ensure that the puller's centre bolt locates securely against the end of the shaft and will not slip when pressure is applied. Also ensure that puller does not damage the shaft end.

5.4 Where no access is available to the rear of the bearing, it is sometimes possible to draw off the adjacent component

● Operate the puller so that its centre bolt exerts pressure on the shaft end and draws the bearing off the shaft.
● When installing the bearing on the shaft, tap only on the bearing's inner race - contact with the balls/rollers or outer race with destroy the bearing. Use a socket or length of tubing as a drift which fits over the shaft end **(see illustration 5.5)**.

5.5 When installing a bearing on a shaft use a piece of tubing which bears only on the bearing's inner race

● Where a bearing locates in a blind hole in a casing, it cannot be driven or pulled out as described above. A slide-hammer with knife-edged bearing puller attachment will be required. The puller attachment passes through the bearing and when tightened expands to fit firmly behind the bearing **(see illustration 5.6)**. By operating the slide-hammer part of the tool the bearing is jarred out of its housing **(see illustration 5.7)**.
● It is possible, if the bearing is of reasonable weight, for it to drop out of its housing if the casing is heated as described opposite.

5.6 Expand the bearing puller so that it locks behind the bearing . . .

5.7 . . . attach the slide hammer to the bearing puller

If this method is attempted, first prepare a work surface which will enable the casing to be tapped face down to help dislodge the bearing - a wood surface is ideal since it will not damage the casing's gasket surface. Wearing protective gloves, tap the heated casing several times against the work surface to dislodge the bearing under its own weight **(see illustration 5.8)**.

5.8 Tapping a casing face down on wood blocks can often dislodge a bearing

● Bearings can be installed in blind holes using the driver or socket method described above.

Drawbolts

● Where a bearing or bush is set in the eye of a component, such as a suspension linkage arm or connecting rod small-end, removal by drift may damage the component. Furthermore, a rubber bushing in a shock absorber eye cannot successfully be driven out of position. If access is available to a engineering press, the task is straightforward. If not, a drawbolt can be fabricated to extract the bearing or bush.

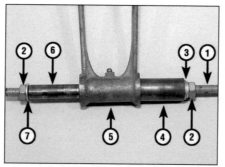

5.9 Drawbolt component parts assembled on a suspension arm

1 Bolt or length of threaded bar
2 Nuts
3 Washer (external diameter greater than tubing internal diameter)
4 Tubing (internal diameter sufficient to accommodate bearing)
5 Suspension arm with bearing
6 Tubing (external diameter slightly smaller than bearing)
7 Washer (external diameter slightly smaller than bearing)

5.10 Drawing the bearing out of the suspension arm

● To extract the bearing/bush you will need a long bolt with nut (or piece of threaded bar with two nuts), a piece of tubing which has an internal diameter larger than the bearing/bush, another piece of tubing which has an external diameter slightly smaller than the bearing/bush, and a selection of washers **(see illustrations 5.9 and 5.10)**. Note that the pieces of tubing must be of the same length, or longer, than the bearing/bush.
● The same kit (without the pieces of tubing) can be used to draw the new bearing/bush back into place **(see illustration 5.11)**.

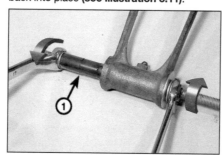

5.11 Installing a new bearing (1) in the suspension arm

Temperature change

● If the bearing's outer race is a tight fit in the casing, the aluminium casing can be heated to release its grip on the bearing. Aluminium will expand at a greater rate than the steel bearing outer race. There are several ways to do this, but avoid any localised extreme heat (such as a blow torch) - aluminium alloy has a low melting point.
● Approved methods of heating a casing are using a domestic oven (heated to 100°C) or immersing the casing in boiling water **(see illustration 5.12)**. Low temperature range localised heat sources such as a paint stripper heat gun or clothes iron can also be used **(see illustration 5.13)**. Alternatively, soak a rag in boiling water, wring it out and wrap it around the bearing housing.

> ⚠ **Warning: All of these methods require care in use to prevent scalding and burns to the hands. Wear protective gloves when handling hot components.**

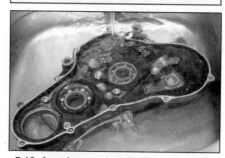

5.12 A casing can be immersed in a sink of boiling water to aid bearing removal

5.13 Using a localised heat source to aid bearing removal

● If heating the whole casing note that plastic components, such as the neutral switch, may suffer - remove them beforehand.
● After heating, remove the bearing as described above. You may find that the expansion is sufficient for the bearing to fall out of the casing under its own weight or with a light tap on the driver or socket.
● If necessary, the casing can be heated to aid bearing installation, and this is sometimes the recommended procedure if the motorcycle manufacturer has designed the housing and bearing fit with this intention.

● Installation of bearings can be eased by placing them in a freezer the night before installation. The steel bearing will contract slightly, allowing easy insertion in its housing. This is often useful when installing steering head outer races in the frame.

Bearing types and markings

● Plain shell bearings, ball bearings, needle roller bearings and tapered roller bearings will all be found on motorcycles (see illustrations 5.14 and 5.15). The ball and roller types are usually caged between an inner and outer race, but uncaged variations may be found.

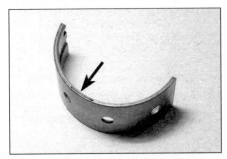

5.14 Shell bearings are either plain or grooved. They are usually identified by colour code (arrow)

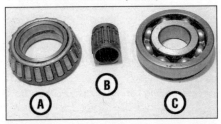

5.15 Tapered roller bearing (A), needle roller bearing (B) and ball journal bearing (C)

● Shell bearings (often called inserts) are usually found at the crankshaft main and connecting rod big-end where they are good at coping with high loads. They are made of a phosphor-bronze material and are impregnated with self-lubricating properties.
● Ball bearings and needle roller bearings consist of a steel inner and outer race with the balls or rollers between the races. They require constant lubrication by oil or grease and are good at coping with axial loads. Taper roller bearings consist of rollers set in a tapered cage set on the inner race; the outer race is separate. They are good at coping with axial loads and prevent movement along the shaft - a typical application is in the steering head.
● Bearing manufacturers produce bearings to ISO size standards and stamp one face of the bearing to indicate its internal and external diameter, load capacity and type (see illustration 5.16).
● Metal bushes are usually of phosphor-bronze material. Rubber bushes are used in suspension mounting eyes. Fibre bushes have also been used in suspension pivots.

5.16 Typical bearing marking

Bearing fault finding

● If a bearing outer race has spun in its housing, the housing material will be damaged. You can use a bearing locking compound to bond the outer race in place if damage is not too severe.
● Shell bearings will fail due to damage of their working surface, as a result of lack of lubrication, corrosion or abrasive particles in the oil (see illustration 5.17). Small particles of dirt in the oil may embed in the bearing material whereas larger particles will score the bearing and shaft journal. If a number of short journeys are made, insufficient heat will be generated to drive off condensation which has built up on the bearings.

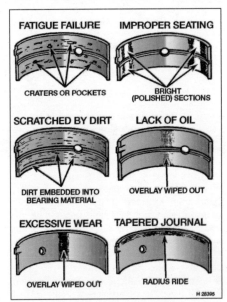

5.17 Typical bearing failures

● Ball and roller bearings will fail due to lack of lubrication or damage to the balls or rollers. Tapered-roller bearings can be damaged by overloading them. Unless the bearing is sealed on both sides, wash it in paraffin (kerosene) to remove all old grease then allow it to dry. Make a visual inspection looking to dented balls or rollers, damaged cages and worn or pitted races (see illustration 5.18).
● A ball bearing can be checked for wear by listening to it when spun. Apply a film of light oil to the bearing and hold it close to the ear - hold the outer race with one hand and spin the

5.18 Example of ball journal bearing with damaged balls and cages

5.19 Hold outer race and listen to inner race when spun

inner race with the other hand (see illustration 5.19). The bearing should be almost silent when spun; if it grates or rattles it is worn.

6 Oil seals

Oil seal removal and installation

● Oil seals should be renewed every time a component is dismantled. This is because the seal lips will become set to the sealing surface and will not necessarily reseal.
● Oil seals can be prised out of position using a large flat-bladed screwdriver (see illustration 6.1). In the case of crankcase seals, check first that the seal is not lipped on the inside, preventing its removal with the crankcases joined.

6.1 Prise out oil seals with a large flat-bladed screwdriver

● New seals are usually installed with their marked face (containing the seal reference code) outwards and the spring side towards the fluid being retained. In certain cases, such as a two-stroke engine crankshaft seal, a double lipped seal may be used due to there being fluid or gas on each side of the joint.

● Use a bearing driver or socket which bears only on the outer hard edge of the seal to install it in the casing - tapping on the inner edge will damage the sealing lip.

Oil seal types and markings

● Oil seals are usually of the single-lipped type. Double-lipped seals are found where a liquid or gas is on both sides of the joint.
● Oil seals can harden and lose their sealing ability if the motorcycle has been in storage for a long period - renewal is the only solution.
● Oil seal manufacturers also conform to the ISO markings for seal size - these are moulded into the outer face of the seal (see illustration 6.2).

6.2 These oil seal markings indicate inside diameter, outside diameter and seal thickness

7 Gaskets and sealants

Types of gasket and sealant

● Gaskets are used to seal the mating surfaces between components and keep lubricants, fluids, vacuum or pressure contained within the assembly. Aluminium gaskets are sometimes found at the cylinder joints, but most gaskets are paper-based. If the mating surfaces of the components being joined are undamaged the gasket can be installed dry, although a dab of sealant or grease will be useful to hold it in place during assembly.
● RTV (Room Temperature Vulcanising) silicone rubber sealants cure when exposed to moisture in the atmosphere. These sealants are good at filling pits or irregular gasket faces, but will tend to be forced out of the joint under very high torque. They can be used to replace a paper gasket, but first make sure that the width of the paper gasket is not essential to the shimming of internal components. RTV sealants should not be used on components containing petrol (gasoline).
● Non-hardening, semi-hardening and hard setting liquid gasket compounds can be used with a gasket or between a metal-to-metal joint. Select the sealant to suit the application: universal non-hardening sealant can be used on virtually all joints; semi-hardening on joint faces which are rough or damaged; hard setting sealant on joints which require a permanent bond and are subjected to high temperature and pressure. **Note:** Check first if the paper gasket has a bead of sealant

impregnated in its surface before applying additional sealant.
● When choosing a sealant, make sure it is suitable for the application, particularly if being applied in a high-temperature area or in the vicinity of fuel. Certain manufacturers produce sealants in either clear, silver or black colours to match the finish of the engine. This has a particular application on motorcycles where much of the engine is exposed.
● Do not over-apply sealant. That which is squeezed out on the outside of the joint can be wiped off, whereas an excess of sealant on the inside can break off and clog oilways.

Breaking a sealed joint

● Age, heat, pressure and the use of hard setting sealant can cause two components to stick together so tightly that they are difficult to separate using finger pressure alone. Do not resort to using levers unless there is a pry point provided for this purpose (see illustration 7.1) or else the gasket surfaces will be damaged.
● Use a soft-faced hammer (see illustration 7.2) or a wood block and conventional hammer to strike the component near the mating surface. Avoid hammering against cast extremities since they may break off. If this method fails, try using a wood wedge between the two components.

Caution: If the joint will not separate, double-check that you have removed all the fasteners.

7.1 If a pry point is provided, apply gently pressure with a flat-bladed screwdriver

7.2 Tap around the joint with a soft-faced mallet if necessary - don't strike cooling fins

Removal of old gasket and sealant

● Paper gaskets will most likely come away complete, leaving only a few traces stuck

Most components have one or two hollow locating dowels between the two gasket faces. If a dowel cannot be removed, do not resort to gripping it with pliers - it will almost certainly be distorted. Install a close-fitting socket or Phillips screwdriver into the dowel and then grip the outer edge of the dowel to free it.

on the sealing faces of the components. It is imperative that all traces are removed to ensure correct sealing of the new gasket.
● Very carefully scrape all traces of gasket away making sure that the sealing surfaces are not gouged or scored by the scraper (see illustrations 7.3, 7.4 and 7.5). Stubborn deposits can be removed by spraying with an aerosol gasket remover. Final preparation of

7.3 Paper gaskets can be scraped off with a gasket scraper tool . . .

7.4 . . . a knife blade . . .

7.5 . . . or a household scraper

7.6 Fine abrasive paper is wrapped around a flat file to clean up the gasket face

7.7 A kitchen scourer can be used on stubborn deposits

the gasket surface can be made with very fine abrasive paper or a plastic kitchen scourer **(see illustrations 7.6 and 7.7)**.

● Old sealant can be scraped or peeled off components, depending on the type originally used. Note that gasket removal compounds are available to avoid scraping the components clean; make sure the gasket remover suits the type of sealant used.

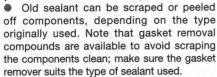

8   Chains

Breaking and joining final drive chains

● Drive chains for all but small bikes are continuous and do not have a clip-type connecting link. The chain must be broken using a chain breaker tool and the new chain securely riveted together using a new soft rivet-type link. Never use a clip-type connecting link instead of a rivet-type link, except in an emergency. Various chain breaking and riveting tools are available, either as separate tools or combined as illustrated in the accompanying photographs - read the instructions supplied with the tool carefully.

⚠️ **Warning: The need to rivet the new link pins correctly cannot be overstressed - loss of control of the motorcycle is very likely to result if the chain breaks in use.**

● Rotate the chain and look for the soft link. The soft link pins look like they have been

8.1 Tighten the chain breaker to push the pin out of the link . . .

8.2 . . . withdraw the pin, remove the tool . . .

8.3 . . . and separate the chain link

deeply centre-punched instead of peened over like all the other pins **(see illustration 8.9)** and its sideplate may be a different colour. Position the soft link midway between the sprockets and assemble the chain breaker tool over one of the soft link pins **(see illustration 8.1)**. Operate the tool to push the pin out through the chain **(see illustration 8.2)**. On an O-ring chain, remove the O-rings **(see illustration 8.3)**. Carry out the same procedure on the other soft link pin.

> **Caution: Certain soft link pins (particularly on the larger chains) may require their ends to be filed or ground off before they can be pressed out using the tool.**

● Check that you have the correct size and strength (standard or heavy duty) new soft link - do not reuse the old link. Look for the size marking on the chain sideplates **(see illustration 8.10)**.

● Position the chain ends so that they are engaged over the rear sprocket. On an O-ring

8.4 Insert the new soft link, with O-rings, through the chain ends . . .

8.5 . . . install the O-rings over the pin ends . . .

8.6 . . . followed by the sideplate

chain, install a new O-ring over each pin of the link and insert the link through the two chain ends **(see illustration 8.4)**. Install a new O-ring over the end of each pin, followed by the sideplate (with the chain manufacturer's marking facing outwards) **(see illustrations 8.5 and 8.6)**. On an unsealed chain, insert the link through the two chain ends, then install the sideplate with the chain manufacturer's marking facing outwards.

● Note that it may not be possible to install the sideplate using finger pressure alone. If using a joining tool, assemble it so that the plates of the tool clamp the link and press the sideplate over the pins **(see illustration 8.7)**. Otherwise, use two small sockets placed over

8.7 Push the sideplate into position using a clamp

8.8 Assemble the chain riveting tool over one pin at a time and tighten it fully

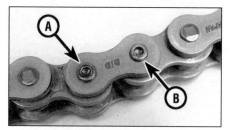

8.9 Pin end correctly riveted (A), pin end unriveted (B)

the rivet ends and two pieces of the wood between a G-clamp. Operate the clamp to press the sideplate over the pins.

● Assemble the joining tool over one pin (following the maker's instructions) and tighten the tool down to spread the pin end securely **(see illustrations 8.8 and 8.9)**. Do the same on the other pin.

> ⚠ **Warning: Check that the pin ends are secure and that there is no danger of the sideplate coming loose. If the pin ends are cracked the soft link must be renewed.**

Final drive chain sizing

● Chains are sized using a three digit number, followed by a suffix to denote the chain type **(see illustration 8.10)**. Chain type is either standard or heavy duty (thicker sideplates), and also unsealed or O-ring/X-ring type.

● The first digit of the number relates to the pitch of the chain, ie the distance from the centre of one pin to the centre of the next pin **(see illustration 8.11)**. Pitch is expressed in eighths of an inch, as follows:

8.10 Typical chain size and type marking

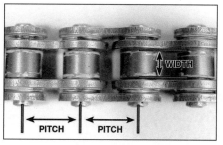

8.11 Chain dimensions

| Sizes commencing with a 4 (eg 428) have a pitch of 1/2 inch (12.7 mm) |
| Sizes commencing with a 5 (eg 520) have a pitch of 5/8 inch (15.9 mm) |
| Sizes commencing with a 6 (eg 630) have a pitch of 3/4 inch (19.1 mm) |

● The second and third digits of the chain size relate to the width of the rollers, again in imperial units, eg the 525 shown has 5/16 inch (7.94 mm) rollers **(see illustration 8.11)**.

9 Hoses

Clamping to prevent flow

● Small-bore flexible hoses can be clamped to prevent fluid flow whilst a component is worked on. Whichever method is used, ensure that the hose material is not permanently distorted or damaged by the clamp.

a) A brake hose clamp available from auto accessory shops **(see illustration 9.1)**.
b) A wingnut type hose clamp **(see illustration 9.2)**.

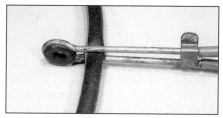

9.1 Hoses can be clamped with an automotive brake hose clamp . . .

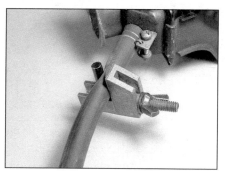

9.2 . . . a wingnut type hose clamp . . .

c) Two sockets placed each side of the hose and held with straight-jawed self-locking grips **(see illustration 9.3)**.
d) Thick card each side of the hose held between straight-jawed self-locking grips **(see illustration 9.4)**.

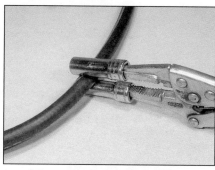

9.3 . . . two sockets and a pair of self-locking grips . . .

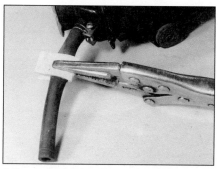

9.4 . . . or thick card and self-locking grips

Freeing and fitting hoses

● Always make sure the hose clamp is moved well clear of the hose end. Grip the hose with your hand and rotate it whilst pulling it off the union. If the hose has hardened due to age and will not move, slit it with a sharp knife and peel its ends off the union **(see illustration 9.5)**.

● Resist the temptation to use grease or soap on the unions to aid installation; although it helps the hose slip over the union it will equally aid the escape of fluid from the joint. It is preferable to soften the hose ends in hot water and wet the inside surface of the hose with water or a fluid which will evaporate.

9.5 Cutting a coolant hose free with a sharp knife

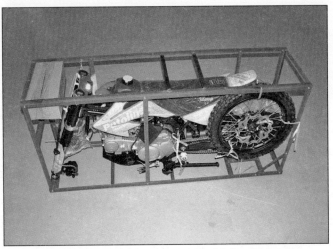

1.1a The Pit bike will be mounted inside its steel crate

1.1b Check that all parts are provided

Building a bike from the crate

2.2 Unbolt and remove the steel tube (arrowed)

1 Uncrating the bike

1 Once the packaging has been removed, you'll need to free the bike from its steel crate **(see illustration)**. Release all the wire ties and remove the individual components, then unbolt the top and ends of the crate. Check that everything you expect to find is there **(see illustration)**. The supplier will usually enclose a list of the assembly tasks and adjustments/ checks you should perform. This effectively is much like the dealer's PDI (pre delivery inspection).

2 Building the bike

1 We recommend that you leave the bike attached to the bottom part of the crate until the front wheel is fitted.

Rear shock

2 Start by mounting the rear shock in place – its top mounting is usually already connected. Some models will have a short length of steel tube between the bottom mounting and frame to stop the back end collapsing; unbolt this and discard the support **(see illustration)**.

2.3a Shock lower mounting is secured by pivot bolt and nut

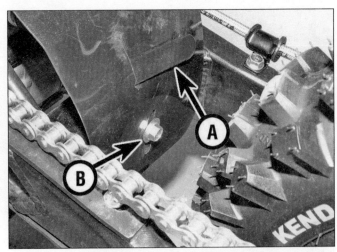

2.3b Deflector retaining bracket tab (A) and securing bolt (B)

2.5a Assemble the clamp around the handlebar...

2.5b ...align the knurled section with the mounting points

3 Bring the shock down to fit between the mounting points on the swingarm and secure it with the pivot bolt and nut **(see illustration)**. If the bike is equipped with a plastic mud deflector, fit its bracket to the shock rear mounting and bolt the deflector lower mounting in place **(see illustration)**.

Handlebars

4 At this point it's a good idea to fit the handlebars, the benefit being that it's more stable with them in place and something to grab if the bike falls to one side. Remove any protective packaging from around the handlebar grips and levers.

5 Identify the handlebar clamps and their bolts. Align the handlebar knurled areas with the clamp base and fit the top half of the clamp and set the angle of the bars so that

they are angled slightly rearwards. Thread the bolts into place and tighten the front bolt down first, following by the rear; note that the resultant gap at the rear of the clamp is intentional. Several different bolt fixings may be found **(see illustrations)**.

Rear brake pedal (disc brake)

6 Take a few minutes to work out how the pedal return spring ends wrap around the pedal, frame and pivot – it's not the easiest thing to fit because of the tension in the spring. There should be a plain washer and split pin provided for securing the pedal on its shaft and for securing the brake rod link to the pedal – take these off if they come fixed in place. Position the pedal return spring over the pivot shaft followed by the pedal, whilst locating the rear end of the spring under the

2.5c On this type secure the handlebar bolts with the nuts under the top yoke

2.5d Gap at rear of clamp is intentional

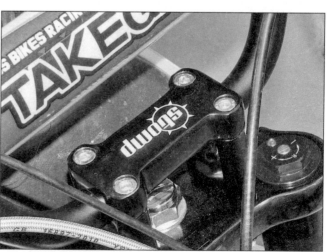

2.5e One-piece clamps are fitted on some models

2.6a Fit the return spring around the pedal pivot shaft

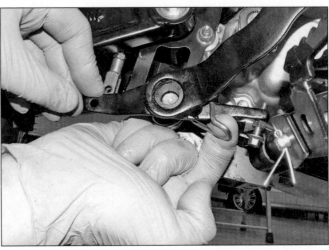

2.6b As the pedal is fitted over its pivot hook the front end of the spring under the pedal

2.6c Use of a flat-bladed screwdriver to ease the spring coils onto the pedal shoulder

2.6d Check that the spring ends (arrowed) are correctly in place

2.6e Pedal pivot correctly secured on its shaft with washer and split pin

2.6f Brake link from master cylinder correctly secured to pedal with washer and split pin

frame and the longer front end under and around the pedal (see illustrations). This may take several attempts and you may find a flat-bladed screwdriver is useful in levering the spring coils over the pedal shoulder (see illustration). Check the spring ends are located correctly and that the pedal returns to its 'at rest' position once released (see illustration). Finally fit the large plain washer over the pivot shaft and insert the split pin through the hole in the shaft. Bend the ends of the split pin around to secure it (see illustration). Now connect the brake link to the end of the pedal, fit the plain washer and secure it by inserting the split pin through the hole and bending its ends around to lock it in place (see illustration).

7 Refer to Chapter 5, Section 3 where the brake pedal is secured by a bolt.

Rear brake pedal (drum brake)

8 On models with a drum rear brake, the rear brake pedal arrangement is slightly different. Fit the brake pedal onto its pivot shaft, having applied a smear of grease to the pivot if it looks dry (see illustration). The pedal return spring connects between the hole in the pedal and the post on the frame. Connect it to the pedal and stretch it so that its top hook goes over the post. This isn't easy because of the tension in the spring. We spaced out the spring coils with plain washers (you'll need a lot) so that its length was extended and eased the top hook over the post with a screwdriver (see illustrations). Simply operate the pedal to withdraw the washers. Check that the pedal returns to its 'at rest' position once released, then fit the plain washer to the pivot shaft, insert the split pin through the shaft hole and bend its ends around to secure it (see illustration). Now connect the brake rod to the pedal extension and secure it with the plain washer and split pin (see illustration).

HAYNES HiNT

2.8a This is how you can use washers to extend a spring

2.8b Lube pivot and slide pedal onto its shaft

2.8c Connect the spring between the pedal and post then remove the spacer washers if you used this method

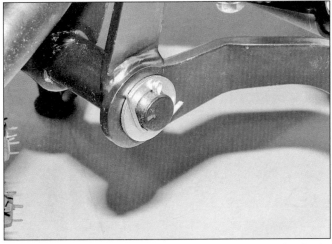

2.8d Pedal correctly secured to its pivot with washer and split pin

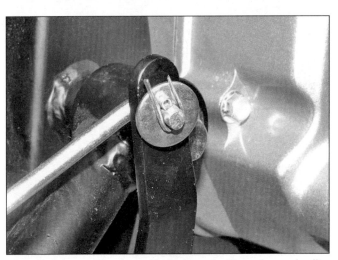

2.8e Pedal correctly secured to brake rod with washer and split pin

2.9a Connect the return spring...

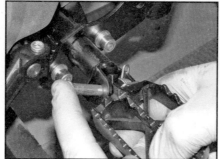

2.9b ...insert the pivot pin...

2.9c ...fit the split pin through the hole in the pivot and bend its ends around to secure it

Footrests

9 If the footrests aren't already fitted, identify the right from the left footrest. Before fitted the pivot pin, check the fitting of the return spring ends **(see illustration)**; the footrest must be able to pivot rearwards and the spring tensioned so that it snaps the footrest back to normal position. Insert the pivot pin fully and secure it with the split pin, bending the split pin ends around to lock it in place **(see illustrations)**.

Front mudguard and numberboard

10 Bolt the front mudguard to the underside of the bottom fork yoke, noting that you'll need to include the number board mounting bracket on most models **(see illustration)**. It's a good

idea to use a drop of locking compound (non-permanent type) on the bolt threads.

11 Check that the numberboard is secured top and bottom and that the cables are routed corrected behind it. The front brake hose passes through a guide on many models **(see illustration)**.

Front wheel

12 At this point detach the bike from the base of the crate. It'll be held by its wheel axle, a couple of spacers and a nut **(see illustration)**. Have someone hold the bike steady whilst you remove the axle. Manoeuvre the bike off the crate and place a support (blocks of wood are fine) under the engine bashplate to raise the front end up sufficiently to fit the wheel **(see illustration)**.

13 Check for a plastic wedge fitted between the brake pads and remove it **(see illustration)**. You may also find a small plastic spacer fitted between the front brake lever and the master cylinder – remove this too **(see illustration)**. Both are there to prevent the brake lever being applied accidentally during assembly and forcing the pads out of the caliper. Insert a flat-bladed screwdriver between the brake pads and gently apply pressure to ease them apart slightly – this will give extra clearance when fitting the disc **(see illustration)**.

14 On disc brake models, retrieve any wheel axle components supplied with the bike and use any spacers and the axle nut provided instead of those used to secure the bike to the crate. Locate the shouldered ends of the

2.10 Three bolts normally secure the mudguard to the bottom yoke

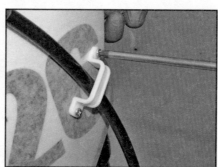

2.11 Secure the guide once the front brake hose has been routed through it

2.12 Unbolt the bike from the base of the crate

2.13a Remove the plastic wedge from the caliper mouth...

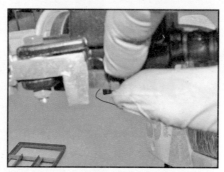

2.13b ...and from the brake lever

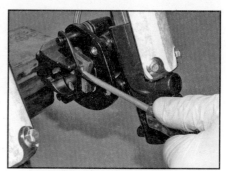

2.13c Gently ease the pads apart. You won't need to move them more than a millimetre

2.14a On this model both wheel spacers are shouldered. The shorter spacer fits into the right-hand side...

2.14b ...and the longer spacer into the left-hand side

2.14c Slide the wheel axle through from the left side...

spacers in the wheel grease seals, working out beforehand which goes in which side if they are of different lengths **(see illustrations)**. Check this by offering the wheel up to the forks – the brake disc should align with the caliper mouth and the wheel should be central within the forks. If correct, slide the axle into place making sure the disc locates correctly between the brake pads **(see illustration)**. Fit the new axle nut and tighten it whilst holding the axle head from the other side **(see illustrations)**. Spin the wheel and check that it rotates freely. Remove the support from under the engine bashplate. Apply the front brake lever a few times to bring the pads into contact with the disc.

15 A variation on the above is shown here. The spacer locates in the left side of the wheel hub. The axle has an extended head

2.14d ...and secure it with the nut on the right-hand side

which when inserted through the right-hand fork butts against the wheel hub on that side. Slacken off the axle clamp bolts on the right-hand fork and retighten them

2.14e Hold the head of the axle with one spanner and tighten the nut with the other

once the axle is in position and the axle nut tightened. We found it necessary to detach the caliper from the fork leg to enable wheel fitting.

2.15a Unbolt the caliper from the fork leg...

2.15b ...and remove the wedge from between the pads

2.15c Insert the spacer into the hub left-hand side

2.15d Slide the axle in from the right

2.15e Tighten the axle clamp bolts

2.15f Bolt the caliper back into place

2.16a Insert the brake shoe assembly into the drum inside the wheel hub...

2.16b ...and on the other side fit the spacer

2.16c As you insert the wheel axle, engage the slot in the brake plate each side of the lug on the inside of the fork

16 On models with a front drum brake, the wheel axle is shouldered and only one wheel spacer is fitted. Insert the brake shoe plate into the drum and insert the spacer into the other side of the wheel (see illustrations). Guide the wheel into place between the forks so that the lug on the inside of the left fork fits between the cast lugs in the brake plate (see illustration). Slide the axle into place and fit the new axle nut. Hold the axle head and tighten the nut, then check that the wheel rotates freely (see illustration). Slot the trunnion into the brake arm and insert the threaded adjuster rod through the hole in the trunnion (see illustration). Thread the adjuster nut onto the end of the rod then continue threading it on until the correct freeplay exists at the handlebar (see illustration). Note that for small hands, the lever reach shouldn't be set too far from the grip yet still have enough movement for the brake to be applied fully (see illustration).

2.16d Hold the axle head with one spanner and tighten the nut with the other

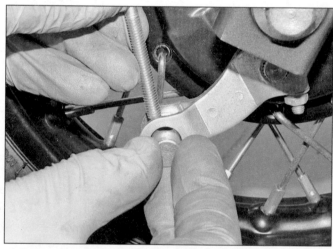

2.16e Insert the threaded end of the brake cable through the trunnion...

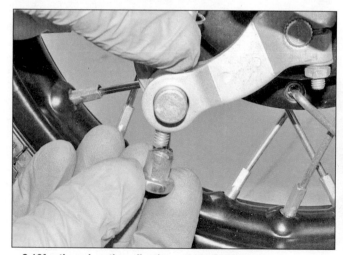

2.16f ...thread on the adjusting nut turning it so that its curved surfaces meshes with the trunnion...

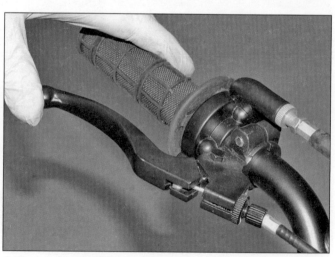

2.16g ...and setting it so that the freeplay at the handlebar lever is correct

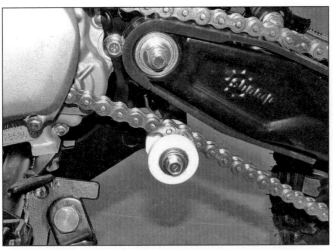

2.18a The chain must run over the while nylon roller

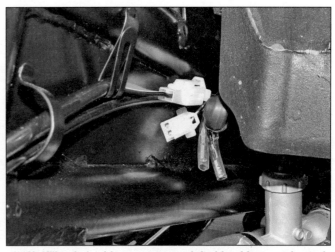

2.18b Kill switch wiring connects on left side of frame at front of fuel tank

17 Make a general check of the wheels, especially the spokes, checking that none are loose. The wheels should be perfectly in line otherwise handling will be affected. You can check this easily by using two perfectly straight edges or string (see Chapter 6). Poor alignment could be caused by incorrect position of the front wheel spacers or incorrect chain adjustment.

18 Check that all cable-ties have been removed from the gear lever and footrests. Check that the drive chain lower run is on top of the nylon roller **(see illustration)**. Check that the engine kill switch wiring is connected – you can see the wires by looking between the fuel tank and frame at the front on the left side **(see illustration)**.

19 Remove the protective film from the exhaust pipe. Peel the protective layer off the bodywork graphics. Use cable-ties where necessary to keep things tidy and prevent them being snagged when riding, a typical example being the kill switch wiring to the handlebar. Check that the cables and hydraulic hoses are routed correctly and through their guides where provided. Some bikes come with a brake snake; this can be

fitted by slipping the closed end through the hole in the pedal and looping the free end through the frame or engine bashplate before locking it down with the clamp **(see illustration)**.

20 Starting at the rear of the bike, work your way to the front on both sides checking that all nuts, bolts and screws are tight. Don't assume that because it's new from the factory that everything will be tight. A drop of thread locking compound (non-permanent type) is advised on the threads of the brake caliper bolts and engine mounting bolt nuts.

- Rear wheel axle nut
- Chain aduster locknut
- Rear shock bolt and nut at top and bottom of shock
- Swingarm nut pivot bolt nut
- Rear brake caliper bolts
- Rear brake disc bolts
- Rear sprocket bolts
- Chainguard bolts and chain roller bolt
- Rear master cylinder bolts
- Rear subframe bolts (where applicable)
- Engine mounting bolt nuts
- Engine bashplate bolts
- Engine oil drain bolt

- Engine oil cooler mounting bolts (where fitted)
- Kickstart lever and gear lever pinch bolts
- Footrest bracket bolts (where applicable)
- Rear brake pedal bolt
- Sidestand bolt nut
- Exhaust pipe bolts/nuts
- Handlebar bolts
- Front brake master cylinder clamp bolts (disc brake models)
- Front brake lever clamp bolt (drum brake models)
- Clutch lever clamp bolt
- Clutch and brake lever pivot bolt/nuts
- Front fork pinch bolts
- Front mudguard bolts
- Steering head bolt
- Front wheel axle nut
- Front wheel axle clamp bolts (where fitted)
- Front brake caliper bolts
- Front brake disc bolts

3 Checking the settings

1 Check the engine valve clearances (tappets) with the engine set to TDC compression. Pit bikes are often supplied with zero valve clearance from the factory. This must be adjusted to the correct clearance **(see illustration)**. You'll need a set of feeler gauges. The procedure is slightly fiddly especially on the exhaust valve but is essential to the correct running of the engine. Failure to get this right will result in the valves not sealing fully against their seats. Refer to Chapter 1, Section 12 for the procedure.

2 Check for a small amount of freeplay in the throttle twistgrip. Your should be able to feel this as 'slack' when turning the grip. Open the throttle fully and check that it returns smoothly when released and doesn't stick at any point.

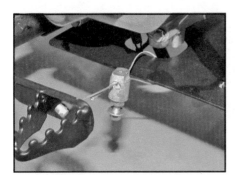

2.19 Brake snake tethered to bashplate

3.1 Valve adjusters are under removable covers, one for intake (shown) and one for exhaust

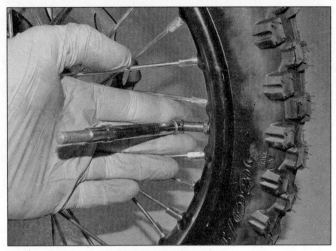
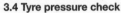

3.4 Tyre pressure check

3.6 Chain freeplay check

3 On manual gearbox models, operate the clutch lever and check that the lever returns smoothly when released. There should be a small amount of freeplay in the cable, otherwise the clutch will drag. Feel for cable freeplay 'slack' as you operate the lever – it should represent no more than 4 to 5 mm measured at the lever stock.

4 Check the tyre pressures, setting them to 26 psi (see illustration). For off-road use the pressure can be anywhere between 20 and 30 psi according to personal preference.

5 Check that both brakes are capable of locking the wheels when fully applied and that they free off fully when released. On disc brake models check the hydraulic fluid level through the sight glass in the reservoir – it should be above the LOWER line in each case. Note that the 'at rest' height of the brake pedal can be adjusted via the pedal stop bolt and locknut.

6 With the bike's rear wheel off the ground rotate the wheel and check the run of the chain. The chain should be evenly aligned on both sprockets if the bike's wheels are in-line. It should also run over the top of the chain roller and must not touch the chainguard or any other component. Check the chain freeplay with a ruler. It should have about 15 mm of slack up and down from the mid-position (that's a total of 30 mm slack) (see illustration). See Chapter 1 if it needs adjusting. Use an aerosol chain lube to spray the outer rollers of the chain.

7 Where the suspension is adjustable, make a note of the current settings. After the first ride you may well want to make adjustments to suit rider weight and riding style. Note that any settings on adjustable front forks must be the same in each fork.

8 Check the engine oil level. Unscrew the dipstick and wipe it clean on a rag. Hold the bike upright and re-insert the dipstick

but don't screw it in (see illustration). Withdraw the dipstick and note the oil level on the hatched area of the dipstick (see illustration). It should be up to the higher extent of the hatched area. If necessary top up with semi-synthetic 10W/40 motorcycle oil until the level is correct. Note that the oil put in at the factory may be sufficient for start up and initial running – check with the bike supplier or dealer. if there's any doubt drain the oil and put in fresh as the expense is minimal. In any case the engine oil should be drained and replaced after the first use of the bike.

4 Fluids and getting it running

1 Fill the fuel tank with unleaded petrol (gasoline) and set the fuel tap lever to ON (see

3.8a Dipstick threads just rest of casing for oil level check

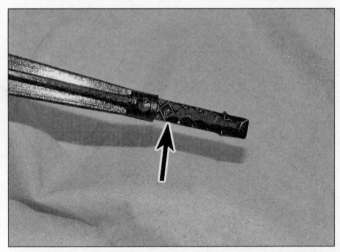

3.8b Oil level should be up to top of hatched area (arrowed)

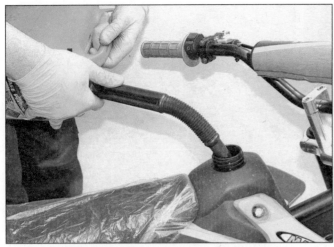

4.1a Fill the tank with unleaded petrol (gasoline)...

4.1b ...turn the tap lever so it points to the ON position...

illustrations). The fuel filler cap is supplied off the tank, so make sure it threads properly into place and that the short breather tube is fitted **(see illustration)**. Check that no fuel is leaking from the fuel hose or from the carburettor. Leaks from the carb body indicate that the float height is incorrect and should be adjusted (see Chapter 3).

2 Set the choke to ON, make sure the kill switch is set to RUN, and start the engine **(see illustrations)**. Let it warm up and tick over, then stop it, let it cool and repeat the same procedure. Increase the engine speed during further start ups and cool downs – this will help the rings to seat in. When full warmed up and the choke is OFF if the idle speed seems too high or not high enough and likely to stall, adjust the idle screw (throttle stop screw) on the carburettor body accordingly **(see illustration)**. Only a slight adjustment will be necessary.

Caution: Don't confuse the idle screw

4.1c ...and fit the filler cap

(central in relation to the vertical throttle slide) with the mixture screw.

3 There's no specific running-in procedure, just bear in mind that because everything is new it will take time to seat in. After using the bike for the first time it's recommended

4.2a Choke in the ON position for starting

you change the engine oil and clean the oil strainer just to make sure any debris from the manufacturing and assembly processes is flushed out. Also brake pads (and shoes on models with drum brakes) need time to bed-in before reaching optimum effeciency.

4.2b Move choke to the OFF position once engine is warm

4.2c Idle speed being adjusted

Lubricants and fluids

A wide range of lubricants, fluids and cleaning agents is available for motor-cycles. This is a guide as to what is available, its applications and properties.

Four-stroke engine oil

● Engine oil is without doubt the most important component of any four-stroke engine. Modern motorcycle engines place a lot of demands on their oil and choosing the right type is essential. Using an unsuitable oil will lead to an increased rate of engine wear and could result in serious engine damage. Before purchasing oil, always check the recommended oil specification given by the manufacturer. The manufacturer will state a recommended 'type or classification' and also a specific 'viscosity' range for engine oil.

● The oil 'type or classification' is identified by its API (American Petroleum Institute) rating. The API rating will be in the form of two letters, e.g. SG. The S identifies the oil as being suitable for use in a petrol (gasoline) engine (S stands for spark ignition) and the second letter, ranging from A to J, identifies the oil's performance rating. The later this letter, the higher the specification of the oil; for example API SG oil exceeds the requirements of API SF oil. **Note:** *On some oils there may also be a second rating consisting of another two letters, the first letter being C, e.g. API SF/CD. This rating indicates the oil is also suitable for use in a diesel engines (the C stands for compression ignition) and is thus of no relevance for motorcycle use.*

● The 'viscosity' of the oil is identified by its SAE (Society of Automotive Engineers) rating. All modern engines require multigrade oils and the SAE rating will consist of two numbers, the first followed by a W, e.g.

10W/40. The first number indicates the viscosity rating of the oil at low temperatures (W stands for winter – tested at –20°C) and the second number represents the viscosity of the oil at high temperatures (tested at 100°C). The lower the number, the thinner the oil. For example an oil with an SAE 10W/40 rating will give better cold starting and running than an SAE 15W/40 oil.

● As well as ensuring the 'type' and 'viscosity' of the oil match the recommendations, another consideration to make when buying engine oil is whether to purchase a standard mineral-based oil, a semi-synthetic oil (also known as a synthetic blend or synthetic-based oil) or a fully-synthetic oil. Although all oils will have a similar rating and viscosity, their cost will vary considerably; mineral-based oils are the cheapest, the fully-synthetic oils the most expensive with the semi-synthetic oils falling somewhere in-between. This decision is very much up to the owner, but it should be noted that modern synthetic oils have far better lubricating and cleaning qualities than traditional mineral-based oils and tend to retain these properties for far longer. Bearing in mind the operating conditions inside a modern, high-revving motorcycle engine it is highly recommended that a fully synthetic oil is used. The extra expense at each service could save you money in the long term by preventing premature engine wear.

● As a final note always ensure that the oil is specifically designed for use in motorcycle engines. Engine oils designed primarily for use in car engines sometimes contain additives or friction modifiers which could cause clutch slip on a motorcycle fitted with a wet-clutch.

Two-stroke engine oil

● Modern two-stroke engines, with their high power outputs, place high demands on their oil. If engine seizure is to be avoided it is essential that a high-quality oil is used. Two-stroke oils differ hugely from four-stroke oils. The oil lubricates only the crankshaft and piston(s) (the transmission has its own lubricating oil) and is used on a total-loss basis where it is burnt completely during the combustion process.

● The Japanese have recently introduced a classification system for two-stroke oils, the JASO rating. This rating is in the form of two letters, either FA, FB or FC – FA is the lowest classification and FC the highest. Ensure the oil being used meets or exceeds the recommended rating specified by the manufacturer.

● As well as ensuring the oil rating matches the recommendation, another consideration to make when buying engine oil is whether to purchase a standard mineral-based oil, a semi-synthetic oil (also known as a synthetic blend or synthetic-based oil) or a fully-synthetic oil. The cost of each type of oil varies considerably; mineral-based oils are the cheapest, the fully-synthetic oils the most expensive with the semi-synthetic oils falling somewhere in-between. This decision is very much up to the owner, but it should be noted that modern synthetic oils have far better lubricating properties and burn cleaner than traditional mineral-based oils. It is therefore recommended that a fully synthetic oil is used. The extra expense could save you money in the long term by preventing premature engine wear, engine performance will be improved, carbon deposits and exhaust smoke will be reduced.

● Always ensure that the oil is specifically designed for use in an injector system. Many high quality two-stroke oils are designed for competition use and need to be pre-mixed with fuel. These oils are of a much higher viscosity and are not designed to flow through the injector pumps used on road-going two-stroke motorcycles.

Transmission (gear) oil

● On a two-stroke engine, the transmission and clutch are lubricated by their own separate oil bath which must be changed in accordance with the Maintenance Schedule.
● Although the engine and transmission units of most four-strokes use a common lubrication supply, there are some exceptions where the engine and gearbox have separate oil reservoirs and a dry clutch is used.
● Motorcycle manufacturers will either recommend a monograde transmission oil or a four-stroke multigrade engine oil to lubricate the transmission.
● Transmission oils, or gear oils as they are often called, are designed specifically for use in transmission systems. The viscosity of these oils is represented by an SAE number, but the scale of measurement applied is different to that used to grade engine oils. As a rough guide a SAE90 gear oil will be of the same viscosity as an SAE50 engine oil.

Shaft drive oil

● On models equipped with shaft final drive, the shaft drive gears are will have their own oil supply. The manufacturer will state a recommended 'type or classification' and also a specific 'viscosity' range in the same manner as for four-stroke engine oil.
● Gear oil classification is given by the number which follows the API GL (GL standing for gear lubricant) rating, the higher the number, the higher the specification of the oil, e.g. API GL5 oil is a higher specification than API GL4 oil. Ensure the oil meets or

exceeds the classification specified and is of the correct viscosity. The viscosity of gear oils is also represented by an SAE number but the scale of measurement used is different to that used to grade engine oils. As a rough guide an SAE90 gear oil will be of the same viscosity as an SAE50 engine oil.
● If the use of an EP (Extreme Pressure) gear oil is specified, ensure the oil purchased is suitable.

Fork oil and suspension fluid

● Conventional telescopic front forks are hydraulic and require fork oil to work. To ensure the forks function correctly, the fork oil must be changed in accordance with the Maintenance Schedule.
● Fork oil is available in a variety of viscosities, identified by their SAE rating; fork oil ratings vary from light (SAE 5) to heavy (SAE 30). When purchasing fork oil, ensure the viscosity rating matches that specified by the manufacturer.
● Some lubricant manufacturers also produce a range of high-quality suspension fluids which are very similar to fork oil but are designed mainly for competition use. These fluids may have a different viscosity rating system which is not to be confused with the SAE rating of normal fork oil. Refer to the manufacturer's instructions if in any doubt.

Brake and clutch fluid

● All disc brake systems and some clutch systems are hydraulically operated. To ensure correct operation, the hydraulic fluid must be changed in accordance with the Maintenance Schedule.
● Brake and clutch fluid is classified by its DOT rating with most motorcycle manufacturers specifying DOT 3 or 4 fluid. Both fluid types are glycol-based and can be mixed together without adverse effect; DOT 4 fluid exceeds the requirements

of DOT 3 fluid. Although it is safe to use DOT 4 fluid in a system designed for use with DOT 3 fluid, never use DOT 3 fluid in a system which specifies the use of DOT 4 as this will adversely affect the system's performance. The type required for the system will be marked on the fluid reservoir cap.
● Some manufacturers also produce a DOT 5 hydraulic fluid. DOT 5 hydraulic fluid is silicone-based and is not compatible with the glycol-based DOT 3 and 4 fluids. Never mix DOT 5 fluid with DOT 3 or 4 fluid as this will seriously affect the performance of the hydraulic system.

Coolant/antifreeze

● When purchasing coolant/antifreeze, always ensure it is suitable for use in an aluminium engine and contains corrosion inhibitors to prevent possible blockages of the internal coolant passages of the system. As a general rule, most coolants are designed to be used neat and should not be diluted whereas antifreeze can be mixed with distilled water to provide a coolant solution of the required strength. Refer to the manufacturer's instructions on the bottle.
● Ensure the coolant is changed in accordance with the Maintenance Schedule.

Chain lube

● Chain lube is an aerosol-type spray lubricant specifically designed for use on motorcycle final drive chains. Chain lube has two functions, to minimise friction between the final drive chain and sprockets and to prevent corrosion of the chain. Regular use of a good-quality chain lube will extend the life of the drive chain and sprockets and thus maximise the power being transmitted from the transmission to the rear wheel.
● When using chain lube, always allow some time for the solvents in the lube to evaporate before riding the motorcycle. This will minimise the amount of lube which will

'fling' off from the chain when the motorcycle is used. If the motorcycle is equipped with an 'O-ring' chain, ensure the chain lube is labelled as being suitable for use on 'O-ring' chains.

Degreasers and solvents

● There are many different types of solvents and degreasers available to remove the grime and grease which accumulate around the motorcycle during normal use. Degreasers and solvents are usually available as an aerosol-type spray or as a liquid which you apply with a brush. Always closely follow the manufacturer's instructions and wear eye protection during use. Be aware that many solvents are flammable and may give off noxious fumes; take adequate precautions when using them (see Safety First!).

● For general cleaning, use one of the many solvents or degreasers available from most motorcycle accessory shops. These solvents are usually applied then left for a certain time before being washed off with water.

Brake cleaner is a solvent specifically designed to remove all traces of oil, grease and dust from braking system components. Brake cleaner is designed to evaporate quickly and leaves behind no residue.

Carburettor cleaner is an aerosol-type solvent specifically designed to clear carburettor blockages and break down the hard deposits and gum often found inside carburettors during overhaul.

Contact cleaner is an aerosol-type solvent designed for cleaning electrical components. The cleaner will remove all traces of oil and dirt from components such as switch contacts or fouled spark plugs and then dry, leaving behind no residue.

Gasket remover is an aerosol-type solvent designed for removing stubborn gaskets from engine components during overhaul. Gasket remover will minimise the amount of scraping required to remove the gasket and therefore reduce the risk of damage to the mating surface.

Spray lubricants

● Aerosol-based spray lubricants are widely available and are excellent for lubricating lever pivots and exposed cables and switches. Try to use a lubricant which is of the dry-film type as the fluid evaporates, leaving behind a dry-film of lubricant. Lubricants which leave behind an oily residue will attract dust and dirt which will increase the rate of wear of the cable/lever.

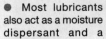

● Most lubricants also act as a moisture dispersant and a penetrating fluid. This means they can also be used to 'dry out' electrical components such as wiring connectors or switches as well as helping to free seized fasteners.

Greases

● Grease is used to lubricate many of the pivot-points. A good-quality multi-purpose grease is suitable for most applications but some manufacturers will specify the use of specialist greases for use on components such as swingarm and suspension linkage bushes. These specialist greases can be purchased from most motorcycle (or car) accessory shops; commonly specified types include molybdenum disulphide grease, lithium-based grease, graphite-based grease, silicone-based grease and high-temperature copper-based grease.

Gasket sealing compounds

● Gasket sealing compounds can be used in conjunction with gaskets, to improve their sealing capabilities, or on their own to seal metal-to-metal joints. Depending on their type, sealing compounds either set hard or stay relatively soft and pliable.

● When purchasing a gasket sealing

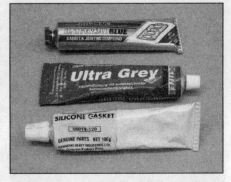

compound, ensure that it is designed specifically for use on an internal combustion engine. General multi-purpose sealants available from DIY stores may appear visibly similar but they are not designed to withstand the extreme heat or contact with fuel and oil encountered when used on an engine (see 'Tools and Workshop Tips' for further information).

Thread locking compound

● Thread locking compounds are used to secure certain threaded fasteners in position to prevent them from loosening due to vibration. Thread locking compounds can be purchased from most motorcycle (and car) accessory shops. Ensure the threads of the both components are completely clean and dry before sparingly applying the locking compound (see 'Tools and Workshop Tips' for further information).

Fuel additives

● Fuel additives which protect and clean the fuel system components are widely available. These additives are designed to remove all traces of deposits that build up on the carburettors/injectors and prevent wear, helping the fuel system to operate more efficiently. If a fuel additive is being used, check that it is suitable for use with your motorcycle, especially if your motorcycle is equipped with a catalytic converter.

● Octane boosters are also available. These additives are designed to improve the performance of highly-tuned engines being run on normal pump-fuel and are of no real use on standard motorcycles.

Length (distance)

Inches (in)	x 25.4	= Millimetres (mm)	x 0.0394	= Inches (in)
Feet (ft)	x 0.305	= Metres (m)	x 3.281	= Feet (ft)
Miles	x 1.609	= Kilometres (km)	x 0.621	= Miles

Volume (capacity)

Cubic inches (cu in; in³)	x 16.387	= Cubic centimetres (cc; cm³)	x 0.061	= Cubic inches (cu in; in³)
Imperial pints (Imp pt)	x 0.568	= Litres (l)	x 1.76	= Imperial pints (Imp pt)
Imperial quarts (Imp qt)	x 1.137	= Litres (l)	x 0.88	= Imperial quarts (Imp qt)
Imperial quarts (Imp qt)	x 1.201	= US quarts (US qt)	x 0.833	= Imperial quarts (Imp qt)
US quarts (US qt)	x 0.946	= Litres (l)	x 1.057	= US quarts (US qt)
Imperial gallons (Imp gal)	x 4.546	= Litres (l)	x 0.22	= Imperial gallons (Imp gal)
Imperial gallons (Imp gal)	x 1.201	= US gallons (US gal)	x 0.833	= Imperial gallons (Imp gal)
US gallons (US gal)	x 3.785	= Litres (l)	x 0.264	= US gallons (US gal)

Mass (weight)

Ounces (oz)	x 28.35	= Grams (g)	x 0.035	= Ounces (oz)
Pounds (lb)	x 0.454	= Kilograms (kg)	x 2.205	= Pounds (lb)

Force

Ounces-force (ozf; oz)	x 0.278	= Newtons (N)	x 3.6	= Ounces-force (ozf; oz)
Pounds-force (lbf; lb)	x 4.448	= Newtons (N)	x 0.225	= Pounds-force (lbf; lb)
Newtons (N)	x 0.1	= Kilograms-force (kgf; kg)	x 9.81	= Newtons (N)

Pressure

Pounds-force per square inch (psi; lbf/in²; lb/in²)	x 0.070	= Kilograms-force per square centimetre (kgf/cm²; kg/cm²)	x 14.223	= Pounds-force per square inch (psi; lbf/in²; lb/in²)
Pounds-force per square inch (psi; lbf/in²; lb/in²)	x 0.068	= Atmospheres (atm)	x 14.696	= Pounds-force per square inch (psi; lbf/in²; lb/in²)
Pounds-force per square inch (psi; lbf/in²; lb/in²)	x 0.069	= Bars	x 14.5	= Pounds-force per square inch (psi; lbf/in²; lb/in²)
Pounds-force per square inch (psi; lbf/in²; lb/in²)	x 6.895	= Kilopascals (kPa)	x 0.145	= Pounds-force per square inch (psi; lbf/in²; lb/in²)
Kilopascals (kPa)	x 0.01	= Kilograms-force per square centimetre (kgf/cm²; kg/cm²)	x 98.1	= Kilopascals (kPa)
Millibar (mbar)	x 100	= Pascals (Pa)	x 0.01	= Millibar (mbar)
Millibar (mbar)	x 0.0145	= Pounds-force per square inch (psi; lbf/in²; lb/in²)	x 68.947	= Millibar (mbar)
Millibar (mbar)	x 0.75	= Millimetres of mercury (mmHg)	x 1.333	= Millibar (mbar)
Millibar (mbar)	x 0.401	= Inches of water (inH₂O)	x 2.491	= Millibar (mbar)
Millimetres of mercury (mmHg)	x 0.535	= Inches of water (inH₂O)	x 1.868	= Millimetres of mercury (mmHg)
Inches of water (inH₂O)	x 0.036	= Pounds-force per square inch (psi; lbf/in²; lb/in²)	x 27.68	= Inches of water (inH₂O)

Torque (moment of force)

Pounds-force inches (lbf in; lb in)	x 1.152	= Kilograms-force centimetre (kgf cm; kg cm)	x 0.868	= Pounds-force inches (lbf in; lb in)
Pounds-force inches (lbf in; lb in)	x 0.113	= Newton metres (Nm)	x 8.85	= Pounds-force inches (lbf in; lb in)
Pounds-force inches (lbf in; lb in)	x 0.083	= Pounds-force feet (lbf ft; lb ft)	x 12	= Pounds-force inches (lbf in; lb in)
Pounds-force feet (lbf ft; lb ft)	x 0.138	= Kilograms-force metres (kgf m; kg m)	x 7.233	= Pounds-force feet (lbf ft; lb ft)
Pounds-force feet (lbf ft; lb ft)	x 1.356	= Newton metres (Nm)	x 0.738	= Pounds-force feet (lbf ft; lb ft)
Newton metres (Nm)	x 0.102	= Kilograms-force metres (kgf m; kg m)	x 9.804	= Newton metres (Nm)

Power

Horsepower (hp)	x 745.7	= Watts (W)	x 0.0013	= Horsepower (hp)

Velocity (speed)

Miles per hour (miles/hr; mph)	x 1.609	= Kilometres per hour (km/hr; kph)	x 0.621	= Miles per hour (miles/hr; mph)

Fuel consumption*

Miles per gallon, Imperial (mpg)	x 0.354	= Kilometres per litre (km/l)	x 2.825	= Miles per gallon, Imperial (mpg)
Miles per gallon, US (mpg)	x 0.425	= Kilometres per litre (km/l)	x 2.352	= Miles per gallon, US (mpg)

Temperature

Degrees Fahrenheit = (°C x 1.8) + 32   Degrees Celsius (Degrees Centigrade; °C) = (°F - 32) x 0.56

It is common practice to convert from miles per gallon (mpg) to litres/100 kilometres (l/100km), where mpg x l/100 km = 282

This Section provides an easy reference-guide to the more common faults that are likely to afflict your bike. Obviously, the opportunities are almost limitless for faults to occur as a result of obscure failures, and to try and cover all eventualities would require a book. Indeed, a number have been written on the subject.

Successful troubleshooting is not a mysterious black art but the application of a bit of knowledge combined with a systematic and logical approach to the problem. Approach any troubleshooting by first accurately identifying the symptom and then checking through the list of possible causes, starting with the simplest or most obvious and progressing in stages to the most complex.

Take nothing for granted, but above all apply liberal quantities of common sense.

The main symptom of a fault is given in the text as a major heading below which are listed the various systems or areas which may contain the fault. Details of each possible cause for a fault and the remedial action to be taken are given, in brief, in the paragraphs below each heading. Further information should be sought in the relevant Chapter.

Engine doesn't start or is difficult to start

- [ ] No fuel flow
- [ ] Engine flooded
- [ ] No spark or weak spark
- [ ] Compression low
- [ ] Stalls after starting
- [ ] Rough idle

Poor running at low speeds

- [ ] Spark weak
- [ ] Fuel/air mixture incorrect
- [ ] Compression low
- [ ] Poor acceleration

Poor running or no power at high speed

- [ ] Firing incorrect
- [ ] Fuel/air mixture incorrect
- [ ] Compression low
- [ ] Knocking or pinking
- [ ] Miscellaneous causes

Overheating

- [ ] Engine overheats
- [ ] Firing incorrect
- [ ] Fuel/air mixture incorrect
- [ ] Compression too high
- [ ] Engine load excessive
- [ ] Lubrication inadequate

Clutch problems

- [ ] Clutch slipping
- [ ] Clutch not engaging (drag)

Gearchanging problems

- [ ] Doesn't go into gear or lever doesn't return
- [ ] Jumps out of gear
- [ ] Overselects

Abnormal engine noise

- [ ] Knocking or pinking
- [ ] Piston slap or rattling
- [ ] Valve and cam chain noise
- [ ] Other noise

Abnormal driveline noise

- [ ] Clutch noise
- [ ] Transmission noise
- [ ] Final drive noise

Abnormal frame and suspension noise

- [ ] Front end noise
- [ ] Rear end noise
- [ ] Brake noise

Excessive exhaust smoke

- [ ] White smoke
- [ ] Black smoke
- [ ] Brown smoke

Poor handling or stability

- [ ] Handlebars hard to turn
- [ ] Handlebar shakes or vibrates excessively
- [ ] Bike pulls to one side
- [ ] Poor shock absorbing qualities

Braking problems

- [ ] Brakes are spongy, don't hold (disc brake)
- [ ] Brake lever or pedal pulsates
- [ ] Brakes drag

Engine doesn't start or is difficult to start

No fuel flow

- ☐ No fuel in tank or fuel tap turned OFF.
- ☐ Fuel tank breather hose obstructed.
- ☐ Fuel filter blocked (see Chapter 1).
- ☐ Fuel hose kinked. Fit a new hose.
- ☐ Carburettor jets clogged. If the bike has been unused for months, the fuel turns to a varnish-like liquid, which can cause the small holes in the jets to block and sediment to build up in the float chamber. Drain the carburettor if the bike is going to be laid up (see Chapter 3).

Engine flooded

- ☐ Carburettor float valve worn or stuck open. A piece of dirt or other debris between the float valve surface and its seat will prevent the fuel shutting off and cause flooding of the carburettor. Clean the float valve, and if worn fit a new one (see Chapter 3).
- ☐ Fuel level too high in carburettor float chamber. Float height setting incorrect. Measure the height and adjust (see Chapter 3).
- ☐ Starting technique incorrect. Under normal circumstances the bike should start with the choke ON (if cold) and the throttle grip closed. If flooded, disable the engine by turning the kill switch to OFF, turn the choke OFF, hold the throttle grip open, and with the gearbox in neutral kick the engine over five times.

No spark or weak spark

- ☐ Kill switch OFF.
- ☐ Kill switch wiring shorted to earth or switch internal contacts failed. Take the switch off and spray its contacts with electrical contact cleaner (see Chapter 4). Remove the bodywork and check the wiring from the switch – make sure the black (or black/white) wire isn't earthed at any point.
- ☐ Spark plug cap not making good contact. Make sure that the cap fits snugly over the plug.
- ☐ Spark plug dirty, defective or worn out. Identify reason for fouled plug using spark plug condition chart on the inside back cover. Fit a new plug (see Chapter 1).
- ☐ Incorrect spark plug. Wrong type or heat range. Check and install correct plug (see Chapter 1).
- ☐ Ignition coil or HT lead defective. Test and replace with new one if necessary (see Chapter 4).
- ☐ Ignition source coil defective (see Chapter 4).
- ☐ Ignition pick-up coil defective (see Chapter 4).
- ☐ CDI unit defective (see Chapter 4).
- ☐ Wiring shorted or broken. Make sure all wiring connections are clean, dry and tight. Look for chafed and broken wires.

Compression low

Refer to Chapter 2A, 2B, 2C or 2D.

- ☐ Spark plug loose. Remove the plug and inspect the threads. Reinstall and tighten securely (see Chapter 1).
- ☐ Cylinder head not sufficiently tightened down. If the cylinder head is suspected of being loose, then there is a chance that the gasket or head is damaged if the problem has persisted for any length of time. The cylinder head nuts should be tightened to the proper torque and in the correct sequence.

- ☐ Improper valve clearance. This means that the valve is not closing completely and compression pressure is leaking past the valve. Check and adjust the valve clearances (see Chapter 1).
- ☐ Cylinder and/or piston worn. Excessive wear will cause compression pressure to leak past the rings. This is usually accompanied by worn rings as well. A top-end overhaul is necessary.
- ☐ Piston rings worn, weak, broken, or sticking. Broken or sticking piston rings usually indicate a lubrication or fuelling problem that causes excess carbon deposits to form on the piston and rings. Top-end overhaul is necessary.
- ☐ Piston ring-to-groove clearance excessive. This is caused by excessive wear of the piston ring lands. Fit a new piston and rings.
- ☐ Cylinder head gasket damaged. If the head is allowed to become loose, or if excessive carbon build-up on the piston crown and combustion chamber causes extremely high compression, the head gasket may leak. Retightening the head is not always sufficient to restore the seal, so a new gasket is necessary.
- ☐ Cylinder head warped. This is caused by overheating or improperly tightened head nuts. Machine shop resurfacing or head renewal is necessary.
- ☐ Valve spring broken or weak. Caused by component failure or wear; the springs must be renewed.
- ☐ Valve not seating properly. This is caused by a bent valve (from over-revving or improper valve adjustment), burned valve or seat (incorrect air/fuel mixture) or an accumulation of carbon deposits on the seat. The valves must be cleaned and/or renewed and the seats lapped. If the seats are badly pitted, fit a new cylinder head and valves.

Stalls after starting

- ☐ Faulty choke. Check the choke lever or plunger stays in position until manually shut-off.
- ☐ Engine idle speed incorrect. Turn idle screw to adjust (see Chapter 1).
- ☐ Blocked fuel tank breather causing a vacuum in the tank (see Chapter 3).
- ☐ Fuel contaminated. The fuel can be contaminated with either dirt or water, or can change chemically if the machine has been unused for several months. Drain the tank and carburettor then refill the tank with fresh fuel (see Chapter 3).
- ☐ Intake air leak. Check for loose carburettor-to-intake stub bolts/nuts (see Chapter 3).

Rough idle

- ☐ Idle speed incorrect (see Chapter 1).
- ☐ Blockage in carburettor pilot jet (see Chapter 3).
- ☐ Fuel/air mixture incorrect (see Chapter 3).
- ☐ Fuel contaminated. The fuel can be contaminated with either dirt or water, or can change chemically if the machine has been unused for several months. Drain the tank and the carburettor then fill the tank with fresh fuel (see Chapter 3).
- ☐ Intake air leak. Check for loose carburettor-to-intake stub bolts/nuts (see Chapter 3).
- ☐ Air filter clogged with dirt. Clean the air filter element or fit a new one (see Chapter 1).

Poor running at low speeds

Spark weak

☐ Spark plug cap not making good contact. Make sure that the cap is pushed fully onto the spark plug.

☐ Spark plug dirty, defective or worn out. Locate reason for fouled plug using spark plug condition chart on the inside back cover and fit a new plug (see Chapter 1).

☐ Incorrect spark plug. Wrong type or heat range. Check and install correct plug (see Chapter 1).

☐ Ignition coil or HT lead defective. Test and replace with new one if necessary (see Chapter 4).

☐ Loose or corroded connections on low tension side of coil. Check security of the black/yellow wire terminal and clean connections.

Fuel/air mixture incorrect

☐ Fuel tank breather hose obstructed.

☐ Fuel filter blocked (see Chapter 1).

☐ Fuel hose kinked. Fit a new fuel hose.

☐ Carburettor jets clogged. In some cases, if a machine has been unused for several months, the fuel turns to a varnish-like liquid, which can cause the small holes in the jets to clog. Drain the tank and carburettor and refill the tank with fresh fuel (see Chapter 3).

☐ Intake air leak. Check for loose carburettor-to-intake stub bolts/ nuts (see Chapter 3).

☐ Carburettor mixture screw maladjusted (see Chapter 3).

☐ Air filter clogged. Clean the air filter or fit a new one (see Chapter 1).

Compression low

Refer to Chapter 2A, 2B, 2C or 2D and check by carrying out a compression test.

☐ Spark plug loose. Remove the plug and inspect the threads. Reinstall and tighten securely (see Chapter 1).

☐ Cylinder head not sufficiently tightened down. If the cylinder head is suspected of being loose, then there is a chance that the gasket or head is damaged if the problem has persisted for any length of time. The cylinder head nuts should be tightened to the proper torque and in the correct sequence.

☐ Improper valve clearance. This means that the valve is not closing completely and compression pressure is leaking past the valve. Check and adjust the valve clearances (see Chapter 1).

☐ Cylinder and/or piston worn. Excessive wear will cause compression pressure to leak past the rings. This is usually accompanied by worn rings as well. A top-end overhaul is necessary.

☐ Piston rings worn, weak, broken, or sticking. Broken or sticking piston rings usually indicate a lubrication or fuelling problem that causes excess carbon deposits to form on the piston and rings. Fit new rings.

☐ Piston ring-to-groove clearance excessive. This is caused by excessive wear of the piston ring lands. Fit a new piston and rings.

☐ Cylinder head gasket damaged. If the head is allowed to become loose, or if excessive carbon build-up on the piston crown and combustion chamber causes extremely high compression, the head gasket may leak. Retorquing the head is not always sufficient to restore the seal, so a new gasket is necessary.

☐ Cylinder head warped. This is caused by overheating or improperly tightened head nuts. Machine shop resurfacing or head renewal is necessary.

☐ Valve spring broken or weak. Caused by component failure or wear; the springs must be renewed.

☐ Valve not seating properly. This is caused by a bent valve (from over-revving or improper valve adjustment), burned valve or seat (improper fuelling) or an accumulation of carbon deposits on the seat (from fuelling or lubrication problems). The valves must be cleaned and/or renewed and the seats lapped, or if the seats are badly pitted fit a new head.

Poor acceleration

☐ Timing not advancing. The pick-up coil or the CDI unit may be defective (see Chapter 4).

☐ Engine oil viscosity too high. Using a heavier oil than that recommended in Chapter 1 can damage the oil pump or lubrication system and cause drag on the engine.

☐ Brakes dragging. A brake which doesn't free off when released could be due to corrosion of the caliper piston, dry caliper slider pins or a bent disc (disc brakes), or a jammed operating arm, dry cable or broken shoe return spring (drum brakes) (see Chapter 6).

Poor running or no power at high speed

Firing incorrect

- [ ] Spark plug cap not making good contact. Make sure that the cap is pushed fully onto the spark plug.
- [ ] Spark plug dirty, defective or worn out. Identify reason for fouled plug using spark plug condition chart on the inside back cover and fit a new plug (see Chapter 1).
- [ ] Incorrect spark plug. Wrong type or heat range. Check and install correct plug (see Chapter 1).
- [ ] Ignition coil or HT lead defective. Test and replace with new one if necessary (see Chapter 4).
- [ ] Faulty CDI unit (see Chapter 4).

Fuel/air mixture incorrect

- [ ] Fuel tank breather hose obstructed.
- [ ] Fuel filter blocked (see Chapter 1).
- [ ] Fuel hose kinked. Fit a new fuel hose.
- [ ] Carburettor main jet clogged. In some cases, if a bike has been unused for months, the fuel turns to a varnish-like liquid, which can cause blockage of the small holes in the jet. Drain the tank and carburettor and refill with fresh fuel (see Chapter 3).
- [ ] Intake air leak. Check for loose carburettor-to-intake stub bolts/nuts (see Chapter 3).
- [ ] Air filter clogged. Clean the air filter element or fit a new one (see Chapter 1).

Compression low

Refer to Chapter 2A, 2B, 2C or 2D and carry out a compression test.
- [ ] Spark plug loose. Remove the plug and inspect the threads. Reinstall and tighten securely (see Chapter 1).
- [ ] Cylinder head not sufficiently tightened down. If the cylinder head is suspected of being loose, then there's a chance that the gasket or head is damaged if the problem has persisted for any length of time. The cylinder head nuts should be tightened to the proper torque and in the correct sequence.
- [ ] Improper valve clearance. This means that the valve is not closing completely and compression pressure is leaking past the valve. Check and adjust the valve clearances (see Chapter 1).
- [ ] Cylinder and/or piston worn. Excessive wear will cause compression pressure to leak past the rings. This is usually accompanied by worn rings as well. A top-end overhaul is necessary.
- [ ] Piston rings worn, weak, broken, or sticking. Broken or sticking piston rings usually indicate a lubrication or fuelling problem that causes excess carbon deposits to form on the piston and rings. Fit new rings.
- [ ] Piston ring-to-groove clearance excessive. This is caused by excessive wear of the piston ring lands. Piston renewal is necessary.
- [ ] Cylinder head gasket damaged. If a head is allowed to become loose, or if excessive carbon build-up on the piston crown and combustion chamber causes extremely high compression, the head gasket may leak. Retorquing the head is not always sufficient to restore the seal, so a new gasket is necessary.
- [ ] Cylinder head warped. This is caused by overheating or improperly tightened cylinder head nuts. Machine shop resurfacing or head renewal is necessary.
- [ ] Valve spring broken or weak. Caused by component failure or wear; the springs must be replaced with new ones.
- [ ] Valve not seating properly. This is caused by a bent valve (from over-revving or improper valve adjustment), burned valve or seat (improper fuelling) or an accumulation of carbon deposits on the seat (from fuelling or lubrication problems). The valves must be cleaned and/or renewed and the seats lapped. If the seats are badly pitted fit a complete new head.

Knocking or pinking

- [ ] Carbon build-up in combustion chamber. Remove the head and clean off all carbon deposits from the piston, combustion chamber, valves, seats and exhaust port (see Chapter 2A, 2B, 2C or 2D).
- [ ] Incorrect or poor quality fuel. Old or improper grades of fuel can cause detonation. This causes the piston to rattle, thus the knocking or pinking sound. Drain old fuel from the tank and carburettor and refill the tank.
- [ ] Spark plug heat range incorrect. Uncontrolled detonation indicates the plug heat range is too hot. The plug in effect becomes a glow plug, raising cylinder temperatures. Install the proper heat range plug (see Chapter 1).
- [ ] Improper air/fuel mixture. This will cause the cylinder to run hot, which leads to detonation. A blockage in the fuel system or an air leak between the carburettor and intake stub can cause this imbalance (see Chapter 3).
- [ ] Maladjusted carburettor mixture screw (see Chapter 3).

Miscellaneous causes

- [ ] Throttle valve does not open fully. Adjust the throttle twistgrip freeplay (see Chapter 1).
- [ ] Clutch slipping due loose or worn clutch components (see Chapter 2A, 2B, 2C or 2D).
- [ ] Timing not advancing. The ignition pick-up coil or the CDI unit may be defective (see Chapter 4).
- [ ] Engine oil viscosity too high. Using a heavier oil than the one recommended in Chapter 1 can damage the oil pump or lubrication system and cause drag on the engine.
- [ ] Brakes dragging. A brake which doesn't free off when released could be due to corrosion of the caliper piston, dry caliper slider pins or a bent disc (disc brakes), or a jammed operating arm, dry cable or broken shoe return spring (drum brakes) (see Chapter 6).

Overheating

Engine overheats

☐ Cooling fins of cylinder head and barrel clogged with mud. Engine oil cooler (where fitted) radiator clogged or damaged. Wash and scrub off mud deposits from the engine.

Firing incorrect

☐ Spark plug dirty, defective or worn out. Identify reason for fouled plug using spark plug condition chart on the inside back cover and fit a new plug (see Chapter 1).

☐ Incorrect spark plug. Wrong type or heat range. Check and install correct plug (see Chapter 1).

☐ Ignition coil defective. Test and replace with a new one if necessary (see Chapter 4).

☐ Faulty CDI unit (see Chapter 4).

Fuel/air mixture incorrect

☐ Fuel tank breather hose obstructed.

☐ Fuel filter blocked (see Chapter 1).

☐ Fuel hose kinked. Fit a new fuel hose.

☐ Carburettor jets clogged. In some cases, if a bike has been unused for months, the fuel turns to a varnish-like liquid, which can block the small holes in the jets. Drain the tank and carburettor and refill the tank with fresh fuel (see Chapter 3).

☐ Intake air leak. Check for loose carburettor-to-intake stub bolts/nuts (see Chapter 3).

☐ Air filter clogged. Clean the air filter element or fit a new one (see Chapter 1).

Compression too high

☐ Check by performing a compression test (see Chapter 2A, 2B, 2C or 2D).

☐ Carbon build-up in combustion chamber. Remove the head and clean carbon deposits off the piston, combustion chamber, valves, seats and exhaust port.

☐ Improperly machined head surface or installation of incorrect gasket during engine assembly.

Engine load excessive

☐ Clutch slipping due to loose or worn clutch components (see Chapter 2A, 2B, 2C or 2D).

☐ Engine oil level too high. Too much oil will cause pressurisation of the crankcase and inefficient engine operation. Drain to proper level (see Chapter 1).

☐ Engine oil viscosity too high. Using a heavier oil than the one recommended in Chapter 1 can damage the oil pump or lubrication system as well as cause drag on the engine.

☐ Brakes dragging. A brake which doesn't free off when released could be due to corrosion of the caliper piston, dry caliper slider pins or a bent disc (disc brakes), or a jammed operating arm, dry cable or broken shoe return spring (drum brakes) (see Chapter 6).

Lubrication inadequate

☐ Engine oil level too low. Friction caused by intermittent lack of lubrication or from oil that is overworked can cause overheating. The oil provides a definite cooling function in the engine. Check the oil level (see Chapter 1).

☐ Blocked oil filter (see Chapter 1) or filter screen (see Chapter 2A, 2B, 2C or 2D).

Clutch problems

Clutch slipping

Refer to Chapter 2A, 2B, 2C or 2D.

☐ Clutch cable incorrectly adjusted (see Chapter 1, Section 6).

☐ Clutch plates worn or warped. Overhaul the clutch assembly.

☐ Clutch springs broken or weak. Old or heat-damaged (from slipping clutch) springs should be renewed.

☐ Clutch operating mechanism freeplay setting incorrect (see Chapter 2A or 2B).

☐ Clutch centre or housing unevenly worn. This causes improper engagement of the plates. Replace the damaged or worn parts.

☐ Incorrect oil used in engine. Oils designed for car engines often contain friction modifiers, which if used in an engine with a wet clutch can promote clutch slip. Always use a semi-synthetic 10W/40 motorcycle engine oil, not fully synthetic (see Chapter 1).

Clutch not engaging (drag)

Refer to Chapter 2A, 2B, 2C or 2D.

☐ Clutch cable wrongly adjusted (see Chapter 1).

☐ Clutch plates warped or damaged. This will cause clutch drag, which in turn will cause the machine to creep. Overhaul the clutch assembly.

☐ Clutch springs fatigued or broken. Check and renew the springs.

☐ Engine oil deteriorated. Old, thin oil will not provide proper lubrication for the plates, causing the clutch to drag. Renew the oil and filter (see Chapter 1).

☐ Engine oil viscosity too high. Using too heavy an oil can cause the plates to stick together. Change to 10W/40 oil.

☐ Clutch housing bearing seized on the shaft. Lack of lubrication, severe wear or damage can cause the bearing to seize. Overhaul to repair the damage.

☐ Faulty clutch release mechanism. Renew any defective parts.

☐ Loose clutch nut. Causes housing and centre misalignment putting a drag on the engine. Engagement adjustment continually varies. Overhaul the clutch assembly.

Gearchanging problems

Doesn't go into gear or lever doesn't return

Refer to Chapter 2A, 2B, 2C or 2D.

☐ Clutch not disengaging (see above).
☐ Gearchange mechanism stopper arm spring weak or broken, or arm roller broken or worn. Replace the spring or arm with a new one.
☐ Selector fork(s) bent, worn or seized. Overhaul the transmission.
☐ Gear(s) stuck on shaft. Most often caused by a lack of lubrication or excessive wear in transmission bearings and bushes. Overhaul the transmission.
☐ Selector drum binding. Caused by lubrication failure or excessive wear. Replace the drum and/or its bearing with a new one.
☐ Gearchange mechanism return spring weak or broken.
☐ Splines stripped out of gear lever. Fit a new lever (see Chapter 5, Section 3).
☐ Selector arm pawls worn.

Jumps out of gear

Refer to Chapter 2A, 2B, 2C or 2D.

☐ Selector fork tips worn.
☐ Stopper arm roller damaged or return spring weak or broken.
☐ Gear pinion dogs or dog slots worn or damaged. The gear pinions should be inspected and renewed. No attempt should be made to repair the worn parts.

Overselects

Refer to Chapter 2A, 2B, 2C or 2D.

☐ Gearchange stopper arm spring weak or broken, or arm roller broken or worn. Renew the spring or arm.
☐ Gearchange shaft return spring weak or broken.

Abnormal engine noise

Knocking or pinking

☐ Carbon build-up in combustion chamber. Remove the cylinder head and scrape the carbon deposits from the piston, combustion chamber, valves, valve seats and exhaust port (see Chapter 2A, 2B, 2C or 2D).
☐ Incorrect or poor quality fuel. Old or improper grades of fuel can cause detonation. This causes the piston to rattle, thus the knocking or pinking sound. Drain old fuel and always use the recommended fuel grade.
☐ Spark plug heat range incorrect. Uncontrolled detonation indicates the plug heat range is too hot. The plug in effect becomes a glow plug, raising cylinder temperatures. Install the proper heat range plug (see Chapter 1).
☐ Improper air/fuel mixture. This will cause the cylinder to run hot, which leads to detonation. A blockage in the fuel system or an air leak can cause this imbalance (see Chapter 3).

Piston slap or rattling

Refer to Chapter 2A, 2B, 2C or 2D.

☐ Cylinder-to-piston clearance excessive. Cylinder and/or piston worn, usually accompanied by worn rings as well. A top-end overhaul is necessary.
☐ Piston ring(s) worn, broken or sticking. Fit new rings.
☐ Piston pin, piston pin bore or connecting rod small-end worn or seized due to lack of lubrication.
☐ Piston seizure damage. Usually from lack of lubrication or overheating. Fit a new cylinder barrel and piston.
☐ Connecting rod big-end clearance excessive. Caused by excessive wear or lack of lubrication. Replace worn parts.
☐ Connecting rod bent. Caused by over-revving, trying to start a badly flooded engine or from ingesting a foreign object into the combustion chamber. Fit a new crankshaft.

Valve and cam chain noise

Refer to Chapter 2A, 2B, 2C or 2D.

☐ Incorrect valve clearances – check and adjust (see Chapter 1).
☐ Valve spring broken or weak. Fit new springs.
☐ Camshaft, camshaft bearings or rockers worn or damaged. Lubrication failure at high rpm is usually the cause of damage due to insufficient oil or failure to change the oil at the recommended intervals. Fit new components or renew the cylinder head complete.
☐ Cam chain rattle, due to worn chain or defective tensioner. Also check the chain guide blades and rollers for wear.

Other noise

Refer to Chapter 2A, 2B, 2C or 2D.

☐ Cylinder head gasket leaking. Check around the joint for blowing with the engine running.
☐ Exhaust pipe leaking at cylinder head connection. Caused by incorrect fit of pipe, loose exhaust flange or damaged gasket. All exhaust system fasteners should be tightened evenly and carefully to avoid leaks (see Chapter 3).
☐ Crankshaft runout excessive. Caused by a bent crankshaft (from over-revving) or damage from an upper cylinder component failure.
☐ Engine mounting bolts loose – ensure all the bolts are tight.
☐ Worn primary drive gears.
☐ Generator rotor nut loose. Check tightness.
☐ Clutch loose on its shaft. Check tightness of nut.
☐ Crankshaft bearings worn.
☐ Cam chain rattle, due to worn chain or defective tensioner. Also worn chain tensioner/guide blades.

Abnormal driveline noise

Clutch noise

Refer to Chapter 2A, 2B, 2C or 2D.
- [ ] Clutch housing/friction plate clearance excessive.
- [ ] Wear between the clutch housing splines and shaft splines.
- [ ] Worn release bearing.

Transmission noise

Refer to Chapter 2A, 2B, 2C or 2D.
- [ ] Gearbox shaft bearings worn. Also includes the possibility that the shafts are worn. Overhaul the gearbox.
- [ ] Gear teeth worn or chipped. Fit new gear shafts.
- [ ] Metal chips jammed in gear teeth. Probably pieces from a broken clutch, gear or selector mechanism that were picked up by the gears. This will cause early bearing failure.
- [ ] Engine oil level too low. Causes a howl from transmission. Also affects engine power and clutch operation (see Chapter 1, Section 3).

Final drive noise

- [ ] Chain chattering noise. Chain not adjusted properly and sprockets worn (see Chapter 1).
- [ ] Front or rear sprocket loose. Tighten fasteners (see Chapter 6).
- [ ] Sprockets and/or chain worn. Fit new sprockets and chain (see Chapter 6).
- [ ] Rear sprocket warped. Fit a new sprocket (see Chapter 6).

Abnormal frame and suspension noise

Front end noise

- [ ] Low fluid level or improper viscosity oil in forks. This can sound like spurting and is usually accompanied by irregular fork action (see Chapter 5).
- [ ] Spring weak or broken. Makes a clicking or scraping sound. Fork oil, when drained, will have a lot of metal particles in it (see Chapter 5).
- [ ] Steering head bearings loose or damaged. Clicks or knocks when braking. Check and adjust or replace with new ones as necessary (see Chapters 1 and 5).
- [ ] Fork yoke clamp bolts loose – ensure all the bolts are tightened to the specified torque (see Chapter 5).
- [ ] Forks bent. Good possibility if machine has been dropped. Replace the tubes with new ones as required (see Chapter 5).
- [ ] Front axle nut or axle clamp bolt (where fitted) loose (see Chapter 6).
- [ ] Loose or worn wheel bearings. Check and fit new bearings (see Chapters 1 and 6).

Rear end noise

- [ ] Fluid level incorrect. Indicates a leak caused by defective seal. Shock will be covered with oil. Replace shock with a new one (see Chapter 5).
- [ ] Defective shock absorber with internal damage. This is in the body of the shock and can't be remedied. The shock must be replaced with a new one (see Chapter 5).
- [ ] Bent or damaged shock body or mounts. Check the mounts. If the shock absorber itself is damaged replace it with a new one (see Chapter 5).
- [ ] Loose or worn wheel bearings. Fit new bearings (see Chapters 1 and 6).

Brake noise

- [ ] Squeal caused by dust or glazing on brake pads/shoes. Fit new pads or shoes (see Chapter 6).
- [ ] Metallic sound from pad backing plate contacting the disc. Pad friction material worn down beyond safe level. Fit new pads and possibly new disc (see Chapter 6).
- [ ] Disc warped. Can cause a chattering, clicking or intermittent squeal. Usually accompanied by a pulsating lever and uneven braking. Fit a new disc and new pads (see Chapter 6).

Excessive exhaust smoke

White smoke

Refer to Chapter 2A, 2B, 2C or 2D.
- [ ] Piston rings worn or broken, causing oil from the crankcase to be pulled past the piston into the combustion chamber. Fit a new piston and rings.
- [ ] Cylinder worn or scored. Fit a new cylinder barrel, piston and rings.
- [ ] Valve stem oil seal damaged or worn. Fit new seals.
- [ ] Valve guide worn. Fit a new cylinder head.
- [ ] Engine oil level too high, which causes the oil to be forced past the rings. Drain oil to the proper level (see Chapter 1).
- [ ] Head gasket broken between oil return and cylinder. Causes oil to be pulled into the combustion chamber. Replace the head gasket with a new one and check the head for warpage.

Black smoke

- [ ] Air filter clogged. Clean the air filter or fit a new one (see Chapter 1).
- [ ] Carburettor main jet too loose or wrong size. Check the jet (see Chapter 3).
- [ ] Fuel level too high. Check the float height (see Chapter 3).
- [ ] Mixture too rich. Check mixture screw setting (see Chapter 3).

Brown smoke

- [ ] Air filter poorly connected or missing (see Chapter 1).

Poor handling or stability

Handlebars hard to turn

- [ ] Steering head bearing adjuster nut too tight. Check adjustment (see Chapter 1).
- [ ] Bearings damaged. Roughness can be felt as the bars are turned from side-to-side. Fit new bearings (see Chapter 5).
- [ ] Races dented or worn, from front-end impact, hitting a pothole or from dropping the bike. Fit new bearings (see Chapter 5).
- [ ] Dry bearings. Caused by grease getting forced out by use of pressure washers. Repack bearings with fresh grease (see Chapter 5).
- [ ] Steering stem bent. Caused by a front-end impact, hitting a pothole or by dropping the bike. Fit a new stem/lower yoke. Don't try to straighten the steering stem (see Chapter 5).
- [ ] Front tyre air pressure too low (see Chapter 1).

Handlebar shakes or vibrates excessively

- [ ] Swingarm bearings worn. Fit new pivot bearings (see Chapter 5).
- [ ] Wheel rim(s) warped or damaged. Inspect wheels for runout (see Chapter 6).
- [ ] Wheel bearings worn. Worn front or rear wheel bearings can cause poor tracking. Worn front bearings will cause wobble (see Chapters 1 and 6).
- [ ] Fork yoke clamp bolts or handlebar clamp bolts loose. Tighten them (see Chapter 5).
- [ ] Engine mounting bolts loose. Will cause excessive vibration with increased engine rpm – ensure all the bolts are tight.

Bike pulls to one side

- [ ] Frame bent. May be accompanied by cracking near the steering head, swingarm mountings or engine mountings. Replace the frame with a new one (see Chapter 5).

- [ ] Wheels out of alignment. Caused by improper location of axle spacers or from bent steering stem or frame (see Chapter 5).
- [ ] Forks bent. Fit new forks (see Chapter 5).
- [ ] Swingarm bent or twisted. Fit a new swingarm (see Chapter 5).
- [ ] Fork oil level uneven. Change the oil in both forks and make sure you put in the same quantity (see Chapter 5).

Poor shock absorbing qualities

Too hard:

- [ ] Fork oil level excessive.
- [ ] Fork oil viscosity too high. Use a fork oil between 5W and 10W (see Chapter 5).
- [ ] Fork tube bent. Causes a harsh, sticking feeling (see Chapter 5).
- [ ] Fork internal damage (see Chapter 5).
- [ ] Rear shock pre-load too high. Adjust to a lower setting (see Chapter 5).
- [ ] Shock internal damage.
- [ ] Tyre pressure too high (see Chapter 1).

Too soft:

- [ ] Fork oil level too low.
- [ ] Fork oil viscosity too light. Use a fork oil between 5W and 10W (see Chapter 5).
- [ ] Fork springs weak or broken (see Chapter 5).
- [ ] Fork or shock oil leaking (see Chapter 5).
- [ ] Shock pre-load too low. Adjust to higher setting (see Chapter 5).
- [ ] Shock internal damage (see Chapter 5).

Braking problems

Brakes are spongy, don't hold (disc brake)

- [ ] Low brake fluid level (see Chapter 1).
- [ ] Air in hydraulic system. Caused by inattention to master cylinder fluid level or by leakage. Locate problem and bleed brakes (see Chapter 6).
- [ ] Brake fade due to excessive use and heat build-up.
- [ ] Pads worn, damaged or contaminated. Fit new pads (see Chapter 6).
- [ ] Brake fluid deteriorated. Fluid is old or contaminated. Drain system, replenish with new DOT 4 fluid and bleed the system (see Chapter 6).
- [ ] Master cylinder internal seals worn or damaged causing fluid to bypass. Fit new master cylinder (see Chapter 6).
- [ ] Master cylinder bore scratched by foreign material or broken spring. Fit a new master cylinder (see Chapter 6).
- [ ] Disc warped. Replace disc with new one (see Chapter 6).

Brake lever or pedal pulsates (disc brake)

- [ ] Disc warped. Fit a new disc and pads (see Chapter 6).
- [ ] Wheel axle bent. Fit a new axle (see Chapter 6).
- [ ] Brake caliper bolts loose. Tighten the bolts (see Chapter 6).
- [ ] Wheel warped or otherwise damaged (see Chapter 6).
- [ ] Wheel bearings damaged or worn (see Chapters 1 and 6).

Brakes drag (disc brake

- [ ] Master cylinder piston seized. Caused by wear or damage to piston or cylinder bore. Fit a new master cylinder (see Chapter 6).

- [ ] Lever bent, balky or stuck. Check pivot and lubricate (see Chapter 6).
- [ ] Brake caliper piston seized in bore. Caused by corrosion behind dust seals or ingestion of dirt past deteriorated seal. Fit a new caliper (see Chapter 6).
- [ ] Caliper sticking on slider pins due to corrosion. Clean and lubricate pins and check dust boots (see Chapter 6).
- [ ] Pads improperly installed (see Chapter 6).

Brake doesn't hold (drum brake)

- [ ] Front brake cable stiff or too much freeplay. Lubricate and adjust cable (see Chapter 1).
- [ ] Rear brake pedal freeplay too great. Adjust (see Chapter 1).
- [ ] Brake shoes worn or glazed (see Chapter 6).
- [ ] Brake drum surface worn or build-up of dust in drum (see Chapter 6).

Brake lever or pedal pulsates (drum brake)

- [ ] Drum warped. Renew wheel (see Chapter 6).
- [ ] Wheel axle bent. Renew axle (see Chapter 6).

Brake drags (drum brake)

- [ ] Shoe return spring broken (see Chapter 6).
- [ ] Operating lever/pedal or linkage stiff (see Chapter 6).
- [ ] Front brake cable dry. Lubricate cable (see Chapter 1).
- [ ] Rear brake pedal return spring disconnected or broken (see Chapter 6).

Note: *References throughout this index are in the form - "Chapter number" • "Page number"*

A

Air filter – 1•12, 3•2

B

Bike stands – 0•8
Bleeding brakes – 6•7
Bodywork – 5•1
Brake (disc)
  bleeding and fluid change – 6•7
  caliper – 6•5, 6•6
  disc – 6•7
  fluid level check – 1•16
  hoses and fittings – 6•7
  lever – 5•7
  master cylinder – 6•5, 6•6
  pads – 1•16, 6•1, 6•4
  pedal – 5•3
  system check – 1•18
Brake (drum)
  cable – 6•10
  lever – 5•7
  lever/pedal freeplay check and
    adjustment – 1•18
  pedal – 5•3
  shoes – 6•9
Building a bike from the crate –
  REF•20 *et seq*

C

Cable
  clutch – 1•8, 2B•12, 2C•15
  front brake (drum) – 1•18, 6•10
  lubrication – 1•20
  throttle – 1•10, 3•10
Caliper
  front – 6•1, 6•2, 6•5
  rear – 6•6
Cam chain, tensioner and guides – 2A•17,
  2B•22, 2C•25, 2D•15

Camshaft, rockers and valves – 2A•7,
  2B•8, 2C•9, 2D•5
Carburettor
  float height adjustment – 3•4, 3•6, 3•8, 3•10
  idle speed adjuster – 3•3
  jet needle setting – 3•4
  mixture adjuster – 3•3
  overhaul (JingKe PD) – 3•6
  overhaul (JingKe PZ19) – 3•5
  overhaul (Molkt) – 3•8
  removal and refitting – 3•4
CDI unit – 4•4
Cam chain – 2A•17, 2B•22, 2C•25, 2D•15
Chain (drive) – 0•7, 6•19
  checks and adjustment – 1•3
Clutch – 2A•9, 2B•12, 2C•15, 2D•8
  cable – 1•8, 2B•12, 2C•15
  lever – 5•7
Coil (ignition HT) – 4•2
Compression test – 2A•2, 2B•2, 2C•2
Conversion factors – REF•33
Crankcase separation – 2A•18, 2B•23,
  2C•26, 2D•15
Crankcases and bearings – 2A•19, 2B•24,
  2C•28
Crankcase breather – 1•9
Crankshaft and connecting rod – 2A•19,
  2B•25, 2C•28
Cylinder barrel – 2A•7, 2B•9, 2C•13, 2D•7
Cylinder head – 2A•4, 2B•5, 2C•6, 2D•2

D

Disc brake
  bleeding and fluid change – 6•7
  caliper – 6•5, 6•6
  disc – 6•7
  fluid level check – 1•16
  hoses and fittings – 6•7
  lever – 5•7
  master cylinder – 6•5, 6•6
  pads – 1•16, 6•1, 6•4

  pedal – 5•3
  system check – 1•18
Drive chain – 0•7, 6•19
  checks and adjustment – 1•3
Drum brake
  cable – 6•10
  lever – 5•7
  lever/pedal freeplay check and
    adjustment – 1•18
  pedal – 5•3
  shoes – 6•9

E

Engine
  cam chain, tensioner and guides – 2A•17,
    2B•22, 2C•25, 2D•15
  camshaft, rockers and valves – 2A•7,
    2B•8, 2C•9, 2D•5
  compression test – 2A•2, 2B•2, 2C•2
  crankcase breather – 1•9
  crankcase separation – 2A•18, 2B•23,
    2C•26, 2D•13
  crankcases and bearings – 2A•19, 2B•24,
    2C•28
  crankshaft and connecting rod – 2A•19,
    2B•25, 2C•28
  cylinder barrel – 2A•7, 2B•9, 2C•13, 2D•7
  cylinder head – 2A•4, 2B•5, 2C•6, 2D•2
  generator – 2A•15, 2B•21, 2C•24, 2D•14
  idle speed – 0•7, 1•14, 3•3
  kickstart – 2A•15, 2B•20, 2C•22
  oil pump – 2A•14, 2B•18, 2C•20, 2D•13
  piston and rings – 2A•9, 2B•11, 2C•14,
    2D•8
  primary drive gears – 2A•13, 2B•17,
    2C•15, 2D•8
  removal and installation – 2A•2, 2B•2, 2C•2,
  running-in – 2A•21, 2B•27, 2C•31, 2D•20
  sprocket – 6•21
  valve clearances – 0•7, 1•12
  valves – 2C•10

Note: *References throughout this index are in the form - "Chapter number" • "Page number"*

Haynes Motorcycle Manuals – The Complete List

Title		Book No
APRILIA RS50 (99 – 06) & RS125 (93 – 06)		4298
Aprilia RSV1000 Mille (98 – 03)	♦	4255
Aprilia SR50		4755
BMW 2-valve Twins (70 -96)	♦	0249
BMW F650	♦	4761
BMW K100 & 75 2-valve models (83 - 96)	♦	1373
BMW F800 (F650) Twins (06 – 10)	♦	4872
BMW R850, 1100 & 1150 4-valve Twins (93 – 06)	♦	3466
BMW R1200 (04 – 09)	♦	4598
BMW R1200 dohc Twins (10 – 12)	♦	4925
BSA Bantam (48 – 71)		0117
BSA Unit Singles (58 – 72)		0127
BSA Pre-unit Singles (54 – 61)		0326
BSA A7 & A10 Twins (47 – 62)		0121
BSA A50 & A65 Twins (62 – 73)		0155
CHINESE, Taiwanese & Korean Scooters		4768
Chinese, Taiwanese & Korean 125cc motorcyles		4781
Pulse/Pioneer Adrenaline, Sinnis Apache, Superbyke RMR (07 – 14)	◊♦	5750
DUCATI 600, 620, 750 & 900 2-valve V-twins (91 – 05)	♦	3290
Ducati Mk III & Desmo singles (69 – 76)	◊	0445
Ducati 748, 916 & 996 4-valve V-twins (94 – 01)	♦	3756
GILERA Runner, DNA, Ice & SKP/Stalker (97 – 11)		4163
HARLEY-DAVIDSON Sportsters (70 – 10)	♦	2534
Harley-Davidson Shovelhead & Evolution Big Twins (70 -99)	♦	2536
Harley-Davidson Twin Cam 88, 96 & 103 models (99 – 10)	♦	2478
HONDA NB, ND, NP & NS50 Melody (81 -85)	◊	0622
Honda NE/NB50 Vision & SA50 Vision Met-in (85-95)	◊	1278
Honda MB, MBX, MT & MTX50 (80 – 93)		0731
Honda C50, C70 & C90 (67 – 03)		0324
Honda XR50/70/80/100R & CRF50/70/80/100F (85 – 07)		2218
Honda XL/XR 80, 100, 125, 185 & 200 2-valve models (78 – 87)		0566
Honda H100 & H100S Singles (80 – 92)	◊	0734
Honda 125 Scooters (00 – 09)		4873
Honda ANF125 Innova Scooters (03 -12)	♦	4926
Honda CB/CD125T & CM125C Twins (77 – 88)	◊	0571
Honda CBF125 (09 – 14)	♦	5540
Honda CG125 (76 – 07)	◊	0433
Honda NS125 (86 – 93)	◊	3056
Honda CBR125R (04 – 10)		4620
Honda CBR125R, CBR250R & CRF250L/M (11 – 14)	♦	5919
Honda MBX/MTX125 & MTX200 (83 – 93)	◊	1132
Honda XL125V & VT125C (99 – 11)		4899
Honda CD/CM185 200T & CM250C 2-valve Twins (77 – 85)		0572
Honda CMX250 Rebel & CB250 Nighthawk Twins (85 – 09)	◊	2756
Honda XL/XR 250 & 500 (78 – 84)		0567
Honda XR250L, XR250R & XR400R (86 – 04)		2219
Honda CB250 & CB400N Super Dreams (78 – 84)	◊	0540
Honda CR Motocross Bikes (86 – 07)		2222
Honda CRF250 & CRF450 (02 – 06)		2630
Honda CBR400RR Fours (88 – 99)	◊♦	3552
Honda VFR400 (NC30) & RVF400 (NC35) V-Fours (89 – 98)	◊♦	3496
Honda CB500 (93 – 02) & CBF500 (03 – 08)	◊	3753
Honda CB400 & CB550 Fours (73 – 77)		0262
Honda CX/GL500 & 650 V-Twins (78 – 86)		0442
Honda CBX550 Four (82 – 86)	◊	0940
Honda XL600R & XR600R (83 – 08)	♦	2183
Honda XL600/650V Transalp & XRV750 Africa Twin (87 – 07)	♦	3919
Honda CB600 Hornet, CBF600 & CBR600F (07 – 12)	♦	5572
Honda CBR600F1 & 1000F Fours (87 – 96)	♦	1730
Honda CBR600F2 & F3 Fours (91 – 98)	♦	2070
Honda CBR600F4 (99 – 06)	♦	3911
Honda CB600F Hornet & CBF600 (98 – 06)	◊♦	3915
Honda CBR600RR (03 – 06)	♦	4590
Honda CBR600RR (07 -12)	♦	4795
Honda CB650 sohc Fours (78 – 84)		0665
Honda NTV600 Revere, NTV650 & NT650V Deauville (88 – 05)	◊♦	3243
Honda Shadow VT600 & 750 (USA) (88 – 09)		2312
Honda NT700V Deauville & XL700V Transalp (06 -13)	♦	5541
Honda CB750 sohc Four (69 – 79)		0131
Honda V45/65 Sabre & Magna (82 – 88)		0820
Honda VFR750 & 700 V-Fours (86 – 97)	♦	2101
Honda VFR800 V-Fours (97 – 01)	♦	3703
Honda VFR800 V-Tec V-Fours (02 – 09)	♦	4196
Honda CB750 & CB900 dohc Fours (78 – 84)		0535
Honda CBF1000 (06 -10) & CB1000R (08 – 11)	♦	4927
Honda VTR1000 Firestorm, Super Hawk & XL1000V Varadero (97 – 08)	♦	3744
Honda CBR900RR Fireblade (92 – 99)	♦	2161
Honda CBR900RR Fireblade (00 – 03)	♦	4060
Honda CBR1000RR Fireblade (04 – 07)	♦	4604
Honda CBR1000RR Fireblade (08 – 13)	♦	5688
Honda CBR1100XX Super Blackbird (97 – 07)	♦	3901
Honda ST1100 Pan European V-Fours (90 – 02)	♦	3384
Honda ST1300 Pan European (02 -11)	♦	4908
Honda Shadow VT1100 (USA) (85 – 07)		2313

Title		Book No
Honda GL1000 Gold Wing (75 – 79)		0309
Honda GL1100 Gold Wing (79 – 81)		0669
Honda Gold Wing 1200 (USA) (84 - 87)		2199
Honda Gold Wing 1500 (USA) (88 – 00)		2225
Honda Goldwing GL1800	♦	2787
KAWASAKI AE/AR 50 & 80 (81 – 95)		1007
Kawasaki KC, KE & KH100 (75 – 99)		1371
Kawasaki KMX125 & 200 (86 – 02)	◊	3046
Kawasaki 250, 350 & 400 Triples (72 – 79)		0134
Kawasaki 400 & 440 Twins (74 – 81)		0281
Kawasaki 400, 500 & 550 Fours (79 – 91)		0910
Kawasaki EN450 & 500 Twins (Ltd/Vulcan) (85 – 07)		2053
Kawasaki ER-6F & ER-6N (06 -10)	♦	4874
Kawasaki EX500 (GPZ500S) & ER500 (ER-5) (87 – 08)	♦	2052
Kawasaki ZX600 (ZZ-R600 & Ninja ZX-6) (90 – 06)	♦	2146
Kawasaki ZX-6R Ninja Fours (95 – 02)	♦	3451
Kawasaki ZX-6R (03 – 06)	♦	4742
Kawasaki ZX600 (GPZ600R, GPX600R, Ninja 600R & RX) & ZX750 (GPX750R, Ninja 750R) (85 – 97)	♦	1780
Kawasaki 650 Four (76 – 78)		0373
Kawasaki Vulcan 700/750 & 800 (85 – 04)	♦	2457
Kawasaki Vulcan 1500 & 1600 (87 – 08)	♦	4913
Kawasaki 750 Air-cooled Fours		0574
Kawasaki ZR550 & 750 Zephyr Fours (90 – 97)	♦	3382
Kawasaki Z750 & Z1000 (03 – 08)	♦	4762
Kawasaki ZX750 (Ninja ZX-7 & ZXR750) Fours (89 – 96)	♦	2054
Kawasaki Ninja ZX-7R & ZX-9R (94 – 04)	♦	3721
Kawasaki 900 & 1000 Fours (73 – 77)		0222
Kawasaki ZX900, 1000 & 1100 Liquid-cooled Fours (83 – 97)	♦	1681
Kawasaki ZX-10R (04 – 10)	♦	5542
KTM EXC Enduro & SX Motocross (00 – 07)	♦	4629
LAMBRETTA Scooters (58 – 00)	♦	5573
MOTO GUZZI 750, 850 & 1000 V-Twins (74 – 78)		0339
MZ ETZ models (81 – 95)	◊	1680
NORTON 500, 600, 650 & 750 Twins (57 – 70)		0187
Norton Commando (68 – 77)		0125
PEUGEOT Speedfight, Trekker & Vivacity Scooters (96 – 08)	◊	3920
Peugeot V-Clic, Speedfight 3, Vivacity 3, Kisbee & Tweet (08 – 14)	◊♦	5751
PIAGGIO (Vespa) Scooters (91 – 09)	◊	3492
SUZUKI GT, ZR & TS50 (77 – 90)	◊	0799
Suzuki TS50X (84 – 00)	◊	1599
Suzuki 100, 125, 185 & 250 Air-cooled Trail bikes (79 – 89)		0797
Suzuki GP100 & 125 Singles (78 – 93)	◊	0576
Suzuki GS, GN, GZ & DR125 Singles (82 – 05)	◊	0888
Suzuki Burgman 250 & 400 (98 – 11)	♦	4909
Suzuki GSX-R600/750 (06 – 09)	♦	4790
Suzuki 250 & 350 Twins (68 – 78)		0120
Suzuki GT250X7, GT200X5 & SB200 Twins (78 – 83)	◊	0469
Suzuki DR-Z400 (00 – 10)	♦	2933
Suzuki GS/GSX250, 400 & 450 Twins (79 – 85)		0736
Suzuki GS500 Twin (89 – 08)	♦	3238
Suzuki GS550 (77 – 82) & GS750 Fours (76 – 79)		0363
Suzuki GS/GSX550 4-valve Fours (83 – 88)		1133
Suzuki SV650 & SV650S (99 – 08)	♦	3912
Suzuki DL650 V-Strom & SFV650 Gladius (04 – 13)	♦	5643
Suzuki GSX-R600 & 750 (96 – 00)	♦	3553
Suzuki GSX-R600 (01 – 03), GSX-R750 (00 – 03) & GSX-R1000 (01 – 02)	♦	3986
Suzuki GSX-R600/750 (04 – 05) & GSX-R1000 (03 – 06)	♦	4382
Suzuki GSF600, 650 & 1200 Bandit Fours (95 – 06)	♦	3367
Suzuki Intruder, Marauder, Volusia & Boulevard (85 – 09)	♦	2618
Suzuki GS850 Fours (78 – 88)		0536
Suzuki GS1000 Four (77 – 79)		0484
Suzuki GSX-R750, GSX-R1100 (85 – 92) GSX600F, GSX750F, GSX1100F (Katana) Fours (88 – 96)	♦	2055
Suzuki GSX600/750F & GSX750 (98 – 02)	♦	3987
Suzuki GS/GSX1000, 1100 & 1150 4-valve Fours (79 – 88)		0737
Suzuki TL1000S/R & DL V-Strom (97 – 04)	♦	4083
Suzuki GSF650/1250 Bandit & GSX650/1250F (07 – 14)	♦	4798
Suzuki GSX1300R Hayabusa (99 – 14)	♦	4184
Suzuki GSX1400 (02 – 08)	♦	4758
TRIUMPH Tiger Cub & Terrier (52 – 68)		0414
Triumph 350 & 500 Unit Twins (58 – 73)		0137
Triumph Pre-Unit Twins (47 – 62)		0251
Triumph 650 & 750 2-valve Unit Twins (63 – 83)		0122
Triumph 675 (06 – 10)	♦	4876
Triumph Tiger 800 (10 – 14)	♦	5752
Triumph 1050 Sprint, Speed Triple & Tiger (05 -13)	♦	4796
Triumph Trident & BSA Rocket 3 (69 – 75)		0136
Triumph Bonneville (01 – 12)	♦	4364
Triumph Daytona, Speed Triple, Sprint & Tiger (97 – 05)	♦	3755
Triumph Triples & Fours (carburetor engines) (91 – 04)	♦	2162
VESPA P/PX125, 150 & 200 Scooters (78 – 12)		0707
Vespa GTS125, 250 & 300 (05 – 10)		4898
Vespa Scooters (59 – 78)		0126

Title		Book No
YAMAHA DT50 & 80 Trail Bikes (78 – 95)	◊	0800
Yamaha T50 & 80 Townmate (83 – 95)	◊	1247
Yamaha YB100 Singles (73 – 91)	◊	0474
Yamaha RS/RXS 100 & 125 Singles (74 – 95)		0331
Yamaha RD & DT125LC (82 – 87)	◊	0887
Yamaha TZR125 (87 – 93) & DT125R (88 – 07)	◊	1655
Yamaha TY50, 80, 125 & 175 (74 – 84)	◊	0464
Yamaha XT & SR125 (82 – 03)	◊	1021
Yamaha YBR125 & XT125R/X (05 – 13)		4797
Yamaha YZF-R125 (08 – 11)	♦	5543
Yamaha Trail Bikes (81 – 03)		2350
Yamaha 2-stroke Motocross Bikes (86 – 06)		2662
Yamaha YZ & WR 4-stroke Motorcross Bikes (98 – 08)		2689
Yamaha 250 & 350 Twins (70 – 79)		0040
Yamaha XS250, 360 & 400 sohc Twins (75 – 84)		0378
Yamaha RD250 & 350LC Twins (80 – 82)		0803
Yamaha RD350 YPVS Twins (83 – 95)		1158
Yamaha RD400 Twin (75 – 79)		0333
Yamaha XT, TT & SR500 Singles (75 – 83)		0342
Yamaha XZ550 Vision V-Twins (82 – 85)		0821
Yamaha FJ, FX, XY & YX600 Radian (84 – 92)		2100
Yamaha XT660 & MT-03 (04 – 11)	♦	4910
Yamaha XJ600S (Diversion, Seca II) & XJ600N Fours (92 – 03)	♦	2145
Yamaha XJ6 & FZ6R (09 – 15)	♦	5889
Yamaha YZF600R Thundercat & FZS600 Fazer (96 – 03)	♦	3702
Yamaha FZ-6 Fazer (04 – 08)	♦	4751
Yamaha YZF-R6 (99 – 02)	♦	3900
Yamaha YZF-R6 (03 – 05)	♦	4601
Yamaha YZF-R6 (06 – 13)	♦	5544
Yamaha 650 Twins (70 – 83)		0341
Yamaha XJ650 & 750 Fours (80 – 84)		0738
Yamaha XS750 & 850 Triples (76 – 85)		0340
Yamaha TDM850, TRX850 & XTZ750 (89 – 99)	◊♦	3450
Yamaha YZF750R & YZF1000R Thunderace (93 – 00)	♦	3720
Yamaha FZR600, 750 & 1000 Fours (87 – 96)	♦	2056
Yamaha XV (Virago) V-Twins (81 – 03)	♦	0802
Yamaha XVS650 & 1100 Drag Star/V-Star (97 – 05)	♦	4195
Yamaha XJ900F Fours (83 – 94)	♦	3239
Yamaha XJ900S Diversion (94 – 01)	♦	3739
Yamaha YZF-R1 (98 – 03)	♦	3754
Yamaha YZF-R1 (04 – 06)	♦	4605
Yamaha FZS1000 Fazer (01 – 05)	♦	4287
Yamaha FJ1100 & 1200 Fours (84 – 96)	♦	2057
Yamaha FJR1300 (01 – 13)	♦	5607
Yamaha XJR1200 & 1300 (95 – 06)	♦	3981
Yamaha V-Max (85 – 03)	♦	4072
ATVs		
Honda ATC 70, 90, 110, 185 & 200 (71 – on)		0565
Honda Rancher, Recon & TRX250EX ATVs		2553
Honda TRX300 Shaft Drive ATVs (88 – 00)		2125
Honda Foreman (95 – 11)		2465
Honda TRX300EX, TRX400EX & TRX450R/ER ATVs (93 – 06)		2318
Kawasaki Bayou 220/250/300 & Prairie 300 ATVs (86 – 03)		2351
Polaris ATVs (85 – 97)		2302
Polaris ATVs (98 – 07)		2508
Suzuki/Kawasaki/Artic Cat ATVs (03 – 09)		2910
Yamaha YFS200 Blaster ATV (88 – 06)		2317
Yamaha YFM350 & YFM400 (ER & Big Bear) ATVs (87 – 09)		2126
Yamaha YFZ450 & YFZ450R (04 – 10)		2899
Yamaha Banshee and Warrior ATVs (87 – 10)		2314
Yamaha Kodiak and Grizzly ATVs (93 – 05)		2567
ATV Basics		10450
SCOOTERS		
Twist and Go (automatic transmission) Scooters Service and Repair Manual	◊	4082
TECHBOOK SERIES		
Motorcycle Basics Techbook (2nd edition)		3515
Motorcycle Electrical Techbook (3rd edition)		3471
Motorcycle Fuel Systems Techbook		3514
Motorcycle Maintenance Techbook		4071
Motorcycle Modifying		4272
Motorcycle Workshop Practice Techbook (2nd edition)		3470

◊ = not available in the USA ♦ = Superbike

The manuals on this page are available through good motorcycle dealers and accessory shops.
In case of difficulty, contact: **Haynes Publishing**
(UK) **+44 1963 442030** (USA) **+1 805 498 6703**
(SV) **+46 18 124016**
(Australia/New Zealand) **+61 2 8713 1400**

MCL 07.05.15

Preserving Our Motoring Heritage

< *The Model J Duesenberg Derham Tourster. Only eight of these magnificent cars were ever built – this is the only example to be found outside the United States of America*

Almost every car you've ever loved, loathed or desired is gathered under one roof at the Haynes Motor Museum. Over 300 immaculately presented cars and motorbikes represent every aspect of our motoring heritage, from elegant reminders of bygone days, such as the superb Model J Duesenberg to curiosities like the bug-eyed BMW Isetta. There are also many old friends and flames. Perhaps you remember the 1959 Ford Popular that you did your courting in? The magnificent 'Red Collection' is a spectacle of classic sports cars including AC, Alfa Romeo, Austin Healey, Ferrari, Lamborghini, Maserati, MG, Riley, Porsche and Triumph.

A Perfect Day Out

Each and every vehicle at the Haynes Motor Museum has played its part in the history and culture of Motoring. Today, they make a wonderful spectacle and a great day out for all the family. Bring the kids, bring Mum and Dad, but above all bring your camera to capture those golden memories for ever. You will also find an impressive array of motoring memorabilia, a comfortable 70 seat video cinema and one of the most extensive transport book shops in Britain. The Pit Stop Cafe serves everything from a cup of tea to wholesome, home-made meals or, if you prefer, you can enjoy the large picnic area nestled in the beautiful rural surroundings of Somerset.

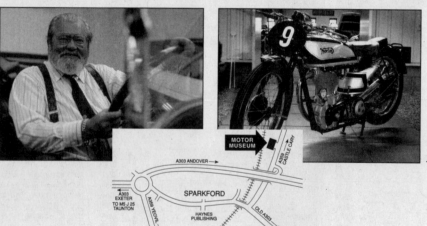

> *John Haynes O.B.E., Founder and Chairman of the museum at the wheel of a Haynes Light 12.*

< *The 1936 490cc sohc-engined International Norton – well known for its racing success*

The Museum is situated on the A359 Yeovil to Frome road at Sparkford, just off the A303 in Somerset. It is about 40 miles south of Bristol, and 25 minutes drive from the M5 intersection at Taunton.
Open 9.30am - 5.30pm (10.00am - 4.00pm Winter) 7 days a week, *except Christmas Day, Boxing Day and New Years Day*
Special rates available for schools, coach parties and outings Charitable Trust No. 292048